THE POPE'S BOOKBINDER
A MEMOIR

THE POPE'S BOOKBINDER

A MEMOIR

David Mason

A JOHN METCALF BOOK

BIBLIOASIS
WINDSOR, ONTARIO

FIRST PAPERBACK EDITION

Library and Archives Canada Cataloguing in Publication

Mason, David, 1938-, author
     The Pope's bookbinder / David Mason.

Includes index.
ISBN 978-1-77196-005-2 (pbk.)

     1. Mason, David, 1938-. 2. Mason, David, 1938- --Books and reading. 3. Antiquarian booksellers--Canada--Biography. I. Title.

Z483.M327A3 2014   381'.45002092   C2014-903808-9

Edited by John Metcalf
Copy-edited by Dan Wells
Typeset by Chris Andrechek
Cover Designed by Kate Hargreaves

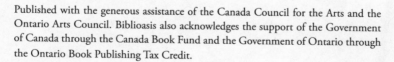

Published with the generous assistance of the Canada Council for the Arts and the Ontario Arts Council. Biblioasis also acknowledges the support of the Government of Canada through the Canada Book Fund and the Government of Ontario through the Ontario Book Publishing Tax Credit.

PRINTED AND BOUND IN CANADA

Contents

For Debra
and
For Michael Patrick Mason

Without whom it
wouldn't mean much.

First to possess his books, for without them
He's but a sot, as I am, nor hath not
One spirit to command. They all do hate him
As rootedly as I. Burn but his books.
—Caliban, plotting against Prospero

Wisest are they who read old books—
drink old wine—converse with old friends—
and let the rest of the world go by...
—John Cowper Powys

"He cannot lock us all up."
"He has prisons enough."
"For bodies, yes. But what are bodies? He can take our goods,
but God will prosper us. He can close the booksellers, but still there will be
books. They can have their old bones, their glass saints in windows, their
candles and shrines, but God has given us the printing press."
—Hilary Mantel
Wolf Hall

"What I do is me: for that I came."
—Gerard Manley Hopkins

Family Album

My earliest memories are reflected by one of the earliest photos in the family album. We are living in a small Ontario town called Mount Forest, where my father is the temporary manager at the Royal Bank. In those years my father was a sort of troubleshooter for the bank. Whenever a manager in one of the branches in the towns of Southern Ontario dropped dead, or absconded with some of the money or the minister's wife, or both; or whose alcoholism became too blatant to cover up any longer and they had to haul him off to the asylum, the bank would send my father out from head office to handle things until a new manager was appointed.

We lived in a big wide two-storey house with a veranda running the entire width, an exact match of the house next door, except that I remember the next-door neighbour's kids taking me to their second floor and opening a door at the back of a closet, a secret door which revealed stairs ascending into a dark mysterious unknown— an attic. I remember being very incensed that we had no such attic; it seemed grossly unfair, and I concluded that it must be due to my father's being the bank manager: he was just too respectable to have an attic full of the sorts of secrets and mysteries I was sure the kids next door experienced daily. I now believe a significant part of my character was evident in this attitude; I think it illustrates that sense of curiosity and wonder which, in spite of my timid outer response to the world, was already evident and which for the rest of my life has caused me an enormous amount of trouble, landed me in lots of messes, a few of them very serious, but which also has been responsible for most of the greatest triumphs I have experienced. I guess I've been going into that mysterious attic ever since.

That first photo shows a group of five or six kids of various sizes sitting in a circle. I recognize only my older sister. To one side, three or four feet away, sits a child of maybe three years of age, watching this group but noticeably not part of it. This is me, and every time I look at this photograph it evokes feelings of both sadness and some wonder at how clearly it captures my personality, now and obviously then, too.

One can also discern in this photo another central component of my character, apparent even then. I am watching this group with a sense of awe—I find them fascinating. I am the observer—the eternal outsider, that just about every writer whose autobiography I have ever read describes. That I became a bookseller rather than a writer speaks only to natural talent—that is, my lack of it—the reason I never considered the writer's path.

CHAPTER 1

My Earliest Heroines and Heroes

My father's parents were of farm stock, from small Ontario towns. Settling in Toronto, my grandfather, a plumber and tinsmith, had his business at College and Bathurst. The father of my friend and sometime business partner, Malcolm Lester, the publisher, owned a movie theatre a few blocks along College. I like to imagine that my grandfather would have been called in when the pipes in the theatre burst in the cold.

Across the street was College Street United Church, which, as a kid, I always assumed was owned by my mother's family, the Baillies, since the minister, a personal friend, visited us regularly. My Uncle Bob was the choirmaster at the Church, and my Aunt Mina played the piano in the Sunday School. Most of the first two rows were always full of Baillies, so it was not an illogical assumption for a kid to make.

I never met my grandfather Mason, as he died before I was born. My grandma Mason was one of those severe Methodists, a stern judgmental woman, disapproving of all childish exuberance. She lived with us until her death in the fifties. I suspect it was not easy for my mother to have her continually severe presence in her house, but I never heard my mother say a word against her. I guess she and my mother had worked out some sort of truce over the years. But, to be fair, I don't recall my grandmother ever chastising my sister or me in my mother's presence, although she was quite strict when our parents were out. I avoided her, as she had that Methodist quality of making you feel guilty without ever quite understanding what you were supposed to be feeling guilty about.

The Baillies, my mother's people, were a very different lot. Grandpa Baillie immigrated from Borthwick, Scotland, while his wife Gertrude Dore was from England, where family legend places her as a descendant of Sir Francis Elderfield of Sutton Courtney, near Oxford. Many years later I was delighted when I learned that one of my heroes, George Orwell, was buried in the graveyard of that village, buried there by David Astor who owned the manor house once owned by my distant ancestor.

I never knew Grandfather Mason but I did know my other grandfather, Grandpa Baillie, a silent man who said little. He fathered eleven children, of whom eight survived to adulthood, and he was a carpenter by trade. His claim to fame was that as an employee of the Hospital for Sick Children he had built the first iron lung in Canada. As a child I was mystified by how, if an iron lung was made of iron, a carpenter could build it.

Grandpa Baillie also seldom seemed to smile, but I clearly remember his gentleness with me. My mother was close to her mother and we visited often at their house on Admiral Road, where he would take me down in the basement to his workshop, a place of great mystery and wonder to a child. There was sawdust everywhere, and I would always be given a few little sanded wooden blocks, so beautifully smooth to the touch, worthless scraps which to a child were like precious jewels. I guess my love of wood comes from that. I have always loved to handle wood, real wood, not that disgusting veneered pressboard which passes as a substitute for it today. In five separate stores, I have always built my own bookshelves, starting on Ward's Island, where I had begun selling books by catalogue from my home and sometimes to friends on the ferry. I built my first bookshelf from some discarded wood siding I scrounged from a demolished house. It took me three evenings to build that first shelf. I did everything wrong, but I gradually evolved a system (which I naturally named *The Mason System*) where I could construct an 8' x 4' shelf in twenty minutes.

Constructing a shelf in twenty minutes is not an insignificant accomplishment when you need a hundred or so of them, and really quickly, economic reality always prodding you. All my friends laughed at my boasting, but they all ended up adopting my system. In those days in Toronto, all the booksellers were good friends and when a new bookstore opened we would go down and spend a day or two working for our friends for free. We were all so poor that we all understood how important it was to open as quickly as possible so that one could start bringing in some money to pay for it all.

Like probably every man who spends too much time thinking, I regret that I didn't know my father better. The intricate connection between fathers and sons is universal and probably ultimately inexplicable. A man of my age knows that, but still compulsively wrestles with whatever clues his memory retains. I expect women have the same problems with their mothers, only different in content.

My father seemed a simple man. He seemed to care about only two things, his work and his family. I never had a philosophical conversation with him; in fact, I never had a political conversation with him. At home, he didn't seem to care about the great world outside. One of my loveliest childhood memories involves his coming home from work every night. My sister and I would run to the door to greet him with hugs, screaming "Daddy's home!", he bringing in with him the chill and all the smells of that great mysterious world out there, that I was certain he had been arranging properly every day.

I don't think his capacity for intimacy extended much past us. He had a huge, beautiful smile, which I have decided was a defense against intimacy with strangers. It was probably very useful in business too, as was his always-impeccable dress. There are family photos showing him and my mother before their marriage, standing beside his shining Model A Ford, impeccably dressed even then and with that beautiful warm smile that seemed to radiate confidence.

My mother was the traditional wife of the period, keeping a perfect house. Her hobby, as we called it, was sewing, and she was very good at it. She made clothes for all her friends and because she charged ludicrously low prices for her work she was constantly solicited by all sorts of people for dresses and such. Amongst other things, she made by hand the wedding dresses of my sister and probably every Baillie niece, alongside those of the daughters of all her friends.

It was only when I was middle-aged that I realized that sewing wasn't a "hobby"—it was her vocation. In those days women weren't supposed to have a vocation, but that is what she had. She sewed every day all her life and she was sewing the last time I saw her, on the day she died, going to sleep that night and not waking up. We should all be so lucky to end so easily.

The nursing home in which we had had to place her the week before offered only a single room, and when Debbie and I and her parents visited that last day I could see she found it humiliating, her sense of dignity affronted that she had to greet guests in what was, in effect, her bedroom.

I believe she died on purpose, refusing to continue such an affront to her sense of propriety. When they called me the next morning from the nursing home to inform me that "they couldn't find any signs of life," I went up and sat with her for a couple of hours and waited for the funeral people. She must have succumbed quickly after she went to bed because her hair was still perfectly coiffed, not a hair out of place.

As I sat there for that two hours, that became a point of great comfort to me. She would be so pleased to know that she was properly arranged for wherever she now was.

About a month earlier she had called me in the shop where I was negotiating a purchase of books with Bob MacDonald, one of the best book scouts I've known.

"I think I'm having a heart attack," she said.

"Call 9-1-1," I replied, alarmed.

"I most certainly will not," she replied.

I didn't drive then, but Bob offered to drive me to her place on Bloor, out past Keele.

When we arrived, she was standing outside in a suit, elegantly dressed, including a hat and her fur wrap. There was no way she was going to the hospital improperly dressed, not even for a heart attack. She was in and out of the hospital three or four times before the nursing home, mostly staying in the emergency room. One day the doctors told us she wouldn't last the day. She lay unconscious all day making rasping noises, surrounded by her children. But she didn't go and they finally sent us all home promising to call if she went in the night.

We returned the next morning to find her sitting up in bed eating her breakfast.

"I'm not supposed to be here, you know," she said, a smug smile on her face.

My sister Marguerite was everything to me as a child. Three years older than me, she was both my minder and my mentor, my protector and my persecutor. Sturdy, very strong and of very determined character, she could not only outsmart me and easily subdue me, but in the time-honoured tradition of older sisters everywhere she often did. My partner Debbie, also an older sister, has told me many stories of her youthful persecutions and manipulations of her younger brother. They are so eerily similar that I have come to believe it is a biological phenomenon. I believe that it is in their role as older sisters that women learn, very young, how easy it is to manipulate men, no doubt a useful tool when they grow up. Studying this as an adult, a perceptive man will likely conclude that biology, not viciousness or cruelty, is the centre of this trait.

But, to be fair, she could also beat up most of the bigger boys in the neighbourhood and often did, too. Especially Blake, who lived next door and who, although part of my small neighbourhood gang of friends, was a bully. His outweighing me by a fair bit meant that he only needed to sit on me and I was helpless. I think Marg especially enjoyed beating up Blake when he bullied me. Twenty-five years later when, as an adult, I met Blake and renewed our friendship, I happened to tell my sister about that meeting, and her response seemed to imply that if she were to see him again she'd again enjoy beating him up.

Marguerite always seemed to know everything about our family (she still does) and she continues to fascinate me with arcane family details that I never knew about.

It was Marguerite who told me when I was about seven years old that she and I had both been adopted, even showing me, secreted in some drawer, the newspaper death notices of our adoptive parents' two natural children, one dead of an early staph infection, the other of the complications of hydrocephalus and spina bifida. Both died very young.

But, another clue to my character: even though this profoundly affected me, I never asked my parents about it. And they never mentioned it. It was never talked about, ever.

In later years, when I caused my parents so much pain and grief, I couldn't help wondering if their thoughts didn't return to their two lost boys, and if they didn't also speculate on what weird personality defects of my natural parents they might be paying for.

I was born and mostly raised in Toronto, in the area north of Yonge and Lawrence Ave. After some years on small-town assignments with the Royal Bank my father was permanently posted to the head office in Toronto, and we settled in a nice house on Elm Road. That area remains much the same as it was then except that the cheaper houses, mostly bungalows, have disappeared, replaced by monstrous houses filling entire lots, which upsets the aesthetic symmetry of the neighbourhood. Once, some thirty years later, buying a library in that area, I parked afterwards and studied the old house. Except for paint on the trim everything was the same, except for some inexplicable feeling of difference which I couldn't pin down. I woke in the middle of the night, realizing what the confusing difference was. It was the trees I had climbed as a child, now thirty years bigger. No child would ever climb them again as I had done, familiar with every branch and crotch.

I don't know who taught me to read, but someone must have very early, because I have no recollection of a time when I couldn't. Sometimes I like to think that I was born already knowing.

However, I grew up in a house in which there were no books, except for the books my sister and I received at Christmas and on birthdays, or the occasional ones loaned to my parents by friends. On Christmas day, with all the presents opened, when the inevitable let-down occurred, I would always retreat to my bedroom to read whatever book I had received.

But, as with just about everything else, this book deprivation had some positive benefits—the greatest one being that it introduced me to libraries. And it also meant that I not only read and reread all the books I received as seasonal presents, like the Hardy

Boys, but as a voracious reader, after I read my boys' books, I devoured all my older sister's books too. So I have read all the Nancy Drews, the Bobbsey Twins, and the Pollyanna books and many more meant for young girls. And while I have to admit that all those young lady heroines were "plucky," they didn't really meet my criteria for adventure.

And, like many another insatiable young reader, I also read some inappropriate books, simply because they were there, loaned to my parents or left by a guest. Which is how, at around eight years old, I read perhaps the first book of many which profoundly altered my life. This was *The Royal Road to Romance*, by Richard Halliburton. Halliburton was a rather strange American, who spent his whole life travelling the world and writing books about it. He did things like climb the Matterhorn by himself and sneak into the grounds of the Taj Mahal to swim in the pool in front of it. He also swam across the Hellespont, copying Byron, and then swam the entire length of the Panama Canal, for which he was charged the lowest toll recorded in history—36¢. Halliburton wrote many books of his adventures, which culminated in his building a replica Chinese junk in Hong Kong and sailing off to conquer the Pacific, never to be seen again. He was a real hero to me, and his infectious sense of adventure and daring profoundly affected me, causing me some years later to take off myself, to spend several years travelling in Europe and North Africa, seeking adventure. Books really can change your life!

Aside from these occasional loans, the only books I remember seeing in our house were compilations of facile platitudes called *Tony's Scrapbook*, issued yearly by a man called Tony Wons, which my mother religiously bought as they came out— although I can't remember ever seeing her read one. As a pointless aside, I can't resist mentioning that I now have an almost complete set of this man's puerile, cliché-ridden books, partially because seeing them on the shelves provides a sentimental renewal of the connection to my mother. But more practically, because another of my collecting interests is publisher's design bindings, and all the covers of Tony Wons' books are wonderful examples of the best in that period's Art Deco design. So are their dust jackets. And since I also collect early dust jackets I have here a double justification. Being a collector demands finding plenty of justifications for your collections, and I've become very good at that.

So, my first thirteen years were spent in a respectable middle-class neighbourhood with the same neighbours, my own gang of friends, with whom I shared all those boyhood adventures and all those experiences every child has, and I walked every day to the same school. There, except for the trading of comics and Big Little Books with some of the kids I knew, no one read books. I did—incessantly—but since none of my pals did, it became a private passion. I never felt that was strange, but neither did I ever feel the need to attempt to share it with any of my friends.

My friend Blake's parents were members of the Book-of-the-Month Club, and one day Blake handed me a book with a page marked saying, "Read this part—it's really sexy." He leered, knowingly.

We would have been eleven years old, just becoming enthralled with the mysteries and possibilities of women and sex.

I read the "sexy" part, which could only have been sexy to an eleven-year-old who was still so naïve as to think that two adults disrobing in front of each other just before the fade-out could be wildly exciting.

Of course, being a reader, after I read the sexy part, I then read the whole book, which wasn't really appropriate for an eleven-year-old, it being George Orwell's *1984*. I still remember how bleak everything was, from the decrepit slums to the life led in Orwell's fictional London. Years later I read all of Orwell, even those terrible novels which made all of Britain appear a dull, filthy and depressing place. When as a nineteen-year-old I went to Britain by ship and got on the Liverpool-to-London train and passed through the soot-encrusted slums of Liverpool all I could think was, "Jesus, Orwell was right."

Once I spent a night in a doss house in London and Orwell was right about them too. It was horrible, a room with a dozen cots, bedbugs, the freezing damp making the smell of unwashed bodies and filthy socks even worse.

Since I grew up in a house where books seldom entered, my reading really began when my older sister and I started visiting the library every Saturday. The closest library was the St. Clements branch, which was then, I think, the only library branch in North Toronto. But its real importance was that half of it was devoted entirely to children's books, and it featured regular Saturday storytellings.

I have three indelible memories of St. Clements in those early days. One was sitting in a circle with a bunch of other kids being read to by one of the librarians. The second, of a librarian examining the books I was returning from the previous week and, based on them, recommending new ones. The third and perhaps key memory involves the thrill of excitement I felt every Saturday morning when my older sister led me by the hand to return last week's books and borrow ten more. The thrill of anticipation I felt then, returning home with ten new books, has continued to this day some sixty years later. And the excitement I still feel, as I head home to solitude and the wonder of our incredible human imagination with a new book by an author I love, still provides that thrill, one of the few patterns of my character which has never changed.

I also remember, with some satisfaction, my attempts to con my mother into thinking I was sick on Monday mornings so I could stay home from school and read. At first my mother was too smart and too strict for such transparent ploys, but I quickly learned that if one started demonstrating the symptoms of some dire illness on Sunday afternoon, before dinner—after cleverly hiding food under the bed to replace the dinner which you claimed to be too sick to eat—even the most suspicious mother could be fooled into accepting fraudulent symptoms. And it didn't take long before I realized that it was pointless to stage such elaborate productions for only one day off school— why not two or three days? So, I have a family history of having endured a sickly childhood without ever actually having been sick.

Just recently I read an interview with the late Jack McClelland of McClelland & Stewart, who suffered from asthma as a child. McClelland relates that all he had to do was fake a wheezy cough on Monday mornings for his mother to say "Oh, another asthma attack—you'd better stay home from school." McClelland, like me, was an indifferent student who was happiest at home by himself, reading.

Because St. Clements served the entire north end of Toronto it must have been well-used, and I presume that it therefore influenced a lot of kids as it did me. One of those kids who became well-known was James Houston, the man most responsible for bringing Inuit art to the attention of the world and who initiated much of the commercial success in the dissemination of Eskimo art and sculpture, which now is known and collected worldwide and is perhaps Canada's sole indigenous art form.

James Houston, now dead, gave a talk at The Osborne Collection—the world-famous collection of children's literature, one of the greatest treasures held by the Toronto Public Library—which I unfortunately missed, but part of which was recounted to me afterwards by my friend Margaret Maloney, the retired past director. As Margaret told it to me, Houston talked of proposing marriage to one of the librarians when he was nine years old. The librarian apparently responded by suggesting that it might be better if they waited awhile. I told this wonderful anecdote in a talk once and suggested that anyone with the wisdom to give such a reply should have been running the country, not a children's library.

So, my earliest heroines were those nameless librarians at St. Clements. Except, of course, for my sister.

Although I mustn't leave out Poor Mrs. Quack, Mrs. Peter Rabbit and Old Mother West Wind. For the first books I clearly remember reading were the wonderful nature stories written by Thornton W. Burgess. Reddy Fox, Paddy the Beaver and all their friends so filled my imagination that when I couldn't find any new ones I hadn't read I reread them countless times. When I became a bookseller I started a collection of them, constantly upgrading as I found better copies. I was surprised to find at International bookfairs how expensive first editions and signed copies of Burgess' books are. I shouldn't have been; it is another indication of the universality of Burgess and the nostalgia he arouses in so many.

A few years ago I finally turned over my collection of Burgess to the Osborne. I was surprised how good it made me feel. I felt I was giving back something in memory of those wonderful librarians who did so much to influence my life, and I also felt I might be helping to influence some future generation into a love of reading and books. And, of course, the next day I started acquiring more Burgess for the next gift.

When the George Locke Branch of the Toronto Public Library opened at Yonge and Lawrence in 1950 I started going there and dropped St. Clements. Since I was now 12 years old it made sense anyway. I had graduated from Burgess through Doctor Doolittle, the series of the Twins from various countries—like the Dutch Twins and the Chinese Twins—and a similar series I liked, the Little Cousin series (*Our Little Japanese Cousin, Our Little German Cousin*, etc.), all of which I have collections of. All were intended to teach kids the customs of foreign countries. It instilled the idea that even with all these different customs and beliefs we were all remarkably similar in our humanity. It seems to me that we could use a bit more understanding of this fact these days.

And, of course, I devoured all of Arthur Ransome's wonderful sailing adventures, including *Swallows and Amazons*.

But one of my great disappointments is that somehow I missed all those great British juvenile stories by G.A. Henty, Westerman, Manville Fenn, Brereton and others. But at least I got Tarzan and, in the Big Little Books, all the now-mythic American superheroes, Buck Rogers, Dick Tracy and Terry and the Pirates. Very recently I appraised a gift of six hundred Big Little Books gifted to The Osborne Collection by an eighty-two-year-old who had collected them all his life. What a wonderful experience. I actually wanted to read (or reread) most of them, but I had to keep a professional distance.

It would be around this time that I read what would certainly be my all-time favourite children's book, *The Wind in the Willows*. I still reread it every few years, and while I loved the pompous blustering Toad, and still do, I strongly identified with Mole with his cozy underground sanctuary which I always envisioned, and still do, as being lined with bookshelves.

The Wind in the Willows is another of my many personal collections, copies now numbering over two hundred variant editions and formats. It even includes the first edition, a very expensive book, which I found with damaged covers and which I then had rebound in a stunning design binding commissioned from Michael Wilcox, the Canadian bookbinder who some people, including me, consider the best in the world.

This collection will someday be donated to the Osborne, although I'm not certain the Wilcox binding will accompany it. I may leave that to my son. That is, unless he continues to argue with me and I have to disinherit him.

But by then I was beginning to discover some of the great classic children's literature, like Mark Twain and Dickens and Dumas' great adventure novels, all of which I still read.

For some reason I found comic books a bit lacking, just as I'm not much taken by the graphic novels we're seeing so much of these days, but I did read them. So, besides my library visits I also read and collected some comic books. But mostly I loved the Big Little Books, which some of my pals and I bought, read, discussed and passionately traded. *Dick Tracy*, *Tarzan*, *Little Orphan Annie*, and *The Shadow* enthralled us. And also about that time I discovered the fairly new Classic Comics, which were a brilliant innovation, rendering some of our great classical literature into comic book formats designed for children. I bought these avidly, blowing my allowance regularly on them, even sacrificing the sweets we usually spent our meagre allowances and gift money on.

I still recall with great pleasure the part Classic Comics played in my education. As an adult I often cannot remember if I have actually read a famous book as a child, or only the Classic's version of it. When that happens the only thing to do is to read the actual book to find out, which continues to introduce me to great literature.

After I left school at fifteen and was working, a different part of my education began.

Still living with my parents and still reading late into every night, I discovered another kind of literature, for like all young men of fifteen or sixteen I was obsessed by sex. Every night after a quick dinner I would head for the local pool hall where, along with pool, I was learning life lessons from an assortment of businessmen, hustlers, conmen, losers and gamblers and, of course, other delinquents like me.

And every night on the way home I would stop at the corner store (they were then called cigar stores) where I would explore the paperback racks in search of the texts relating to my new educational obsession: sex.

Paperbacks of the time took certain liberties with their cover design. I guess they still do. The publishers knew that I, and many people much older than me, read paperbacks seeking sex. Even women, no matter their denials, sought the same, albeit somewhat disguised, the phenomenal success of the Harlequin Romances compelling proof of that. And in the fifties, with paperbacks revolutionizing the reading habits of many, the publishers sought an edge by promising rather different rewards than the text might provide. Lurid covers sporting near-naked women and suggestive blurbs designed to sell to the sex-starved worked—certainly they worked on me.

All of this led me to read some unlikely books in those days. The novels of Louis Auchincloss or Wright Morris are no doubt literature, but not exactly what sex-besotted fifteen-year-old boys are looking for. And the same with *Madame Bovary*; it was sex, not sin and its consequences, that I sought.

One night, going home from the poolroom and suffering from a recurring pain which I knew from experience would only be alleviated by a night spent in a bathtub full of hot water, I stopped to get the necessary reading material.

David Mason

This night I chose a book on Roman orgies, the cover picturing all sorts of toga-clad men surrounded by voluptuous women whose breasts threatened to pop out at any moment. The cover blurbs reinforced their lurid promise: "Depraved Romans," "Pagan, Corrupt and Debauched," etc. At home everyone was asleep, so I drew a hot bath, got in, feeling some immediate comfort, picked up the book which was to save me from a night of pain, and started reading.

It wasn't anything like what I expected. An old man complained about being a cripple and a stutterer, and his constant humiliations from the laughter of others—it was boring. And worse, the only woman was an old lady, a shrew. There wasn't even a hint of sex, never mind orgies. I was enraged. False advertising, I thought. How dare they. I read two chapters and stopped in disgust. I am reminded of a news item about an elderly lady exiting a movie theatre when *Deep Throat* had popularized pornography in America demanding her money back, disappointed at the film she had just seen. "That's disgraceful," she fulminated, "I paid to see smut and it's smut I want to see." But I had no other book to read. I could have gotten out of the tub, dried off, gone to my bookshelf and found something to reread, but I didn't want to reread—I wanted something new. I had no option: I had to continue with the disappointing book. The next thing I knew the bath water was cold, quite cold, freezing in fact. Looking at the book I saw I was halfway through it, so engrossed had I been that I hadn't even noticed the cold water.

I ran another hot tub and read the rest of the book that night.

I had never read anything like that book before, and given its effect on me I can say that I have never experienced that feeling from any other book I've read. It literally changed everything, forever. The book about Roman orgies was *I, Claudius*, by Robert Graves. And further in, while one didn't get a lot of orgies, one did get all the scurrilous details of the excesses of Tiberius, Caligula and Nero, so I did get my money's worth even in the sex department. I had always loved historical fiction, but it had always been the stories which captivated, the adventures of the swashbuckler fighting the evil Lord in seventeenth-century Scotland, or invading the harems of the despicable infidel corsairs of Barbary (now, of course, it's we who are the despicable infidels). But it was only many years later that I came to see that what I had really loved was the history, the details of life in different times and places.

Robert Graves showed me that Claudius, and all the Romans, were people. Real people with real passions, who had real lives and real problems. From my dry school texts I had believed that all those people from the past were boring. They married, they fought battles, but they didn't seem to have sex like they did in my novels, and of the history they made, we, it seemed, only needed to learn the dates. As far as I could see, passion played no part in history; only who won, and when, counted. They were all cardboard cut-outs with names to me. *I, Claudius* demonstrated, that life offered opportunities for the brave and the daring; and that there were consequences. That was the beginning of my real intellectual life.

That night led to everything. Because of *I, Claudius* I have forever held Robert Graves in great affection, my awe at his stupendous gifts not even slightly dampened when I read many years later that he considered his novels hack work, necessary to earn the money to enable him to survive for his true destiny, the pursuit of the White Goddess.

I had discovered the Romans. And I started some serious exploration of those times, all with the help of those wonderful Penguin Classics translations. Suetonius first, but then all the others, poets, playwrights, suffering with Catullus, conquering Gaul with Caesar. I've heard it said that those Penguin translations are too pedantic, too scholarly, but they weren't for me. For not even a pedant could still that passion and exuberance for life one finds in the classics, and I have come to believe that to be the mark of the true artist. No artist whose muse is passion can ever be boring.

And, of course, it didn't take long to find the Greeks after that.

When I came on Herodotus I devoured him. The first historian, excluding the Bible, it was a wonderful experience; one of those books where you don't care if it's true or not—it should be true, and that's enough.

When I became a bookseller and a passionate collector, it won't surprise anyone to hear that one of my favourite collections became one that encompasses every first printing of every edition of *I, Claudius* and its sequel (if not quite its equal) *Claudius the God*. I have quite a few different editions in this collection, including sixteen copies of that same paperback that so affected me when I was fifteen. Every time I see another one I buy it, and I get the same feeling that you and I would get if we could once again be fifteen years old and could again kiss the first girl we ever loved.

Years later, when I also read and collected T. E. Lawrence, of whom Graves wrote a biography (*Lawrence and the Arabs),* by an incredible stroke of combined luck and coincidence I bought for almost nothing (£25 if I remember) Lawrence's own copy of *I, Claudius* from his Cloud's Hill Library. It's pretty hard to imagine a finer association copy of that book, at least for me.

Starting with the penny tracts of the seventeenth and eighteenth centuries and gradually evolving to the dime novels and pulps of the nineteenth century and such brilliant innovations as the Tauchnitz editions designed as cheap portable reading for English travellers on the continent, paperbacks really came into their glory when Allen Lane invented Penguin Books, generally acknowledged amongst book people as the true advent of the paperback revolution. Penguin's astounding success quickly spread to America. It is perhaps not widely known that amongst the earliest paperback books published in America, and in the minds of many (including me) the finest list of paperbacks in America, Signet Books, was originally published as Penguins. For collectors of those early Signets it is therefore necessary to seek the first hundred or so under their original imprint. Later they became Penguin/Signet and then just Signet. I have a serious collection of Signets (amongst several other U.S. paperback series which I largely collect for the cover art, some of which is truly stunning). Much of my early newsstand reading was in Signets, and lucky for me because in spite of their lurid covers they often published important literature, especially in their reprinting of contemporary novelists.

I collect only the first two thousand Signets (which aren't really even two thousand in number since for some reason the publisher began numbering in the six hundreds as Penguin and didn't become Signet until they were into the seven hundreds).

The history of the modern paperback evolution is fascinating as it becomes revealed. This, as every antiquarian bookseller and every serious scholar well knows, is both the *raison d'être* and the only justification needed for the collecting of books. Of course all collectors share the secret which trumps all other justifications: the pure pleasure of the hunt, the search, then the triumph of possession. We covet books like normal people covet money.

Much of the early "Noir" literature was published in these cheaply produced paperback formats, intended to be read and discarded, and what little has survived tends to be scarce and expensive for that reason.

Now, Noir is respectable—as it should be—because many of its practitioners are very fine writers. The books are also morality tales, direct descendents of those medieval tales of brave deeds and lovely ladies later satirized and exemplified by Don Quixote, but now placed in the context of modern cities. I didn't know any of this then of course—I just was an innocent seeker after sex, driven by frustrated lust.

Chapter 2

Respectability Abandoned

With adolescence I began getting into trouble in school; defiance, disruptions in class, general snottiness, which got me sent to the hall regularly and finally barred permanently from two of my grade nine classes. At this time another ominous character trait became apparent: I seemed to have no fear of authority. Ejected from class, sent to the principal's office, instead of having fear of consequences, I found the confrontations stimulating.

Discovering alcohol, my crowd began to drink on Friday and Saturday nights, getting quickly plastered on the then drink-of-choice, lemon gin (I still marvel at how we came up with such a repugnant choice), which usually ended by us all puking and retching in a field. We would often cause disruptions in our neighbourhood restaurant and the owner would kick us out or, if we were too obnoxious, call the cops. When the cops were called my pals would scatter, but I wouldn't; when the cops arrived I would be waiting for them on the curb and would harangue them with a passionate lecture about my democratic rights. Naturally the police would take me to the station, where my insufferable snottiness usually got me a few cuffs around the head. Then they would call my father.

"Mr. Mason, we have your son here again, you'd better come down here and get him." Of course this was humiliating for my respectable father, even worse because he hadn't a clue why I did these things, nor what to do about it.

This all occurred in Willowdale, where we had moved a couple of years before. I was then in grade nine at Earl Haig Collegiate.

Towards the end of grade nine my parents decided to move back to North Toronto. I suspect it was to get me away from the bad influences that they were certain was getting me in all the trouble. They bought a house near where I had grown up, north of Lawrence Avenue. The move was to occur in November of the next semester. I had failed two subjects in grade nine, but had been sent on to grade ten, where I was expected to make up these two failures.

But unbeknownst to my parents, I went to the office at Earl Haig before the end of June and told them I would be transferring to Lawrence Park Collegiate from the first of the year, not the end of October. In September when school started, I would take the lunch my mother prepared every day and repair to the poolroom, where I pursued my real education. This worked perfectly until sometime in late October, when one day I forgot to take my lunch. My mother delivered it to Earl Haig, only to be told I had moved to Lawrence Park two months earlier. There was a big fuss, of course, and in the end I started at the new school, already hopelessly behind for grade ten, never mind the two subjects from grade nine that I was supposed to be making up.

My form teacher was the Latin teacher. I considered Latin a stupid pointless subject and I quickly managed to get myself permanently ejected from his class too (twenty-five years later I went back to study Latin, at night, at university, since as an antiquarian bookseller I needed to know something of that "stupid pointless subject").

It was really too late to salvage anything of the year, even if I had wanted to, which I didn't.

Before Christmas, my antics, now exacerbated by my defiant indifference to consequences and mixed with a hopeless ignorance of everything being taught, got me permanently suspended. I was fifteen years old.

Even my confused parents now concluded that school for me was pointless and it was decided I could leave. Ignored by everyone was the fact that I spent most nights till 2 or 3 AM reading under the covers with a flashlight. It didn't occur to me either that this should have provided a clue to an astute observer. Having not had a single friend or acquaintance, so far, who read books, reading remained my private vice. It was many years later before I comprehended that reading, even then, was saving my life.

The problem was that in those days no one could leave school before sixteen years of age unless it could be established that the family was poor and needed the help of the kid's income. But my father was not poor and I was only fifteen years old.

I was sent to the headquarters of the Board of Education where a battery of psychologists tested me for a week or so, which resulted in all of them giving up in the face of my obstinate refusal to give them the time of day, and I was allowed to enter the great world—on my own at last. Then began the series of experiences and adventures which led eventually to discovering my vocation some fifteen years later.

Looking at my early years with the perspective of what understanding I've acquired since, I continue to be astounded that none of those teachers or principals, or later the psychologists, managed to even notice the connection between this greasy-haired young delinquent whose defiance they couldn't handle and the imaginative kid who sat up most nights reading incessantly with a flashlight. It's true that I didn't get it either, but they were supposed to be smarter than me.

So, I was fifteen years old, exuberant at my release from the drudgery of school and working at Eaton's, my first full-time job. (I am constantly amazed at how many Canadians I've met who also started their working life at Eaton's.)

My first payday at Eaton's, I took my $49.00 pay (this was for half a month, hence a bit less than $24.00 per week) and walked south to Burnill's Bookshop at Yonge and King to buy the first book I ever remember purchasing in a bookstore. I can still remember my feeling of awe at the beauty of all those wonderful shining dust jackets, each promising unknown adventure and the excitement of new ideas. Indeed I still remember clearly the feelings of awe I had at the realization that I could actually *own* one of those books—it could be mine to take home. It would be mine; I would not need to return it to the library. Using up my entire lunch hour, forgetting to eat, I finally settled on two Modern Library books, Bertrand Russell's *Why I Am Not a Christian* and a book of Freud's essays. I don't think these first two choices were a fluke. They were indicative of the thrust for understanding which goes with youth, an indication of the path all young people should be taking, that search for knowledge and meaning, which never finishes.

But it was another two years before I made another significant step forward in my education. Still buying books, both paperbacks and many Modern Library editions, feeling my way, I had left Eaton's. I worked a year and some for Dr. Scholl's, the foot comfort man, as a shipper, packing and mailing thousands of corn plasters, trying to ease the pain of the world even then, I like to say. And yes there actually was a Dr. Scholl; I met him. Every couple of years he toured his extensive domain and we would all be lined up, at a respectful distance, to do homage, as with the Queen.

But then I became bored with factory life and applied for a job at an insurance company. It was there I met my first book friends, who also worked there. Becoming acquainted, I was astounded to find that Alfred Ames and Don Tough both, like me, were avid readers. We quickly became close friends. Don and I rented an apartment on Bloor Street and Al, still with his parents, spent the weekends partying in our apartment. During the week we spent most evenings, often in a beer parlour around the corner on Bay Street, passionately discussing the ideas we were finding through our incessant reading. Even though we were only seventeen and the legal drinking age was then twenty-one we were regulars and were never questioned. At the same time, we spent most weekends drinking at the Town Tavern and The Colonial, where for the price of a beer (45¢) one could see and hear most of the great jazz men of that greatest period in the history of jazz. We were rabid fans and discovering what only became apparent many years later, that the Toronto jazz scene was right up there with New York's, Los Angeles's and San Francisco's.

But as the excitement, both intellectual and social, fermented and I came to have a larger view of the wonder of the world's potential, my interest in business slipped away. It became harder to take insurance seriously—after all, what we were selling, essentially, was security. But in my reading and in my life I was discovering the excitement of insecurity, of forcing the future, of challenging the status quo. The people were nice enough. Shortly after I had started, they had recognized my potential and started grooming me for better things, moving me up. But the inevitable boredom began to set in and even I was now able to recognize the signs.

That was pretty much the end of my business career; it went downhill from there, and fairly quickly. Within six months I was fired, getting drunk at the company picnic and personally insulting the vice-president. Reporting to work the next morning I was given two weeks' pay and ejected. I had such a massive hangover it took me two days to realize that I was relieved. It took a few years before I realized that, in spite of my drunken stupidity, some instinctual spark had saved me from respectability.

My youthful rebellion was not against my father but rather against all authority, the whole world, in fact. Shy and timid I might have been, facing what I thought to be a sophisticated and confident world, but I was extremely stubborn in the face of the pressures to conform. About that time I discovered another writer who strongly affected me, a man named Robert Lindner, a psychologist famous for a book called *Rebel Without a Cause*. Hollywood bought Lindner's book and used only the title for that famous James Dean movie. But another of his books, the one which so affected me, was called *Prescription for Rebellion*. Its thesis was, essentially, that in an insane society—and the fifties was certainly that—the sane man must necessarily be a rebel. This was the first time I was introduced to the idea that maybe it wasn't me who was some sort of weird misfit psycho, that maybe I was right in my disgust at and defiance of society. It gave me heart.

Lindner was a friend of Norman Mailer's, who became an early intellectual mentor of mine. Lindner was attempting to reinstate hypnosis as a respectable medical tool, but he died at the criminally young age of forty-one, his great promise unrealized.

I have all Lindner's books in my library, in first editions, many bearing presentation inscriptions, my homage to this man, another of the many to whom I owe so much.

The restlessness initiated by the influence of Richard Halliburton's travels then caused me to go hitch-hiking across America to San Francisco, and, after a bit, to Vancouver, where I continued my education in real life, this time learning some important truths about poverty.

It was a very bad year economically and there was no work. I applied for unemployment insurance (the only time in my life I ever did, and I still suffer guilt). I got $17.00 a week, and the sleazy room with two cots, a chair and table my friend Don and

I rented in a rooming house at Richards and Pender Streets cost $10.00, if I remember. So we had to live each week on what remained. I learned what real hunger is like, not just missing a few meals, but a continual, never-satisfied hunger. We lived on bread and peanut butter, occasionally Cheez Whiz, which we considered a luxury. The hunger was mostly a mental affliction—the proof of this was that we would between us eat a loaf of bread in a sitting, stuffing ourselves, but the constant hunger never let up. The first thing that goes in that state of extended starvation is sex—one loses interest completely. Thoughts of sex are replaced by constant fantasies of food. Meals we had eaten as children would be recounted in obscene detail, our mothers' cooking praised, arguments arising over the merits of our respective mothers' special gifts at apple pie or chicken stuffing. Food and eating became an obsession, and stuffing ourselves with six peanut butter sandwiches filled our stomachs temporarily but didn't eliminate the lust for diversity.

I learned some important truths. I learned, for instance, that the poor are not poor because they drink; they drink because they are poor. The constant worry about money, or its lack, creates tension; the obsession with trying to stretch insufficient funds to cover an entire week causes periodic psychic explosions. The occasional beer, taken as a rare treat, was dangerous. The relaxed expansiveness would cause one to have a second, and then lose all restraint, resulting in a drinking binge and a rare evening of pleasure. But, of course, there are rules—this meant two or three days of no money for food, until the Friday line-up at the pogey office.

Every day we went there looking for work, but there was none.

But books continued to fill the long days without work and the void of constant hunger was forgotten in the wonder of

David Mason

literature. And with no money for movies or any other entertainment, a library card became a passport to civilization.

Christmas saved us. We got taken on as extras at the post office (that adventure itself worthy of an essay) and afterwards, with a month's pay in hand, set out for Mexico.

But, being somewhat naïve, we made a few mistakes, the first one being that we bought one-way bus tickets to Bellingham, the first town south of the border. America was also suffering a recession and they were watching for us. Naturally we were unaware that American customs officers were used to having hundreds of kids like us, who claimed to be visiting friends in Bellingham for a few days. It took the border guard about five minutes to see through our stupid story and we were turned back.

Indeed we were turned back at every border point in British Columbia (and I shall ever remember the three days we spent buried in snow, in Osoyoos B.C., unable to hitch a ride).

Finally, we found ourselves in windswept Fort McLeod, Alberta, and realizing we weren't ever going to talk our way across the border, we decided our only alternative was to return to Toronto.

Still dressed in suits, ordinary leather shoes and topcoats, we were inappropriately dressed for the Canadian Prairies in January and completely unaware of what we were in for.

Just as well.

It took thirteen days to reach Thunder Bay and I've never been so cold before or since.

We went into police stations asking to sleep in cells but the RCMP, who were the police in all the towns of the west, didn't much care when we told them we had been graciously accommodated in jails in the United States. Once after they had turned us away, we demanded to be arrested. They relented and let us sleep on the floor in the stinking urinal of the jail; I guess they didn't want any non-criminals soiling the blankets in the cells.

Hitch-hiking often means you are let off in the middle of a town, which then necessitates walking right on through the town to get to the highway again. People would come up to us on the street and tell us to get inside. "You'll lose that nose (or ear) if you don't." Once inside, we understood, as we experienced the excruciating pain which comes with thawing. Unlike the RCMP the shopkeepers were friendly and accommodating, even though we didn't buy anything.

By the time we experienced our final humiliation, walking through Winnipeg (easily twice the size of Toronto, I thought) an agony exacerbated by gale force winds at Portage and Main, I'd had it with winter, especially in western Canada. Knowing a fair number of westerners (I even married one) I realized a long time ago that the weather is not their fault and I don't hold it against them. They also are victims. But I've never forgiven the RCMP. And I've never been back, not in winter anyway.

Back in Toronto I got a job at a stockbroker's where I started at the bottom. It was around this time that I discovered used books in Old Favorites, then the only used bookstore I had known about in Toronto. (Britnell's still had a couple of tables of used books, as did Eaton's—and maybe Simpsons, but I didn't know that.)

My mentor and first boss in the trade, Jerry Sherlock (Joseph Patrick), got *his* start at Eaton's used book tables. He was working as a reporter, covering the crime courts at City Hall, and he would spend his noon hour browsing the 10¢ table in Eaton's. One evening at his church the priest showed Jerry a list of books he was seeking for the church library. Jerry spotted one that he had bought that day for 10¢ at Eaton's.

"I have that book," he told the priest, and sold it to him for 75¢. So was begun the career of the best bookseller Canada has yet seen.

Back from the west and also by necessity back living uncomfortably in my parents' home, I didn't waste any time looking for work. As I said, a stockbroker on Adelaide Street called Davidson & Company needed a clerk and I applied and got the job. I was an assistant to the man who processed the transaction slips from the client sales on the floor of the Toronto Stock Exchange, around the corner on Bay Street. Several times a day the slips would be brought up to the office where my immediate boss and I recorded them and passed them to the people who recorded them against the customer's accounts.

The best part of that job was the Saturday overtime. Friday, being often the busiest day in the markets because it was the last day of the week, often caused enough backup that my boss Dick and I would need to come in Saturday mornings to clean up the residue. At noon or so Dick would repair to the pub next door and I would head out with my extra overtime money—which was usually about $17.00—to Old Favorites Bookstore, then in its second venue on Front Street, between Yonge and Bay.

I still remember clearly the first time I had entered Old Favorites. I was awed, filled with the sort of wonder that would have been more appropriate to a cathedral than a bookstore. Earlier I had browsed there when I was seeking a break from the onerous and humiliating process of looking for work. In fact I had asked Lou Morris, the amiable, gentle owner, for a job. After a lengthy conversation he had pretty much decided to hire me when a chance question revealed that I couldn't type. So I didn't get the job. Typing was essential to Lou, for the job involved quoting from the huge file of customer-wants that Old Favorites maintained.

Surrounded with high shelves, seemingly endless rows of them, their height resulting in an atmosphere of gloom which caused the whole place to even more resemble a cathedral, all I could do was wonder at such a profusion of riches.

I spent the rest of that day, till closing time, looking, removing books from the shelves to examine them, all without any of the familiarity which I might have possessed had I had a normal education to fall back on.

Almost everything was new, unknown, mysterious, each book a possible experience waiting to happen. It was as though each book was trying to speak to me, with its title, or its colour, or even its bulk. Take me, read me, they seemed to be silently begging.

From this uncountable treasure trove I had to choose titles, and I had nothing to work with except the odd name of a known writer that I had read.

I would spend the rest of each Saturday deciding on which books I would spend my $17.00. General used books then sold for an average $2.00 to $5.00, so I could buy three or four books every visit. But measuring a book not as a monetary cost, but as a reflection of an hour-to-two hour's work, made final decisions seem even more significant—a mistake could be seen as what it was, a waste of valuable time. And with no literary education or much experience to fall back on, I ended up reading some pretty weird stuff.

Within a year, the pull of adventure, so insidiously ingrained in me by Richard Halliburton, plus increasing boredom at the stock market, caused me and my pals to decide to go to Europe. That we had no money seemed irrelevant. Landing in England with hardly anything, we found that we could at least get work in London; I tried a few different jobs, some of which seemed incredible to spoiled young North Americans. Jobs under medieval conditions in factories where one worked from 6 AM to 6 PM (compulsory overtime it was called.) Sometimes one saw two or three generations of the same family in the factory. Probably at fifteen or so dad took his son to the factory, so he too could put in a lifetime of drudgery. We were starting to get a taste of how horribly pampered North Americans were.

We lived in Bayswater, then still fairly rundown, while in adjoining Notting Hill Gate, there had been recent race riots.

Freezing to death in the worst climate I'd experienced (at least in western Canada you were warm as soon as you got inside), we learned what the English had put up with after the war. There were still huge craters all over the east end, shilling meters for electricity and gas, heat so pitiful that we had to gather in the kitchen every evening with the oven on and its door opened, hoping to keep warm until bedtime, when we donned our sweaters and overcoats before climbing under the covers. It's a wonder that the English as a race has survived. I still don't understand how they propagated in that cold.

But London was still a wonderful place to be young and poor. Free galleries, museums and the greatest neighbourhood libraries I've ever seen. And as always, books provided so much.

I went on to spend several years living in London in the winters and hitch-hiking all over Europe from April to November. There were several countries where one could easily get work, although it was naturally the work assigned to immigrants everywhere, those who couldn't speak the country's language: washing dishes, digging ditches (and graves), cleaning highways; the lowliest work, anything, in fact, which would provide the food to go on. I learned a lot about prejudice and xenophobia. When you are on the lowest levels you get a reprise of what I had learned as a young kid working as a caddy. You are of no importance, beneath the radar. In foreign countries you are subjected to that ancient instinctive dislike and distrust of the different. In Europe, if you were poor, you learned the real structure; you lived in parks, under bridges, in abandoned buildings. You also lived with the indifference and contempt of those people who operate on assumption and prejudice. My real education was always going on. But being so poor, it was always necessary to be somewhere which would allow a quick return to England. Which meant I never did visit Italy or Greece or the Middle East, although I spent most of a year in Tangiers and several years in Spain, through the great good luck of getting a job in a printing plant.

It was a communal atmosphere we seekers lived in. The grapevine would provide means to keep contact with a growing crowd of fellow travellers in most of the cities of western Europe.

Always there were books and talk of books; ideas were fuel, knowledge, the search for truth our passion.

In Paris, I hung around the Beat Hotel, mostly full of British and American writers or pseudo-writers, where we would congregate, stoned on the ubiquitous marijuana and the other drug of choice then, amphetamines, which caused us to sit up for days without sleep, reading the latest writing and passionately discussing it. Heroin was just then insinuating itself into the scene and later several of my friends and acquaintances succumbed to overdoses.

Once I got quite sick, along with being strung out on amphetamines. Taking pity, an American from Boston who lived there allowed me to sleep on the floor of his room during the days—the floor only, the bed was forbidden. I couldn't really blame him, as we never bathed; the only washing we ever managed was the occasional cold-water sponging. But along with the amphetamines, the constant clatter of typewriter keys from the next room ensured I rarely slept, at best dozing for brief periods. The man in the next room typed all day, every day, until 6 PM or so, when he would go down to the narrow bar downstairs. That man was William Burroughs, already treated with deference and respect because of *Naked Lunch*. We didn't then know how important *Naked Lunch* would become, but we did know it was a very powerful book. We didn't know its eventual effect on American literature, but we certainly knew that it had already changed our generation's literature forever.

That summer, living in the back of a truck parked under Pont Neuf in Paris, Burroughs' *Naked Lunch*, just published, had been passed around from hand to hand and read with great excitement. It was, of course, the first edition, which got rattier and rattier as everyone read it. Now, a fine copy of that first edition sells for $7,000.00 to $10,000.00. My crowd certainly contributed to its present scarcity.

I then went to Morocco and Spain for most of four years. I loved Spain and I loved the noble people who live there, an affection which has never diminished. I wanted to stay in that wonderful place which so fascinates foreigners, especially North Americans, and I studied the language and seriously sought work. Which is how I came to get a job in a publishing and printing plant. When I adanced far enough with the language and could read a bit, a Spanish friend gave me a volume of Lorca's plays and as ever, when I could use books, my language skills blossomed and I became quite fluent. I read little modern Spanish history because Franco's censors allowed only their version of events to be published. But so deep was my fascination that back in Canada I ended up with a major collection of some five hundred books on the Spanish Civil War, now in the University of Toronto.

After three years, during which I learned the essentials of bookbinding, I left Spain and returned to Paris where I lived in a seedy hotel (even then, $2.00 a night meant just what you can imagine).

My parents, by now uncertain if they would ever see me again, offered to pay the fare back to Canada, but I took a couple of weeks to decide. I was starving again, surviving on less than a $1.00 a day for food, wandering the Paris streets, looking in shop windows at food I was unable to buy. The only safe places were the English language bookshops, George Whitman's Shakespeare and Company, across from Notre Dame, and the shop run by, I think, a Swedish woman on the Rue de Seine.

But I was now also experiencing a recurrence of my old nemesis: boredom. But this time it came in an entirely novel way: instead of the old familiar boredom of jobs, I realized I was bored by my lifestyle. I was sick of drugs and inane pointless conversations with stoned hippies. I was sick of listening to putative writers and artists prophesying their eventual triumph and fame. And I was sick of trying to figure out how to get enough money to eat everyday, of the incessant conversations about attempts to bleed more money from helpless parents so one could relax for a week or a month.

For a bunch of people who considered ourselves refugees from capitalism and respectability, we spent an inordinate amount of time discussing money. It was like my starving period, where all we talked about was food. This crowd, intent on changing society, was obsessed I came to realize with what we purported to despise.

I was depressed and dismayed by the number of junkies amongst my friends and acquaintances, especially when word would filter back through the grapevine about those who had succumbed to overdoses or other drug-related deaths. A few years later that would include old friend Don Tough, one of my original "reading" pals, who had travelled to Europe along with Alfred and me all those years ago. He had become an addict, and stayed in England where he could legally maintain his habit. Except for one short visit back to Canada he made some years later I never saw him again. Another overdose.

But mostly I was bored and disgusted by the aimlessness of it all. I was almost thirty and I knew now what all those years of reading and experience demanded: some aim, a mission. Intelligence needs some direction, some challenge, it needs to be applied to practical aims or it will atrophy.

I began to realize what was necessary. It was time to go home. This phase of my life, this part of my education, was done. I picked up the ticket my parents had sent to the Canadian Embassy and flew back to Canada.

CHAPTER 3

The Pope's Bookbinder

One of the things about history which most fascinates me is how events which can be seemingly so insignificant when they occur can have such resounding consequences later. This is what learning bookbinding did for me.

I got into bookbinding by a fluke, just as I later did with bookselling. There are deep parallels. The truth is bookbinding, like bookselling, is not really a job; it is a vocation. For anyone who might not know the difference between a job and a vocation, a vocation is a job where you don't earn enough to live on.

As I mentioned earlier, I lived in Spain for a while, and one day I got a job in a printing plant. I thought it would be more interesting doing printing than my usual work in those European countries, but I hadn't counted on the difficulty of setting type in a language which I spoke abominably, albeit fluently. And the linotype machines were so primitive they scared me. They must have been the original models, belching gasses and liquids of unknown composition but of obvious chemical danger. Even with the lax safety standards prevalent then in Spain they only allowed the operators to work a year or so without a break because of the lead, so I wasn't about to tempt fate. But I discovered that they had a small bookbinding department of three or four guys, mostly binding periodicals and government publications, and one man who bound leather to order under the direction of the maestro of the bindery. He, it turned out, was a master binder who had been properly trained in the European apprenticeship tradition.

When I got a chance I grabbed the opportunity to take up binding. I thought it would be an interesting potential hobby when I was back in Canada since it was both creative and practical—after all, damaged books could be rescued from oblivion—and it was a solitary activity, which suited my temperament, and most important, it involved handling books, my lifelong passion and love. And of course, being ignorant, it seemed to me fairly simple.

I was able to join the binding department and was put to work at the bottom, that is, preparing books for sewing, taking them apart, cleaning off the signatures, and then sewing them. As it happened, I liked sewing, I liked the preparation, getting the signatures ready and the methodical stacking and sewing gave me plenty of time to daydream—perfect work for the lazy kid I was. I loved to watch a pile of signatures rising neatly until a full book manifested itself, ready for covering.

I gradually advanced, learning most of the basic techniques and, more importantly, practicing them incessantly. For as anyone who has done binding will know, the basic techniques are fairly straightforward, but what is needed is practice—and yet more practice.

I was soon made assistant to the guy who bound leather to order and was then able to watch all the advanced techniques and, gradually, to practice them myself under the eye of my teacher. As a bonus I was allowed, on my own time, to bind my own books if I paid for the materials, and eventually I had all of the few English books I possessed in leather bindings. Not always appropriately bound I'm afraid, as those who have seen them know. Because I only owned a few English books, about half paperbacks, and because of a complete lack of any historical knowledge of bookbinding, my bindings are often inappropriate for two reasons: one being a lack of relation between form and content (in the most extreme case this resulted in a Penguin paperback being bound in full morocco with raised bands, gilt); and more embarrassing, books which were bound in somewhat questionable taste.

In my defence, it should be understood that this bindery was commercial and I saw only work that was done there, so there was no criteria with which to compare except the work of the maestro and my boss, who himself owed his skills to the maestro. Both these men were of the excess school of binding, that is, the more garish the better: this meant more and bigger false bands and tons of gilt, gilt and more gilt; and edges gauffered with four colours of dye hammered into them. All this embarrassing excess is also evident in my own bindings: in other words, the more or bigger-must-be-better syndrome.

Curiously, the only exceptions to this are my earliest attempts, when I was so concerned with simply finishing a binding properly that I kept to basic technique. Those earliest bindings are the most aesthetically pleasing, a compelling argument against too much education. The worst example of any of my bindings, one which gets shown only to my closest friends, exhibits all those vulgar elements I mentioned, combined with excruciatingly bad taste. The book in question is the Modern Library Giants edition of Freud's *Collected Works*. I have to digress here. This was, after all, the sixties—just about every kid in Europe had Freud's *Collected Works* in his knapsack. In fact, while I'm at it I might as well tell you some of the other books I rebound: *The Tao Te King*, *The Bhagavad Gita*, *The I Ching*, Dostoevsky's *Crime and Punishment*, Hemingway's *For Whom the Bell Tolls* (then banned in Spain, incidentally), and Joyce's *Ulysses* (also then banned in Spain). And Petronius. And my beloved Knut Hamsun, who along with Ezra Pound and Celine is one of those great writers who continue to embarrass their admirers by their flirtations with Nazism. There was also my morocco-bound Penguin edition of what I, along with Somerset Maugham, consider perhaps the greatest novel ever written: *The Charterhouse of Parma*. As you can see, I was educating myself and searching for answers, an honourable activity for twenty-year-olds, then and now. In spite of what they say about the sixties today, those were interesting times in which to be growing up.

Anyway, I bound my Freud in half-scarlet calf without raised bands, although a book that fat cries out for something to detract from its squat bulk, and with scarlet leather corners so big they ruined the symmetry from the side. And then I added black cloth sides which created a contrast truly startling. And when you open the covers, as you tend to do quickly to escape such a gross spectacle, you confront marbled endpapers, also of bright red and black, so that there is no escape from the vulgarity. Even the top edge is stained bright red. One can only wonder what Freud would have said. Some of my other bindings show other faults and questionable taste, but the Freud is exceptional for its lack of any redeeming features. But still, in spite of the excesses, I love them all; they are my babies, especially since they are my complete collected works, so to speak, for my career was almost over and I will never bind another book.

I stayed at the plant a year and a half, not nearly enough time to learn more than the basics, but I enjoyed it a lot. Probably the highlight of that early phase of my binding career was when we bound a book for the Pope. The book was a religious publication, which the Spanish Government wished to present to His Holiness, and we bound it in full white morocco, a horror to work with. So easily marked is white morocco that we had to wash our hands every time we approached the book, just like surgeons, and our incessant smoking also had to be curtailed, for a falling ash could ruin a skin, just as any nick could result in a mark the equivalent of a tattoo. Actually, to be quite precise, I wasn't allowed to touch it after we put on the white cover, although in a moment of personal triumph, I was allowed to heat up the brass wheels with which the gold-man applied the gilt. This is more important than it sounds because the proper application of gold demands precise heating. But before all that, I did all of the preparation and sewing and cut and attached the boards. So I can therefore state justly that I used to work for the Pope.

Back in Canada, when I contemplated setting up as a binder, I thought of having a card printed like those used by some English firms such as, "Tea Merchants. By appointment to Her Majesty the Queen." Mine was going to read "D. Mason. Bookbinder, By Appointment to His Holiness, Pope John XXIII." In the end I decided that might appear a touch vulgar, although everywhere one looks one sees people presenting credentials no less fraudulent than mine.

I found in Canada that there was not much opportunity for a guy whose resumé for almost ten years was blank, so out of curiosity, but with a growing awareness that bookbinding might be one of the few options open to me, I decided to check out the scene.

Well, any of you who know what it was like in the late sixties in Toronto will know what I found, and it didn't take long either. I found Robert Muma, about the only binder practicing the craft then in Toronto. There may have been others, but I didn't find them. I went and spent an afternoon with Bob Muma, that very kind and gentle man, and while he was great fun what he told me wasn't encouraging. He did commissions, mostly family bibles and such, but he did other leatherwork too, and when he showed me some of that work it was apparent that designing wallets and other leather things was his real love. If I remember correctly he was a self-taught bookbinder and, while highly competent technically, his bookbindings often looked like wallets. Do not presume that I denigrate Muma's work; twenty-five years later I bought from his widow a half dozen of his design bindings, for which I paid a fair bit and considered myself lucky to get the chance to do so. He was generous with his knowledge and seemed as delighted to find someone interested in his work as I was happy to find him. I would have loved to work for him but there simply weren't enough jobs. He made it plain that he believed it would be impossible for me to get enough work to set up for myself, and further depressed me by pointing out a problem which hadn't even occurred to me. There was no bookbinding equipment to be had in Toronto. And even if there had been I didn't have any money anyway.

It all seemed too depressing, so I looked into some of the commercial binderies, but not with any real hope I would get a job. Furthermore, knowing how inexperienced I was, I was actually somewhat afraid of being hired because I feared I would then be exposed for the fraud I knew myself to be.

I walked into the Ryerson Press in this mood one day carrying samples of my work and was stunned to be hired as a bookbinder on the spot. I reported the next day and was shown around the bindery. Ryerson was of course a publisher, but they printed and bound their own books so the bindery was full of machinery—which to my eyes seemed as primitive as what I had known in Spain.

But it was the hand bookbinding that stunned me. No fear there of being exposed as a fraud. Compared to the guys they had there I *was* a master binder. Now I could see why the man had hired me when he saw my work. These men, all central Europeans, were butchers. None of them had ever done any proper apprenticeship, and they seemed to relish the mutilations they inflicted on books. Hack and slice like all beginners, and oh—how they loved the guillotine, that single most dangerous natural predator of the bookbinding world.

I must here digress to mention the Bookbinders' Hell. Bookbinders' Hell is large, there's lots of room for everybody, and there is a special punishment for each sin bookbinders commit. But the largest area in that Bookbinders' Hell is reserved for those who trim books. If you have ever read rare book dealers' catalogues you will have noticed numerous descriptions of books which have been trimmed until all the margins, the catchwords and often even half the text, have disappeared. What this means is that books rebound two or three times over a few hundred years have been hacked at by each successive generation of binders, seemingly never learning from their predecessors' depredations. All in the name of neatness. In the Bookbinders' section of Hell, binders guilty of trimming are themselves trimmed every day, a bit from the fingers, a bit from the toes, and finally some from the tongue to quiet the piteous pleas for mercy.

That, then, was the situation in Canada at that time. One bookbinder who really preferred leathercraft, a large publishing company whose bookbinding department contained the worst sort of book butchers, trimming and hacking away, no tools available and not the slightest sign that anyone cared or was even aware of that sad state.

And to make matters worse, this new bookbinder on the scene was a fraud; he hardly knew what he was doing, and, worse, couldn't even talk bookbinding talk in English.

I didn't know the English words for the technical terms used by binders. I had learned everything I knew in Spain, so naturally I only knew Spanish words for the tools and techniques.

I still occasionally see a book which I recognize as Ryerson work, and it still causes me to wince. One happy event, though, was that I joined the Bookbinder's Union, the only union I've ever joined, and I still retain my union card, of which I am inordinately proud, I don't know why. It was a provisional one, for there was a six month probationary period. But, unfortunately, I didn't work six months. In fact I only lasted eight days, after which I was laid off along with about a dozen others from the bindery. In case you are thinking that they did in fact discover I was a fraud, I don't think so. I may have been, but so were all of my co-workers. At least I knew it. Most likely, being laid off had more to do with the general incompetence which put Ryerson into bankruptcy a few years after my brief stint with them.

Anybody who attended the sale in Varsity Stadium that Ryerson put on when they went bankrupt could only be amazed that they had lasted as long as they did. What a mess of junk. Two and three volume sets of the memoirs of forgotten soldiers. Or worse, the exciting adventures of some protestant clergyman subduing the Devil in rural Saskatchewan. And thousands of leftover copies from the Ryerson Chapbook series, which included every amateur hack in Canada who ever wrote a poem; thousands of books that they could hardly give away, even at giveaway prices.

Anybody who knew anything about books, seeing that turgid mixture of pointless books which should never have been published, understood at once why and how Ryerson went under.

On the other hand, if you are partial to conspiracy theories, there is another possible explanation for my being laid off. The Ryerson Press had been founded as The Methodist Church publishing house and was still owned by the United Church of Canada. Perhaps they had somehow learned of my Vatican connections. Whether I was in fact the victim of some anti-papist conspiracy is now unprovable, but whatever the true explanation this ended my professional bookbinding career, all eight days of it. But by amazing good luck, in a series of flukes surely too significant to be a coincidence, I found myself in another career, bookselling, which ensured that I would spend the rest of my life unappreciated on the margins, culturally and socially, and, most important, well below the official poverty line in income. Just like bookbinding after all.

Chapter 4

Marty Ahvenus—Out of the Wilderness

Back in Canada after all these years, I spent an uncomfortable couple of weeks at my parents, then moved in with my old friend Alfred Ames and his new wife Nancy, sharing their house on Ward's Island. This was when I got to know Bob Mallory, Gwendolyn MacEwen's 'Magician', who lived behind us in a tumble-down shack which, in some schizophrenic extravaganza, he had completely covered in tinfoil. Through him I met Gwen, who still visited and tried to help him. As with many schizophrenics, Bob had many weird characteristics of dress which made him appear similar to a genie or an eastern magician, especially his constant wearing of a large turban; along with his otherworldly and often incomprehensible conversation it's not hard to see that Gwen probably got the idea and the model for her novel *Julian the Magician* from Bob.

I needed work right away but wasn't sure how to set about getting it. Close to ten years' absence washing dishes and digging ditches is hardly going to impress any potential employer.

A neighbour on the Island had a part-time job in a bookstore, but was leaving town and offered the job opportunity to Alfred, with whom I was sharing the cottage. He was going to apply for it and I accompanied him on my way to seek work myself.

We entered the tiny shop on Yonge, just south of Dundas, and met the owner. Al told him he wanted the job, but when the owner, Barry Young, heard that we were neighbours of his last employee he said no.

"I don't want another person from Ward's Island. She was always missing the early ferry and she'd get here at noon, when I was arriving. That's no good to me," he said.

As a one-man operation he needed the assistant for the three hours each day he needed to go to the publishers to pick up books and orders. This job also included all day Sunday, so with the three hours in the morning it came to 23 hours a week at $3.00 an hour, $70.00 or so a week, not much, but possible with a rent of $60.00 a month. Al was as desperate as me, and he also had a wife to support.

But it was obvious that Young was not going to relent. Knowing our neighbour, we knew that she had probably missed the ferry at least two or three times a week, and if she missed it on Sunday he wouldn't even know.

I said nothing, but in spite of Al's pleas that he wouldn't miss the ferry I could see that Young wasn't about to be talked into another Islander.

But something made me act quite out of character; I suddenly spoke up.

"Listen: why don't you hire us both? We'll switch every other day and one of us will always make it on time. Why not try us out?"

Still skeptical, Young considered it—it would solve his problem because he was well aware that it wasn't that easy to get someone·willing to commit themselves for $70.00 a week—so I pressed: "Why not try this? Give us a two week trial, if one ferry gets missed we'll call it quits. What's to lose?"

He weakened and agreed.

So we started the next day and it turned out fine—we easily managed the ferry and took turns, alternating Sundays as well. After a few months Al and Nancy decided to move to Northern Ontario and I got the entire job to myself. I also took over the entire house, since by then, I had met my future wife, Kathleen, become enamored and she had moved in with us too. So, with her working we were able to handle the rent on our own. And Barry Young, who was a great guy, was himself very eccentric, so he prepared me for all the eccentric used booksellers I would soon engage with.

Like many another in the antiquarian book trade I therefore started in new books. The new book trade, of course, is so different from used books that the only real experience gained for an antiquarian is in gaining some knowledge of how people buy books, a small part of what's needed in the antiquarian trade, but a necessary preliminary. But really the most important part is the experience of dealing with that uncontrollable monster known to all small businessmen as "The Public." I found I loved talking to people about books—or at least that part of the public who actually love books and are reasonably sane.

I never have figured out what compelled me to act so out of character to gain entry into the book business. Were some subconscious factors at play?

I have no idea, but what I do know is that I was a natural from day one. Young's was a tiny shop, so small he could only have any variety by confining his stock to paperbacks. All the walls were lined with the normal paperback racks, as was the centre, leaving barely enough space to navigate aisles. Therefore, to have any selection, it was necessary to have each rack, which in a normal store would contain multiple copies of the same book, filled with as many different titles as it could hold. By the second day I suggested that I spend my three hour shift putting the books in alphabetical order so we would have a hope of finding a book when it was requested.

By the time I was done I had discovered that I had a phenomenal memory for books and authors, even if I had never read them. Someone would inquire of a title and I would name the author. Where did that come from? More important, for a budding bookseller, if I had handled a book I remembered and could go to the appropriate rack at once. In later years, with my own stock, this great gift made me many sales and often astounded the staff of other stores. Often, a few days after scouting a store in San Francisco or Vancouver or Calgary, I might regret not buying a book, phone the store, request the book, and give explicit directions as to its location in the store ("It's on the second floor, third aisle of the literature section, second shelf from the bottom, fifth or sixth book from the left.") There must be *some* explanation for this phenomenon, because I've met many other dealers who can also do this.

Perhaps all those years of libraries and then Old Favorites had imparted some of this remarkable ability to retain authors and titles, but it's still a mystery to me. And it never went away, at least not until very recently when following the nature of things in aging, everything seems to be going away, especially my memory.

And I also found I loved the job, loved talking to people, discussing books and, since my only real job after answering questions was to sit at the cash desk and take money, I also had a fair amount of time to read.

After a while, when my interest didn't lead to boredom, I started thinking that maybe this was what I should be doing with my life. It had literally never occurred to me. All those years of reading in solitude had convinced me that reading books was a vice, not something that one could consider doing for a living. Almost thirty, a failure at everything I had ever tried, I was desperate to find a challenge, to find some work that mattered to me and that would test the capacity of my mind and challenge my intelligence. But I feared that the old familiar boredom would again appear, as it always had in the past. That fear lasted for several years. For almost my first ten years in business I woke every morning fearing that this would be the day my interest in bookselling evaporated. Finally, I caught on that, after that long, it wasn't likely to happen.

That it took so long to realize I had found my vocation indicates, I think, something of the depths of my despair at not having found anything I could engage with earlier.

Of course, now that I have had forty more years to think about such things, I have realized that most people go through life that way; they do work they hate only for the money they need to keep them going as they count the days until they can retire.

Realizing how incredibly lucky I had been to discover book-selling has more than made up for the pitiful living booksellers can look forward to.

For, of course, I whine at any opportunity about my poverty, but in truth that's only to keep up appearances. All booksellers whine, it goes with the territory. I wouldn't want to hurt my colleagues' feelings by admitting that I don't care about the lack of financial reward. But the fact is, I don't.

So I find myself, like all old men, lecturing the young, as my father had me. "Try and find some work to do that you can love; and do it the best you can," he would say, perhaps a cliché, but for a banker in that terrible conformist decade, the fifties, as close to a radical thought as my father ever uttered.

So, on June 15th, 1967 I entered the Village Bookstore on Gerrard Street in the old Bohemian village in Toronto and announced to my recent acquaintance, Marty Ahvenus, the proprietor, that I had decided to open a used bookshop.

I had no knowledge of books, except of some of their contents, no experience, and most crucial, no money. I had only my part-time job in Young's store, now earning $3.50 an hour, but such was my ignorance that none of these factors bothered me at all.

Furthermore, a good part of my motivation was based on my near complete lack of qualification for just about any other type of work.

I had become acquainted with Marty Ahvenus because his shop on Gerrard Street was fairly close to Young's and he had made an arrangement that when he needed a recent publication for a customer Barry Young would order it for him. I became friendly with Marty on these visits. I took to going there often. Marty gave everyone generous discounts, but he was even more generous to young people with little money. It didn't take me long to realize that dealing in used books was a hundred times more interesting than in new ones.

Marty, through his friendship with so many of the young Canadian writers, found himself by the accident of those friendships stocking the new, often self-published books of those young writers. His shop had become a center for those writers to meet and discover the books of their peers. It's unlikely that any of those writers who used Marty's store as their unofficial meeting place in Toronto were aware that they were part of the beginnings of a true Canadian literature, anymore than we young booksellers were aware that we also were laying the foundation of a true antiquarian trade in Canada.

We were, all of us, just having a good time, as we struggled to embark on our vocations and survive, whether it was in writing or bookselling. We may not have known it at the time, but the modern literature renaissance was going on everywhere in North America, with the ascendance of the Beats in New York and San Francisco and with young writers in every city testing the limits both in form and in law. With bookselling, renaissance is an inappropriate term, because there had existed little before in Canada—a few decent shops and dealers in the whole country, though mostly part-timers dealing in Canadiana from home. The closest we had had to a real general used bookstore in Toronto was Old Favorites.

I was already intrigued by the idea of becoming a bookseller. I knew I had only one place to go for help, my father, and I knew that I couldn't subject him to an appeal unless I was certain. But hanging around Marty's listening to all the fascinating conversations with readers and collectors and the many writers who dropped in regularly convinced me that if I was to become a bookseller, used books was the way to go.

So, I went to my father, who was less than enthusiastic, knowing as he did my track record. And he would be aware that bringing him my scheme meant I was going to hit him up for money.

Here's how I described it in a talk I once gave at the Fisher Library:

Having decided to become a bookseller, I went to my father, who was a banker, to tell him the important news. But his enthusiasm didn't match mine—probably because he suspected what was coming next. Now, any of you who have had children and have heard all the great schemes that are going to make them millionaire entrepreneurs before the age of twenty-five will know, as my father did, that the very core of all such schemes always begins with dad laying out some money. After extensive negotiations we arrived at a deal, which was that I got a one-time loan of $500.00 (to be paid back for sure this time and not a penny more ever no matter what great opportunities or disasters not one penny more period, if you want to ruin your life with your crazy schemes I can't stop you but please leave your mother and me in peace for the few years left us etc. etc.). We all know that scenario. The funny thing was that I paid him back the five hundred and never did ask him for another cent, but until he died some fifteen years later, whenever I entered his home he always looked at me a bit quizzically, as though he was expecting me to broach the subject of a loan once again. In later years, whenever I told him that I had just bought a library, his instant response was "I don't have any money."

I've never been certain whether my father was convinced by my obvious seriousness or if he was just doing what desperate fathers do: trying to give his son another boost, hoping against hope that this time ....

But he signed a cheque for $500.00 and I began my new life. The truth is, I was as skeptical—and as terrified—as my father probably was. But I was determined to give it my best. If I went down in flames, again, I knew it would be back to the factory, doomed to a life of drudgery.

As I entered the Village Bookstore that day in 1967 Marty was talking to a man, to whom, when I made my profound announcement, Marty introduced me.

"This is Gord Norman," he said, informing me that Gord was also a bookseller. Gord Norman, it turned out, operated from his home issuing catalogues in his specialty, Modern First Editions. Gord was cordial, asking me at one point how big my stock was. When I informed him that I had no books, he inquired how long I thought it would take to acquire sufficient books to stock a store. I replied with the confidence of the abysmally ignorant, "Oh, I figure about six months." (I also thought that my $500.00 loan was going to be enough money to stock a shop, too.)

Neither man laughed in my face, although I'm sure they were both quietly amused at my incredible naïveté. (In fact, when I went out on my own two and a half years later I had some seven hundred books, about two shelf sections.)

But both of them took me seriously, demonstrating a generosity of spirit I've never forgotten. And both of them immediately began a process I only became aware of quite a long time later, quietly and subtly instructing me, guiding me with gentle suggestions, mentoring in the time-honoured traditions of the book trade. They knew what I then didn't know, that there being no schools for booksellers, the responsibility for educating future generations of the trade falls to other booksellers. The continuity of five hundred years of tradition demands that the older pass it on to the younger.

They didn't know whether I was one of the worthy ones or just another of those who show up often, do it for a while and disappear. They did what I have done ever since I realized the importance of these traditions; they took me seriously and were prepared to do so until I proved myself unworthy of their attention.

My new acquaintance, or I guess my new colleague, Gord Norman told me that he was just going up to a sale of books run by Hadassah, the Jewish women's organization, and asked if I wanted to accompany him. I did. It was an outdoor street sale on Markham Street in the Mirvish village.

Rummaging through the assorted books I realized I hadn't any idea what I should be interested in buying—reality was starting to intrude.

I finally found a book by Somerset Maugham, whom I was then reading with great pleasure. It was a late novel, and it had no dust wrapper, but I didn't know that it should have. On the verso of the title it clearly stated "First Edition," although it wasn't. More properly it should have read "First U.S. Edition," but even that was not true. It was in fact the Book-of-the-Month Club issue. In that period the Book Club would simply purchase a part of the first printing and the only certain way to tell the issues apart for one who didn't know the other signs was if it retained its dust wrapper, where the book club details could be found.

But I couldn't get into too much trouble because the price was only 25¢. I bought it.

A few minutes later Gord showed me a book called *The Buddhist Praying-Wheel*, by a man called Simpson. It looked very serious and obscure. I didn't know enough to realize that that was a good sign. It looked too dry and scholarly to me, which is exactly what it was. A real bookseller would have known that was what made it desirable.

But Gord advised me to buy it, and since it was only 50¢ I suppressed my skepticism, bowing to his superior experience (at that stage my experience of the used-book business being of about ten minutes duration; I guess every other used bookseller in the world had more experience than me). So my first expenditure as a bookseller was two books: cost 75¢.

Travelling home that same afternoon on the Ward's Island ferry I met my friend Blake Stevens, to whom I proudly announced that I was now a bookseller, showing him my entire stock, all two books. He astonished me by showing great interest in the Maugham and asked if he could buy it. I agonized for a moment about what to ask for it, my first experience of that anxiety-laden existential dilemma booksellers come to know so well: needing to arrive at a price on the spot, no time for reference, no time to properly think. After years and years one gets better at this but never comfortable. I bit the bullet and suggested 75¢. He paid me, thus completing my first sale, on my first day as a bookseller. Part of my shock and indecision at Blake's request indicates another of my worst dilemmas as a bookseller, then and now. I didn't really want to sell the Maugham to him because I had intended to read it that night. In the forty-five years since that day I have countless times faced the same dilemma; wanting to keep a book which I should actually be trying to sell. And countless times I have solved my problem by deciding to form yet another of the many collections I have built over the years, my justification being that some time in the future I would sell the whole as a collection. It works very well too. Another first on my first day, this one a pretty dumb one as my father always pointed out. I had bought two books for a total of 75¢, sold half my entire stock and got all my money back, being left with Simpson's *The Buddhist Praying-Wheel* as my eventual profit. My first sale as a bookseller was therefore conducted on a boat, perhaps, I like to think, the only career in the annals of the book trade begun thus. Later I also sold a book on that same ferry to my friend (and first publisher) Karen Mulhallen, who also lived on Ward's Island then.

And, furthermore, my first day as a bookseller, I now realize, may very well have been my most successful day as a bookseller, in spite of all those years since.

A library bought, half of it sold at once for an enormous profit-ratio, paying for everything and retaining one very good book as my profit.

Forty-five years later I still have Simpson's *The Buddhist Praying-Wheel*. Its history illustrates a lot about the used-book business, and probably me as well. After much thought and anguish I decided that it should be worth $15.00. That was a considerable price when used books were mostly priced from $1.50 to $3.00 and the more common first editions only sold for $5.00 to $10.00. But it *was* a good book, and scarce, as I later found, having only ever seen one other copy of it since then.

A few months later I began working for Jerry Sherlock at Joseph Patrick Books. I have been asked and have explained thousands of times about Joseph Patrick. There is no Joseph Patrick; Joseph Patrick is Jerry. He didn't want to use his own name so he used his middle names. His full name is Gerald Joseph Patrick Sherlock (yes, his people came from Ireland). I have cursed Jerry thousands of times for all of the time I've wasted explaining that. Still, during the two years I worked for him and in the forty-five years of friendship since then, that would probably be the only thing that has ever given me real cause to curse him. Jerry very generously gave me some space in his shop to put up some of my books for sale. *The Buddhist Praying-Wheel* lasted through those two years and then accompanied me to my new office, where after a few months I raised the price to $17.50. There it sat for a few years more, before I raised the price again, to $20.00, then $22.50 and up in those increments until it reached $35.00. Finally, after fifteen or twenty years, with the price now at $75.00, I looked at it one day—but now with the eyes of someone who had gained the sense of tradition and continuity which all booksellers inevitably acquire through time—and realized that I should not sell that book; after all it was the first book I ever bought as a bookseller. I removed it from the shelf, gave it to my bookbinder, instructing him to make a folding protective box, and put it in my private library, where it affords me great comfort and pleasure every time I look at it.

This is precisely the sort of book anecdote which infuriated my father, the banker. "Oh fine," I can hear him say, "you buy a book that nobody wants, pay rent to keep it on the shelf for twenty years, then spend even more than it's worth to put it in a special case. And somehow you convince yourself that you are running a successful business. You need your head read." (This was one of my father's favourite expressions, which he directed at me my entire life. It wasn't until many years later, when I seriously began buying books on phrenology, that pseudo-science which believed that character could be ascertained by the shape of the head, that I realized where it came from. His parents' generation had actually *believed* in phrenology, and no doubt his father had said that to him a few thousand times too, but seriously.)

So, now a bookseller, at least in my own mind, I worked my three hours a day at Young's, scouted the Crips and Sally Ann in the afternoons, and spent a lot of time in Marty's store watching and listening and learning.

One curious detail of which I was then completely unaware, was that Young's Books was the only bookstore on Yonge Street then right up to the Batta Bookstore north of Wellesley Street which wasn't a porn store. I never went into any of them (there was one directly across the street from Young's) so I never realized this until I became friends with Nicky Drumbolis. Nicky Drumbolis is an extraordinary bookseller for whom I have enormous affection and respect. He is a remarkable man, unlike any other bookseller I've known well personally.

At that time I didn't know Nick, nor was I aware that he was the distributor for all those stores, almost all of them owned or controlled by "The Mob." Every month Nicky (he told me years later) would travel to New York to pick up a truckload of pornography and bring it up to Toronto to supply these stores. These stores were all the same, usually having a small front room stocked with a few ordinary new publications or soft-core porn magazines, and a larger back room where the very lucrative hard-core porn was displayed. When I walked up Yonge Street I would notice that the front windows often displayed the avant-garde work of the time: the Beats, lots of pamphlets, poetry published by Ferlinghetti's City Lights in San Francisco, and similar publications from the New York underground. In fact, much of the poetry and prose displayed in these shops were by writers now considered among the giants of Modern American literature, writers such as Williams, Ginsberg, Kerouac, Olson, Spicer, McClure, and Burroughs, who were then considered scum, perverts, *communist* perverts in fact. Nicky had many funny anecdotes about his dealings with Canadian customs, but what was curious were his motives. As he told me, his bosses had no interest in what was displayed in the front windows of those shops, so he had a free hand; he could buy, bring in and display anything he wanted. Their profit came from the back rooms. Nicky believed it was his duty to bring those books into Canada, believing if he didn't Canadians would have no opportunity to be exposed to these writers and their books, who he believed were transforming American literature and who would one day influence the world. He believed that if he didn't do it, no one would. He considered it his moral obligation to expose Canadians to their influence. He was like those crazy missionaries, so many of them Canadian, who sailed to the Pacific Islands to convert the natives to Christianity. But in Nick's case his religion was literature, and just as quite a few of those dedicated Christians were eaten by the natives, so has the indifference and contempt of our society attempted to eat Nicky's idealism. But while he's starved for thirty or forty years, he persists. And if God doesn't reward him, I believe history, literary history, will. I consider Nicky to be probably the most remarkable bookseller Canada has produced. Drumbolis is a true visionary but is considered a fool by many of his contemporaries who can only understand profit. But remember William Blake was also considered nuts in his time.

Another thing which Nicky told me during our many conversations about books in Toronto in those arid times continues to fascinate me. The Mob, who muscled out the original pioneers in the porn trade in Toronto and elsewhere, eventually controlling it, refused to traffic in gay porn. They were apparently too straightlaced. So they ruthlessly controlled pornography, prostitution, and later drug traffic, but they drew the line at gay porn. Contrary to their morals, apparently. Another irony pointed out to me recently relates to Nicky Drumbolis. Nicky recently sold a huge and extremely important collection of very contemporary literature to the University of Toronto. Nicky knows more of the minutiae of modern literature than any dealer I've ever met, and he learned all this and acquired much of the collection that he sold because of his experiences and his purchases during the time that he was working for the Mob.

So, as my friend took great delight in pointing out, it appears that the Mob is largely responsible for buying and supplying this great collection to the University of Toronto.

One day, shortly after meeting him, Gord Norman asked if I wanted to accompany him on a scouting visit to see the books of a man called Mr. Honsberger. Mr. Honsberger dealt books from his home, and as we travelled there Gord gave me instructions.

"He specializes in occult or astral projection, also spiritualism (books generally categorized in the trade as 'nutbar') and he believes in it strongly himself. All his books will be very cheap except anything otherworldly. Don't," admonished Gord, "under any circumstances, put anything with remotely that kind of content in your pile. None of the books will be priced but they will be very cheap. If you put any books in your pile which he believes to be important—which means an occult book—he will ask a lot for them.

"And, if you don't take it at whatever crazy price he asks, it will be the end of us both. He will become cranky and kick us both out without any books. Make sure none of your books could even remotely fall in the occult genre. And, also, when he answers the door, whatever you do, don't laugh. Don't even smile."

I didn't understand what he meant and spent the rest of the trip trying to figure it out.

We knocked on Honsberger's door. When he opened it Gord's warning became clear. Mr. Honsberger was an elderly gentleman and, as book people often do, he radiated gentleness and courtesy. The only mildly disconcerting thing was his appearance.

He was wearing huge flying goggles, with really thick lenses held in place by a thick rubber strap encircling his head, and a World War I airman's leather helmet with big earflaps, along with a heavy floor-length canvas coat, even though it was mid-summer. He obviously saw nothing worthy of explanation in his bizarre get-up so we pretended that we didn't either. It turned out that the goggles were really specifically-made glasses, for he was extremely short-sighted. The coke-bottle lenses so enlarged his eyes that with the leather flying helmet he looked like some sort of demented Red Baron.

There was an English actor named Marty Feldman who suffered, I believe, an eye defect which caused him to have bulbous eyes. And with this as comic equipment he sustained an acting career. The first time I saw him in a film I thought, "It's Honsberger's son," because that's exactly how Honsberger looked.

I wanted to ask him if his biplane was parked in the back-yard, or if maybe he was dressed for a trip to some alien world in another universe, but my natural book greed kept my smart-alec instincts reined in.

We descended to a basement so full of books it was difficult to move, where Gord and I rummaged for a couple of hours, piling up huge stacks of books. At one point I thought I would test Gord's admonition about Honsberger, for despite his outfit and his disconcertingly magnified eyes, he seemed so gentle that I couldn't imagine that what Gord had told me could be true. I spied a hard-cover edition of *The Third Eye*—in fact it was the first edition, the only one I've seen before or since—by the Tibetan Lama Lobsang Rampa, who had started life as a pipe fitter in St. Catharines or Manchester or some such place. "That's a good book," I essayed to Honsberger, holding it up under his nose, which one had to do, for even with the magnifying goggles it was obvious he was near blind.

His whole demeanor changed. He drew himself up and focused his bulbous eyes on me, glaring.

"That is a *very* important book. I would need to get $100.00 for that book," he said, his manner now both menacing and con-frontational, his magnified eyes unblinking.

"Oh," I quickly replied, "I know it is. I've read it twice. I only wish I could afford it. Are you sure it's only $100.00? That seems a very cheap price."

Mr. Honsberger was mollified and reverted back to the gentle dreamer. Sure enough, when he totaled up our purchases everything was 25¢ or 50¢.

We left Mr. Honsberger content, with his *real* treasures safe.

CHAPTER 5

My Second Mentor:
Jerry Sherlock and Joseph Patrick Books

By now I was becoming known to the Toronto trade through Marty and Gord Norman, and I started getting job offers, although I couldn't understand why. I was certainly no catch, as I knew practically nothing and had no experience. Much later I figured it out. The pool of available people around the bookworld then in Toronto was made up of eccentrics, misfits and losers, so that when someone came along who seemed halfway sane and presentable everyone tried to hire them. One day I was in Old Favorites and Lou Morris, who hadn't hired me in my first attempt to enter the trade years earlier—because I couldn't type—offered me a job.

"I still can't type, Lou," I said.

"I'll get you doing other things," he said.

I didn't know if I should. I had begun to see that, great as it was for browsing or scouting, I wasn't going to learn a lot in Old Favorites. Already influenced by Gord Norman, I wanted to specialize in Modern Firsts, but it was obvious I'd be on my own if I accepted; nobody at Old Favorites knew or cared about first editions. Still, I figured, I should accept just to get access to all those books. I would have been able to scout for books as I worked, a decided advantage.

Lou and Kay Morris were going on holidays for two weeks so we agreed I would give my answer when they returned.

In the meantime I'd been amassing a small pile of Canadiana. When I had met Jerry Sherlock he had told me I should offer him Canadian books. Like all good dealers he was known to pay well, making good offers—sometimes very high ones. We ignorant scouts lived in anticipation that Jerry would shock us going through our pile by offering $150.00 for what we had considered a $5.00 book. And he often did so. I had a couple of shopping bags full of Canadiana saved up, all bought because they were either very cheap or seemed interesting. But the neophyte lacks the necessary experience to know the one essential for rare books—rarity. The rules of condition can be learned quickly, as can relative importance to some degree, but scarcity, that other essential component of the three prime requisites of rare books, needs years of experience to learn.

I visited Jerry's shop at Wellington and Yonge; I had never seen anything like it. It was beautiful. The premises had previously been some sort of outlet for fine China and had built-in wooden display counters on the walls, which worked wonderfully to display antiquarian books. As I later learned it was also very cheap, being owned by one of the big banks, which intended to build a new head office across the road. They were just keeping it rented until they needed it.

It looked like a rare bookshop should look; all dark old wood and old leather.

Jerry bought about half my books and then offered me a job. I didn't know what to say. I was stricken with indecision and guilt. Lou had asked me first. Could I be one of those superficial greedy opportunists who would eschew proper behaviour and decency for his own personal benefit?

I went to Marty for advice.

"It's a no-brainer, Dave. If you want to be a bookseller, take Jerry's offer. You'll learn a hundred times more there. And a hundred times faster."

I phoned Jerry and accepted, but still felt constrained to go to Lou after his return and apologize for my crass opportunism. Lou took it well, with the same gentle acceptance with which he seemed to accept all human foibles. I actually think he even agreed with me.

I worked for Jerry for two years, way too short a time to learn much about books, but in retrospect I see that what was really important to learn, I did learn: how to approach things if one wants to be a real bookseller, a professional.

Before I met Jerry Sherlock I already disliked him; and I was sure that when I did meet him I was going to despise him. This was because for the few months, between my beginning to scout for books and meeting Jerry, other scouts and booksellers would often ask if I'd met him yet, always adding, when I said that I hadn't, that when I did, I would like him. He's a great guy, they would say. And so many people said that so often, that I got sick of hearing about this Mr. Nice Guy. I was sure he would turn out to be one of those professional phonies, who pretend congeniality, but when one gets past their hypocritical façade are revealed as self-centered egoists. But, as so often is the case when one prejudges, I couldn't have been more wrong. Another problem which I figured would ensure my dislike of him was the constant references I heard beforehand describing Jerry as a devout Catholic. I was an atheist, had been since my eleventh or twelfth year, so I expected, again, the pompous superiority one gets from the true believer with all the answers. But Jerry was none of the things I had expected.

When we met he was friendly, completely unpretentious and exhibiting none of the pompous superiority that I had expected from someone so often described as the most important bookseller in Toronto (it was only later, when I had some experience, that I realized that he was the best bookseller in Canada and, along with Bernard Amtmann, one of the two most important this country has had so far.)

It's hard for me to try and describe Jerry Sherlock because knowing him has been so important to me on so many levels. He has affected me as strongly as anyone I have ever known. His character affected me professionally and personally—he was my true mentor and my most important teacher, but also after being my mentor he became and remains a close friend.

Insofar as Jerry had faults they were pretty minor, except for one which caused constant irritation, but sometimes also great amusement to his friends. I expect it wasn't so amusing to his family. This was his memory. Jerry was the perfect example of the absent-minded professor; he would forget anything and everything, incessantly. Everything except books.

After I'd been working for him for a few months I applied to become an associate member of the ABAC, the Antiquarian Booksellers Association of Canada, something that was then straightforward. An associate member of the ABAC had no voting privileges. It was really just a way to attend meetings and have the association's initials on your business card, a small convenience when dealing with bankers or crossing borders, or sometimes when buying books privately. All you needed to become an associate was to be a full-time employee of a full member and for $25.00 a year you were eligible. The problem was that your employer had to apply for you, but Jerry kept forgetting. It became very vexing. Before every ABAC meeting I would press Jerry to put me up, resorting to notes after a few times. I had never joined anything since Boy Scouts (which I abandoned quickly after I discovered the pool hall) and the Bookbinder's Union.

But I knew by now that I was born to be a bookseller and I badly wanted some tangible mark of my admittance to that noble society of peddlers of culture.

But Jerry always forgot to apply on my behalf. He would return from an ABAC meeting and start to give me the latest trade gossip, when I only wanted to hear if I was a member.

When I could no longer contain my eagerness and asked, he would become embarrassed and admit that he'd forgotten. I finally had to ask a friend, already a member, to remind Jerry openly, right in the meeting, before I was finally allowed in.

You couldn't stay mad at Jerry for those lapses—they were obviously beyond his control, and when another incident occurred he was always sheepishly embarrassed. It must have been truly difficult for his family.

His daughter Anne, who herself became a bookseller and once rented part of Jerry's store for her stock and that of her business partner, once issued a catalogue with a rather strong note, one I've never seen before or since in a bookseller's catalogue. It went something like this:

When ordering from this catalogue under no circumstances leave a message with any person answering the phone other than the proprietor. Certain people here never pass on messages.

Jerry would extend very generous discounts to other booksellers, especially beginners, and then forget he had done so. Once, two newish booksellers came into the shop and Jerry gave them over 50% off and told them to pay later.

They never paid at all and when they appeared again a year later he was doing the same when I whispered to him, "Jerry, these sons-of-bitches haven't paid you for the last time yet."

"Oh," he shrugged, "didn't they? Well I'm sure they will when they can."

I made sure they did.

Some of Jerry's memory lapses became the stuff of legend amongst his friends. A couple of them I told for years, often right in front of Jerry. He would give the same sheepish laugh, happy to see his friends amused, resigned to his reputation for forgetfulness.

The best one he told me himself. It seems that one day, a few years after he and Bernice had moved into their new home in High Park, he was riding the streetcar and met an old neighbour from the previous neighbourhood. During the pleasantries the woman inquired of Jerry how many children he and Bernice now had. "Five," replied Jerry. The neighbour congratulated him. Then by great coincidence the same old neighbour met Bernice a week or so later on the same streetcar and greeted Bernice by congratulating her on her five children.

Bernice was forced to inform her old neighbour that they actually had six children. Jerry tried claiming that this had only occurred because when he had met the neighbour he had been engrossed in reading a bookseller's catalogue and was justly distracted by the bargains it contained. This made his friends laugh even louder.

Sometimes, in the store, the phone would ring and it would be one of Jerry's kids calling for something. After a bit Jerry would have to say, "What's your name?" or "Which one are you?"

I only stopped telling stories about Jerry's memory lapses when I began experiencing the same problems myself. Now my memory is almost as faulty as his was then, and I find myself doing the same sheepish laugh and attempting the same pathetic excuses about too much useless arcana in my head.

But even though Jerry couldn't be counted on to remember why he had gone from the back of the store to the front, he could supply you endless details about any Canadian book ever published, its scarcity, its importance, and its value.

On my first day at Jerry's shop I got my first lesson in how previous experience in a different context can be important later. Just as scouting golf balls prepared me for scouting books (and caddying, incidentally, prepared me for dealing with the wealthy as well. Caddies, like the most menial of servants, are largely unnoticed—invisible, in fact—and therefore they see their wealthy employers, not only without the outward signs of wealth, their expensive suits, but also, golf being what it is, they often witness character defects without the façade of self-control. There is nothing like golf to bring out the worst in people), other jobs taken out of necessity prepared me with experiences that became invaluable in entirely different contexts years later.

One such stint found me, as I mentioned earlier, as a shipper for a couple of years for Dr. Scholl's, the foot comfort man. I would ship out the corn plasters, and I became very good at constructing neat, compact parcels. So when, on that first day, Jerry explained that the first thing one learned in an antiquarian bookstore was how to properly pack books, I told him I already knew how to pack, thanks to Dr. Scholl. He was surprised, but skeptical. He watched me closely as I made a package, carefully slicing and folding in the ends until a perfect brick-like package resulted. Jerry couldn't believe his luck. An apprentice who not only wasn't a simpleton (except about Canadiana) but one who could pack! In fact, he admonished me, "Dave, you packed that too well. We don't slice the ends, we force the excess corrugated cardboard into the ends. Your package is beautiful, but that much care is not necessary."

The packing of books is not only the first thing an apprentice is taught, it is one of the most important. Real booksellers believe that they have a moral responsibility to ensure that a client receives a book in exactly the state it was in when it was on his shelf. A very good indication of how professional any bookseller is can be ascertained by how they ship their books. If the books are carelessly packed it is safe to assume that such people are probably prone to cutting other corners as well. And you should assume as much. I do.

We get compliments regularly, from all over the world, on our packing. The best ones come as veiled complaints when someone, pretending to be irritated, informs us it took fifteen minutes to open the package.

Working at Joseph Patrick Books, it turns out, taught me plenty, even if it wasn't what I thought I was learning at the time.

I wasn't really interested in Canadiana, probably a residue from my intense boredom as my ninth- and tenth-grade teachers had attempted to teach me that dates and names constituted history. It was only much later, when I read Pierre Berton's marvellous popularizations, that I came to see that our history contains as many fascinating characters as any country, anywhere. Ever since, I have been reading Canadian historians. I give them, just as I give novels, fifty pages (or three chapters.) If they haven't got my attention by then, too bad—that's it. Life's too short, there's too many books—too many worthy books.

What has to be learned in a rare bookstore is overwhelming in the beginning. My lack of interest in Canadiana caused me to believe I was ignorant. People would come into Jerry's shop, ask a question, and my standard response would be, "I'm sorry I've only been here a short time. I don't really know anything."

Finally Jerry called me aside. "Dave," he said, "it's all very well to be honest, but what you should realize is that, little as you think you know, you already know more than most of them. I don't want you to lie, but why don't you just not say anything?"

This was pretty good advice. From where I sit now, I see that I had actually learned a fair bit, even if I hadn't yet caught on that it was these customers who were already teaching me as much as Jerry was. People who collect books start with an interest which, coupled with that weird acquisitive instinct common to all collectors, becomes transformed into a passion—often a compulsion—which can and does result in the expenditure of lots of money. Significant money, even for single acquisitions. It also confers a commensurate level of knowledge, a fact seldom understood by outsiders. A person who spends $500.00 or $1,000.00 or more for an historical artifact changes their perspective of what is really important. Many collectors pursue books to the exclusion of almost everything else.

The greatest privately owned collection of Canadiana I ever saw was formed by a postman, and this in the days before their incessant blackmail of the rest of us rendered postmen well-to-do. This man lived in a tiny rundown house which hadn't seen paint in many years. Certainly his collection was probably worth three times as much as the house.

At Jerry's I started to meet serious collectors, some very successful businessmen and some as eccentric as a lot of the scouts I knew from the Crips and Sally Ann.

In about my second week I started to plumb the depths of this eccentricity. One day that week Jerry said to me, "Well Dave, I have an appointment, I'll see you later. Just take messages, write everything down, you'll be fine."

I was terrified. I was in charge. I was sure something would happen that I wouldn't know how to deal with, and Jerry would lose money or something. About an hour in the phone rang.

"Do you buy books?" asked a woman.

"Depends what they are," I replied. (I had learned that at least, the first answer, always, to that common question.)

"They're Canadian books, all of them. There's around 10,000 of them, my husband's collection," she said.

Ten thousand books! Even I knew that was an enormous number, almost unheard of outside of a library.

"We specialize in Canadiana," I said, unable to mask my excitement. "My boss is out right now but I know he will be interested. I'll have him phone you as soon as he returns."

"Well, you'd better hurry up," she said. "They're all out on the front porch right now."

"The front porch? Books on the front porch?"

This was strange, but I was so excited I didn't pursue that thought.

Jerry returned.

"Anything to report?" he asked.

"Not much, Jerry," I suavely replied. "Except for a library of 10,000 Canadian books I got offered."

"10,000?" said Jerry. "That's huge. You got the name and number?" he asked, his excitement now matching mine.

"Yes. And we have to move quickly. She said they're on the front porch. I can't figure that one," I said.

Jerry's face fell.

"I know what that means," he said sadly. "What's the name?"

I showed him.

"Oh, it's him again. I should have realized. Every few years his wife gets sick of him bringing books into the house, puts them all out on the porch and threatens to leave him. He runs away and hides, she tries to sell them, then in a few more days she forgives him and they go back in the house. I should have realized it was him, but it's been four or five years since the last time."

We were both now dejected. Jerry explained.

"The worst part is that I went out to look the first time and everything he had was junk. It was all Canadian, but he had bought the whole lot at the Sally Ann over the years, at 10¢ each, and there wasn't a decent book in the lot. Whenever he did have a good book it would be ex-library or falling apart."

So my first Canadian library was a flop. Maybe they still appear on the porch every few years. Obsessives like that man don't stop until they die.

At Jerry's things became somewhat schizophrenic. Not interested myself in Canadiana, I worked for a man who not only specialized in Canadiana but was hardly interested in other kinds of books, except for his own personal interests, which were Catholic books and authors such as Belloc and Chesterton. Jerry was as close to a self-taught bookseller as it's possible to be, I think, which makes his achievement even more remarkable. You will hear me go on and on in this memoir about the traditions of the trade and the proper way a professional should act, and I learned much, if not most of that, from Jerry. But where did he learn it? There *were* no professionals before Jerry, at least in Toronto, or if there were I didn't meet them. There were several dealers who knew books and did things properly, especially some of those earlier part-timers like Fred Ketcheson. And Dora Hood, whose memoir *The Side Door* I recently reread after forty years. This caused me to change my long-held view that she hadn't really been a real bookseller, but only a nice, amateur, hobbyist.

Rereading her memoir, I realized that I had been unfair to her all those years. From the perspective of thirty-five years more experience I can only shudder in embarrassment at my ignorant dismissal of her for all that time. I think I was guilty of a sort of reverse snobbery mixed with the arrogant ignorance I have despised all my life. Mea culpa.

In fact, *The Side Door* demonstrates that Dora Hood *was* a real bookseller and a good one too, and, like Jerry Sherlock, self-taught. Only a born bookseller could have survived with neither experience or teachers, nothing but her natural experience and her instincts. She knew her Canadian history well, she learned quickly, and more interesting to me now, her book reveals a quiet, gentle humour and all the signs of someone who recognized the foibles of human nature that all booksellers need to learn in order to deal with the eccentricities of collectors.

David Mason

I never met Dora Hood, but years ago I bought a photographic study of her from John Reeves, the Canadian photographer. I guess I thought I was buying it as another ephemeral component of my collection on the history of bookselling in Canada. It has sat on a shelf in my office all these years, so I guess I've been at least honouring her historical significance. I now know that had I met her I would have liked her and respected her. And I like to think we would have become friends. As a belated attempt to atone I shall frame her portrait and hang it in my shop.

Probably part of my early dismissal of her related to her too-gentle descriptions of some of her clients. I never met any of the people she describes but Jerry knew some of them. His descriptions of them went from "nice, but a cheapskate" to "a harmless fool". Or, "he thought he knew books, but he wouldn't have lasted a day in the trade."

I realize now that a good part of my cruel and ignorant dismissal of Dora Hood was based not on my lack of interest in Canadiana, but on my impression of her successors. When Dora Hood retired, the business was owned and run by Julia Jarvis and Jean Tweed. Julia Jarvis I only met once, but that was enough. She was a type I knew well, having grown up in the era when Toronto, probably all of Canada, was run by people just like her. She was the worst sort of self-satisfied unquestioning snob. She could barely bring herself to acknowledge me when we met. I, with jeans and beard, obviously wasn't the "right sort." When I was growing up, Toronto names were all English and Scottish, the social lines more rigid than even those of the British class system which they so slavishly copied. It was largely that pathetic assumption of some innate superiority which made the Toronto of the time (Canada?) so deadly boring, and which caused me, when I left for Europe at nineteen, to say that I would never return. Luckily, by the time I did return, we were being saved from that cultural suicide by the influx of people from all over the world. We owe a lot more to this influx of different customs and attitudes than these immigrants will ever know. They saved us from ourselves.

Jean Tweed, conversely, I liked a lot. She was earthy and friendly. Once, when she and I and Hugh Anson-Cartwright had the thoroughly embarrassing and unpleasant duty of going to the apartment of a thief we had caught who had stolen from all of us, and whose explanation for his betrayal of our trust was his drinking, where, he said he "lost all moral control," Jean gave him a passionate but gentle lecture on alcohol, which demonstrated pretty clearly that she was herself a reformed alcoholic. I liked her a lot, but not enough to forgive her partner her stupid snobbery.

A friend of mine, who started bookselling about the same time I did, very cleverly made a good part of his living off Dora Hood's Bookroom for a couple of years, based on the stupid systems which Hood's successors considered a proper way to buy books. They had taken Dora Hood's system and without thinking through the implications applied them as "rules" in an entirely different era.

They used a system whereby they paid one half of the retail price of any Canadian book they had stocked previously. No doubt this was fair for books for which they had a back order. Commendable even, when these were good books, books which sold for $100.00 or $200.00. But for really valuable books, where desirability and rarity would cause a knowledgeable dealer to pay 70 or 80% for a book which they could sell the next day, they were cheating the seller, whether they knew it or not. But what did them in was the $5.00 to $20.00 books, which at 50% meant they were paying half-price for what they shouldn't have bought for any price. This stupidity, in my opinion, is what eventually brought them to ruination, as unquestioned axioms and methods usually will. This may have worked well for Dora Hood when her sources of supply would have largely been from the dispersal through death and moving of her acquaintances and collectors, but when the next generation—my own—introduced not just a bunch of sharp young dealers who were intent on actually making a living at bookselling as a profession, but also a bunch of scouts who went out seeking Canadiana in every possible source, many more copies of books became available quickly, just as the advent of the Internet a generation later showed everyone that many books once thought to be scarce were a lot more common than had been assumed.

My friend, learning this, took them all his cheap, common Canadiana that he got for free and that every other dealer knew one couldn't pay anything for. Paying half price on $7.50 to $15.00 books ignores the obvious, that they're in that range because they are common. In a capitalist society everything must have a price but acting on the idea that price *is* value is what did them in.

Adding up a large number of books at $3.75 or $5.00 will result in a fair amount of money. I believe this eventually bankrupted Dora Hood's successors. While I and most of my friends may be terrible businessmen, we're not stupid. Vanity and snobbishness and the unquestioned assumption of the rightness of one's position in the world is the basis of the old saying "Shirtsleeves to shirtsleeves in three generations," a fate of many dynasties. The tragedy of the Eatons, considered by so many Canadians as our own home-grown royalty, was no tragedy; it was another shirtsleeves scenario, as Rod McQueen's admirable book *The Eatons* illustrates.

Working for Jerry I started to absorb a sense of the booktrade in Canada.

In the booktrade in Montreal there were Bernard Amtmann and Grant Woolmer, both very good booksellers. There were also

Heinz Heinemann, of Mansfield Bookmart, William Wolfe and Isobel McKenzie, but when I showed up the trade was just beginning in Toronto, with Jerry, Hugh Anson-Cartwright, Marty Ahvenus, and Gord Norman. Within a very few years another whole group of young booksellers, including me, appeared.

It is for that reason that I consider those above-mentioned people the first true generation of real booksellers in Canada. Myself, Steven Temple, Gail Wilson, Larry Wallrich, Paul Lockwood, and Joyce Blair of Abelard, Bela Batta, Bob Russell even, I like to think of us as generation 'one-and-a-half', since all of us came along during the next ten years.

By some curious inexplicable coincidence, a similar thing occurred in the States, with a whole wave of new booksellers appearing in the middle-to-late '60s. When we started having bookfairs in the early '70s a whole bunch of young Americans showed up. Some twenty or so years later, with some sense of historical perspective, I took to calling all of these people, all of whom I recall with the same nostalgic affection one finds in people's accounts of their university friends, the class of '67. Now that some of those people have died or are dying off my nostalgia is even more intense, probably another effect of the strong sense of history and tradition that becomes imbued in all booksellers in time.

To continue with the historical minutiae, in the summer of 1969 I began to feel constricted by many of the hassles which went with living on Ward's Island, especially the ferry schedule, which demanded precise timing, and my by-now normal habit of carrying one or two shopping bags of books each way every day. But most important was the impending birth of my son, due some time around early December. Even though the ice in the bay didn't usually impede the ferry that early, I had nightmares about being stuck in the ice mid-bay with my wife delivering in primitive conditions on the big boat. It's one thing to start your career as a bookseller on a boat; it's another altogether to enter into fatherhood. My friend Alfred had needed to rush his wife Nancy to the hospital via the police boat with what turned out to be an ectopic pregnancy, which had scared us all. This was, admittedly, irrational, but for a man just about everything about having a child, especially when it is your first, is irrational. We decided it was time to leave the island.

My friend Karen Mulhallen had left the island by then and told us about a basement apartment she had seen on Kendall Avenue, on the edge of the Annex, so we took it.

Then Joseph Patrick Books was evicted from the Wellington Street store. The owners had finally started construction on their new head office across the street and decided they wanted Jerry's building as well.

Jerry decided to move to his house, from which he would issue catalogues. He told me that I was welcome to stay on, but he lived in the east end and I had no wish to travel across town every day to sit in a basement, cataloguing. So, in spite of now having some sense of the extent of my abysmal ignorance, I decided that it was time to go out on my own. This didn't surprise Jerry, because a few months earlier I had almost taken over the Village Bookstore from Marty Ahvenus, who had been offered a much nicer shop further along Gerrard Street. When he offered me 29 Gerrard Street I jumped at it. It was perfect for someone like me, and even better because with a bit of work, we could have lived on the second and third floors. This is way more important to a young, poor, bookseller than it may appear. To live above or behind one's shop means not only saving money, it reduces travel time (and carfare) to work and, most important of all, it allows one to work at odd hours.

Later, in my first shop, I would go up and eat dinner at 6 PM and come back down, staying open till 9 PM. In fact, in those days

I would stay open as long as a customer was in the store. It was very painful on the occasions when a browser would look till 10 PM or so, say thanks and leave without buying a book.

Naturally, they couldn't know that we were only open hoping that they might buy a $10.00 book. Every dollar was crucial in those days.

But Marty's new store fell through, he stayed, and I continued working for Jerry and issuing catalogues for another year.

Jerry had been upset when I told him that I was leaving to set up my own. He had made it plain that if I reconsidered and stayed with him I would soon be in line for a partnership. Jerry being then the best Canadiana dealer in the country, this meant that I would have gone very quickly from a new kid with not much more going for him than some flair and ambition to being a major player. And with me being interested in almost all other areas *except* Canadiana, such a business probably would have become within a few years the most prestigious antiquarian bookshop in Canada. It was very tempting, but some spark of native intelligence caused me to hesitate and then refuse. I was determined to do it my way and I told Jerry I wanted to try it on my own.

Part of my rationale would have been because I had already seen enough of Jerry to know something of his eccentricities. His were similar to mine, but where they were different, there would have been problems. For instance, during the day Jerry and I would talk too much, and then the work didn't get done. Then Jerry would decide he had to work overtime to catch up. Even though I shared his guilt, I didn't want to work overtime. I had both my own work at home plus a beginning family. Jerry would stay half the night. But sometimes the next day I would see that Jerry hadn't got much cataloguing done and he would explain that in going through a book to describe it properly he ended up reading it all night.

Thinking back, I realize that I acted properly, whether by instinct or by accident. Partnerships almost never work in the book business, except those between people who are also partners on a personal level. Character traits which cause affectionate amusement in friends can be very irritating when it means that you are losing money. Jerry Sherlock and I have remained close friends for the forty odd years since I worked for him. I don't like to think about any other possibility.

I have never regretted my decision, mainly because I now have the enormous pleasure of looking around my shop and realizing that I did it all by myself. And from nothing, too ....

I wanted to do things my way, and some residue of caution after ten years of extreme poverty had taught me that growing too fast without commensurate growth in knowledge and experience would be dangerous. (I was exactly right there, I think. The only cases I've seen in forty years where growth not matching experience didn't matter, was where the dealer started off wealthy— usually quite wealthy—so that the inevitable errors based on inexperience could be handled. For all such errors cost money.)

I think I was right. Wonderful as Jerry was, gentle, generous, easy-going, he would have been a difficult partner. All the attributes which made him such a congenial companion might not have been so endearing when his generosity and lack of business ruthlessness was costing a partner money. Jerry's wife Bernice had learned years ago that, as wonderful a father and husband as Jerry was, the future, in fact just the everyday welfare of her six children, meant that she had to be the one that was practical. Jerry was the archetypal absent-minded professor, totally inept at the practicalities of making profit.

In later years, when the kids were all in school, Bernice took on a part-time job and began banking money as insurance that her kids wouldn't starve.

Much later Jerry would joke, when he didn't have the money to buy yet another desirable lot of books, that he knew Bernice had money in her bank account, but he also knew that there was no way she would lend him a penny for books. It's not that he didn't support his family, he gave her a considerable sum every week, for it's not cheap supporting six children. But he knew that he shared the disease of every good bookseller—a desirable book, when seen, must be purchased—and will be by the man who can. And every day brings more opportunities to see and buy another desirable book. So he didn't blame Bernice for ensuring that there would always be food money, knowing she was right. While I refer to Jerry as a great bookseller, that means, to be precise, that he was really a great *book buyer*. He was not an aggressive salesman, in fact, the most potentially dangerous lesson he taught me working for him came from his basic credo. "My job, Dave," he would say to me, "is to find the books and point out their importance. It is the job of the collector and librarian to find me and buy them."

That was too one-sided—even I knew that—but I shared with Jerry the characteristics which cause such a one-sided view; a distaste for the vulgar necessities of commerce, which will cause a shy man, who dislikes confrontation and subterfuge, to retreat into that private defence which says: "I have great books that are properly collated and described and fairly priced. It is the duty of the client to recognize this and buy my books, based on his recognition of those facts."

In retrospect I realize that my instinctive reaction to Jerry's offer, meaning I was again taking the long, hard way, was the proper one. For Jerry and I still remain dear friends forty years later. And my immeasurable admiration and affection for him as a human being was never tested.

Premises were no problem, even though I still had no money. My friend Marty's Village Bookstore was three floors. The second floor was his overstock and storage area, but since he had prospered enough to take an apartment elsewhere, the third floor was empty and he offered it to me for $25.00 a month. It was two small rooms with one wall still holding a built-in shelf.

So here I was, still ignorant, still impoverished, with only about 700 books of questionable quality, a pregnant wife and yet, instead of being terrified, as I should have been, I was exhilarated.

Finally, I was entirely on my own and I could now say, "I'm a real bookseller now."

I took my few shelves, built a couple more and moved in.

When I was ready I had only enough books to cover about half of two walls in one room.

I had an atrocious letterhead on crinkly paper, somebody's idea of sophistication, which had been printed for me and shipped from my old printing plant in Spain, and a rubber stamp with my name on it for the envelopes. Curiously, it was ten years before I had properly printed letterhead and envelopes, and forty years before I even attempted to design a more attractive letterhead. Most booksellers begin with well-designed and beautifully printed letterhead, but I resented every penny spent on anything but books. And so ingrained does the sense of poverty become when one starts with nothing, that it was thirty years before I relaxed enough to spend money on business things that weren't books.

CHAPTER 6

My First Real Shop

After I took over Marty's third floor I began keeping tabs on all the shops on Gerrard Street West, waiting until one came up for rent. The next summer a tiny two-storey house with an attached, even tinier shop, came up on the strip of Gerrard, past Bay Street. It had been the home and business of a masseuse, and the basement, a half-level down from the shop (the main floor of the house being a corresponding half-level up from the shop, reached by three or four stairs), was finished, giving me an extra large room.

It was perfect. There were even two small windowed compartments on the front of the house where I could set up book displays. The rent for the whole thing was $300.00 a month, which seemed an enormous amount to me then. It was a scorching August that year, and I worked long sweaty hours shelving the store, even though I didn't have enough books to fill them.

It was then that I worked out a system whereby I could build an eight-foot shelf in twenty minutes, no small thing for a newcomer with no money who had to get open very quickly. Despite being a lousy businessman, I had been smart enough to con the landlord into allowing me in to work for three weeks before paying my first month's rent.

The upstairs, the living part, was filthy, having been unused for years, but we had it shining in a day, and I moved my wife and young son into it at once, again before paying rent. I have since managed that with every store I've had, opening before I was paying rent, perhaps the only example of business acumen I've ever shown.

David Mason

Beside us was a tiny restaurant called Mary John's, an eatery dating back to the 1920s and famous for having fed artists and writers since that time, including, purportedly, Hemingway, when he lived in Toronto while he was at the *Toronto Star*. And unlike many such claims this one appears to have been true.

On September 1st, 1969, at 10 AM sharp, I descended the short flight of stairs separated from our living room by a curtain into my new shop, made a last brief inspection to make sure everything was still as perfect as it had been at 4 AM, when I had turned off the lights and gone up to bed. I unlocked and opened the door of my first actual open bookshop for the first time.

Standing on the sidewalk waiting were Phil McCready and Bob Pepall. I was shocked and very moved by such a gesture. They both shook my hand as they entered. After compliments on the look of the store and effusive encouragements they looked around a bit, each bought a book for $10.00 or $20.00, we shook hands again, they wished me luck again, and then they left. I was almost in tears at their thoughtfulness. Green as I was, I knew that they didn't need or probably even want the books that they had bought; they were just being quietly generous. They had obviously arranged to be there. My first customers! I still think of them as that, even though I had already been in business for two years and already owed both of them several favours. Several other dealers and friends made the courtesy visit that day, but the rest of that first day remains a blur. I can't even remember if I had one real customer that day. Nor did I care. It just seemed natural that all my first visitors were dealers, although I was a long way from learning what became apparent over the next few years: other dealers are, by far, the best customers in the book business.

My new life as a shopkeeper—a bookshop-keeper—had begun, and continues still, forty years later.

With an open shop, I finally found myself selling books most days, instead of only selling them when I had assembled and published a catalogue. I had calculated that with a rent of $300.00 a month, for both the store and the adjoining house, I needed to put aside the first $13.00 I took in each day to ensure that I would be able to pay the next month's rent. And there were quite a few days when I didn't even take in $13.00. I was still operating under the now deeply-ingrained habit of not spending what I didn't have. All those years in Europe living on the edge of disaster had instilled a caution which made me resent the spending of any money which wasn't essential.

And, of course, with the added responsibility of a wife and a very young child, I had to be even more careful that I could pay the bills.

Waiting for customers, I read bibliographies incessantly, absorbing points about books I hoped to search out and memorizing the pseudonyms so many writers used for whatever reason.

After opening on Gerrard Street I learned the routines all used booksellers develop and very quickly began to devise my own personal variations on those methods. I had already begun to question some of the practices of my two main mentors, Jerry Sherlock and Marty Ahvenus. Both were constantly observed and asked for advice. I quickly saw that both were very good booksellers but both were very lousy businessmen. Furthermore, like Tolstoy's unhappy families, they were both lousy businessmen in very different ways. I learned that, while I could learn plenty from both of them, I needed to weigh what advice they gave me against their known eccentricities.

I watched how Marty handled the purchase of libraries. I had never even bought a large lot of books yet, and I envied him when a huge lot came in, sometimes fifty or a hundred cartons of books. Marty would leave the cartons of books in the store, making it uncomfortable, or impossible, to see the shelved books.

Naturally his customers, the regulars who came in several times a week, wanted to rummage in those boxes, and Marty would let them. They would sort through the boxes and bring an assortment of good books to Marty, who would name some pitifully low price for them. This, of course, is why everybody, customers and dealers, loved Marty: his generosity was legendary.

I would watch Marty give away the cream of a library and be left with the dregs. After that, he would usually call in Bela Batta and offer him what he wanted at 25¢ or 50¢ a book. When Bela was done, he would call in Old Favorites and sell them the residue for a nickel a book or less. Marty thought this was okay, but it wasn't any good for me because I had very few books and needed to build up my stock. But more important, no one was offering me libraries anyway; the best I got were accumulations, very small and of very mixed quality. I had had a bit of wonderful advice from Les Gutteridge, the British dealer, who had been the boss and mentor of my friend Len Kelly (the founder of Volume One Books), who had sold the stock of Epworth Books, the English firm he managed, to the University of Alberta at Edmonton and included himself in the deal, becoming their agent in the acquisition of their special collections. Incidentally, this was one of the few truly clever moves any Canadian university made during the frantic attempt in the 1960's by universities to prepare for the invasion of post-war baby-boomers.

"A young dealer needs to sell books, but he also needs to improve his stock," said Les Gutteridge. "The way to do this is, when you get what you know is a desirable book, find out its value and then price it 10% over that value. Ten percent extra is an acceptable range with any good book. A serious collector who wants it will not be deterred by such a price—$110.00 for a $100.00 book, or $1,100.00 for a $1,000.00 book, will be acceptable to a knowledgeable collector. He will not resent nor hold against you such a minor excess, knowing that if he pays you a bit extra on that book he will certainly make it up on the next one, for you both know that in his narrow area of interest you cannot hope to emulate his knowledge. This is how it should be, and he will know that having bought your good book for more than he might have had to pay elsewhere, you will remember his interests."

A smart collector will know, in other words, that in the long run he will profit.

The cheapskates and the bargain hunters will not buy your book. They, being fuelled by their psychological defect (for a true collector cheapness, the meanness of spirit which measures in pennies rather than value, mixed with that terrible error that causes so many people to equate cleverness with intelligence, will ensure that such a man will not buy your book. The cheapskate will say to himself: "That's a $100.00 book, I'm too smart to pay that man $110.00 for it." That the next copy he might encounter could be $125.00 or $150.00 doesn't occur to him; that he might never again get a chance to own that book also does not occur to him. He's no fool, he thinks to himself, that silly dealer can't put one over on him. I'll show him, he concludes, but he loses the book. Who did he outsmart? Himself).

So, based on my observations of Marty's style, and with Les Gutteridge's very good advice, I worked out my own system.

I had no money and few good books. All I really had was time. I concluded that, surely for someone in my position, I should do the opposite of what Marty did. Instead of buying a lot of books and getting my money back from the cream and then dumping the junk, I should try and get my money out of the junk and keep the good stuff, which would gradually increase the quality and the value of my stock.

It worked. I built a box outside the store, the quarter-box all bookshops use to dispose of what they consider of no value or outside their interests.

I spent a lot of time tending it, feeding books into it and I also kept a running total of what it brought in. I did this for all of the years I had a ground level store, and I was constantly amazed at how much I realized from what most dealers considered *dreck*. In my next store on Church Street, which was a converted three-storey house with covered veranda, I left the quarter-box, a six-foot shelf, out all night, with the porch light on during the warm months. I had restaurants on both sides of me then, and often in the morning I would find $20.00 to $100.00 which had been pushed through the letter slot. Often there would be notes too.

"Dear Mr. Mason. It's so nice to find people who still work on trust." Or, "I took $13.00 worth of books. Here is $20.00. I'll return for my change later." Sometimes they returned for their change, sometimes they didn't. But lots returned and became customers. Once, during a book fair, Michael Thompson said, "If you tried that in L.A., they'd not only steal all the books they'd probably steal the shelf and break all your windows just to teach you not to be so trusting."

Despite four stores since—all bigger and grander—my tiny Gerrard Street shop remains my favourite. It was painful to leave there, even though I knew it was time, for my stock and my ambitions had exceeded the space. Almost no one remembers the Gerrard Street shop. I can think of only two living customers who go back that far, both of them still clients and both now friends of many years: Eric Robertson and Ian Young.

Eric Robertson, a musician and composer, has a magnificent collection of books relating to his native Scotland, especially Sir Walter Scott, but he also owns many of the great books of English literature in first editions. Many years ago he showed me his first edition of Robert Burns' *Poems*, purchased on one of his yearly visits to Edinburgh, the only copy I've ever seen.

Like every bookseller, I've had ten thousand people offer me the first edition of Burns' *Poems,* which their grandfather brought from the old country, every one of them at least a hundred years too late. Eric Robertson's grandson will someday be able to say that *his* grandfather did bring one here and in his case it will be true, maybe for the first time ever.

In a history of the modern British antiquarian trade published in 2006 by the British Association the ABA to commemorate their centenary, Elizabeth Strong, the proprietor of the well-known Edinburgh bookshop McNaughton's, mentions that Eric Robertson was a regular, rummaging through the six-penny boxes outside their shop when he was six years old.

Ian Young, poet, writer, bibliographer (*The Male Homosexual in Literature*, Scarecrow, 1975), publisher, bookseller, and collector, is my other oldest customer.

I once told Ian the anecdote of my discovery of literature through buying books with lurid covers for their promise of sex. He, in turn, demonstrated the secret codes, both in word and cover art, by which a young gay man could recognize literature which contained gay themes, so young gays could do the same as I had done. In those times, when being gay was still illegal, those codes were necessary. I was fascinated by

Ian's explanation, and when I found he had written an essay on the evolution of gay liberation as illustrated in paperbacks, I and my partners in a small publishing company, Malcolm Lester and Wesley Begg, published his account, called *Out in Paperback* (LMB, 2007).

CHAPTER 7

Los Angeles

About this time Richard Landon brought Michael Thompson into my Gerrard Street store. Thompson was an American dealer who greatly influenced me and became a good friend. Thompson was in Toronto with two large trunks of early books on behalf of his employer Jake Zeitlin, of Zeitlin and Ver Brugge in Los Angeles. He was here to sell books to the University of Toronto, especially the early science books which were Zeitlin's chief specialty and naturally of great interest to the University's rapidly growing rare book department.

Thompson spent his days selling books to David Esplin and Marion Brown, still then the head of the rare book department, with Richard Landon absorbing all this new experience of books, just as I was. Late into every night Landon, Thompson and I, with our women and other booksellers, drank, ate and gossiped.

Except for the occasional visit from scouting dealers, this was my first contact with the foreign trade. I found Michael's anecdotes about all those dealers I didn't know and all those great books I'd never seen, much less owned, fascinating.

My friendship with Thompson led to many new things. Michael pressed me to visit Los Angeles. The Americans had been mounting book fairs for a few years, and in California they were coalescing into their current system of alternating yearly between Los Angeles and San Francisco. Michael suggested that I visit Los Angeles, stay with him and participate in the fair.

I certainly hadn't the necessary stock to even consider exhibiting, but it seemed like a fun idea. I thought about it, especially when around that time my banker offered to lend me up to $30,000.00. I should mention that, though I was at that time specializing in Modern Firsts, everyone else here except Hugh Anson-Cartwright and Gord Norman dealt only in Canadiana. Hugh had good books in most fields, while Gord only sold Modern Firsts and general literature, like me.

While I was slowly building up a small stock of eighteenth- and nineteenth-century books, thanks to Britnell's, few in Toronto had much experience with this type of book. Indeed, most people here, whether they were dealers or collectors, didn't much care about first editions then. When I had been working for Jerry and starting to specialize in Firsts, I had been astounded by Jerry's answer when, on compiling a catalogue of Canadian Literature, I noted that Jerry had not differentiated between first editions and reprints in a long run of Stephen Leacock he was cataloguing.

"Librarians in Canada don't give a damn about first editions, Dave," Jerry explained, "They just want a copy of the book."

The presence or absence of the dust jacket was of no concern here then either, a pretty good indication of the complete lack of sophistication in collecting in Canada, with the exception of Canadiana. All bibliographic expertise was centered on Canadiana, everything else being ignored as of no significance.

But I wanted literature and especially earlier books, in particular British nineteenth-century literature, increasingly my fascination.

"You can't sell early first editions here, nor fancy leather bindings either," the older experienced dealers told me. I didn't understand how they could be so certain. They'd never tried to sell such things, and I was determined to do so. Later, I realized their negativity was merely another example of that old contradiction—making assumptions and acting on them without testing them first.

With the encouragement of Thompson and my new $30,000.00 credit line I decided to make my first trip into the larger international book world.

When I got to L.A., Thompson took me around the stores to introduce me. I was astounded at how high book prices were. Of course, they *seemed* high to me only because I hadn't seen many of those sorts of books. I quickly realized that the earlier books on my own shelves were quite underpriced compared with what was usually encountered here; my sophistication as a bookseller was being raised another notch.

At first, I was stunned at the array of beautiful books I was presented with, but at those prices I thought I wouldn't be able to buy any. But in a day or so, as I became more acclimatized to the wealth of material before me and its shocking cost, it became clear that I was the one who was naïve. These dealers and their prices were not out of line.

I decided that I must bite the bullet and just buy nice books. And so I did. I decided my only safeguard was to buy things which I had never seen in Toronto, my idea being that if no one had seen these books they couldn't question my prices.

In one store I agonized over a nice nineteenth-century book called *Death's Doings*, by Richard Dagley (London, 1827), with nice steel-engraved illustrations, in two volumes, bound in a nice half-leather binding. It was pretty and it seemed interesting. The price of $45.00 was intimidating, but I decided to buy it anyway. The same day, two stores later, I found another copy, also attractive, this one priced at $35.00. Naturally my insecurity made me certain that I had paid $45.00 for a $35.00 book, but it didn't take long to realize that I needed to bite the bullet and buy this one too. If I'd liked it at $45.00, surely I should like it better at $35.00, in spite of the apparent evidence that it must be a very common book. I sold both copies fairly quickly back in Toronto and didn't see another copy for some fifteen years—two copies in a row having been just a fluke. Bernard Amtmann, the founder of the Canadian booktrade, would say often, "You should never hold a book in contempt just because you have two copies of it." This experience taught me the truth of Bernard's statement.

Working on the standard 20% discount dealers offer each other, I also hit on another great bookselling truth which, matched up with the great advice I'd received from the English dealer Les Gutteridge, I've been using happily for the forty years since. As Les had told me, no serious collector will find fault with a price on a good book being 10% over what he expected; such a price will only make the fool and the cheapskate balk. So it followed that with higher priced books, say $150.00 or more, with a discount of 20% and adding 10% one would be working with an acceptable profit ratio of 30% (except to realists like my father, the banker).

What that meant is that a dealer can buy any book he can afford to pay for if he doesn't much care about money. Since I was already discovering that money, for me, was not a goal, but only part of the means to obtain my real goal—to own good books—I realized that the only danger would be if my taste was deficient.

And where my taste was deficient, it followed, experience, if I lasted long enough to gain some, should develop. And this system did work. And still does work. That's why my advice to beginning collectors is always the same. Buy what you like. Buy the best copy of a book your resources allow, and always remember the rules of condition. A defective book is never a bargain (or at least hardly ever).

If you follow that rule, the only further advice is to keep buying. Putting out hard cash for things teaches quickly. Costly errors grate every time they are noticed. I used my own advice years later when I became interested in buying art.

Follow your own instincts. Your early mistakes, no matter how costly or how embarrassing they will be to you later, will, in the end, just be more evidence of your increasing sophistication.

All my early life, my father's favourite condemnation of my behaviour had always been "You always need to learn everything the hard way, don't you?" I always ignored this, because I believed that what he meant was that his so-called "easy way" was to do what he advised me. I never thought there was an "easy way," and I still don't.

The major purchase of that trip also provided the most pleasure. It was a first edition in two volumes of Pepys' *Diary* (London, 1825). Because it had taken most of two hundred years to break the cipher Pepys had used, it wasn't published until that date. The two large folio volumes I found in the shop of one of the major dealers there was priced at $250.00.

I could hardly believe it: $250.00 for a first edition of one of the great classics of English literature. I sold that copy for about $450.00 very quickly in Toronto, and I found that over the next few years I was able to buy other copies on almost every trip. I bought a lot of wonderful books on that first trip and found on my return to Toronto that my colleagues had indeed been way off in their untested assumptions—the Toronto collectors bought a lot of them quickly, allowing me to make that trip every year thereafter and to buy even more expensive books each time.

Even better was the rest of the trip. At that time Air Canada had a special deal where one could fly to Los Angeles, then Vancouver and back to Toronto for a special rate. And this deal included free stops in any one city in between. Naturally between Los Angeles and Vancouver I stopped in San Francisco, where I met many of the booksellers who later became friends or mentors, including Franklin Gilliam, Barney Rosenthal, John Windle and David Magee. A lot of the advice I received from them also proved to be wrong; I was increasingly learning that the advice of others often proves to be merely the untested assumptions of people who prefer a comfortable opinion to actually trying something new.

"Don't bother going to John Howell Books," I would be told. "He's too expensive. You won't be able to buy anything from him."

David Mason

In fact, I spent $1,000.00 in Warren Howell's shop (Warren Howell, the son of John Howell, and Jake Zeitlin were then the two most prominent dealers in western America). I bought there a very good inscribed Jack London for a good client, and several desirable books for stock, including a Canadian book which proved a great sleeper. After that, I never again listened to that sort of conventional wisdom. Mostly, the sort of people who make these silly assumptions really only demonstrate their own lack of imagination.

Being confident in the rightness of your opinions is certainly comfortable, but I find myself dismissing as second-rate those dealers who I hear voicing untested nonsense.

In Vancouver that first trip I met all the dealers there and bought a lot of books. I spent most evenings getting drunk and arguing with either Bill Hoffer or Ned Bowes, but never with both together as they were already enemies. I also spent some time soliciting Vancouver dealers to join the Antiquarian Booksellers Association of Canada (ABAC). I was by then a director on the executive of the ABAC, and I had been mandated by the board to talk western dealers into joining our group.

After Vancouver I went to Calgary, where my wife was from. She had taken our son there to visit her mother and I spent several days there doing the bookstores, especially Jaffe's, the Old Favorites of Calgary, where I probably paid for the entire trip three times over just in their basement. The enormous profit from Jaffe's was largely based on what I consider the greatest single discovery I made in my earliest period—Canadian editions.

The Jaffe's of the time was a huge dimly-lit mess run by two old men who I gathered were long-time factotums, the original Jaffe seemingly long gone. Jaffe's was a great used bookstore of the sort that makes scouts salivate—in the class of the Holmes Book Shops in San Francisco and Oakland, Acres of Books in Cincinnati and Long Beach, and who knows where else, Old

Favorites in Toronto, Foyles in London and from what I've read half the now-defunct stores on 4th Avenue in New York. For a book scout, whether a dealer or collector, these stores are prime territory—any astute collector or a young dealer can and will find treasures in such places, things that might have sat there unseen by the casual browser for fifty years, and priced accordingly.

The two old guys who ran Jaffe's were so pleased to encounter a dealer who actually loved books that they offered every amenity.

They took me up and turned me loose on a balcony with a huge desk piled high with books, which I suspect had been the office of the original Jaffe. There was between ¼" and ½" of layered dust covering everything, for which they apologized. "We've been meaning to clean up for a while," said one, echoing almost every dealer I've known.

"I don't mind a bit of dust," I replied, trying to hide my excitement. The heavy layer of dust told me that no one had been up there for years. I knew that there would be sleepers here—and dust does no harm to books unless it is allowed to get damp.

Amongst other things, I found a fine copy of the first edition of Poe's *The Conchologist's First Book* (Philadelphia, 1839) which, because of the very low price asked, I assumed couldn't be the first—it had to be an early reprint. Many books from that century (and, of course, earlier) are almost impossible to ascertain as firsts unless you've had them before or are certain of the precise date. Publishers of the time did not consider the dealers and collectors who would generations later appreciate some indication of a book's edition or printing. (They still don't—publishers don't care about the books they published in the past; they care about the ones they're publishing now and next year.) A young dealer learns to gamble when he finds a book that *could* be significant, but of which, since it's new to him, he can't be sure. A fairly high percentage of those gambles disappoint, probably about 70-80% in the early years. But in later years those percentages should be reversed.

That Poe was a first and paid all the expenses of the whole trip. But it was in Jaffe's basement that I hit the jackpot. Already a large store, Jaffe's somehow had the basement space in the adjoining three or four stores as well.

Maybe they owned the building and rented out the adjoining stores, but whatever the reason they had a huge space all shelved with orange crates stacked in narrow aisles, where they had fiction filed in alphabetical order. All that fiction was priced from $1.50 to $3.00, and starting at "A" I went right through the alphabet picking out first editions of the secondary authors, mostly British, that I found there. I had learned by studying the sales in my first catalogue that many American institutions lacked these British authors in their collections, and I had realized why. Authors of the sort I was finding, such as Arnold Bennett, Chesterton, Belloc, Bernard Shaw, and H.G. Wells, had been popular enough in their time to warrant U.S. publishers issuing their own edition. But in Canada, with our branch-plant mentality, we had merely distributed the original English editions, and these were what I was finding here. Serious research libraries in North America were now intent on filling out their holdings of the first editions of those authors. Although not then considered as important as writers like Eliot, Lawrence or Yeats, they had become very saleable in the $15.00 to $25.00 range. I bought hundreds of them, interspersed along with books which were by then-collected authors.

I bought enough, just in Jaffe's, to fill out my next three catalogues.

And even better, this alphabet was also jammed with Canadian editions, which I now considered not only one of my major specialties, but my own private personal territory. By now I was buying not just the Canadian issues of collected authors, I was buying everything I saw. And I was already becoming adept at spotting the Canadian publisher's imprint, denoting a Canadian edition, at the foot of the spine.

CHAPTER 8

Reflections on Scouting

A few years ago I had a visit from Justin Schiller at my store, and that visit initiated a lengthy period of meditation on an aspect of bookselling which, while largely unknown or of no interest to the public, is so central to bookselling that dealers constantly dwell on it. For anyone who doesn't know who Justin Schiller is, I will briefly explain. Justin Schiller is generally acknowledged to be the greatest authority on children's books in the booktrade. Although he is only in his sixties, he has been a bookseller for longer than many other people's entire careers. He was issuing mimeograph lists of books for sale from his bedroom in his parents' home in his early teens, and there is a famous photograph of him in the front of the auction catalogue of his first great L. Frank Baum collection, auctioned in 1978, where he appears to be about twelve years old.

That photograph shows Justin with braces on his teeth, but also wearing a warm, toothy smile. Now, Justin wears three piece tweed suits and exhibits signs of portliness (aren't we all), but the toothy smile remains the same. Just don't make the mistake of thinking there isn't a very determined mind behind that smile.

Not being much of a traveller anymore and seldom participating in foreign book fairs, I don't see many of the dealers of whom I once saw a lot. I hadn't seen Justin in probably ten years. I expected, from various reports I had heard, that this would be the sort of visit one expects from a highly successful and very specialized bookseller. This is more or less how it works. The dealer enters, passes a few minutes in pleasantries and catching up on old mutual friends, praises your store, spends a few minutes, (in this case) in the children's section, and then asks if anything not readily visible might pertain to him. And then after a purchase—even a token courtesy purchase is usually welcomed by both parties in this trade ritual—the visiting dealer departs. But on this occasion this standard ritual did not occur. Justin instead started in the children's book area but then proceeded to look at every other subject section in my rather large stock. After a couple of hours he brought a foot-high stack of books to my desk to be totted up.

On examination everything became clear. When adding up the total of a dealer's choices, the owner always takes mental note of the titles chosen, both out of curiosity and, if he is smart, as a way of learning. This is the time when many dealers get that sinking feeling which occurs when they suddenly realize that they have missed the significance of a book, and that a sleeper—an undervalued book—has once again slipped through to someone with more knowledge. Or, in my view, because of a more lively imagination on the part of the purchaser. In this case, every book in Justin's pile, extracted from every part of my store, from religion, science, art, literature, travel, and even crime, instantly told me why he was buying them. Every single one had some connection to the world of children. It was a compelling demonstration of the consummate pro in action.

And so, after the goodbyes, Justin left, leaving me musing on how seldom these days one goes through that practiced ritual with one's colleagues. And in the ensuing days I found myself musing more and more on the significance of this experience. For what Justin was doing was not simply buying a few books from another bookstore: he was scouting, the central preoccupation of bookselling to many dealers, and the part most like a game, where dealers hone their skills and test their knowledge and imagination against their colleagues, the prize being profit, a book found worth more than the seller realizes—sometimes significantly so. And as with professional gamblers and sports figures, while the profit is not negligible, the real significance is the feeling of winning. A professional athlete may earn or win millions, but the core of his triumph is in winning, the feeling of being the best. Book scouting is no different.

So, unlike some successful booksellers, who expect to be shown the best books in a bookstore, Justin Schiller hadn't lost either his scouting skills or his love of searching out good books himself. His visit renewed my respect for his justly acknowledged depth of learning and, more important, it led to this ongoing philosophical meditation.

I have been scribbling notes and meditations ever since, another attempt to make sense of my now lengthy time in the trade.

I officially started in the book trade in 1967 when, as I have recounted, I consciously decided to be a used bookseller, and began buying books for the store I intended to open. But I now see that my scouting career really began one afternoon, probably in 1946 or 1947, when two pals and I were walking through the bush adjoining the Rosedale Golf Club, the prime spot for kids from North Toronto in winter for skiing and tobogganing and in summer for exploration and adventure. On that late summer day my friends and I were stumbling through shrubbery when I suddenly came across a lost golf ball lying at my feet, shiny and white, perfect, glowing up from its hollow, no less beautiful than a diamond would have seemed to an adult. I was awed, then excited. If there was one, there must be more. Our aimless wandering now focused on the search for more of these treasures. We spent the rest of the day searching. I quickly learned the trick of not looking directly, but flicking my eyes over the surface of the rough, glancing from the side of the eye, which allowed that eye to register flashes of white on the brain, stopping me while each flash was investigated. Looking without looking, a skill which, when cultivated later, was essential to scouting books. Often the white flash would be nothing more than a discarded scrap of paper or an empty cigarette box, but by the time increasing darkness warned us we were in for trouble at home and we desisted I had five shiny white golf balls. My friends had not a single one between them. I was a scout; I had the eye. I had the gift. A shy, timid kid with not much self-confidence, I had found something I was better at than my companions, perhaps the first such thing. Selling the golf balls later in the caddy shack, my first monetary rewards for scouting, also led me to take up caddying, which I did until I was around fourteen and discovered the pool hall. But during all those years I continued to scout and sell golf balls. A scout was born.

While a good part of the excitement in finding a significant book is the eventual profit, the imaginative scout comes to realize that he has a higher purpose; he is rescuing from obscurity something which has historical or aesthetic value to society. And having rescued it, his next social function is to then place it somewhere where its contribution to the record of civilization will be understood. He is serving the future by saving the past, a noble activity.

There are two basic, but quite different, categories of scouts. The first group—in which I include myself—is the one I am most concerned with here. It is made up of either booksellers or serious and very knowledgeable scouts who are often affiliated with a single bookseller in some sort of exclusive arrangement or partnership.

The second category of scout is much more common than the dealer/scout, and will be found in every major city which contains used and rare bookshops. Most cities have several of these guys trolling daily, who deal in whatever they can turn over for a profit. They usually have a hand to mouth existence, buying in the morning and needing to sell in the afternoon. They are from a variety of backgrounds, although usually they are people who fit in to conventional society even less than most of the dealers they deal with. Often—but not always—bachelors living in weekly rented rooms, they have discovered scouting through scrounging at antique flea markets, the Sally Ann, garage sales, church sales, anywhere, in fact, where a book could be found. Most do not last more than a few years—some because they never learn anything, or because they don't have the eye, or even an approximation of that essential skill, but mostly because they often alienate the dealers they depend on as their only customers. This sort of scout, even if they last, can be counted on to die broke, often with a room jammed with the detritus of their mistakes.

They are often eccentric and they are almost invariably what people call 'characters'. They buy as cheaply as they can, a necessity when you don't know much, and since they depend on the goodwill of their dealer-customers they generally settle on a few different dealers whom they count on to buy their finds. Some never learn anything, even though most work very hard. It's not easy to start at seven AM, hit the Crips and the Sally Ann, read newspaper ads and flyers for church sales, garage-sale ads and posters, and run around a huge city trying to find a decent book, especially when most of them don't really know what a decent book is. And many of them cannot even afford to own a car. But the usual reason for their downfall is that their ignorance, and their need to sell quickly, means they are at the mercy of those they sell to. This, in my experience, often causes them to become a bit paranoid, which is a progressive disease, the results of which are often crippling resentment and anger.

Time after time I have heard scouts lament that such and such a dealer has cheated them, paying little or nothing for what they later came to believe was a valuable book. These accusations usually stem directly from their ignorance, and it contradicts what I think smart dealers always do in their dealings with scouts, which is to treat them fairly. Many dealers—and I am one of them—tend to *overpay* scouts, or to buy things they don't really want, both practices an attempt to encourage the scout to bring you more.

For the good general scout, it is a balancing act. They need to take some of their better finds to all their main dealer-customers so that the dealer will not assume that all the best books are going to his competitor. (It is obvious here that dealers tend to share the scout's paranoia only in reverse—they also have to use the balancing act.)

The better scouts are quite different. They will generally be as knowledgeable as any dealer, indeed sometimes they are ex-dealers, guys who got sick of the responsibility of running a store and returned to their first love.

In forty years of observing the book trade, I have come to believe that deep in his secret heart of hearts every bookseller who runs a shop believes that he is one of the great scouts just taking a short break. On rainy days in a shop empty of customers and between raising the prices of books to keep his spirits up, his private fantasies are of the day when he will throw up all this boring, respectable crap and revert to his original vision of himself as a fearless scout pillaging the shops of his innocent and ignorant colleagues, exiting in triumph with their unrecognized treasures. No overhead except small rooms somewhere and maybe a car or van—often his hotel for the night—to transport the booty. In reality, the pressures of overhead and responsibility weigh him down more each day, and each day his fantasy becomes more delusional, his escape less likely. Just as marriage, mortgage and children capture the young, narrowing their focus, so does success capture an older man with the bigger and more impressive premises, more staff to handle, the increased volume and extended hours to help absorb the escalating costs. Scouting, the freedom and excitement of the chase, is relegated to an occasional indulgence when responsibilities allow.

But no real bookman ever gives up scouting.

The better scouts are trained to see significance where others see only garbage. One night, stumbling along Queen Street half-pissed, my drinking companion, another bookseller, stopped to examine some boxes of garbage outside a building we knew was inhabited by a group which was one of the warring factions of the Communist Party of Canada. I was too lazy to stop, continuing on to our destination—a pub of course. But I had second thoughts when my colleague came in soon after with an entire carton he had found in the garbage, which was full of pamphlets in Russian. We started to examine them. I quickly came across an imprint (an imprint denotes the place a book is published, in either a city or a country) which I recognized, which automatically marked the item as Canadiana. Although I knew no Russian, I had had occasion earlier to research other such pamphlets, so I knew that the city name in the Cyrillic alphabet was the Russian version for Winnipeg, Manitoba. Winnipeg had been the final immigration stop of a fairly large contingent of European Jews and Eastern-European immigrants, in the early part of the twentieth century. A surprisingly large percentage of the major social reformers, and even many current public figures in Canada, came from that Jewish community's offspring. One of my favourite ironies in being a Canadian is knowing that so many of our most important politicians and social activists, business successes and cultural figures, have been either United Church ministers or the offspring of European Jews. And sure enough, a couple of pamphlets later I spied one which had the Cyrillic script version for Toronto. "I'll give you $50.00 right now for the whole box, sight unseen," I said. "Sold," replied my drunken colleague, and then had fun for the rest of the evening informing our drinking companions of his cleverness in seeing the possibilities in garbage. He bought us all beer for the rest of the evening, announcing loudly every time he ordered another round to "Drink up. The commies are paying. There's a lot more where that came from." We spent the rest of a raucous evening praising "the commies" for providing half the pub with an evening's drunkenness. And, of course, my friend blew the whole $50.00. Somehow I got my drunken self and my box of pamphlets home safely.

The next day, sober, I examined my carton and found, as I had hoped, quite a few more Canadian imprints. I sold several, all in Russian, right away for $300.00-400.00, and eventually realized a fair bit of profit from the rest of the box. But more important, I learned a serious truth, namely that scouts can't be snobs. I also made it up to my colleague by buying him quite a lot of beer over the following months. "Thank the commies," I would say when he thanked me for another free round.

When I started out, as ignorant as any other beginning scout, the obligatory first stop every morning at 8:15 AM was the tiny bookshop run by the Crippled Civilians on Jarvis Street, familiarly known to the regulars as "The Crips," but now renamed more politically correctly as Goodwill Services. It adjoined their large central headquarters which, like the Sally Ann, solicited donations of almost anything. In fact, most of us scouts and booksellers who frequented it regularly furnished our homes and dressed ourselves in the cast-offs of people who had died or moved.

The tiny bookshop opened at 8:30 AM, but arrival fifteen minutes earlier ensured that one was close to the head of the line, where one attempted to guess the prices of the new titles in the display windows and hoped that the scouts ahead in line were ignorant of these titles. The first in would usually point at the four or five decent newly displayed books in the window, making a pile which he would then sort through at his leisure, checking price and condition before putting the desirable ones in his pile to buy, and leaving his rejects for his fellow scouts.

Those not close enough to the head of the line when the door opened would dash to the special sections, usually the Canadian section, which most often would contain the sleepers. For this, of course, was what we all sought—the sleeper. The pricing system was as follows: Fiction 15¢ a book or ten books for a $1.00. This meant that if one found five or more fiction titles it was cheaper and certainly better to fill out the number to ten, since between six or seven meant all the rest were free. This was the first opportunity I had to learn how booksellers regularly out-fox themselves, buying unsaleable books, thinking they are saving money, when they are really just loading themselves down with useless crap that no one will ever want and to which they must give expensive shelf space, probably forever.

Like everyone else who has read too many books, I have many useless quotations which pop unsolicited into my mind on almost any pretext. The one that fits here is from William S. Burroughs, and I find it always pertinent: "Hustlers of the world, there's one mark you cannot beat: the mark inside."

A pointless aside: one book I had read and really liked was *The Ides of March*, by Thornton Wilder. One day, I found one clearly marked "First Edition" on the verso of the title. It was in a fine dust wrapper and priced at 10¢. A week later I found another. And then another, and another, one almost every week. It took about three months for me to catch on that if an ignorant neophyte like me could buy a dozen copies of a first edition in fine condition for 10¢ each in a single thrift store in one city then there must be something wrong. And there was. In fact there were two things wrong. First, they weren't first editions, they were the Book-of-the-Month Club issues, in spite of the printed notice of "First Edition" (it took me ten years to acquire the true first edition, which in my experience is scarcer than the special limited signed edition that was also issued at publication).

Second, and more significant, nobody wanted that book anyway. No one, it seemed, except me, thought it was a great book. I probably still have ten of those dozen books somewhere forty years later and there is a very important lesson here. What value does anything have if no one wants it? One of the first book jokes I can remember went like this: a book scout offers a book to a dealer, naming his price. The dealer hesitates, the scout gets nervous. After all, this is his dinner at stake, maybe his hotel room for the night too. "That's a very rare book you know," he says anxiously to the dealer. (Just in case the dealer doesn't realize this.) "Yes, I know," says the dealer. "It certainly is. Almost as rare as customers for it." There are several lessons here.

Other books at this Crips store were priced 35¢, or 50¢, 75¢ or $1.00, and if really desirable up to $2.00, $3.00, or $5.00. The rarely asked $10.00 meant a really good book, or one thought to be so by Mr. Fraser, the pricer and head bookman, and a man not to be trifled with. He ran the place like a fiefdom and woe to the one who tried anything shifty which, of course, many did. But seldom twice, because Mr. Fraser would explode at any perceived insult, or any infringement of his unwritten code, and any behaviour which he considered uncivilized was grounds for instant and very loudly conducted banishment. In other words, he was like a teacher dealing with a lot of unruly schoolboys. Mr. Fraser (I never knew his first name, nor would I have ever used it if I had known) was in fact just that: a retired school teacher. He was also a bit of a snob. I think he didn't want anyone to think he was the usual type of Crips employee. And he wasn't. He was there because he was blind, or at least almost blind. He had a degenerative ocular disease which had resulted in his being blind in one eye, and with only five percent vision in the other. So he could make out a face if it was very close, but mostly he recognized his regulars by their voices. He priced books by the same method, putting his one decent eye about an inch from the title page to ascertain what it was. Not too many years later even that eye deteriorated so badly that management supplied him with a helper, usually a not-too-swift young man whose sole task was to bring a box of books to Mr. Fraser's desk, then to read him titles one by one, then hand them to him for pricing. Mr. Fraser had a distinctive writing style which was instantly recognizable by everyone who frequented that shop, and I still occasionally open a book to find his price on the endpaper. This always causes a sensation of acute nostalgia.

The Sally Ann and St. Vincent de Paul also had shops, but St. Vincent seldom got anything one would want and the Sally Ann was generally very poor as a source of books because, as was widely known, the fix was in. That is, bribery prevailed. Every so often someone would complain loudly and an investigation ensued with the corrupted manager being fired. Then books would magically appear untouched, sometimes for as long as two to three weeks, until the newly appointed manager also succumbed to the blandishments of bribery. Then—no more good books. We all thought we knew who was guilty of the bribing, a local bookseller, but we never had any hard evidence. Curiously, although we were all officially incensed that this dealer was bribing the manager, I always felt that what *really* bothered us was that we didn't actually know how to go about bribing someone ourselves. Our friend, of European origins, had centuries of custom to fall back on, but the rest of us were probably too naïve to even know how to attempt such corruption.

One day, a friend of mine who had started scouting for an antique business she planned to open, saw that the door to the private back room was open and that a man who she knew worked for a local bookseller was rummaging through books. Naturally, she assumed she could too, so in she went, only to be summarily kicked out by the Sally Ann employee. Her sense of justice sorely offended, she went right to the top with her complaint, which resulted in the manager being fired, and we enjoyed another short period of book supply democracy. But more important, when she told me who the rummager was, a long-time employee of a certain local dealer, we finally had irrefutable evidence as to which dealer was bribing the book manager. In those days the Toronto dealers socialized a lot with each other, and at a bookseller's party soon after I slyly positioned myself in a group which contained the briber (who was, and still is, a dear friend of mine, but the opportunity to place a barb in front of a receptive audience outweighs that). I waited for a lull, and suddenly interjected, "Hey guys, you'll never guess. We finally have definite proof who's been bribing people at the Sally Ann all these years." I had everybody's attention. We had all suspected this dealer for many years and his innate cunning showed itself again, as he attempted to divert attention by piping up instantly. "Really? Who is it? Tell us!" It couldn't have been more perfect. Without a pause I struck. I looked him in the eye. "You, that's who." The roar of laughter from the assembled dealers drowned out even my friend's embarrassed spluttering. Finally, even he sheepishly joined the laughter, but he never did respond to the accusation. Nor, come to think of it, was he embarrassed enough to stop the bribery, which soon recommenced.

But back to Mr. Fraser. I was always very polite with Mr. Fraser and I never presumed to ask for any considerations. There was an ugly, fat cat in the shop, Mr. Fraser's special favourite. It was horribly spoiled and cranky. It slept wherever it cared to, stretched out almost always, it seemed, over books you wanted to look at, and if you attempted to move it you could get clawed or badly bitten. Even worse if you riled the cat enough he might just piss on the books to teach you a lesson, ruining some pretty good volumes over the years. The whole place stunk of cat urine, but it would be a fatal error if you had the temerity to complain to Mr. Fraser about the cat's behaviour. Out you would go, banned for life. I saw this a few times when people unaware of Mr. Fraser's affection for the cat spoke up about the stink.

As I said, I was always very polite to Mr. Fraser. Of course, I had a serious edge because I worked for Jerry Sherlock, whom everybody liked and respected. Jerry was then the major Canadiana specialist in the country, and Mr. Fraser acted like the three of us were the only cultured people to be found in that cesspool of hustlers and losers. Sometimes Mr. Fraser would break his own rules for dealers he liked and hold something for them. One day another scout saw Mr. Fraser bring out a couple of books, saying to me "Mr. Mason, I put these aside thinking you might like them." When he did that I always thanked him profusely and bought them, whatever they were, and whatever the price because I didn't want to discourage him from repeating such gestures. However I heard later, that this unwise scout, seeing this, made the fatal error of asking Mr. Fraser the next day to hold books in a certain area for him. That was the last time we saw him in there. Sometimes a banned scout would attempt to infiltrate back in by using the ploy of not speaking, counting on Mr. Fraser's blindness to protect him. But someone would eventually call him by name or he would forget and say something and Mr. Fraser would recognize him by his voice, and once recognized he would suffer a second and even more humiliating ejection.

One day Mr. Fraser brought out a book, offering it to me by saying, "Mr. Mason, I've put a huge price on this because it is the first edition of a Canadian classic and it's in mint condition." Even with his bad sight he could see that it was in very fine condition. It was William Kirby's *The Golden Dog*, dated 1877, which indeed is a Canadian classic, and it was in literally new condition. (Proper dealers never use the term "mint condition"; we leave that for the coin dealers.) But it was not the first edition, although the date was right. I could tell this instantly, because on looking at the title page I found a long written tirade, signed by William Kirby, bitterly complaining that this was a piracy stolen by those despicable thieves who were intent on seeing him in the poorhouse. Mr. Fraser had not seen the inscription, nor the signature, and I thought it better not to tell him about it, not wanting to hurt a blind man's feelings, especially one doing me a favour. He had priced it at $10.00, a rare price in the Crips, but acceptable given that I very quickly sold it for $500.00. For many years afterwards I boasted about buying a great sleeper from a blind man. "How disgusting," the looks on the faces of my colleagues seemed to say, "stealing from a blind man." But I knew better; I was aware those looks were actually manifestations of envy, the bitter chagrin of the loser. (The reason this was scouting, not stealing, was because of another old protocol of the trade: a priced book is fair game.)

The first edition of *The Golden Dog* was published in New York and Montreal in 1877. It was printed in Rouses Point, NY, just across the border, a ploy by the publisher to protect Kirby by securing a U.S. copyright, but which backfired, because Lovell, the publisher, after printing in the States, neglected to register it for U.S. copyright. And then, because it was published first in the U.S., he also lost Canadian copyright protection as well, leaving Kirby with no legal rights at all. Many editions were issued for years, both pirated and legal ones, and it continues to be reprinted, but I have never seen any copy of any of those many editions signed by Kirby. The whole story is fascinating and it can be found in the bibliographical essay published by Dr. Elizabeth Brady in the Papers of the Bibliographical Society of Canada, #15 for 1976 (Toronto, 1977). In fact I sold that copy to Elizabeth Brady's then husband, as a gift for her, and as her essay shows it is part of her important Kirby collection which is now at Queen's University.

I will say little about the scout as collector because a scout collecting is much the same as a collector collecting, although his experiences as a dealer or scout will have taught him a few of the necessary lessons perhaps a bit earlier and perhaps a bit more forcefully because of his experiences in bookstores.

I will, however, reiterate what I concluded many years ago and state at every opportunity—my belief that one can't really excel at any function which relates to books unless one is a collector and frequents used bookshops. That is, you can't be a good librarian, a good archivist, or even a good academic if you have no experience amassing a collection on your own for your personal use by frequenting bookshops. This said, it follows that I also believe neither can one be a good bookseller if one doesn't collect. This view would be widely disputed in the trade. Indeed, I would guess that a very high number of dealers would disagree.

I think many—maybe half—of dealers would claim that a dealer who collects causes problems with clients, especially a conflict of interest, and that it is generally not proper for someone who is supposedly trying to make a living. This view is often as vehemently held as my contention that the opposite is true.

Having considered all the arguments against the dealer/scout as collector, I remain adamant: a dealer who does not collect cannot experience the emotional passion which fuels all collecting, thereby omitting from the equation its very essence. And with that lack of perspective he loses the ability to emotionally connect with his clients—and for that matter, even with books. We have all experienced the Doctor who is so accustomed to his own omnipotence that he has forgotten that he is also a human being and becomes so emotionally distanced from the suffering and fears of his patients as to get the reputation as "very good perhaps, but cold".

When one considers the collector as a scout it is of course necessary to drop a major part of the motivation which we have ascribed to the dealer/scout: profit.

True collectors do not collect with profit in mind. In my experience, profit doesn't seem to be even a long-term concern with most collectors. Sometimes, chatting with a collector about their collection, the collector might mention some horrendous price he has paid for a single item; but I can't really remember ever hearing one speculate what their outlay for a fairly big long-term collection may have cost them, even in general terms. And it is only with collectors who are getting quite elderly that one even has conversations about the eventual dispersal of their collection.

I am certain that profit has never been a concern of all of the real collectors I have known. If this assumption is correct we can infer therefore that collectors who are concerned with and constantly stress monetary value are essentially speculators and not real collectors. Maybe that's why so many of them disappear so quickly.

Collecting is an emotional process, a hobby which seems to so engage the collector and which provides so much pleasure and comfort that I believe monetary reward is of little interest. When collectors sell their collections or put their books up at auction I think the price realized is for the collector only a measure for himself—a tribute perhaps to his cleverness and passion—but not really a monetary concern. Some collectors plan to give their collections to institutions on their death—and some do it before. Some are of the school that believes that they should return their books to the open market to give later collectors a chance to own them. Mostly though, a man who has spent many years acquiring books and assembling a coherent collection by imposing his knowledge, experience and passion on a subject will be very proud, and rightfully so, of his accomplishment, and will want to have what in effect is his creation left intact both for future scholars and as a tribute to himself. For that is what a collection is. Whatever other value it might contain, a collection is a monument to the person who builds it.

We have a man in Toronto who obsessively collects all of modern philosophy (this would be from the early nineteenth-century to today). This man previously formed the greatest collection of the work of Bertrand Russell in the world. A professor of philosophy, unmarried and therefore free of many constraints, he spent almost every summer scouting every bookshop in Britain and would return with three or four hundred additions to his Russell collection every year, in later years mostly magazine appearances, and often books where the index merely cited Russell, sometimes only once. Obviously he had the book-collecting disease badly and incurably by this time, the compulsion for completeness having become an obsession.

He once gave an address about collecting where he began by telling his audience that his collecting career had started when he collected the printed cards used to separate layers in the old style Shredded Wheat boxes. The roar of laughter which this elicited from the audience indicated that most of the rest of us had done the same thing as kids.

Anyway, this man, when he pretty much ran out of Russell to buy, focused his obsessional habit on the entire field of modern philosophy, and did so with the same intensity he had applied to Russell. Both his Russell collection and, later, his philosophy collection were gifted to the University of Toronto, and every five years or so two appraisers are called in to value the latest addition, which is so large it generally takes most of a week to appraise. This professor (his name is John Slater, as almost any dealer in the world will have guessed by now) usually drops by when we are about to start on the latest batch to point out things which might escape our notice. This is usually necessary because much of it is so obscure only another philosophy professor might know who some of these people are.

It was very common for John to show us a book, the author completely unknown to us, and inform us what a sleeper it was at £1 or £2 or whatever. This would no doubt be a very scarce book, but the real point is that no one else seeing that book would even know who the author was, nor care. So it was a sleeper only to the man who found it, as in this case.

One year John casually mentioned to me, "You know, Dave, my collection will now be the most complete modern philosophy collection anywhere in the world."

"Well, John," I replied, "I guess you mean the largest in private hands."

"No, I mean anywhere *in the world*. I know that because I've checked my collection of American philosophy and it's better than that of the British Library, and my holdings of English philosophy are better than what is in the Library of Congress."

As I meditated on that later I realized that it indeed would be true. An important point. What that means is that one person, on his own, with imagination and passion, can supercede the resources of perhaps the two greatest public repositories in the English-speaking world. Think about that before you dismiss the private collector as a befuddled eccentric.

Vanity is the downfall of many scouts. The urge to boast of great finds often causes the scout to reveal his secret triumphs, especially late at night when the alcohol is flowing. And it's not just scouts and dealers who do themselves in, figuratively—collectors do it too. A smart dealer always has his ears attuned for the verbal slips which mean useful knowledge for the future. But just in case you might think I am revealing these secrets out of some innate superiority, let me admit right now that this syndrome is so familiar to me because I share the character flaws which cause it. I am also guilty. The temptation to tell the story of a great find, especially when you are the brilliant hero of the story, can prove overwhelming even when you know that in the telling you will be revealing things better kept secret. An example: many years ago when the Canadian art-collecting market became popular it overflowed into books. The new collectors of art, educating themselves, sought reference and history books on Canadian art, causing the field to become very expensive, rising prices reflecting both demand and intrinsic importance. Art collectors began to frequent bookshops. It became a common occurrence that an unknown visitor would casually inquire of a

David Mason

bookseller if he had any issues of a book-collecting magazine called *The Colophon*. We always knew what *that* meant.

The Colophon, perhaps the most beautiful and ambitious magazine on book collecting ever produced, appeared as a quarterly from 1930 to 1950. It was originally issued in ornate decorated board covers, with a number of different articles in every issue, each one designed and printed by a different fine printer. It was a beautiful piece of work, and because of the interest in book illustration it often contained etchings and woodcuts commissioned for articles, or simply on their own. So it was that in 1932 they commissioned a print from David Milne, a drypoint etching, entitled *Hilltop,* which has become very collectable, partly because it is one of very few signed Milnes that is accessible to a Milne admirer who is not rich.

The perhaps apocryphal story about it is that Milne did the etching by running the plate through the wringer of a washing machine, which caused wear to the plate, which ended up resulting in four states of the plate. This plate, extracted from the *Colophon*, readily sold from $1,500.00 to $2,000.00 then, and those of us who knew that often would put out feelers to American dealers and friends to supply us that issue. In those days single issues sold for $20.00 to $25.00.

Some art collectors learned where it had been published, which explains the seemingly casual inquiries for the *Colophon* we started to receive. Some dealers would even buy a complete run of the *Colophon*, expensive even then due to its importance and beauty—not to mention it's very interesting content—just to get the Milne print. Even today, when one see complete runs of the *Colophon* offered in the market they are usually described as "missing a plate from issue No. Five." Once, scouting in a huge used bookstore in San Francisco, I went to the Books on Books section to find that it contained only one issue of *The Colophon* and it was No. Five! Probably part of a bigger run, it had remained unsold because half of the back-strip was missing. My great good luck, because it was priced at $7.00 and the Milne plate was still in it. That find paid for the whole trip.

All this was ruined by the vain boasting of Richard Landon, the Director of the Fisher Library at the University of Toronto, a known frequenter of bookstores and a serious private book collector himself. Landon once found in Michael Thompson's shop in Los Angeles a copy of No. Five for $10.00 or $20.00, and later over drinks couldn't resist one-upping Thompson by boasting of the sleeper he had just bought from him. This was particularly galling for me because until then I had been buying an average of two or three copies every trip to Los Angeles from Thompson and other dealers—mostly for $20.00 each. Thompson, being a very smart bookseller, continued to offer them to me, but rather than $20.00 I now had to pay $100.00 (US) and, of course, even that price rose in time. But I still bought them and Thompson and I continued to move them along for a while—a nice lucrative sideline for us both. However, gossip being what it is, that only lasted a couple of years before too many others caught on and another sleeper disappeared, the result of Landon's loose lips. But that wasn't Landon's only sin. Another Canadian book often found cheaply in the States was Louis Hemon's *Maria Chapdelaine*, illustrated by the important Canadian artist Clarence Gagnon, published in Paris in 1933. Because the book had been first published in 1916 and the French-Canadian artist Gagnon was not well-known outside Canada, it appeared to be just another of those later illustrated editions of literary classics that the French so love to issue, to the wonder of the rest of the world.

The bubble burst one year when the *New Yorker* published a profile of Larry McMurtry, the writer and Academy-Award-winning screenwriter, who has been an antiquarian bookseller for some fifty years. One of the people the author of the profile chose to interview was Landon, who could not resist boasting that he had bought a copy of *Maria Chapdelaine* from McMurtry's Washington store for $10.00. Even worse, he revealed its value, (it was then selling for upwards of $2,000.00), to the entire readership of the *New Yorker*. Soon we were getting offered the Milne print for $1,000.00 to $1,500.00 by our American colleagues and *Maria Chapdelaine* for even more. Landon seemed unperturbed when he was informed that his loose lips significantly lowered the average yearly income of half the dealers in Canada.

Now I find myself back where I started, Justin Schiller's visit, which prompted these musings and memories of my forty-some years in the trade.

While my general purpose has been to amuse, with some of the many stories that long-time dealers can relate endlessly, it seems clear to me that the real purpose in this and all anecdotal histories of the booktrade, is to impart some sense of the sheer richness of the bookseller's life and how important what we do is. I have come to believe that, more important than my or my colleague's petty concerns or our personal ambitions, the true significance of our work is social, and our main contribution is the salvaging and retention of important artifacts of our civilization. The sense of continuity and the importance of the long-established traditions of the trade are, I hope, apparent here, as they are so well-reflected in the sadly few memoirs left by my betters in the trade.

For many years, in discussions about the literature of the trade, I tended to praise Charles Everitt's *Adventures of a Treasure Hunter* as a wonderful book for booksellers. It has always been the first book I give to recently hired employees to introduce them to the literature of bookselling, but it has always been received with a mixed reaction. Some liked it—or said they did—others barely bothered to mask their indifference, and quite a few have eventually expressed open contempt for my choice.

My choice for second best is David Randall's *Dukedom Large Enough*, but the book most book people seem to prefer is David Magee's *Infinite Riches*, which is a delightful book by a delightful man and presents civilized reminiscences by a very witty Englishman who transplanted to San Francisco and never left. That Magee personally collected Wodehouse will tell you what to expect from his own book. The first time I met Magee he welcomed me into his house, where he was ensconced in a sunken living-room space having a gin and tonic with a visiting collector and exchanging gossip and witticisms. It was not yet eleven AM. The bookshelves in the area behind this space had huge gaps. "Yes it's those Heritage boys," he said, "they're up here buying books about once a month. I can't keep the shelves full." The Heritage boys: Ben and Louis Weinstein had founded Heritage Books in Los Angeles in the early-to-mid-sixties. They were very aggressive buyers for many years, building one of the most impressive and successful bookselling firms of the twentieth century. Magee was, by this time I guess, buying back the libraries of those of his collectors who had died before him, and like many older long-experienced dealers he was either out-of-date with the aggressive pricing favoured by ambitious young dealers or perhaps—what I prefer to believe—he just didn't much care about profit at this stage of his life. He was very cordial and inscribed a copy of his book "To my young Canadian colleague." I was so impressed by Magee that those images played in my mind for a long time. That's how I want to end my so-called career, I thought—not so much swilling gin and tonic at eleven AM, but enjoying the fruits of all those years of struggle, surrounded by old friends, cronies, and the learned and civilized people that booksellers get to deal with, ambition and money being relegated to where they belong at that age—down near the bottom of the list.

Now I'd like to provide an answer to a philosophical dilemma which has haunted the booktrade certainly during my time and probably since some Babylonian or Greek manuscript peddler hawked his wares in some early pre-Christian marketplace. For as long as I've been around there has existed a controversy over whether bookselling should be considered a trade or a profession. Well, here is the answer, and like all great truths it is succinct: Bookselling is a trade; bookscouting is a profession.

CHAPTER 9

Britnell's

The Albert Britnell Bookshop was a great bookstore, probably the best in the country, and by the time it petered out, another victim of the tumultuous changes we are still in the process of absorbing, it was being run by the fourth generation of the Britnell family.

Albert Britnell had emigrated to Canada around 1887 and founded the original shop, which was on Yonge Street, down near Eatons. By the '30s it was run by his son, Roy Britnell, one of the great characters of the book trade and a man for whom I had an enormous respect and affection.

Every year Albert or Roy or maybe both of them had travelled back to Britain and brought back huge loads of books for stock. This was in the time when England supplied the English-speaking world with what was no doubt seen as an endless source of wonderful and very cheap books.

I doubt there's a book person in Toronto who doesn't pass that grand old store with Albert Britnell's name still embossed on the lintel in ever-more-green copper letters without experiencing the feelings of distaste and depression that its present occupant, Starbucks, arouses in me every time I go by.

Albert Britnell's bookshop had moved up to Yonge Street north of Bloor during the worst of the depression. Although I don't know for sure, it can't have been much later than this that the focus on new books pushed the used books into near oblivion. From what surfaced when Roy began to clear the basement it was obvious that most of them had been in the storage crates at least since that depression move, some of them much longer, probably from the nineteenth century. By the time I began to go in, in the late sixties, there was a single table in the front holding used books and a shelved office in the rear of the store which occasionally was stocked from the basement.

Roy handled all the used books and he seldom bought libraries by that time.

Roy Britnell loved to talk to the collectors and dealers who came in. It seemed to me that, successful as the new book business was, he missed the old and rare trade and the sort of people he had met through it.

He told me many stories about all the people he had dealt with over those many years, from Robert Service to the Canadian Prime Minister who, knowing Roy wielded great power in the downtown Toronto business community, invited him to lunch, only to be refused bluntly: "I told him I had work to do, unlike some." Roy told this anecdote with enormous self-satisfaction. For a long time I assumed it was Lester Pearson, the Prime Minister then, but as I got to know Roy I learned as everybody did that he was a life-long passionate Liberal. I was confused until I realized that it must have been John Diefenbaker and that Roy was reliving a triumph which he must have savored for at least ten years or so.

Now, with Roy getting elderly and his son Barry, who owned and ran the shop, both uninterested in and ignorant of used and rare books, Roy realized that he had better start disposing of these books while he could still handle them. Up till then there had been a couple of tables in the store containing used books, priced very cheaply, and a 25¢ bin set up outside the store in warm weather.

So Roy began filling a glass case a couple of times a week with desirable books, rendered even more desirable because Roy had not been active in rare books for many years, and his feel for values was thirty to forty years out of date. Once Roy held a Saturday sale, even advertising it in the newspaper, a sale entirely of Canadiana. The line-up on sale day was long and so cheap were the books that I've never forgotten the displays of almost insane greed I witnessed.

People were grasping and pulling whole piles right from Roy's arms as he brought up fresh stock. That many of the people who demonstrated such disgusting displays of avarice I knew to be quite wealthy astonished me.

Or it did until I read years later Graham Greene's masterful fictional study *Doctor Fischer of Geneva*, perhaps the greatest book I've ever read on that disease. For avarice is a disease as deadly as any psychological disease I've seen, easily as repugnant in its effect on observers as the many cases I've witnessed of self-destruction from alcohol and drugs. For as with alcohol and drugs, greed seems to feed on itself; wealth, rather than assuaging greed, seems to inflame it, often pathologically.

Britnell's basement had been legendary for a long time. No one had ever been down in it, although I was told that Edwin Harris, a tiny, pugnacious Yorkshireman and a lifelong collector (who will appear in these pages later), had simply walked down there one day uninvited. Roy kicked him right back out again. During many late-night sessions in the backroom of the Village Bookstore we dealers and collectors plotted elaborate ruses to get access to that fabled basement treasure trove. When the Hudson's Bay Company was being built next door ("They offered me $3,000,000.00 for my store, Mr. Mason," Roy would chortle: "I told them I didn't need the money"), we discussed sneaking into the excavation site in the night and tunneling through into the basement. One of my many ideas, and my favourite, involved us all dressing up as firemen and rushing through the store carrying firehoses and yelling "Fire!" as we ran into the basement. Our firemen's coats would have special large pockets sewn inside to carry out the loot. This will give some indication of the quality of some of the treasures which came out of Roy's basement.

During the famous Canadiana sale, Roy brought out in one pile about ten copies of the very scarce and desirable three-volume *History of the North-West* by Alexander Begg, published in 1894 and even then $150.00 to $200.00 a set. All the copies were in brand new condition, telling me that Britnell's had probably bought them new in 1894 and that they had sat in the basement ever since. They were $15.00 that day.

Only two people ever got calls from Roy before he put books out: Allan Fleming and Hugh Morrison. One day Hugh called me and advised that it might be a good idea if I dropped into Britnell's. Roy had that evening put out a whole case full, of which Allan and Hugh had chosen a few but left most. I went the following morning and found wonderful books in this case. Literature from the 1890s to the 1920s, all in new condition and all from the library of one of the most interesting and mysterious collectors Canada has known, a man called W. MacDonald McKay. All McKay's books bore his distinctive bookplate (I now own examples of three distinct McKay bookplates). There were prime first editions and special editions from the significant writers of the time, from Oscar Wilde through Yeats and "AE" (George Russell) to those beautiful limited editions of the contemporary writers of the 1920s. My hands were shaking as I made a huge pile, partially because even at their prices of $1.00 to $3.00 they were so ludicrously underpriced as to be essentially free. But still there was enough that my bill that day added up to close to $1,000.00.

How I would pay Britnell I neither knew nor cared; I knew I just had to take them. And, of course, part of my anxiety was that some other dealer might appear before I had secured all the real plums. I found myself leaving things like limited signed editions of vellum-bound special issues by people like Galsworthy and Masefield at $1.00 each because of worry about the size of the bill. One of the books I found was an 1893 edition of Christina Rossetti's *Goblin Market,* with illustrations and a cover designed by Laurence Housman, in a large-paper edition of one hundred and sixty copies. This large-paper issue had the Housman illustrations coloured by hand (one source claims the colouring was done by the Guild of Women Binders). This book is considered not just one of Laurence Housman's greatest designs but a highlight of that wonderful flurry of incredible publisher's design-bindings of the nineties. In new condition, in the dust wrapper, the book was priced at $1.50. After much research where I found literally no trace of it I worked my courage up and priced it at $12.50. That was the first book I sold to Sybille Pantazzi, the self-described Fifty-cent Queen, librarian at the Art Gallery of Ontario and one of the greatest collectors I've known, whose flamboyant personality was such that anyone who met her was unlikely to ever forget her. Sybille liked to claim that she never paid more than 50 cents for any book. In spite of that claim, when she saw it in my window shortly afterwards, she entered the store, her chequebook open, already writing in it. "Young man, I'll have that *Goblin Market* book in your window, if you please. I'll just finish making out this cheque when you tell me the price. Thank you. Thank you, young man. I'm sure this is merely the first of many mutually profitable exchanges we shall conduct in the future," she said, as she marched out with her prize.

I watched for that book to appear in the market for many years, very aware that my lack of experience had caused me to grossly underprice it, but unsure by how much. Thirty-five years later I saw it in a prominent U.S. dealer's catalogue, a nice copy, but not nearly as nice as mine had been, for $4,500.00 (US). This when our dollar was 60¢ U.S., so the Canadian price would have been close to $7,000.00.

Another book I got at this time from Britnell's was a German edition of Oscar Wilde's *Ballad of Reading Gaol*, done in an edition of fifty copies with stunning woodcut illustrations by Frans Masereel. This copy was handbound in a beautiful full morocco binding, and I priced it at $25.00. At our first ABAC book fair at York University I overheard a librarian say to another librarian, "$25.00 he wants for that. And it's not even signed." I expect $500.00 would have been cheap for it then and $5,000.00 would be cheap for it today.

One day I found a book in the quarter-box called *The Fiend's Delight* by one Dod Grile. Only a couple of days earlier I had been reading about Ambrose Bierce, the great cynic, and had found that, although he was an American, his first two books had been published in England under the pseudonym Dod Grile. This book, a fine copy, priced at 25¢ was the English edition, the true first edition of his first book, and I sold it the next day for $75.00. Twenty-five years later, with a modest collection of my own of Bierce's work, I had to pay $750.00 to get a lesser copy of that book for myself. This anecdote allows me to quote here my favourite Bierce quote, and one of my all-time favourite quotes, a pretty good example of why Bierce is still so worthy. Says Bierce, "We wouldn't worry so much about what people think of us if we realized how seldom they do."

Bierce also wrote one of my two favourite short stories ever, *An Occurrence at Owl Creek Bridge,* yet another of the many stories turned into a movie which doesn't come close in emotional impact to its literary source.

Not long after, reading somewhere about Willa Cather, I learned that, working for the publisher S.S. McClure, she had ghostwritten or rewritten a life of Mary Baker Eddy by one Georgine Milmine, in 1909, which had become rare because the Christian Scientists did not like it and bought every copy they could find and destroyed them. The very next morning I found a copy in Britnell's, this time for 75¢. A perfect copy, I sold it quickly as well for $75.00, $75.00 apparently being what I thought the highest possible price in those days.

Ever since that great find I have gone through the religious sections in used bookstores looking for another copy, but so far I've not found it again. Another book one looks for in religious sections is Strauss' *The Life of Jesus* in its English translation, in three volumes (London: Chapman, Brothers, 1846). The translation was by George Eliot and was her first book publication, preceding all her novels. I found that book at a bookfair recently and bought it for $600.00, curiously in a booth right beside that of one of my most despised competitors. Entering my colleague's booth I couldn't resist casually asking him why he hadn't bought it, as I changed the price right in front of him from $600.00 to $13,000.00.

He was suitably chagrined. And yes, you're right, that was a petty, malicious thing to do. But a lot of fun.

But what I hadn't counted on was that this activity was raising my education in the art of scouting to a new and higher level, even though prices at Britnell's were not much more than at the Crips.

Because my bill at Britnell's seemed to be permanently at around a $1,000.00 and because Roy, when he filled the back shelves with a large load, could double that amount in one shot, I had to buy with those financial consequences in mind.

Indeed, I had already devised a system where I tried to go in and navigate the aisles to the back room without meeting Roy, because from time to time he would confront me with the extent of my indebtedness.

There were in fact two Britnell shops a couple of blocks apart. The other, John Britnell's Gallery, up near Davenport, sold art and antiques and usually had books in the basement. I believe John Britnell was a cousin of Albert's and had emigrated at around the same time. Sometime in the intervening years there had been a parting of the family ways and the two branches spoke neither to each other nor of each other in my experience. To differentiate, us book people referred to John Britnell's store as Junky Britnell's. It had a staff as ignorant, sleazy and down-right repugnant as Roy's bookshop staff was upright, competent and proper.

I have plenty of stories about Junky Britnell's, almost all of them nasty, and I've heard plenty of anecdotes from others. The books in the basement were never priced. An old woman, greed and guile etched on her face, would assess you, not the books you were interested in, no doubt measuring you to see how much she could get away with gouging. Those of us who were dealers would never have admitted that we were or we would never have got to buy a book. After these sessions became too repugnant for me to care about profit in the face of such disgusting displays of greed, I severed our relationship one day by very quickly handing her the $5.00 she asked for a book, breaking into a large smile and repeatedly saying "Wow, wow they'll never believe this!" as I walked away. Naturally she thought she'd sold a very valuable book for $5.00, and the look of rage and spite on her face made up for the many instances I had seen where she showed smug satisfaction after cheating another innocent. I never went back.

The John Britnell shop is long since closed but at an antique show a few years ago I bought a painting which bore a printed description of the artist as "A famous West Coast artist. He is considered one of the best scenery artists (sic) in B.C." Curious, given that the artist, whose work I know well, is in fact a woman, and all her paintings are of P.E.I. It was quite cheap and as I left the booth I noticed the name, "John Britnell." So they got the gender wrong, and the ends of the country wrong—but at least the price was right, although that could never have been their intention. As with so many money-grubbers I've seen, their guile and crookedness was regularly and ultimately defeated by their ignorance.

In the world of collecting, knowledge will always triumph over ignorance and greed. If you want to be an effective and successful collector take the trouble to educate yourself. Of course, as an added bonus, learning what you're doing also adds greatly to the subtle pleasures of collecting. "Connoisseur," that ultimate compliment paid to all collectors, comes from the French 'to know', and properly denotes that knowledge is the essence of the pleasures to be derived from beautiful things.

Living around the corner on Church Street, my first stop every day was Britnell's, just before nine AM. First, one hit the quarter-box outside, which often held novels from the very early twentieth century, which were usually found in new condition, indicating they had probably been in the basement from the time they were published. They became a major source for my Canadian editions project and were especially important to my already serious collection of publisher's bindings. Most of these books would be priced at 25¢.

Or one would find such things as multiple copies of poetry series, like the Ariel Poems. These last would usually be 5¢ or 10¢

David Mason

each and sold in the market for $7.50 to $15.00. The quarter-box scouted, it was quickly to the back room, which would be replenished often by Roy from the crates which had often remained untouched in the fabled basement.

My great daily rival for these treasures was Bob Stacey, then a student at the University of Toronto but working part-time at the Rare Books Department, then situated in a temporary space on Charles Street while the Robarts and Fisher libraries were being constructed.

We competed fiercely, both at the quarter-box and in the rear, but shared the same basic problem at Britnell's. Which was how to make our way through the store to the back room without being accosted by Roy Britnell. This was because Bob and I had no money at all and generally would owe Roy up to $1,000.00 each, no small sum then, especially for a starving, fairly new bookseller and a student. For years afterwards Bob and I would trade stories of our pathetic excuses to Roy when he did confront us about the level of our debt. I usually blamed institutions for their slow payment systems, whereas I think Bob blamed the accounting systems at the University of Toronto for errors which slowed up his salary. I don't think Roy believed any of that, but he liked us both, and no doubt recognized our lust for books. He was really just reminding us that he was aware of our debt load.

One day I approached the quarter-box to find Bob ahead of me. As I approached he maliciously waved a handful of the Yeats' Ariel poem issue, which then sold for $15.00. "10¢ each Mason. Beat you this time," he chortled. Quickly assessing the situation I passed right by him without answering and went directly to the back room, my only hope being to beat him there. When Bob entered five minutes later I waved at him a large handful of a much better Yeats pamphlet, a play then selling for $35.00 per copy, "25¢ each, Bob," I gloated, his chagrined grimace more fun than my anticipated profit.

Another day I entered the back room one morning to find some ten or fifteen copies of a four-page pamphlet by Robert Louis Stevenson, which, from the short preface, by whomever had printed it, seemed to be an introduction by Stevenson to a book by Andrew Lang, the nineteenth-century poet and essayist, mostly remembered now for the series of fairy tales he edited (*The Golden Fairy Book*, *The Purple Fairy Book*, etc., all of which are important; but even more significant, all published in beautiful and elaborately gilt, decorated bindings).

I didn't know what these pamphlets were. I was going to buy a couple, but then I realized that at 10¢ each I should probably buy all of them just to protect my investment. Whatever they were, I would at least control the source. So I bought them all. But the next day when I went in there was another big pile of them, this time priced at 5¢ each. Using the old principle "in for a penny," etc., I decided, even though I figured I would probably die with them all, I should buy them too. So I did.

No more came out. When I counted them I had twenty-nine copies of this weird pamphlet, at a cost of approximately $2.00 to $2.50. I did a fair bit of research but never found out much. Then about a year later in a catalogue from John Howell Books, a very prominent San Francisco firm, then in its second generation, I found a copy offered. It was described as a piracy of a preface by Stevenson for a book which never got published, until then unrecorded, and of great rarity. It was priced at $200.00 (US). I had twenty-nine copies of this great rarity. Some years later I found in the collection of the Fisher Library a copy with an annotation added in the hand of the man who had in fact printed that piracy, the famous

W. MacDonald McKay, probably the most important of the early Canadian collectors outside the field of Canadiana, stat-ing that he had printed it in an edition of fifty copies. So I had twenty-nine copies of a fifty-copy edition. I still have twenty-five or so of them but I have sold three or four. Even with several lifetimes' supply, at $200.00 each I've already done pretty well. There are many such stories about the bargains which came from Britnells.

In my time Albert Britnell's was almost entirely new books. I would often meet Roy, who seemed to spend his days puttering, usually humming all the while, resplendent in his famous spats. Roy would regale me with stories of days during the depression when not a customer would enter, and tell me his favourite stories of how he had put usurpers in their place. He told me many stories of people who had opened bookstores between his store and Bloor Street—not one had survived. "There's more to selling books than getting between Roy Britnell and Bloor Street, Mr. Mason," he would roar with obvious pleasure.

While he regaled me, all the while Roy would be straightening the shelves in front of us, but without looking at them. He would arrange the books from left to right, starting with the tallest book at the left and arranging them in a perfect downward slope by feel, with the shortest book at the right side. When he was alone, this ritual would be accompanied by toneless humming, but whenever I started a conversation he would launch into a fascinating anecdote or monologue, always waving his arms around to emphasize his latest triumph, like telling off the Prime Minister, or throwing out Bert Kenny, an elderly and very scholarly collector who had been a lifelong member of the Communist party. ("We don't need any of that Commie stuff around here," he'd roared at

Bert as he banished him after some innocent jibe of Bert's at one of the sins of capitalism.) All the while he would be compulsively arranging by feel.

I became very fond of Roy—like many men who have ruled their own domain all their lives, he freely exhibited his eccentricities and said exactly what he thought no matter the public stature of the person he was talking to, or the consequences, for that matter.

He was always scrupulously polite to me—a scruffy kid in jeans—and I took it to mean that me being a bookseller, no matter my inexperience, meant to him that I was his equal and worthy of his courtesy. I never saw any evidence which led me to think otherwise, and I was so impressed by his collegial attitude to all booksellers that it has caused me to also afford all respect and trade courtesies to any young bookseller I meet who exhibits the signs of being, or wanting to be, a real bookseller.

My favourite Britnell story, which he told me more than once with great relish, related to another bookseller who had long toiled on lower Yonge Street, and having prospered, had taken premises on Bloor Street. But this man was confronted by a seemingly endless series of hassles from the city over permits and licenses, all initiated by the bureaucratic system that all small businessmen know so well. On investigation the man came to see what his problem was and where it came from. For this man was Jewish, and the staid Bloor Street merchants, full of the genteel anti-Semitism which was so general then, to our shame, were intent on not having a Jew on posh Bloor Street. When the man understood this, he went to Roy Britnell for advice. Roy was a powerful and influential man in that area, and he was not a man to be crossed when he cared about something.

Roy took charge, put an immediate stop to that, and the man opened his shop. "Well, I wasn't going to let them get away with that, was I Mr. Mason," he would chortle. "We couldn't have that after all the man was a good bookseller, wasn't he?"

CHAPTER 10

The Pleasures of Blackmail

I don't know why so many of my most exciting book adventures occurred in the earliest years of my career, but they did.

What I will relate here happened when I was only four years in business, and only two on my own, long before I had amassed any of the experience necessary to deal with this sort of problem.

One of my greatest triumphs as a bookseller—blackmailing the head of a major institution—was completed before I actually realized just what it was that I had been doing.

Some background is necessary.

As I said earlier, my mother was from a large family of those Scottish immigrants who built this country, and they remained very close. All my mother's brothers and sisters were warm outgoing people and we had regular and boisterous family gatherings, where my father, an only child, often seemed lost in all that warmth.

But of all the impressive Baillies, the most impressive and my favourite (and I would guess everybody's favourite) was my Uncle Jim. Jim's great game when we were young was to play 'horsey,' as we called it. He would take a young child, cross one leg over the other, seat you on his foot, and holding you by both hands bounce you up and down, higher and higher, while we would scream with delight, "Higher, higher—Uncle Jim!" Who could not love a man who could always be counted on to make you scream with joy and terror at the same time? Every Baillie kid, and there were a lot of us, would rush him when he arrived at family gatherings yelling "Horsey, Uncle Jim, horsey! We want to play horsey!"

It was a measure of Jim's character that he always complied, and with great good humour. We must have exhausted him with our demands but he seemed to love it as much as we did.

Jim Baillie was an ornithologist. He joined the Royal Ontario Museum at seventeen and spent forty-eight years there running the department of ornithology, even though he was never appointed curator due to that ludicrous institutional rule which stated that a degree trumped all else, including competence, knowledge, passion, and all the other really important human attributes. When I became old enough to understand such things, Uncle Jim's experience became a template for my view of human affairs. That this world values credentials over true merit still irks me today, perhaps partially because of my own grade-nine dropout status.

Jim seems to have left school after grade eight, and although he attended high school at night ten years later, he never got a high school graduation certificate, so we also had that in common.

Jim was famous. He wrote a weekly column on birding for the *Toronto Telegram* for many years and regularly led walks for birders all over Toronto and the rest of Ontario.

Of course, to his family, it was just Uncle Jim and his silly birds. In a short biographical study of Jim by a young woman named Lise Anglin, my mother relates that in the days when young people still living at home were expected to contribute almost all their pay to the family upkeep Jim came home on his first payday with an oil painting of a bird, on which he had spent his entire monthly paycheck of $35.00. He then presented this painting to his shocked mother. A woman trying to feed all those kids on her husband's meagre salary got a bird painting instead of food money. Her reaction, in my mother's account, is described as "less than enthusiastic."

All our houses contained various bird paraphernalia, water-colours, carved birds on bookends and such things, probably Jim's attempt to keep his own house from being inundated by all the gifts given him by his many admirers.

Jim was an enthusiast. He welcomed anyone and everyone who loved birds into his office, giving just as much importance to a ten-year-old kid who showed the necessary signs as he did to the wealthy skin and egg collectors who were his cronies. His example of inclusiveness, of a community based on passion, not credentials, so influenced me that I often spend considerable time with penniless kids whose love of books and learning is apparent. I guess I mean that if one has a vocation the true centre of it is not just personal ambition, but recognizing the signs of vocation in others and helping them, so that important traditions get passed on.

I am often amazed by how many people are bird-watchers. Two of my fellow booksellers, for instance, and two of my librarian friends at the Fisher Library, regularly went on Jim's well-known tours around the Toronto area. I had long been friends with those two librarians before I learned that. When I successfully brought Jim's library to the Fisher I found out that these two women were more enthused that his great ornithological library was in the Fisher because they were birders than because of their loyal connections to their library. Since he died I have met literally hundreds of people who knew and admired him. The province named a bird sanctuary at Point Pelee after him, where thousands of birders flock every year to indulge in their seasonal rites, rites which confound all of us who don't share their passion. But, I'm in favour of passion, even obsession, wherever it is found. That's what changes the world. There are two funds named after him which award grants for research in birding; he was also given a centennial medal in 1967 for "valuable service to the nation."

Birders as a species have become subjects of some interest to me. They share a similar circumstance with book collectors, in that their families and friends often consider them eccentric, if not deranged. They will travel for miles on a regular basis to stand for hours in the cold with expensive binoculars, hoping for a chance to catch a glimpse of some obscure species of bird which they may or may not properly recognize by its markings. In Jim's memoir, a friend notes that in the early days they all had to carry their binoculars in paper bags to escape derisory comments by people.

As children, we would be taken in behind the public displays at the Royal Ontario Museum to Jim's office, a place of great wonder and mystery to me. There were real birds in there; you could touch them even. They were dead, we would be told, and stuffed so that they would be here forever. And those were real feathers, you could tell when you touched them. That's how you knew they were really dead too, because when you touched them they didn't fly away. Jim always made a great production of ignoring the adults while he gave the kids a lesson in whatever he was currently working on. In a happy coincidence that I only became aware of years later, Michael Wilcox, the world-renowned Canadian bookbinder, worked in that department gluing together bird skeletons, and later married Jim's secretary.

When I became a bookseller I would offer Jim Canadian bird books when Joseph Patrick got them, but he always had them. He had a very good collection of books, offprints, and pamphlets on North American birding which he had left to the ROM in his will. And his vast network of friends amongst birders had resulted in many donations of eggs and skins to the ROM and, of course, amongst the still-living, promises to donate current collections when the collector died.

Aside from his papers and articles on bird subjects, Jim had been working for many years on a biography of Charles

Fothergill, the Postmaster of Port Hope and an amateur naturalist. He had some manuscript journals borrowed from Fothergill's family and there was some confusion as to who should eventually have them, the ROM or the University of Toronto. There had been other problems of jurisdiction which had arisen when the ROM and the University of Toronto separated in 1968, so that there were less-than-cordial relations between the two institutions.

But Jim's great coup, to his mind, was the campaign he mounted—successfully—to buy a Great Auk for the ROM, one of the few surviving examples of that now extinct Canadian species, and the only specimen in Canada. After my old friend and patron Bob Pepall learned that Jim had been my uncle he often referred to that project. He had contributed a fair amount to it, being another of Jim's many friends.

Gordon Sinclair, also a friend of Jim's, devoted his CFRB radio spot one day after Jim's death to an eulogy, where he stressed with great warmth and admiration Jim's great generosity of spirit, especially with the young.

After forty-eight years with the ROM, Jim was due to retire in 1970, but had been hospitalized with heart problems a couple of weeks before. We were all concerned that his impaired health might affect his retirement plans.

Then my mother called to tell me that he had died—on the very day he was due to retire! We were devastated. The funeral at College Street United was huge, the church overflowing with Jim's many friends and admirers. Later, when I learned the whole story, I concluded that Jim died that day out of anger and frustration at what they had done to his beloved museum. His life ended on the very day that the centre of that life disintegrated.

I waited a couple of weeks and visited my cousin Florence Wilson, Jim's daughter by his first wife Martha Scadding.

David Mason

Martha Scadding was a descendant of the local historian and antiquary Henry Scadding, whose *Toronto of Old* is still one of the seminal histories of early Toronto. She had died young, leaving Jim a widower, with Florence his daughter to care for. Years later he remarried, a wonderful vivacious Greek woman named Helen Kleon.

Helen, a tiny woman, had a degenerative and progressive disability, a form of arthritis which distorted limbs and made her appear even smaller. It caused physical distortion of her joints and great pain and eventually put her permanently in a wheelchair. In spite of her obviously deformed limbs, her enthusiastic embrace of life and her Greek exuberance shone through her huge, lustrous eyes, and caused us all to love her greatly. She became a treasured member of the family.

I knew that Jim had willed his important library to the ROM, so I was shocked when my mother informed me that shortly before his death he had rescinded that will. I met with his family to offer my services to Helen and Florence to help deal with his library. Jim had always said that he figured that the library was worth $10,000.00, but Helen and Florence told me that Jim had sold a few of the important highlights to help pay for some operations for Helen that they hoped might alleviate some of her pain. They were sure that the library's value was now a lot less than that. I told them that my concern was more that it be placed in a fitting place as a monument to Jim, and I made it plain that, naturally, there would be no fee for my help in doing so.

Then I started to get the real story of what had happened in his final years, which had led him to rescind his will. It first astounded me, then quickly enraged me.

It turns out that while the Museum couldn't make a grade-school dropout the Curator of Ornithology despite his vast knowledge, experience and world-wide reputation in the field, and despite the fact that he had effectively been running it for years as the Assistant Curator, they would and did hire the applicant he recommended to become curator. He had interviewed candidates and finally recommended an American from Kansas by the name of Jon Barlow, who had all the necessary degrees. Although his PhD was not in ornithology, he seemed to be qualified.

Typical of Jim's character, after hiring this man he brought him to Toronto and put him up in his own home while the man acclimatized himself and set himself up in his own place. Then Barlow took over and the transformation started.

I had gone to the ROM to look at the library before I visited Helen and Florence. Barlow had been cordial, the only slightly curious detail being that he didn't seem disturbed that he wasn't getting the library. I had half-expected him to initiate a possible purchase on behalf of the ROM and I couldn't understand how a dedicated curator wouldn't be devastated at losing such a collection. Little did I know that he had lost far more than Jim's library.

Barlow, on arriving five years earlier, had immediately begun bringing in old friends and cronies from the United States. This is not in itself wrong, except when such moves are based on cronyism, without regard to competence.

But Barlow formed his personal circle and began alienating other people in the department, shunting them aside. People like Terry Short, a lifelong friend of Jim's, an illustrator of many Canadian nature books, and like Jim, a long-time employee of the ROM.

But, worse, he began to alienate that large group of collectors and enthusiasts that all public institutions depend on. Barlow insulted collectors, dismissing their efforts to contribute with unveiled contempt. So insulting did his treatment of some of these people become that offended collectors, many of whom contributed many hours of their time to compiling lists of sightings and such things, stopped volunteering and began quitting in disgust, some changing wills and sending their important collections elsewhere. Jim became increasingly concerned that the network of friends of the department and potential donors whom he had cultivated for fifty years was crumbling.

These collectors had loved the idea of their efforts adding to the ROM's great holdings, but when they began to see the contempt and dismissal with which Barlow treated Jim's fifty years of dedication to everything they revered they severed their ties. It seems Barlow was of that type who, gaining academic credentials himself, derides as inconsequential anyone who doesn't have them. I have encountered many such people, and they all seem to share a common characteristic: the mark of the insecure pedant. They are usually rigid, and perhaps because they doubt their own talents and knowledge they tend to become defensive, especially when their actions are questioned by people they consider their inferiors. People like this are a great danger to any institution. All major institutions have evolved systems to include the passionate amateur in their activities. (It should be understood that I use the word 'amateur' in the French sense, where it is a compliment, and not in the English, where it carries a faintly denigratory connotation.)

These amateurs provide an institution with the opportunity to make use of their skills, and provide the collector with the opportunity to contribute to the growth and prestige of the institution. On the personal level, this allows the collector to feel that he is adding significance and sustenance to something he feels is very important.

It's a good system, and every librarian I've known whose library contains any special collections understands this and cultivates these people.

Finally, after some five years of increasingly severe confrontations, Jim wrote a letter, a thirteen-page tirade, typed single space, outlining with specifics the entire deterioration at the ROM and what he saw as the destruction of his life's work. He sent it out to twenty-three prominent people. Helen and Florence gave me a copy of the letter.

On reading this, I could easily see all of the signs of emotional turmoil this caused him; he saw his life's work being destroyed, and the tone of the letter demonstrates a deterioration in his mental balance. He became increasingly strident, obsessive even. It indicated just how seriously Jim viewed the problem and, sadly, it also indicated that his mind, unable to cope with the enormity of the troubles he experienced, was showing signs of such severe stress that it became apparent that his physical health was at great risk.

Reading that letter is a melancholy experience. It shows us a man losing control in the face of blatant unfairness. Starting off in precise methodical order it lists incident after incident where Barlow's incredible insensitivity caused problems. It becomes worse when he talks of a letter from Peter Swann, the director of the ROM, "ordering his retirement on June 30, 1970," his 65th birthday having passed. It becomes obvious that this was Barlow's doing, and a perfect indication of Peter Swann's methods. It was easier for Swann to go along with Barlow and to get rid of Jim than to deal with the complications.

Jim actually lists the retirement record of nine other ROM people who continued working long after retirement age.

At this point the letter is beginning to show evidence of instability. Jim demands that Barlow, not he, be dismissed on June 30, and that the ROM appoint him curator for a five-year term, during which time Jim promised to clean up all the mess that Barlow's stupidities had caused.

It would, of course, take a very brave or very determined director to do that, a man who cared far more about the institution's well-being than his own. And, of course, the ROM did not have such a director.

By the time I finished reading the letter, I knew what had killed my uncle.

Many things, which I have despised all my life, had conspired to ruin his career, and, in fact, killed him: incompetence, followed by the use of power to cover up that incompetence; moral cowardice on the part of people who could have rectified things; self-interest trumping duty or even decency. It goes on and on.

I was filled with disgust, which rapidly turned into anger and determination.

Now in possession of the whole story, I went in to examine the library a second time. I didn't think that the few really valuable books Jim had sold affected the value of the library that much. Rare books can be replaced with patience (and money, of course); what was important was the profusion of minor publications, offprints, monographs, many of them inscribed gifts from Jim's colleagues worldwide. And, most important, the correspondence, also worldwide, with other birders, whether they were professional ornithologists or amateur enthusiasts.

Jim's office was completely lined with bookshelves full of books, magazines and pamphlets, and there were several filing cabinets full of the papers accumulated over fifty years of work.

I was curt with Barlow this second visit and, in fact, was studying him closely, of which I'm sure he was aware. Nervous now rather than cordial, he clearly could see that I had been given the facts and a sheen of sweat was apparent on his face.

I opened a file cabinet and started examining the papers.

"Oh," said Barlow. "No point looking at them. They belong to the museum, you can't take them."

I didn't answer; the sweat became more pronounced.

"I'll be calling in an appraiser, Mr. Barlow," I said (purposely refusing to call him Doctor—by this point I was already taking no prisoners, my rage making me coldly ruthless). I knew the rules; papers generated in public institutions during an employee's tenure are legally considered the property of the institutions.

I went to my friend Richard Landon, at the University of Toronto. I told him the whole story over lunch saying, "I want to sell the University of Toronto this collection. I believe it will certainly be the best such collection in Canada, and Jim Baillie was my favourite uncle and I want it at the U of T. I have complete freedom to act for Jim's family. They'll go along with my judgment. His collection being in the Fisher will show those creeps that some people think he was important."

"Okay," said Richard. "How do we proceed?"

"Because he was family, I'm going to avoid any possibility of suspicions or accusations, so I'm going to have Jerry Sherlock appraise it. Then I'm going to discuss the price and the family's stipulations with Jim's wife and daughter, then I'll offer it to you. There won't be any sales talks or any bullshit."

"Okay," Richard said. "I'll speak to David Esplin and when you're ready we'll make an appointment with him."

I called Jerry Sherlock and we went to the ROM. Barlow hovered again while Jerry worked, getting even more nervous when Jerry, on my instructions, started going through the filing cabinets.

"You can't have those. Why look there?" he said, the sweat on his face the measure of his increasing anger and anxiety.

Till then I was still being civil and correct, if completely formal. It was time to open hostilities.

"I want everything here, Mr. Barlow."

"Everything? You can't have it."

"Well, it's going to be in the appraisal. Perhaps it's time for you to set up a meeting with Peter Swann."

Barlow was furious, he didn't know how to handle such blatant effrontery. Didn't I know how things worked? He was the curator of a whole department in a major institution, and I, a mere punk, was telling him what was going to happen in his domain? What arrogant presumption.

"I'll have an appraised value in a couple of days. Make an appointment anytime after that."

Then I went to David Esplin, Richard's colleague. Esplin had been hired by the university in 1965 to bring the university's research collections up to the level they needed to be for post-graduate programs.

Esplin was abrasive, opinionated, brusque and confident, all the qualities needed to do what the University of Toronto had hired him to do, to build the essential base necessary for a great research collection for the major university in Canada. And to do it quickly.

Jerry Sherlock appraised the collection at $25,000.00, and I discussed it with Jim's family. I suggested we ask less than the appraised value and make two stipulations. That it be called the James L. Baillie Collection, the university agreeing to continue building on it, and that it be confirmed in writing that anyone, no matter their age or qualifications, be allowed full access.

Except for calling it the Baillie Collection, these stipulations were unnecessary. They were really just a reflection of the importance the family and I gave to a proper recognition of Jim's contributions to his field. The University of Toronto would automatically add to any such collection; after all, that's their mandate. Otherwise there would be no point in any serious library buying anything. And, of course, as a public institution, anyone has a right to use it anyway, so both stipulations were pointless; they were just our way of emphasizing what was important to us. It was Jim's passionate attention all his life to so-called amateurs, especially the young, which motivated that stipulation, and I knew Landon and Esplin would understand that.

Richard and I met with Esplin. I could tell that Richard had already explained all the relevant details. I gave Esplin the appraisal, told him the price and stipulations and told him my plans, what I intended to do afterwards and how I was going to do it.

"Okay," said Esplin. "Let's go look at it."

We made an appointment and went to the ROM.

Barlow hovered, watching closely and still sweating.

Esplin looked carefully for half an hour, turned to me and said, "Okay, I'll take it, if you can deliver it. But don't get me in any fights with this institution."

No bargaining, no arguments. I've never forgotten that civilized gesture to a kid he must have known was operating mostly on nerve. He assessed my delicate position and accepted everything, his only stipulation being that I make no extra problems for him by my methods.

I told Barlow on the way out, "Mr. Barlow, let me know when we can meet with Peter Swann."

A few days later Barlow and I entered Swann's office. I had learned a great deal more during my lengthy preparations for the fight, having reread the letter and a relevant exchange of letters between Swann and Uncle Jim in the archive.

Peter Swann was an early example of what is now a quite common type of Canadian institutional executive. He had been hired to be the public face of the ROM, and his function, aside from managing a large institution, was to raise money from private donors to further the expansion of that major public institution. Governments—politicians—are notoriously cheap about delegating funds to culture, at least in North America. (I read recently that the French Government grants $150,000,000.00 a year to subsidize the Paris Opera. An opera house! It took many years of effort by private citizens like Hal Jackman before Toronto finally got an opera house, but we still remember the enraged cries of elitism by those Canadians who seem to believe that hockey is fine, but minority tastes are elitist snobbery.)

Whether Swann was the first institutional head whose primary function was to raise money in Toronto I'm not sure, but he might have been the first who sought public attention as a money-raising tactic, something which is now a primary function of the heads of public institutions. William Thorsell, a later head of the ROM, and Matthew Teitelbaum at the Art Gallery of Ontario, are current examples of that species. When governments increasingly lack the sophistication to understand that feeding souls is as important as building sewers and freeways, private citizens with vision become even more essential to a country's culture, as do the directors of those public institutions which need private help.

Swann was constantly in the news, at public functions and dinners, and he was becoming quite well-known and I believe that he was very effective in raising funds. But what I discovered in my many talks with Jim's friends and colleagues was that inside the museum it was a mess. Time after time I was told that Swann didn't want to deal with the internal problems of the professional staff. I guess he felt he needed to concentrate on raising the public awareness of the ROM, and he therefore neglected inner administrative problems. I blamed Barlow strongly now for almost everything that had gone on, but I also felt Swann had committed sins of omission and bore some of the responsibility. His refusal to act or address the problem had exacerbated matters.

My strategy was to focus on Swann's responsibility for this mess, and that is how I presented it to him.

Barlow and I entered Swann's office, Barlow already sweating. By now my private name for him was Doctor Slippery, and it wasn't just because of the ever-present sheen. Barlow couldn't look me in the eye for more than a second or two. Swann sat us. He was not nervous, but seemed a bit apprehensive and very cautious; he was obviously a pro. He knew he had a problem, and perhaps a serious one. He knew I was family, so my anger would be more personal and therefore much more dangerous. Hurt pride is not to be placated by token offerings. He didn't know where all of this might lead, and he was very alert.

We didn't waste much time on pleasantries—what was the point when we both knew we'd better draw the lines early? Barlow only spoke once.

"Okay," Swann said, "What do you want from me?"

I got right to it, laying out my position and what I would offer.

"Mr. Swann, you have a serious problem. Jim Baillie was a very public man and much loved by many people. Your institution treated him very shabbily. I have studied the evidence. His family is very confused and upset. I am also very angry and upset. But I'm not confused. With Jim's letter and with what I've been told from people inside your institution, I have a very definite plan which I intend to pursue.

"You and I must reach an agreement here, otherwise you can be sure that you are going to have a situation to deal with where your opponent has nothing to lose and, furthermore, doesn't have the slightest concern what it could cost him personally. However I'm going to suggest a solution which could solve the problem."

"And that is?" said Swann, watching me closely.

"I've just sold Jim's library to the University of Toronto," I said. "But I offered them as part of the deal Jim's whole office—the files, everything."

It was here that Barlow spoke for the only time in the entire meeting. "He can't have those, they belong to the museum."

I ignored him and so did Swann. I continued.

"Mr. Swann, there are twenty-three copies of that long letter Jim wrote out there. I have the list he used to send them. If you heard Gordon Sinclair's radio eulogy and read between the lines you will be aware that he has a copy. So do many others, influential and important people here, and throughout the world. Many of those people are ornithologists and academics, but many others are business people, the kind of people you need in order to raise the money that the ROM needs to raise. Here's what I want, and here's what I suggest.

"You let me take the entire contents of that office, and I will undertake to get those twenty-three letters back and destroy them. I, and Jim's family, will get what we want, and you will avoid a public scandal which I assume you don't want. Personally, I'd love a public scandal, but I'm trying to be professional, as a representative of the Baillie family. It's more important to them that a personal monument to Jim be established than that they get revenge, especially when they aren't even sure they understand what has happened. As for me, I would choose revenge, the more public the better, but unless I decide that's necessary, I will let my regard for Jim's family supersede that. That is my offer."

Swann looked at me intently for about five seconds.

"Do you think you can get those letters back?" he asked.

"Yes," I said. "I believe I can."

"It's a deal," he responded at once, confirming my first observation that he was a pro.

We shook hands and Barlow and I went back to Jim's office.

"I have to go through the files before you pack them," said Barlow. "To take out stuff that's obviously the ROM's property. Like official reports, and minutes of meetings, stuff like that." His white face was shining with sweat.

"Weren't you listening, Barlow?" (No longer even the subtle insult of "Mister.") "I guess we'd better go back and see Swann," I said. "Let's go." That was it. Doctor Slippery surrendered.

I packed and delivered the library. I wrote a letter to the twenty-three people explaining what I had done and why and got every letter back. I then wrote to every nature group I could find, from the Ontario Federation of Naturalists to obscure birder clubs everywhere, explaining that Jim's very important library was now at the University of Toronto, and that the library would welcome donations of relevant papers to fill out the collection so that it would continue to be the greatest printed collection relating to ornithology in Canada.

Several of Jim's friends donated much time to working gratis on the papers, transcribing Jim's handwritten notes and advising the Fisher staff, their way of paying homage to their friend and guide.

The response was enormous and very gratifying to me. Regularly, as Jim's old friends and associates have died off, more important material has been left to the university.

So Uncle Jim's legacy is intact and continues to grow. Booksellers get a fair number of opportunities in a lifetime to both further their professional ambitions and to also contribute to the common good, but I can't imagine that anything I do will ever supersede what I managed to do here. And I was fully aware at the time that probably nothing in my future would measure up to that triumph. I peaked early in the glory race, I guess you could say.

It is unlikely that Dr. Slippery will ever read this, having long since gone back to the States. I kept track through occasional queries over the years, and heard that, in the manner of all big institutions, which never fire people unless they commit unmentionable moral transgressions, he was locked in his office (the term universities use to designate people whom they are trying to keep from causing any more damage) and allowed to continue until retirement. He may not even be alive, for all I know.

In a further irony, Swann himself was fired a couple of years later by the ROM Board of Directors. The charges? An article in a newspaper quotes a board member: "Any institution that has a President who … has lost and continues to lose the support of the backbone of the museum, the curatorial staff, doesn't deserve to have his contract renewed."

It's impossible here not to refer to the old cliché: "What goes around, comes around."

Some time after everything was completed, Florence and Helen asked me up to the house. After some hugs and congratulations they presented me with a cheque for $2,000.00. I refused. I tried to explain what it meant to me. To not only triumph over the bad guys, like John Wayne and Alan Ladd, whose films formed my early moral base, but to do so on behalf of that wonderful man, one of my earliest true heroes, was more than enough reward for me. In truth, I didn't want to soil my triumph with profit. But they had their own agenda, and they insisted that I take the money. It became apparent that their insistence was based on the same feelings as my own. Their pleasure at the outcome was based on the same emotions. Family pride, the importance of the recognition of our beloved Jim's importance, and this wonderful result which we believed was his vindication.

I started to see that for them the gesture had nothing to do with money, but by giving me money they wanted to show their appreciation for my part in it. I swallowed my distaste and accepted.

What made it even better was that I badly needed the money then, although I didn't tell my relatives that. An added gift was the pride and pleasure my mother and father took in my accomplishment, even though I never told them all the sordid details of their son's descent into the world of blackmail and chicanery.

And, of course, it should be obvious to the reader, that of the twenty-three copies of the infamous letter, one copy survives. It is in the Baillie collection at the University of Toronto, although access is restricted. I made sure that it was there for the future record.

I do not believe that my promise to destroy them all bound me to do that. I am a bookseller. My vocation demands that I save the written record, not destroy it. To ask a bookseller to destroy part of the historical record would be like asking a doctor to assist in a suicide; it would be a professional sin. No one has the right to ask that. I have in my personal archive a letter to me from a very well-known Canadian poet on certain personal matters. In a postscript she adds: "Dave, please destroy this letter. I know you will." What she should have known is that I wouldn't do that anymore than she would steal lines from another poet.

I hope that this account shows that I was a very accomplished blackmailer and that I had the time of my life being one.

But it's been all downhill from there.

While I held Swann in contempt for his part in this debacle, I found it ultimately sad, for he had impeccable credentials in his field. After an illustrious career at the Ashmolean, which included the publication of two books in his field of expertise, which had given him worldwide respect amongst his peers, he chose to effectively wipe out all of that by foolishly choosing local fame and no doubt attractive financial recompense over his real vocation.

Closer to home, I've known two librarians—both of whom had the real goods—true librarians, a much rarer type than might generally be realized, who opted for what they had mistakenly considered "advancement"—accepting executive positions with much more prestige and, of course, more money. Both came to realize that they had damaged their real careers.

For, as true librarians, their real loyalty was to books, and they exchanged, in effect, their vocations for the illusory rewards of power and advancement.

One of these men bluntly admitted this to me years later. His "advancement" had resulted in him spending the rest of his career chairing stupid meetings. He ended his lament by saying "I never got to play with the books again," as effective a condemnation of power and prestige in the book world as anything I've heard.

The other one, who in his early years showed promise of being one of the two or three greatest librarians in the country, just sort of fizzled out. He and I remained mutually friendly and for years had dealings (although, even there, it was business and administrative matters, not book-related things). He became (I can't bring myself to say "evolved into") a consummate bureaucrat. Whenever I brought him some problem he would invariably reply, "I can't do that Dave. I have to think of the consequences"—that financial restraint, that executive or union-driven decree—"I can't do that—they'll have my scalp if I do."

He was defeated because he chose fancy rewards over his natural vocation. The single saddest aspect of his wrong decision was that, after initially showing such enormous understanding and feel for books, he didn't enter my store or buy a book for himself from me or I expect any other bookseller for the last twenty-five years after he chose "advancement" and security over his vocation.

The moral I extracted from these two examples, among others, is that a vocation is a delicate thing. It must be nurtured and tended with the same sensitivity and intelligence as, say, a marriage. We are all, every day, offered inducements and temptations which seem to offer high rewards. A man with a true vocation must guard the integrity of that vocation with the same zeal that he affords to his family or his country. There can be no compromises of one's truth, just as one can't be a sometime patriot.

Both my friends lived to deeply regret their error, reduced to spending their time waiting for the freedom of retirement.

Learning My Trade 1:
How to Scout

I t might appear as if, in business three or four years and with my first U.S. scouting trip under my belt, I had progressed to a certain sophistication, but the truth is I was merely following my instincts—only forty years later do I see what I didn't know then, that my instincts were pretty good.

It is not surprising that I didn't realize that I was a natural, because I had either failed at everything I'd tried or, worse, lost interest after showing initial talent.

As a skinny twelve-year-old, I once shot an 84 in golf. Playing with mostly wooden-shafted clubs so early in the morning that we would be soaked with dew to the waist before we reached the first green, I was very good but inconsistent. But I didn't, once again, have enough interest to persist.

To understand my real education in scouting it is necessary to go back to my early years in my first store, as it was there that luck gave me a great opportunity to learn my trade.

One day I received a call from Cicely Blackstock, the librarian at the University of Toronto then responsible for book selection in Canadiana and Canadian Literature. She asked if I would be interested in taking on a project with the university. I certainly was. I was excited and flattered to be asked, and I felt that it would be an opportunity to both learn a lot and prove myself with an important client. We made an appointment and Miss Blackstock explained what the University wanted. The project was straight-forward—to supply the University of Toronto with every piece of poetry, fiction and drama written by a Canadian which it didn't own already. Now, when I say every piece of poetry, librarians

David Mason

will know that I mean precisely what I say. Every scrap, vanity publication or self-published piece of junk written by a Canadian was wanted. A collection of that sort may not teach a researcher much about poetry, but it will reflect a lot about Canada and how Canadians think, so amassing all the junk is not as silly as it might first appear. A country's literature is not just the Shakespeares and Miltons: it is also the hacks and mediocrities. To accomplish our project, Miss Blackstock marked the university's holdings on a copy of Watters. I was free to supply listed items that the university didn't hold, as well as any item of Canadian literature that wasn't listed by Watters. Here I should explain that "Watters" is the term used by booksellers and librarians to refer to a major, pioneering bibliographic project undertaken by Reginald Watters, a Canadian librarian. The full title is *A Checklist of Canadian Literature and Background Materials.—To 1950*. Watters' students solicited the holdings of all major Canadian institutions and a few foreign libraries who had large holdings of Canadian literature. These included the British Museum, the Library of Congress, and Brown University in Rhode Island, which has a huge collection of Canadian literature. As far as I can determine, different universities sent copies of their file cards, which often carried erroneous information. Watters and his student assistants used these to compile the *Checklist*. Consequently, new errors were added to existing ones and, of course, many books were missed, but the first result, published in 1959, was the only game in town and a necessary pioneering effort. The second edition, published in 1972, was revised and extended to include the period from 1950 to 1960. It is also faulty, with less justification, but is still the only game in town. Although extended bibliographic treatment is now available on important Canadian writers, Watters remains an essential reference tool for Canadian literature as a whole. I must stress here that the books I was seeking were mostly the obscure titles that the

university hadn't bothered with in earlier years when it had concentrated on buying the work of the important Canadian writers,
but which were now required to fill the gaps in the collection. So
there I was, one minute a used bookseller without books or customers, the next a special agent on a crucial mission.

Having absorbed the excitement of being hired, I had to face
reality. How was I going to supply these books? Where and how
would I find them? I had only one idea, and it was limited. I went
to all of my colleagues and explained my position and asked if I
could go through their stock, take what I needed and pay them
after I got paid. My colleagues were very generous, or probably just
indifferent, and I was allowed access to stock buried in basements
and other repositories of the unsaleable—the long-forgotten and
unwanted junk. I would spend the better part of a day scrounging through places that hadn't been cleaned in many years. The
length of time books had laid there unwanted would be reflected
in their prices and the amount of dust covering them. I would
pick up a book, laboriously check it against my list, and every once
in a while—triumph—a book I needed would surface. At such
moments I felt as though I had discovered pure gold and not only
a $7.00 book that I was going to sell for $8.00. The system was
working! I was too green to know even relative scarcity or values, so
if a colleague's price was $10.00 my assumption was that my col-
league must know more than I did (after all, I knew nothing) and
that, therefore, the book's value was what he said it was. The truth
was that none of these books had anything but a relative value,
based not on merit but on general scales for used books. In those
days, most books, not special or greatly sought-after, sold in the
$3.00 to $10.00 range. The price was based on such important factors as thickness, interest of title, and colour, but I was too raw to
know this. Later I learned that it wasn't just me who was ignorant
about Canadian literature; so was every other dealer except my

old boss Jerry Sherlock. Jerry actually knew scarcity, one of the few safe factors in the book world. My ignorance ensured that I never got to benefit from what we in the trade call "sleepers," books grossly underpriced which, when located by a knowledgeable dealer, can be fairly priced very much higher. So, generally, I would get a twenty percent discount from a colleague and add ten percent to the price. Often I was too frightened to do that with books priced over $15.00, and chose to operate on just the discount. On any given one of these expeditions, I would buy perhaps six to ten books for $60.00 to $75.00, and then send these to the university with a bill for $75.00 to $100.00. This seems a pitifully small amount now for what would usually be most of a day's work, but I was delighted with it. My monthly rent divided by working days was $13.00 a day (this was for both the store and home, for by this time I had opened my first actual store in the old Gerrard Street Village) and each day I put aside the first $13.00 I took in to ensure that I would always have the rent for the first of the month. There were days when I didn't even take in the $13.00. So a gross profit of $15.00 to $20.00 for a day's work was most welcome.

Soon I had scrounged through every filthy basement within travelling distance of Toronto. Unless one of my colleagues bought a big lot of Canadian literature, my resources were exhausted. I had to think of something new, so I started to study Watters, hoping to get ideas. Repeated study of the titles of the books I needed did indeed show a certain pattern. The books I wanted to find were mostly by obscure or unknown writers and had been published in the United States or, less often, in England. Gradually an idea formed. I would prepare want lists of all these obscure authors and titles, one for the United States and one for England. I would then put part of the list in a full page ad in the *AB*, a U.S. trade magazine, and see what happened. If that worked, I would advertise in the *Clique*, the British trade equivalent.

Now a word about the *AB*: *AB* is short for *Antiquarian Bookman,* which was a weekly trade magazine that contained some minor editorial matter and a few obituaries but was mostly devoted to lists of books wanted by dealers and libraries as well as lists of books for sale by dealers. It was the trade vehicle that we used to search for books (usually by title, although small box ads were also used for searches by subject or author—"everything by or relating to ..."). I would advertise and those responding with quotations would be sent my full list. While I was compiling my list it occurred to me to add to it various writers' names who were much sought-after and very saleable here but not needed for my project, the idea being that I might get some quotations for books that I could buy at a good price for regular stock. There were then several Canadian writers who had been very popular in the States and had been largely published there, but whom American quoters would probably not know were sought-after and selling at a premium in Canada. A few examples are Charles G.D. Roberts, Susanna Moodie, Sara Jeanette Duncan, Morley Callaghan, Ernest Thompson Seton, Stephen Leacock (who had been very popular in the United States in his heyday), the humourist T.C. Haliburton, and such poets as Bliss Carman and E J. Pratt. Also, just starting to be recognized, were the major Canadian writers of today: Margaret Laurence, Mordecai Richler, Irving Layton, and Earle Birney. Soon I had a lengthy list, baited with my cunning little additions. I sent in a full page advertisement and waited with great trepidation. No one else had tried such a thing before and I hadn't a clue what might ensue. However, I did know what to expect in the way of quotations since I had advertised before and I knew something about the people who quoted books to that magazine.

When you enter a bookstore such as mine you are viewing something which may appear simple but is not. Perhaps the most common question we get in a store is "Where do you find all these books?," a question booksellers try not to answer, because the system is very complex and any reasonably accurate answer would take far longer than that sort of casual courteous question would warrant. There is a very complex system which has worked reasonably well for centuries, and when you walk into an antiquarian bookshop you are seeing the apex of the pyramid, the upper levels, but even here there is a hierarchy. So if Quaritch and Maggs in London or Kraus in New York represent the pinnacle of the trade, there are books on their shelves that came from a hundred lesser shops from around the world. And underneath the antiquarian shops are the used bookstores, and under these are the junk shops and the antique shops, and under these are the runners, the scouts, the amateurs, and the collectors with a bit of an eye. Please don't think I refer to these lower levels as in any way inferior, for they are, in fact, as necessary and as important to the well-being of the book trade as the loftiest dealer, although often those lofty dealers would like us to think otherwise. Scientists now point out that every part of the world's ecosystem affects every other part and that, perhaps, all systems are the same. When Miss Blackstock hired me, she in fact hired about a thousand people. Or to be more precise, she hired me to handle those thousand other book people on her behalf, and I often wondered if she had any idea of the nuts and eccentrics and downright fools and crooks that came as part of the package.

So we can see that there are many people involved in the antiquarian book world who are invisible to the final customer, and perhaps that is for the best. The people who quoted through *Antiquarian Bookman* were not perhaps the lowest in the scale, but they included the most eccentric. Anyone who has used the *AB* as a means of getting books has hundreds of stories about the eccentricities of the quoters, and anybody who used it regularly kept a file of names to be avoided, usually designated "DANGER."

Actually, most dealers tried not to use it at all, for the paperwork alone could drive you nuts. Most quotations arrived on three-by-five inch file cards or postcards. Now, normal business practice indicates that if you are trying to sell someone something, your first priority is to let potential buyers know what it is you are offering for sale. Not so for quoters from the *AB*. Many quotations arrived completely illegible, some written in huge scrawl and others with tiny crabbed letters. On one occasion I put in the *AB* a small block ad requesting anything by a writer whom I collected personally. I received one quotation which was completely incomprehensible except for the author's surname and the prices for the seven or eight books quoted. I couldn't decipher a single title. I pondered it for a while, trying to figure out what the books were, but had to give up. I was just going to throw the card in the waste basket when I realized that the prices asked weren't very high. I decided to take a gamble. I wrote the man: "Dear Sir, Thank you for your quote. Even though I can't tell what you have quoted me because I can't read your writing, I have decided to take a chance so I enclose $25.00. Please send all the books. P.S. Please print next time. Yours truly,..." A week later seven books appeared, all written by my author, all in a series he had edited which I had not known about and none of which I had in my collection. Furthermore, all of them were in fine condition and were properly packed (another area of great peril). Unfortunately, this sort of happy resolution was rare. More common were exchanges like the following.

In my early days there was a man who quoted $50.00 U.S. for every book he offered for sale, perhaps on the assumption that sooner or later he would quote one at $50.00 which was actually worth that much and he would sell it. He was famous and this went on for years, so maybe he sold lots of them. Another quoted me an original, signed photograph which turned out to be a frontispiece from a book and signed on the plate—not quite worth the $30.00

I had paid, and certainly not worth the six months and three letters it took to get my money back. The real trick is to not offend the quoter when you ask for the return of your money. It takes a fairly high degree of stupidity to make such an error, and it requires the skills of a politician to tactfully suggest that someone could have made such a mistake without letting on that you actually believe your quoter to be an idiot. My favourite example of the perils of the quotation system is that of a friend of mine who, having sent a man a cheque for a needed book which had been quoted as a fine copy, received a book that was badly dog-eared and filthy, with detached covers which were water-stained and soiled so badly that the title had been obliterated. Sending the book back with a rather sharp note demanding his money back, my friend couldn't resist asking (even though he knew he shouldn't get further involved) how someone could possibly describe such a copy as fine. Back came a reply of such unassailable logic that we can only marvel at the quoter's fine sense of the fitness of things. "Well," this quoter replied, "if I had told you what it was really like you would not have ordered it, would you?" Another common occurrence was the receipt of a large group of quotation cards on which the quoter forgot to put his name and address. This was particularly painful if the books were very good and inexpensive, because there was no way to contact such a quoter.

Advertising in the *AB* was therefore an act of considerable courage, and I awaited the mail thereafter with mixed feelings. But, in fact, things started off very well. I was not deluged by quotes, although a lot came in, but the majority were for books that I needed. Early on it became obvious that, after fulfilling the needs of the University of Toronto, I should buy any duplicates offered, since it was logical to assume that if the University of Toronto didn't have a particular book other Canadian institutions would also need it. This assumption proved to be correct and my next few catalogues devoted to Canadian literature contained a large percentage of my surplus purchases. I had also received a good number of quotations for the planted authors. I was able to purchase many of the titles offered, so I was almost immediately supplementing my efforts for the university with unexpected sales. Another thing occurred which I hadn't anticipated. Many quoters, no doubt grasping at straws, quoted me any book they had relating to Canada. I didn't want most of them but the odd one proved worth buying, so I augmented my take that way as well.

As with all books turning up in faraway places, the occasional item appears that, for one reason or another (for example, a book that was privately printed by an ex-Canadian who no one even remembers as such), is not known by anyone. I have learned to look for such books especially in places like California, where a lot of Canadians seem to have migrated, some no doubt for climate, but others for more esoteric reasons, like joining a religious cult. I always check prefaces to see where they were signed and dated. Just a short while ago, I flashed the preface on a book about Tibet by a woman with a Dutch name and found that the preface was signed and dated at "Chatham, Ontario"—usually proof that the author was Canadian. When I checked Watters, I found that she was. Another winner. The word "Chatham" added $100.00 to the value of what otherwise would have been a $25.00 book. Charles Everitt, whose memoirs *Adventures of a Treasure Hunter* is to my mind one of the best books on bookselling, mentions somewhere that after a lifetime of flashing the pages of books, he became quite adept at spotting the word America in unlikely books. When this happens such a book becomes Americana and opportunities are opened for its sale in markets otherwise closed. I have also been doing this for many years and have found 'Canada' or Canadian place names in some very interesting places. Once, I bought and was cataloguing a Victorian triple-decker (a three-volume novel) when the words "New Brunswick" caught my eye. I discovered with a bit of investigation that the author, a British officer, had spent a couple of years serving with his regiment there. Examining the text, I discovered that the entire novel was set in eastern Canada and dealt with the Indians, always an interesting and sought-after subject here. I promptly doubled the price and called Richard Landon. "I have a novel you don't have," I informed him, which translated as "you must buy this book," and he did. I then had the pleasure of boasting to my colleagues about how clever I was, but as it turned out Landon was even more clever than me, for he did his homework, properly checking all other sources and found no other copy anywhere. In other words, it was unrecorded and had I known that I probably could have asked not $300.00 but $1,000.00 or more. Even worse, Landon didn't just boast to all our friends about the wonderful sleeper he had bought from me, he actually went so far as to put it in print in his annual report. I still get to hear about that regularly, and I guess I will till I die or until another copy turns up somewhere, because it, I believe, remains the only copy known. As a result of this humiliation I evolved a clever system. When I found obscure items that didn't appear in the usual bibliographic sources, I phoned Jerry Sherlock. If Jerry said he had never seen it, then I knew I had a real rarity. In fact, I've continued to do that for the last forty years, for no reference book ever equals a good dealer's experience. Even though I haven't worked for Jerry for forty years, I still make use of his good nature. At least I can now return the favour, occasionally myself having some areas of expertise which I can share with him.

My greatest discovery using my new quoting method was a writer I had never heard of, and one that most readers will not have heard of either, although she was the bestselling Canadian author of her time. Her name was May Agnes Fleming, and she wrote perhaps a hundred books or more. (The exact number is difficult to establish because the titles were changed regularly, not just between England and America, but also between publishers—a new publisher, often a pirate, would change a title to make his edition appear to be a new title.) Watters lists sixty-one titles for Fleming but leaves out a lot. It does note some changed titles, in some cases with three different titles for the same book. Wright Fiction, which is the American equivalent of Watters, lists some thirty-nine titles for Fleming, apparently not aware that she was Canadian. These are not always the same titles as those listed in Watters, so it is confusing. I came to feel a special bond with Fleming, for I felt that I had discovered or at least rediscovered her. She is no longer in complete obscurity, as she is given space in the *Dictionary of Canadian Biography*, as well as other reference works such as the *Feminist Companion to Literature*. May Agnes Fleming was born in New Brunswick in 1840. She began her writing career early and at age fifteen she had a short story published in the *Mercury*. She never looked back. A prolific writer, she wrote for four newspapers at one time and from 1868 on she wrote an average of three novels a year. Fleming eventually transferred to the *New York Weekly*, then the most widely circulated newspaper in the United States, while at the same time providing serials for the *London Journal*. She soon became a master of Gothic fiction, manipulating very complex and ingenious plots. Several of her works contain a "villainess of passion, initiative and determination" contrasted with a "virtuous and submissive heroine." Fred Cogswell, in the *Dictionary of Canadian Biography*, compares her plots to those of Wilkie Collins.

Many of her books have wonderful Victorian titles, and I must ask indulgence because I cannot resist quoting some of them. For instance *Erminie, or, The Gipsy's Vow: A Tale of Love and Vengeance.* (We don't get titles like that anymore, do we?) Another: *The Twin Sisters; or, The Wronged Wife's Hate.* Curiously, Watters notes that this was later published as *The Rival Brothers or the Wronged Wife's Hate.* You will notice that she changed the focus from the sisters to the brothers, but she still leaves in the wronged wife. Here's another one: *The Midnight Queen: A Tale of Illusion, Delusion and Mystery.* Now this strikes me as one of the greatest titles for a book, one so good that, as was said about the first sentences of Johnson's *Rasselas,* there is no need to read any further. Could there be a more perfect description of marriage than the subtitle *A Tale of Illusion, Delusion and Mystery?* Her last novel was something of a groundbreaker, as her heroine faces psychologically complex problems and demonstrates initiative only previously attributed to her villains. (Perhaps this is why she qualified for inclusion in *The Feminist Companion.*) It includes a perceptive portrait of a woman who has the courage to escape from a horrible marriage and forge an independent life. Obviously it was based in part on her own experience. For although she did marry and have four children, by all accounts her husband was some sort of drunken wastrel, and she relied on fiction to support herself and her children. That her husband permanently embittered her is indicated by some of her other titles; for instance, *A Mad Marriage,* and an intriguing combination of two titles published in a double volume—the first, *Fated to Marry,* followed by *A Night of Terror.* Other titles include *Wedded for Pique, The Wife's Tragedy, A Wronged Wife,* and perhaps the most evocative of the lot, *The Unseen Bridegroom: or, Wedded for a Week.* Her situation was so grave that she took legal action to ensure that her husband could not get his hands on any of her money, which given her success as a novelist was substantial. From 1870 on she earned about $15,000.00 per year—no paltry sum at the time. Fleming was one of the most successful and popular novelists of her day and was Canada's first bestselling novelist, even if no one knows of her any longer. Her popularity was such that publishers tried to ride the coattails of her commercial success after her death by putting her name on hackwork written by others.

I got quite a few quotations for Fleming, mostly pretty cheap, and I bought everything offered. I listed them in my next Canadian Literature catalogue and was deluged with orders. It seemed no library in Canada had any May Agnes Fleming, and I ended up with many back orders for them all. I put special ads in the *AB* just for her and for the next two or three years I ran a mini-specialty in May Agnes Fleming. Naturally, other dealers caught on and started searching as well, but my headstart ensured that I had all the contacts and I supplied an enormous number of books until, inevitably, the sources dried up and the prices rose dramatically. I still see the odd Fleming title, always with a tinge of affection for that strange woman. She died in 1880, at the age of forty, worn out from all the writing or, more likely, from raising children, writing all night and holding her drunken husband at bay. It seems to me that there is material for an interesting PhD dissertation somewhere in all of this, and when the scholar appears who takes it on they ought to thank Miss Blackstock and me for making it all possible. They won't, of course; they won't even know about us. But we don't care; we did our jobs and the books are where they should be, waiting for future generations to make use of them.

I believe it was through Fleming that I came in contact with a quoter who will serve as an example of the sort of eccentricity I mentioned earlier. One of my earliest quotations was from a man named Clyde King. He had sent a long quotation and I had responded in the usual manner I used with all new quoters— encouraging them by buying as much as possible. He became my largest supplier of May Agnes Fleming and some others, but soon human nature reared its ugly head and prices started to rise. It seemed that the more I bought, the higher the prices were on the next quotation, until finally his prices exceeded what I felt I could ask my clients. I couldn't come right out and tell him: "Clyde you are getting too greedy. Smarten up if you want me to buy books," so I instead stopped buying certain books, at first stating I didn't need them all, but also subtly hinting that some were getting a bit more expensive than I could afford. But subtlety didn't work with Clyde King and he started to become cranky, so I started turning down lots of them, and finally large lists of books, none of which I felt I could buy without gouging my clients. In the end, I stopped answering his quotations.

Previously King had offered me some children's books which I didn't want but which seemed interesting, so I sent him on to my friend Yvonne Knight of St. Nicholas Books, who specialized in children's books. She bought them and he began quoting books for her regularly as well. Later, when I had resorted to the ultimate defense of not answering King's letters, I had a call from Yvonne. "Clyde King is asking me what happened to you," she said. "He says you don't answer his letters." I told her why and inquired how she was doing with him. "Well, he gets a bit querulous when I don't buy everything," she replied. "Just wait," said I, smiling to myself smugly. Then I started getting calls from Yvonne weekly—"Clyde says you don't like him anymore." "Clyde says he sold you wonderful books for nothing and now you don't even reply. He says you made a fortune off him, and now he simply wants his fair share of the huge profits you cut him off from. He called you an ingrate. Clyde says he bought a huge pile of May Agnes Fleming just for you and now he will be stuck with them. He says to tell you he is not sure if he will be able to stay in business." The next week: "Clyde is ill with worry. Can't you do something? If you would buy just a few, he might be able to survive." By this time Clyde's relationship with Yvonne had started to deteriorate too, and his complaints were turning into diatribes. "You are a traitor and a weasel this week," reported Yvonne. Then it became nationalistic: "What's the matter with you Canadians? Don't you understand anything about loyalty or decency?" Finally, one week Yvonne called to tell me that Clyde wanted the address of the President of the Antiquarian Booksellers Association of Canada. "He's going to have you expelled from the association." "For not answering quotes?" I asked. "Well, he calls it 'unprofessional foreign relations'," she informed me. I recognized Clyde's distinctive prose style. Poor Clyde, he was doomed to further frustration, for as chance would have it I had just been elected to the Board of Directors of the Association. Yvonne's next call conveyed yet another whine: "Don't any Canadians answer letters? Are you all ingrates?" By this time Yvonne was sick of being the go-between and wanted to be rid of Clyde, but was much too nice to be as curt with him as I had been. Then one day, I thought we had been saved. The newspaper sports section announced that George Steinbrenner, the owner of the New York Yankees, had once again fired Billy Martin and named a new manager by the name of Clyde King. I immediately phoned Yvonne. "We've been saved; we're saved. Clyde King is the new manager of the New York Yankees. Boy, is Steinbrenner ever going to get it. If he thought Billy Martin was bad he hasn't seen anything yet. By the time Clyde gets through with him the Yankees will be finished for decades." Unfortunately my euphoria was short-lived because it was, of course, a different Clyde King who became manager of the Yankees, although I believe our Clyde would have been perfect for Steinbrenner.

The accusations kept coming through Yvonne, more and more scurrilous, but the amusing thing was that every few months I would receive another letter directly from Clyde. "Dear

Mr. Mason, It's been a while since we were last in touch. I think of you often and I hope you are well. I just got some wonderful May Agnes Fleming books and I wanted to offer them to you first because of old times." I guess Clyde was from the carrot-and-stick school of quoting, but I was smart enough not to start the cycle again and I never answered. I still occasionally wonder who Clyde King is persecuting these days.

All in all, the experiment worked very well. But one day, after four or five years, it became apparent to me that I was no longer supplying very much to the University of Toronto. Most of my sources had been depleted and my business had grown. The university's collection was now only one project among several and I couldn't give it my full attention. I was no longer hungry enough to be as fully effective as this sort of project necessitates. I called Cicely Blackstock and told her that while I was prepared to continue on the project indefinitely, I thought it time we passed things on to a more hungry newcomer who wanted an opportunity to prove himself. She agreed, and the project was given to another dealer. I was very pleased with how things had transpired, for the University of Toronto had become a valued client and I had gotten to know a lot of the librarians, some of whom I am still working with forty years later.

The Fisher Library is the greatest library in Canada, in every sense of the word, and probably one of the top half-dozen in this hemisphere, and that is so, in my view, because it includes all the aspects that a great library must: good professional librarians, interested alumni and students, serious non-academic users and, equally importantly, an interested group of collectors and readers who understand and appreciate that a great library is really a great museum and must be supported in the same manner. My bias is obvious; something for which I don't apologize. Indeed, it is nice to be partisan when the party deserves it.

CHAPTER 12

On the Buying of Books

My father, the banker, despised the book business, as he believed that it operated contrary to all the principles on which all real businesses needed to be conducted.

"Why do you guys always only talk about buying books; why don't you try and *sell* a book once in a while?" was his favourite complaint whenever he was in the company of a bookseller. "It's a good thing no bookseller ever came to me to borrow money when I was working. I wouldn't loan a penny to a bookseller."

In fact, I didn't meet a banker who would until I was ten years in business. It wasn't that my father was a complete fool, he just didn't understand the book business.

When I applied for my first loan ever, I was already in business. My first catalogue had been issued successfully, leaving me with an accounts receivable of some $800.00. And, more important, I had a job too, working for Joseph Patrick Books. I was therefore astounded when my bank manager refused to loan me the $300.00 I had asked for.

"Mr. Mason," he said, "you have a job, so I can loan you $3,000.00 if you want to buy a car or something else personal, but I can't loan you anything for your business. You have no assets."

"I have books," I replied, astounded at his inability to understand the importance of books.

"What would I do with those books, Mr. Mason, if you defaulted? Who would I sell them to?" he said.

In the end, my father came down and they had a banker's talk which resulted in my father giving him $3,000.00 of Bell Canada shares to secure a $3,000.00 loan.

Ten years later a different manager said to me one day: "Mr. Mason, you can tell your father to come and get his Bell shares back. I still haven't a clue how the book business works, but I can see that you aren't going to let me down. You can now borrow on your signature." He then informed me that I now had a $30,000.00 credit line. (Naturally the bank got rid of that man shortly after. That old-fashioned system, used in my father's time, where a banker made a judgment, shook hands on it and the bank backed him up are long gone.)

Buying is the whole key to the antiquarian booktrade. (Any fool can sell a book, we like to say—it takes a pro to buy one.)

I was ten years in business before I got a chance to buy anything which could be called a library—before that it was scrambling for small lots and scouting other stores, flea markets, church sales, garage sales, anywhere one might find a "sleeper" or a saleable book. Painful as that ten-year period of scrambling and scouting was, punctuated by envy and self-pity as the less worthy but wealthy and connected scooped all the desirable libraries in town, I was actually learning the skills necessary to excel in anything.

In Toronto—aside from Canadiana—the large academic accumulations and the fancy leather from the mansions of Rosedale usually went to one man, Hugh Anson-Cartwright, who had spent his entire career it seemed cultivating those people for just that reason. Naturally the rest of us were maliciously spiteful about his constant purchases and were certain, in our gossip, that he didn't pay anything for those libraries. Actually, by chance, years later when I outbid him on two major libraries, I received some evidence of the truth behind our envy, when the owners revealed my competitors' bids after accepting mine.

Here're a few more buying anecdotes.

One time on Church Street I came down early on a Saturday morning to find a woman and her teenage daughter waiting on the front porch with an open box full of books, some of them exhibiting signs of having been neglected in some unheated shed for years. They were grimy, damp-stained, and soiled, all things which render collectable books unsaleable. They were all books by Charles G.D. Roberts, both his poetry and his animal stories—which must have been in his time as popular as those of Ernest Thompson Seton and the jungle books of Rudyard Kipling. They had found them in a shed somewhere up north and it wasn't hard to tell they'd been there for years.

There were also some volumes of Bliss Carman's poetry. Carman, first cousin and friend to Roberts, is in Blanck's *Bibliography of American Literature,* evidence either that they weren't aware he was a Canadian or that they were reversing the usual system where Canadians, grasping at straws, try to claim writers like Malcolm Lowry and Brian Moore as one of us. Now that we have a serious literature we no longer seem to feel the need to do that, especially given the fact that immigration has supplied us with quite a few good writers born in other places in the world.

I didn't even open any of the books. What did it matter if they might be first editions, when they were so soiled. Their damaged state was so obvious that I didn't even bother to check.

The women's disappointment was so evident that I realized that they probably badly needed the money. I decided I should at least be able to eventually scrounge $100.00 or so from the books, and offered her $50.00 for the box. They cheered up as I gave them the cash, so I thought they'd at least be able to pay for their drive to Toronto.

Later I used some of the techniques I'd learned in bookbinding to clean them up. Although the books had looked horrible, it was largely grime and not water damage, so I got most of it off. In the end I was able salvage almost all of them in presentable condition.

But then I got an embarrassing shock. Opening them, I discovered that they all contained lengthy presentation inscriptions signed by Roberts. They were valuable—in fact, quite valuable!

Roberts is known as a signer in the trade. In his day he was a literary celebrity, and was often asked to read at ladies' clubs and literary associations. In those days a poet had some status, and in literary circles it was known that Roberts used his prestige, much like a rock star, to seduce awestruck women. He had a reputation as a womanizer and I've always believed he used those signings as a seduction technique. Elsie Pomeroy, his biographer, was his long-time girlfriend; I'm told that she hated Roberts' chasing of literary groupies, but probably kept quiet, hoping he might marry her.

Anyway, I felt terrible. For $50.00, I'd bought from someone who needed money badly books probably worth $1,000.00 or more. And, worse, I'd not taken their name or address, as I usually did, because I thought I was simply doing an act of charity.

I've felt guilty ever since. Maybe they will read this and come and get another $500.00. Usually, I keep names and numbers in case I overlook something and decide I should have paid more. You might be surprised to hear that I've called people a fair bit over the years to do that. I've written elsewhere of the time I sent Al Purdy $200.00 more for a book he'd sold me two years earlier for $10.00, only to find that Al didn't even remember the book. He didn't, however, think this any reason to refuse the money.

Aside from making me feel good, I believe this approach is simply good business. People talk. Just as you and I are terrified to call a plumber or electrician or to buy a used car out of a fear of being taken advantage of, so other people are similarly wary of booksellers. Most of what I buy from the public now comes from word-of-mouth referrals.

A bookseller learns early. People don't know what their books are worth, and since they think we do they distrust us.

A bookseller knows he can steal, but he also knows that if he cheats people he has to admit, at least to himself, that he is a crook. And he also knows it's like most other issues of morality. There's no point in being half a crook or an occasional crook—it's like pregnancy—you are or you aren't.

One day a woman called me and told me she had some books for sale. I questioned her in the usual manner to try and decide if they warranted a trip out to see them. Booksellers learn many subtle ways to ascertain needed facts over the phone to avoid the waste of time involved in futile trips.

The woman announced that she had sold me a bunch of books some years earlier and mentioned them. I vaguely remembered.

"Yes," she said, "we later saw one of the books you bought from us at a book fair. You paid us $5.00 for it and you were selling it for $200.00," she announced, knowingly.

Now, young dealers learn very quickly never to give individual prices for books when they're buying a lot. I had learned this early on at Joseph Patrick's.

A young man offered three books of Canadian literature and Jerry Sherlock offered $2.00 each for two of them and $50.00 for the third.

"Okay," said the man, "you can have the $2.00 ones but I've just remembered that my mother wanted to read the other one.

(The $50.00 one.) I'll bring it to you when she's read it," he said. Naturally, he didn't.

What actually happened was that several other dealers around town called later informing us that the kid was trying to peddle it to them for $100.00. But, of course, they didn't buy it. They didn't even know it was a scarce book and were actually shocked to find that Jerry had really offered $50.00. I hope that man's mother enjoyed reading it. This, incidentally, is not a bad example of a dictum I adopted and have repeated many times since. It's not the public who need to be protected from rapacious booksellers, it's us who need to be protected from the public.

But in spite of not revealing individual offers, a tactic I'd always used since that time at Jerry's, this woman's accusation was a shock anyway.

I paused to absorb it, then said, "Madam, that's very interesting. But I have two questions for you. The first is based on the fact that I never divulge individual prices for books I buy, unless I'm only buying one—so how do you know that I paid you $5.00 for that $200.00 book?"

"Oh," she said, "you bought about twenty books, so some of them must have only brought us $5.00." Impeccable logic, I guess.

"Well then, Madam, my second question is this: If you think that I cheated you in our first transaction, stole your books, in fact, then why are you calling me again to sell me more? Do you enjoy being robbed?"

"Well," she replied, "You were so nice."

I had to bow before such lovely logic.

I have thousands of anecdotes about people who've tried to cheat me, no doubt justifying their behaviour by the assumption that they're only protecting themselves. Not the most expensive case to me, but for some reason one that still irritates, happened when I travelled all the way to Oakville to view an estate where, knocking on the door of the massive stone house near the front gate, I found that it was only the servant's house. The owners lived in a huge mansion further in. The books were nothing much, but I bought and paid for several shelves of Stephen Leacock firsts. I made the mistake of leaving them, returning the next day to pick them up. When I got them back to my store I discovered that the woman had torn out the free endpapers in every one, considerably diminishing their value, but worse, ensuring that they would be much harder to sell to any collector.

When I phoned her, she admitted she had done it.

"After all," she justified, "our family name was in some of them. What if someone we knew saw one? They might think we had been forced to sell our books."

When I informed her that they were now worth considerably less, she was quite unperturbed. I was learning more of the rich and their attitudes. And I've never not taken away a purchase on the spot since.

It's not just the best buys one remembers. I once had a call from a man who wanted to sell me his deceased mother's library. This man was dressed in that atrocious style from the seventies which we used to refer to as "full Nanaimo" (I don't know why—it still seems unfair to the citizens of Nanaimo) which consisted of low-slung checkered bell-bottoms, with a white belt and shoes, shirt open in front and the ubiquitous medallion nestling on a hairy chest. This type usually switched to a Nehru jacket in winter. The man was as slimy in demeanor as his style of dress promised. When I saw the library I wondered what he could possibly have ever had to speak about with his mother. Her library was an entire room in the basement, all neatly sorted, and the books were evidence of a fine mind and scholarly passion. The focus of her collection was the migration of races throughout history. This subject has always fascinated me, and I wanted these books very badly for that reason. There were no valuable books in the collection except to scholars of that subject and of those areas, to whom every single book would be very valuable for its content.

All were neatly arranged by area, another indication to me that the mother had spent her entire life and probably most of her money on her passion.

Her vulgar son didn't know or care, wanting only as much money as he could wheedle out of me. And he did a pretty good job—I paid him far more than I should have—I wanted those books badly. But I also, having recognized his mother as one of my people, wanted to treat her books with the respect that they—and she—deserved. While we were negotiating (that's an euphemistic way to describe what was really going on—him selling a used car—me buying a monument to civilization) he happened to mention that his mother had written two books, both unpublished.

"Where are the manuscripts?" I inquired. I could tell from the contents and the arrangement of the books that she was a born scholar. If the manuscripts were not ready for publication I suspected that it would be because of her deficiencies in English, or, more probably, that she may have simply been too shy or too insecure about her lack of academic credentials to actively seek a publisher. No one who had amassed such a library could possibly have written a book that didn't have considerable research value.

He didn't know where they were, he said, and he obviously didn't care. They weren't going to bring him any money, so why should he? After I succumbed to what he obviously considered his superior worldly skills, I handed him my card and tried to impress on him that should the manuscripts ever surface I knew several universities which would welcome them as gifts. But it was obvious that with no money involved he would throw my card in the trash just as soon as my cheque cleared the bank. I never expected to hear from him, and I didn't.

When I got the library back to my shop and began that wonderful ritual of sorting, pricing and arranging, my pleasure started to bring me back to normal after the bad taste his sleaziness had left in my mouth. As I opened one book to price it, a sheaf of cash fell out—$200.00. I knew instantly what it was—it was his mother's secret stash of cash, for emergencies. (My mother kept her secret stash pinned between her window drapes and their lining.)

With anyone else there would have been no moral dilemma—I would have called the person and returned it. With this guy my moral dilemma lasted no more than about ten seconds—the time it took me to remember his indifference to his mother's life passion and his obvious contempt for anything so boring as culture. I put the money in my pocket and offered an explanation to the ghost of his mother, with whom I had been communing during the handling of her library.

"He doesn't deserve it. He'd only blow it on booze or some bimbo. I'll use your money to buy some nice books, that I know you'd approve of," I said to the shade of my friend. And I'm sure, however sadly she might have witnessed her son's desecration of her life's passion, she would have preferred that I have it.

I've found lots of other money in books, but except for that one time, it was never again anything I could spend. I've found U.S. Civil War currency and lots of other money from other countries and times. Somewhere I have framed a German banknote, found in a book, in the sum of one hundred thousand Deutschmarks. When I checked it out I discovered it was from 1923 when it would have bought me a loaf of bread—but only if I'd spent it immediately on the morning it was issued, because by the same afternoon it probably wouldn't have bought a single slice of the loaf.

It's a very bad idea to hide anything in a book, but some people do. Whenever I'm pricing a library, if I find, in flashing the pages of a book, any ephemera, I flash all the books in that lot, for people who do that tend to do it as a habit. I've found, along with all that useless money, some pretty interesting ephemera.

Once, in my earliest shop on Gerrard Street, I was pricing a book when the cover of an envelope fell out with a stamp still affixed. It was a nineteenth-century book and the stamp was dark brown with a picture of Queen Victoria on it and a price of 1d (a penny). That could be a penny black, I thought. Although I knew nothing of stamps, I knew Marty up the street did, for he had collected them as a kid.

I phoned him.

"Marty," I exclaimed, "I think I've found a penny black!"

"Don't be silly, Dave," said Marty. "You're acting like one of those people who think a book-club edition is a first edition. It won't be."

But I walked up the street to Marty's with it just to see for certain.

"Jesus, Dave," said Marty, examining it. "It *is* a penny black."

"I'm rich! I'm rich!" I yelled. "What's it worth?" I asked Marty, excitedly.

"It's not perfect, but it's pretty nice," he said. "It's worth about $10.00."

"$10.00? The first stamp ever printed and it's only worth $10.00?"

"They're still not all that rare, Dave," said Marty, amused by first my excitement and now my dejection.

"That's ludicrous," I voiced my disgust. "$10.00? If you had the first book ever printed, a Gutenberg bible, it would be worth at least a million. And you're telling me that the first stamp ever issued is only worth $10.00? That's it for me with stamps."

I put it back in a book, deciding that my career as a stamp collector had both begun and ended in the space of half an hour.

The trouble is, I forgot which book I'd put the bloody stamp back into. Some years later, telling that anecdote to a customer who did know stamps, he casually (too casually, giving away his interest) said that he'd like to see it.

"It would be worth a bit more now," he slyly hinted. "I might be interested in it."

But I couldn't find it, and it's still missing. That's what really taught me never to put money, or anything else, into books for 'safe keeping'.

I've known Robert Fulford for some forty years, during which period, until I could no longer deal with recent review stuff, I would take the books that people like him are regularly inundated with and issue him a credit which he would use to buy other books he actually wanted. Bob would throw his review copies in cartons and when he had ten or a dozen boxes ready he would deliver them and I would assess his credit.

Once, fairly early, I discovered that Fulford, like most people who receive or buy many books, often read several at once and sometimes didn't finish reading them. Bob in those days had formed the habit of using $1.00 or $2.00 bills as bookmarks. One shipment he brought had about $10.00 in ones and twos that he had obviously forgotten he'd left in the books.

I phoned him.

"Bob, you left a fair bit of cash in the last lot of books you brought me," I said. "That's very foolish. And just to teach you to smarten up, I'm going to keep it all."

But my favourite Fulford credit story was the time he delivered a dozen cartons, one of which, when I opened it to look at the books, turned out to contain the contents of his wastebasket. Obviously, he had emptied his trash, put it in a carton and forgotten to put it out, and it had been placed in the stack waiting to come to me.

I naturally went through his trash, which was mostly insignificant, except that I found a very interesting letter from Al Purdy.

I phoned Bob.

"Bob," I said, "you've got to stop sending me your garbage. This is a bookstore, not the dump. And furthermore, I found a Purdy letter in it. And a good one, too. And just to teach you not to throw the letters of important writers in the garbage, I'm confiscating it. I'm not giving you any money, nor even a credit for it. Just to teach you a lesson. And I might just tell Purdy what you think of him, too."

On Church Street, about a week after that bank manager had told me that my father could have his Bell shares back and that he would loan me money on my personal bond, a man came in. He was interested in selling a book which I had never had, but which I recognized at once, for it was housed in that distinctive dark green cloth that John Murray used to bind all of Charles Darwin's books.

It was the first edition of *On the Origin of Species* (London, 1859). It had some problems, the worst one being that someone had put a thick coat of lacquer over the entire book, and the brittleness of that surface layer had caused both outer hinges to crack badly.

Lacquering books in humid tropical areas was a fairly common practice meant to protect the covers from those predatory tropical bugs which would eat right through books. Robert Louis Stevenson, when he moved to Samoa, lacquered his entire library so that it wouldn't be eaten, and the books from his library, when they occasionally appear on the market, are expected to be in that condition. Indeed, the lacquer is seen as an indication of authenticity.

It looked pretty ugly, but it was the first edition of a book which had radically altered human history, changing our view of our origins and creating a controversy which has not disappeared yet, more than one hundred and fifty years later.

There was also a single leaf missing from the table of contents. I figured that due to the brittle lacquer, probably the stiffness had caused readers to open the covers too forcefully and that strain had first loosened, and then caused that leaf to tear out and eventually be lost.

On the free endpaper, in ink, was written "With the author's compliments."

The owner had an accent suggesting that he was from one of the Caribbean islands. His grandfather, he explained, named Richard Hill, had been an amateur naturalist in Jamaica and, in fact, had co-authored with Philip Henry Gosse the *Birds of Jamaica*. Gosse, also a friend of Darwin's, had suggested to Darwin that he contact this man for some specific information on the Jamaican fauna. Richard Hill had been helpful to Darwin, and his grandson showed me a copy of a letter from Darwin to Hill thanking him for his help and telling him he would receive a copy of *On the Origin of Species* on publication.

I told the man I wanted to buy the book, but needed to do some research and would contact him to make an offer within a couple of days. I gave him a receipt and then started by taking the book to the University of Toronto, where they have one of the greatest collections of Darwin in the world, having purchased the private collection of Richard Freeman, Darwin's bibliographer. I found out that there were only twenty-three copies of this monumental work which had presentation inscriptions, none of which had actually been written by Darwin. The custom then was for the author to supply a list to his publisher of those people whom he wanted to be presented with an author's copy and a clerk in the publisher's office would inscribe them "With the author's compliments" and dispatch them to the recipients.

For many years it was thought that no copy bore a gift inscription written by Darwin himself, but in fact several copies with Darwin's personal inscription have surfaced, but none, as far as I know, from the first edition, which had been issued in only 1,250 copies. While Darwin had stalled publication for years out of fear of the controversy which was certain to occur, it seems that neither he nor his publisher had any idea of the extent of the demand which would ensue. Several editions were printed and quickly exhausted.

At the University of Toronto I showed the book to Emrys Evans, the university's master binder, who told me that he thought he could remove the lacquer and undertook to repair the hinges and tip in a facsimile of the missing leaf, which he would do from the University's own copy. He said he would undertake the job as a private commission if I successfully purchased the book. After considerable research I decided that, fixed up, the book should be worth $6,500.00, so I phoned the owner and offered him $4,000.00, which he promptly accepted.

Then I crossed the street to my bank and spoke to my manager, Ian Bain, my second-favourite banker ever since he had told me he would loan me money on the strength of my signature. My father was, of course, my favourite banker, in spite of the fact that after his initial $500.00 loan in 1966 he would never again loan me another penny.

Mr. Bain sat me down in his office and asked what he could do for me.

"I need $4,000.00," I said.

"Oh—buying a library, are you?"

"Well, actually, no. It's for one book."

"One book?!?" His face turned white—I could see that he was questioning his own earlier judgment. "You want $4,000.00 for just one book?" he repeated. You could tell that it had never occurred to him, that any book could cost that much. To place that amount in proper context, my rent for the combined home and shop was $500.00 a month or $6,000.00 a year.

"Well, it's a great book, the greatest book published in science since Newton's *Principia*," I emphasized.

I could see that Mr. Bain, in spite of my earnest name-dropping, wasn't too happy. But he'd said he'd trust my integrity, and he did. He signed the chit and I got the money. I had several other nice experiences with Mr. Bain and his bank, making his branch the last bank where I was taken seriously for the next twenty years, until I finally stalked out in a rage one day and switched to the University of Toronto Credit Union, where they actually treat small businessmen as important customers. I've been there ever since.

By pure coincidence, my old friend Michael Thompson from Los Angeles had been in Toronto selling books and had happened to be in the store when the man brought in that incredible prize. Thompson had observed, open-mouthed and speechless, as I examined the book and gave the man the receipt.

After he left, Thompson, on one of those rare occasions where he seemed genuinely in awe, inquired with disbelief, "Jesus Christ. Do you guys in Toronto get books like that walking in off the street every day?"

He couldn't believe that some stranger could walk in with a first edition of *Origin*, and an inscribed one on top of that. It was preposterous.

I couldn't resist.

"Well, not every day. Probably only once a week or so," I replied, trying to keep a straight face.

I gave the book to Emrys Evans. I could hardly believe its condition when he returned it, even more so when I received his bill, which, if I remember correctly, was only $200.00.

Emrys handed me the book and with it a glass bottle with a layer of solid, thick yellow-brown waste in the bottom.

"That's the lacquer," he said casually. I don't know how he did it, although he tried to explain the technical process. As far as I was concerned it was a miracle.

The book was beautiful, the covers as unfaded and clean as the day it was issued, with not a trace of that ugly lacquer. He had also repaired the cracked hinges (called rebacking in the trade, the process whereby books are rebound with the original cloth replaced and missing areas camouflaged with a cloth of a similar type).

It was a stunning piece of work. It needed very careful examination to even ascertain that Emrys had rebacked it. So beautiful was it, that I immediately upped the price to $7,500.00.

I had that book for quite a while, gradually raising the price every few years to reflect the rising value of Darwin's books in general and especially *Origin*. As always, I didn't mind keeping a book of that importance. Indeed, I wish I still had it because the last copy I saw on the market sold for $150,000.00, and that was for the regular issue without a presentation inscription. Sometime during that lengthy period I had a most distasteful experience with another dealer, a man whom I had first met when he attended one of our early Toronto Book Fairs. The Toronto Fairs became well-known in their heyday. Our Book Fair committee went to great lengths and expense to make Toronto attractive and comfortable for our foreign colleagues. We became fairly renowned for our pre-Book

Fair parties. [There are hundreds of wonderful stories which cannot, unfortunately, be published while some of the protagonists remain alive. There is a rather repugnant book one encounters occasionally called *Hollywood Babylon* by Kenneth Anger (San Francisco, 1975), a purported exposé of the sleazy underlife of the Hollywood stars. The book I might write about those days on the Book Fair circuit will be entitled, I think, *Antiquarian Babylon*. This book will only appear if I outlive all of the other participants from those sordid times.] We went to extraordinary lengths to accommodate our visiting exhibitors' eccentricities. As it happened, I was head of the committee when this man appeared for the first time (and I think the only time), so I bore the brunt of his childish whining. Nothing about his booth suited him, but we rearranged it, replaced his glass display case, and did everything we could to accommodate him, even though I quickly concluded that he was a man whom nothing would satisfy. By the end of the first hour I cordially despised him, but we provided him in the end with probably the best booth in the fair (certainly the most expensive if one considered the amount of time George Flie, our manager, gave him, all with the grace and equanimity George became famous for over the ten or so years he ran our fair).

This man, whose name is Jeremy Norman, was the son of the great twentieth-century science collector Haskell Norman, whose formidable collection is perpetuated in the great catalogues, themselves now collectible, of that collection.

Gossip had it that Haskell Norman had owned half of San Francisco, and it seemed to me that his son was a perfect argument against leaving anything to one's children. One day, years later, Jeremy came into my store and looked at the Darwin. It was obvious he didn't remember our early meetings—indeed I've met him a few times since, and he's never given any indication that he is aware we've ever met.

He looked at my *Origin*, then at the price (which told him he could only buy it if he remembered how much money his father had left him), and sneered "That's not the clerk's hand." I knew instantly what he was doing.

Chagrined that I owned what he coveted but wouldn't pay for, he was attempting to instill insecurity and doubt in my mind; ruining my day was what he wanted to do. He was unaware that I had an impeccable provenance and I'm sure he thought that his credentials as a prominent specialist in that field would suffice to shatter my pretensions, and properly put me in my place.

Actually, I was pleased at this comment, because what he was really telling me was that in addition to being a whiner he was a pretentious, petty bully.

"Oh," I replied casually, relishing it all. "I guess you haven't read the correspondence between Darwin and Hill, where Darwin informs him he will receive a copy. *This copy*. I guess Murray had more than one clerk."

It was great fun. You see, not *all* booksellers are civilized and gracious. And even those who are don't always feel the need to act in a civilized manner when faced with boorishness.

Fifteen or twenty years later, now on Queen Street, a young man came in and introduced himself as a London bookseller. He looked at all of my nicest books, and after considerable examination and some negotiation I sold him the Darwin and a first edition of Wordsworth's *Poems* (two volumes, London, 1807) for, I think, $22,000.00. When he pulled out his chequebook I became a bit nervous—the guy looked about twenty years old and was scruffy, dressed in jeans and running shoes, and I don't think he'd combed his hair before coming out. I quietly excused myself, went into the office and phoned a colleague who travelled frequently to London in order to check him out. My colleague informed me that I could comfortably accept his cheque, adding, "I think he plays polo with Prince Charles."

His name was Simon Finch, and he was later very well-known for having two bookshops in London, one of them specially designed in modernistic fashion where he sold modern first editions. He also apparently had a shop where he sold guitars and other musical instruments to people like the Beatles.

Some years later his empire crumbled into bankruptcy, which occasioned much gossip in the trade, although he seems to be back, establishing himself again, but on a more modest scale.

There is a certain irony in my nervous phone call to my colleague. Here I am, a man who has mostly worn jeans himself for fifty years, getting nervous because another man, dressed in jeans, wants to write a big cheque.

That Darwin is not the most expensive book I've ever sold, but it may be the most important one I've owned, or ever will.

One of the most profitable purchases I ever made I concluded while operating under the effects of a concussion.

One day a man called offering me the opportunity to look at the books of a recently deceased relative, a woman in her nineties, who had never married and who had lived all her life in the same house. The caller informed me that she had been the daughter and the last survivor of William Bell, a publisher. I got quite excited. All the indications hinted at a repository of nearly a century's output of important books, publisher's samples, review copies, perhaps inscribed books from that publisher's authors, or from foreign authors that Bell's firm had distributed in Canada.

I knew who William Bell was. He, along with his partner Cockburn, had been a publisher's rep for many years for the Oxford University Press in Canada. In the early years of the twentieth century they had formed a partnership and started their own company, Bell & Cockburn. They had had a long and friendly relationship with one of the most notable British publishers, John Lane, founder of the distinguished Bodley Head, publisher of many of what were to be Britain's most important writers. John Lane also launched many literary innovations, perhaps the most significant being the publishing of Aubrey Beardsley's risqué work. John Lane knew genius when he saw it and he had that rare gift, moral courage.

Bell & Cockburn, as they were called, may very well have had the confidence to try it on their own precisely because of their good relations with John Lane, for they acquired his distribution rights, a guarantee of sales.

And aside from all those important 1890s writers and illustrators, Lane was also Stephen Leacock's publisher, so Bell & Cockburn got the benefit of selling his books in the Canadian market. Leacock was already enormously popular and sales must have been huge, because Leacock's books are still fairly common here.

Anyway, with that information I was quite excited to see these books and we set up an appointment.

The books were in North Toronto and because I didn't drive the man offered to pick me up at the Eglinton Subway station at nine AM on the day in question. We exchanged descriptions, mine being my usual, jeans and a beard, probably easy to spot at Yonge and Eglinton. I lived then in a second floor flat over a store at Queen and Niagara, and the entrance was not on Queen, but in the alley behind it. It was mid-winter and a bad one, with much ice and cold. Our laneway had ruts where the cars drove and I walked with some care, for a storm, then mildness, followed by extreme cold the day before, had left an ice slick that made everywhere dangerous. But as I headed out of the lane I found a car parked, with a man and a woman sitting in it, talking. I thought it curious to encounter a couple sitting in a lane talking at eight in the morning and assumed that they must be engaged in some sort of questionable relationship to be hiding in this way.

I was irritated as they ignored me, because the ice and snow meant that they were occupying the only safe route. I started to step around their car but I slipped on the icy ridge formed by the ruts, slipped hard, flew in the air right in front of their car and struck the back of my head a strong blow on that ridge. I think I was probably unconscious for fifteen to twenty seconds, for I remember being a bit shocked when I recovered my senses that they hadn't come out of their car to help. I had fallen not two feet from the car and when they didn't respond it further confirmed my supposition that they were involved in some intense lovers' scene.

I slowly got up while they continued to ignore me and was about to yell at them and go on when I felt something run down my neck. Putting my hand to my head I found a lot of blood. Cursing those people, and now beginning to feel anxiety because of my nine AM appointment in the subway (this was long before the ubiquitous cell phone) I hurried back to my apartment. My lady, drinking coffee, asked why I was back.

"I fell," I said.

She looked at the back of my head.

"You're all split open. You have to go to the hospital."

She was towelling my head and the towel was already bloody. I took a few sheets of paper towel, mashed it into a ball and pressed it on the back of my head. I took a beret, put it over this mess, which both held the paper towels in place and hid them and my wound from view, and left again.

The couple was still in their car and I abused them as I passed, but they were too engrossed in their personal drama to even be aware of my insults. I suffered strong anxiety all the way to Eglinton. I was half an hour late, but I instantly recognized my man—he was the well-dressed man fuming and looking at his watch every few seconds. He was barely civil as I greeted him, making my apologies for being late—due to a fall. He barely responded, nor even said much as we drove to the house. My explanation probably seemed phony for I was already, even if I didn't realize it, talking way too much, a common response to a bang on the head. We arrived at the house, the man still angry and surly. We entered and I saw a large dark living room with heavy drapes closed, making it very gloomy. And every wall lined with bookshelves, floor to ceiling. Just what I had hoped to find.

We went into the kitchen where he said, in a barely civil tone, "Okay lets see this cut that you say kept you late."

I removed the beret. The paper towels were completely soaked in blood. He stood behind me looking.

"Jesus!" he exclaimed. "That's serious. I've got to get you to a hospital. Just a second." He opened a cupboard, took out a bottle of whiskey. "Hold still," he admonished and poured a few ounces on my head.

"That's for the outside," he said, his tone now concerned and friendly. "You'd better have one for the inside." He offered me the bottle.

"No thanks. It's too early for me," I replied. In retrospect it was obvious that the blow had concussed me, leaving me indifferent to pain.

"Well, it's not too early for me," he said, as he raised the bottle and chug-a-lugged a big slug.

That told me plenty.

"Let's go, I'll take you to the hospital. You're going to need some stitches."

He handed me some paper towels which I again made into a ball and put it back on my head, holding it in place with the beret.

The beret was damp with blood, but with its dark colour you couldn't tell. He fortified himself further while I did this.

As we headed out, I thought, no doubt irrationally, that I had wasted a trip and would have to come back another time.

"Listen," I found myself saying, "I might as well have a quick look at the books before we go. It will give me some indication of what to expect the next time. It won't take me long to get a feel."

In fact, I felt great. My head didn't hurt except for the burning caused by the scotch although I knew that the wet stuff running down my back was a combination of blood and scotch, meaning that my clothes were probably ruined.

But I was in that disconnected state that could ignore discomfort.

"Are you sure?" he said.

"Yes." I started to look.

A picture quickly emerged. The heavy drapes, once a dark olive green, had turned grey from age and I suspected they hadn't been opened for forty or fifty years. I'd seen that before—old, lonely people, enclosed, maybe by their wealth, in a cocoon of comfort. No financial problems, just a wasted life, waiting for the release of death and often supported by the cupboard full of scotch in the kitchen. A sad waste of life, but much more common than most people might imagine.

All the books were covered, on their spines, with a grimy patina, a combination of time, mixed with dust and humidity, and something else I instantly recognized.

"Your relative smoked, didn't she?" I asked.

"Incessantly," he replied, "I don't know how she ever lasted into her nineties."

I knew the signs, for smoking was not yet then the social abomination it is now. When I had moved from my Church Street store I had used Windex and Kleenex to clean my framed prints and had been very shocked at the disgusting yellow-brown residue left on the Kleenex from fifteen years of tobacco smoke. I could only imagine how my lungs must look.

"These books are ruined," I told him, pulling some off the shelf to demonstrate that the spines were several shades darker than the covers, the covers unchanged because of their proximity to their adjoining neighbours.

The only real value of books like those is in their being first editions. When they are ruined for collectors they are really just used books. I was now sombre, depressed by the implications.

He took me to the second floor to see more. On the way we passed a sun porch, which was enclosed on the outside only by screens. There were two or three open boxes containing books on the floor of the porch, all of them covered by a half-inch of snow which had blown in through the interstices of the screens.

"What's that?" I said.

"Those were children's books we brought down from the attic. I guess that snow is not much good for them, is it?" he replied, taking another swig from the bottle which he'd brought along, maybe in case I needed some more to kill the germs in my wound.

"They'll be ruined too," I said. As soon as it warmed a bit, the snow would melt enough to ruin whatever was there.

The second floor was the same, smoke film on everything.

I knew I didn't need to return, everything I needed to know I'd seen, and as we descended, I explained "These are now just used books, they're ruined for collectors. There will be an enormous amount of work just transporting them and handling them. I can't offer much. I'd give you $1,000.00 for the lot," I ended, apologetically.

"But you barely looked at them," he protested, obviously extremely disappointed.

"I don't need to. It's the damage."

He disappeared into the kitchen for a moment, no doubt for some fresh sustenance. He'd killed the first bottle.

As I looked again I saw something I hadn't noticed, a large poster in an old wooden frame. Even through the smoke-yellowed glass I could see what it was—a Beardsley poster, a very famous one, often reprinted then, showing a distinctive Beardsley woman standing in front of a bookshop, beside her a list of Fisher Unwin's recent publications in their famous Pseudonym and Autonym Library.

That has to be real, I thought. Bell was Lane's rep here and he must have been Unwin's as well. It's got to be an original. The glass was as filthy as everything else, there was no way it could be one of those ubiquitous reprints which were everywhere with Beardsley's recent popularity.

"That's very nice," I said to my man, whose recourse to the kitchen hadn't cheered him up at all. "I'd like to buy that."

I went on, deciding to gamble. I knew, if I couldn't cheer him up, he would not sell me the books.

"Yes," I said. "I'd pay you $1,500.00 for it."

Which was about double what I thought it might be worth, if it was in fact real.

"$1,500.00?" he said, perplexed. "But Waddington's has been in to see the furniture. They said it might bring $500.00 at auction. How can you offer three times that?"

"Because I like it," I replied.

It had worked. I could see that he now knew he was dealing with an honest man and that the offer for the books had been fair.

He accepted on the spot and, not taking any chances, I wrote him a cheque on the spot.

He then drove me to the hospital, where I got six stitches, all the while jabbering on at the doctor who sewed me up.

"Oh, another one," said the doctor, looking at my head. "You're the fifth one I've stitched up so far today. Must be pretty icy out there." It was still only 11 AM.

I spent the rest of the day talking compulsively to everyone I encountered and couldn't sleep at all that night. In spite of that, I got a vehicle and emptied the house the next day. Even the books covered in snow were all right. The snow was so fine I could flick it off like dust, and because it had remained very cold, it hadn't even left a trace. And those boxes contained very nice decorated children's books from the late nineteenth century.

In the end I did extremely well. What I hadn't thought of in my concussed state was that this library would contain many Bell & Cockburn imprints which were on the books of foreign authors, thereby making them eligible for my project of supplying Canadian editions to the National Library.

Therefore I had quite a few immediate sales which I hadn't even considered earlier.

It took a while until I began to see that I was going to do very well from this purchase and I began to feel guilty that I might have cheated them. Luckily, I found a way to repay the owners quickly in kind. They had told me they had a great batch of Leacock manuscript material and letters, and I went to a great deal of trouble to arrange that it be given to the University of Toronto. I further arranged that they get a substantial tax credit. In that period a fair bit of Leacock manuscript material had been auctioned, and I had bought some of it at far less than its real value. Being able to arrange their tax credit at the real value of the Leacock collection allowed me to salve my conscience in the belief that they had been properly compensated. That made me feel better as, book after book, interesting presentation inscriptions to Bell surfaced.

But the real profit proved to be the Beardsley poster. After offering twice what I thought it might be worth and three times what Waddington's said it might bring at auction my research showed that the last copy I could trace had sold at auction some three years earlier for $5,000.00—I had a winner.

Peter Stern, a Boston dealer I had known forever, wandered in by chance, saw it, and tried to buy it. Peter had begun dealing in Sherlock Holmes material, issuing specialized catalogues which he filled out with other detective fiction. He had recently begun widening his range into modern first editions in general, and today he is one of the pre-eminent American dealers in all the most desirable in English literature of the nineteenth and twentieth centuries. I told Peter I was still researching it, whereupon he asked for first refusal when I had arrived at my price. This is a very serious ritual for serious dealers. What it means is that a book on which a dealer gives such assurance cannot be sold elsewhere nor even offered without first being offered and refused by the person who has "first refusal." Professional dealers take this trade protocol seriously, and I shall here show you just how seriously a dealer with integrity takes his word. I kept and studied that poster for some years. Thirteen years after I had promised Peter Stern first refusal Debbie and I decided to participate in the annual Boston Book Fair. I had exhibited at the first four or five book fairs that our international association had sponsored in Boston and had concluded that it was not nearly as good a fair as Toronto's. I had ceased exhibiting there, and in America generally for very different reasons, many years ago. I hadn't been to any American fairs for fifteen years or more, but I now decided that Debbie, who more and more was making the most important decisions for our business, needed to get to know our foreign colleagues just as I had all those years ago. I had forged during those early book fairs friendships that still survive, and I earlier came to believe that Debbie would operate at a disadvantage running our business if she didn't form such friendships herself. So we signed up for the Boston fair. It was quite an experience in several ways I hadn't anticipated. People I hadn't seen in fifteen or twenty years had sometimes changed beyond recognition. A slim curly-haired friend was now bald and fifty pounds heavier. Another I simply didn't recognize till he smiled—everything had changed except his smile. Identifying women proved even harder, though it's best not to go into that.

Before we went I phoned Peter Stern, who remembered the poster but obviously had forgotten that I had given him first refusal on it. I told him the price, which was now $15,000.00 and that we would bring it with us. Peter didn't feel he could buy it at that price. It went through the fair much examined but unsold, and when we returned to Toronto we hung it in the store for a couple of months before deciding that the public had had its chance. We took it home, where it now hangs in our living room, giving us much pleasure.

CHAPTER 13

Canadian Editions

Another project, similar in style if not content to my early Canadian literature project, was conducted with the National Library of Canada, our equivalent of the Library of Congress and the British Library. The mandate of the National Library of Canada is to acquire, quite simply, all things relating to Canada. This project I am about to tell you about was virgin territory, ignored till I happened on it as a very young scout, and which, if the truth be admitted, I believe I invented. It is my most significant contribution to Canadian bibliography. This is the field known now as Canadian editions, that is, books by foreign authors published in Canada.

I can only remember one early major bibliography which properly attempted to cite Canadian editions, and that was James McGregor Stewart's *Rudyard Kipling: A Bibliographical Catalogue* (Toronto: Dalhousie University Press and Toronto University Press, 1959). Stewart was a Canadian and would have been regularly exposed to the Canadian editions of Kipling's books, of which there were quite a few, demonstrating Kipling's importance at the height of the British Empire. Jacob Blanck's *Bibliography of American Literature*, the major attempt to categorize American literature from its beginnings into the early twentieth century in ten volumes (generally now referred to as BAL, or sometimes just Blanck) was a major achievement, and it notes Canadian editions when it locates them. The single most interesting section of BAL for Canadian editions is the entry on Mark Twain, who was constantly pirated in Canada, and some of whose true first editions were thus published in Canada.

It didn't take long for me to discover that Mark Twain had been extensively pirated here in the nineteenth century, because international copyright didn't exist before 1890.

The Americans regularly pirated English authors and I knew that for that reason many true first editions of British authors were actually American piracies. And some of them therefore commanded very high prices due to the rarity of these often cheap paper-covered editions.

It didn't make sense to me that Canadian piracies shouldn't be equally important. The Canadian pirates would steal the text from a periodical, or sometimes directly from the English or American text, printing so quickly that they often were offering their cheap productions within a day or two of the American publication. And when they stole from periodical serials, they were often out with their piracy before the proper first edition was issued, and they thereby usurped that position, becoming themselves the *true* first edition (a phrase loved by booksellers—it makes us appear knowledgeable). So incensed was Twain by his enormous losses at the hands of the Canadian pirates that he moved to Montreal for six months, the legal statutory period to gain Canadian copyright protection. He did this to protect *Life on the Mississippi* (Montreal, 1883), which is therefore a legitimate publication, although there is an earlier pirated version of part of it called *Old Times on the Mississippi*. A Canadian librarian once compiled from Canadian sources his own checklist of Canadian piracies of Twain's books, which is a good 50% larger than BAL's. I have specialized in this field for almost 40 years and I have done well supplying foreign institutions and collectors with the Canadian editions of their writers. I believe the situation in Australia was similar, although I am ignorant as to whether piracy was as prevalent there.

I have made a lot of money over the last forty years with Canadian editions, and so I should have, because until I started buying them they were almost entirely ignored. I will tell the full story of this, but the real significance, I believe, is not these variant issues themselves but the obscurity they rested in until I discovered and exploited them. The first one I discovered—in my second year, still working for Jerry Sherlock and scouting for my own second catalogue—in Bela Batta's Yonge Street store. It was F. Scott Fitzgerald's *Tales of the Jazz Age*. Pulling it off the shelf, thinking it was the first edition, I was surprised to find instead, that it bore the imprint of the Canadian publisher Copp Clark, although the copyright page information was precisely the same as the Scribner's U.S. issue. This was because the Canadian issue were often merely printed from the plates of the U.S. edition, changing only the imprint on the title, the spine, and the dust jacket.

The second surprise was the price—$10.00. The first edition of that title at that time would have been $100.00 to $150.00, the significance of the dust jacket (which this copy lacked) not yet having reached the ludicrous point it occupies today. It didn't make sense to me that there should be such a discrepancy in price, so I bought it. These books were usually part of the first edition and I assumed, and later research confirmed where print-run figures could be learned, that there would have been a very small percentage of an entire edition with a Canadian title page. Sometimes evidence shows the Canadian issue could have been as few as fifty copies. This seems almost a silly number, not justifying even the resetting of type to print another title and stamping on the spine, but it does explain the great scarcity of some of these editions.

Investigation quickly showed that there were lots of these Canadian editions in the Toronto shops, mostly priced as cheap fiction—$2.00 to $5.00, depending on the author. I decided that these should be considered more valuable and I started quietly buying up authors who were then collected.

At first, while just looking for good authors such as Twain, Trollope, Aldous Huxley, D.H. Lawrence and others, I found that there were hundreds of other authors, mostly the ordinary popular writers of the period, who were also issued in Canadian editions. I started to study the subject, but unlike what occurred with bibliography in other areas, I found I was on my own. It was while doing this that I began to understand that I was a nat-ural-born bookseller.

After some time I became very proficient at finding these books on store shelves from spotting the Canadian publisher's name on the spine. Indeed, I eventually got very proficient at guessing, even with no imprint on the spine, what foreign titles in a certain period *should* have been first Canadian editions. Pulling them off the shelf I would be enormously pleased when I was right most of the time; a good example of what I have come to call the "educated instinct."

My Catalogue No. 2, issued in 1968, contained a section devoted to Canadian editions which I prepared with great trep-idation. After much agonizing I priced some of my Canadian editions right up there with nice copies of the first editions, and I was frankly scared as to what the reception would be. After all, I was exploring a field that had been ignored by everyone and had no established bibliographic foundation. This is why I priced the books with such trepidation. I, a relative newcomer, was setting the prices.

When you are a beginner, everything provides a lesson. Some of the ancillary lessons I learned with this Canadian editions project were difficult and in the end painful, although necessary to learn.

The man at the National Library who hired me for the Canadian editions project had to be convinced of the impor-tance of these editions, both bibliographically and for what they illustrated of Canadian publishing, bookselling, and, more important, the reading habits of Canadians in that period.

I did not learn until some years later, that while this man was a librarian, none of his assistants and underlings were librarians—they were, rather, civil servants and bureaucrats. So naïve was I then that it never occurred to me that a library could be staffed by anyone other than librarians, but such was the case in Ottawa, in one of our most important national institutions.

It all began when, after considerable effort, I convinced this man that it was important to amass a collection which showed so clearly what was seen as culturally important reading in Canada during the period covered. I sold him a collection of some seven to eight hundred titles I had formed, but pointed out that since this collection brought together only a relatively small percentage of the total output—from, say, the 1820s to the 1940s—produced in Canada, the really important part of our deal was to find some way of adding the missing titles to their holdings. After I managed to convince him that Canadian editions were a legitimate concern of Canada's National Library, I suggested to him that he hire me to fill out the collection with new acquisitions. I explained that the only way to do such a project was for one person to have an exclusive contract to supply missing books.

It's obvious why it needed to be exclusive, since careful records would need to be kept to avoid buying unneeded duplicates. I knew that though Canadian editions were ignored and cheap in Toronto stores at the time, they would not long remain so when the other dealers finally caught on to what I was doing. The man agreed, the principle being obvious, but he told me that he couldn't put such a thing in writing because someone might consider it fishy, even perhaps a criminal conflict of interest. As a public servant he needed to think of such things.

The way he put it was to say, "I can't sign anything but I'll guarantee that we won't buy anything from any other dealer." He then gave me authorization to send all books $25.00 or under without quoting them; I could simply send them with an invoice. Anything over that amount I had to quote. Within a year he had upped my automatic shipping invoicing limit to $50.00; obviously I had passed the test.

I worked directly with his assistant, a young woman who had been present at all our discussions, and the project worked very well. A couple of years later, though, the young woman, with whom I had forged a very smooth working relationship, called me one day to tell me that she was leaving the National Library. I was upset, as she was very clever and our system of communication had worked marvellously. She had also become a collector of Edna O'Brien, whose red hair and patrician profile she shared.

"Where are you going?" I inquired sadly.

"To the Treasury Department," she replied.

"Treasury? What the hell is a librarian going to do in Treasury?"

"Oh," she replied, astounding me, "I'm not a librarian, I'm a civil servant. They move us around like this all the time."

That's when I learned that our national repository of printed material relating to our history is not staffed by librarians.

I kept a careful record of all transactions, compiling a list as I went, which effectively became the first written record of the publishing of foreign titles in Canada. Indeed, I am now working on cleaning up bibliographic descriptions because I intend to make a book of it. It will be the first published record of actual foreign influence on the Canadian literary psyche.

It was, of course, for this reason that I needed it to be an exclusive contract—even if not a written one—because I bought a very high percentage of the books from other dealers working on my 20% trade discount and adding more only if or when I felt that it didn't inflate the price unduly.

Obviously, if I paid $80.00 for a $100.00 book which turned out to be one they already held I would be left with a $100.00 book on my shelves for who knows how long. That book costing $80.00 would not just obviate the profit from five similar books but would very quickly render the whole project pointless, disastrous, in fact, from any business perspective. I regularly scoured the other bookshops for titles and my colleagues were generally pleased to cooperate on this project because, except maybe for Twain and a few other major authors like Conrad and Fitzgerald, the world had not yet caught up and Canadian editions would have otherwise languished on their shelves for years.

Where my contract with the National Library really paid off was often out in the small towns, or in the really huge stores like Old Favorites in Toronto and Jaffe's in Calgary, which never threw anything away. In those days the popular fiction from, say, the 1880s through the 1930s was still pretty common in used bookshops. Used bookshops generally sorted their stock in subject areas but literature sections were usually filed alphabetically. And since the proprietors of both the small-town shops and the large city ones weren't sure who might want what, they tended to keep everything. The authors who weren't named Hemingway or Faulkner lay forgotten and ignored, waiting for me to notice the Canadian publisher's name on the spine. It became very common for me to pay for visits to shops in small town Ontario with just the Canadian editions I found. By this time it was apparent to the rest of the trade what I was doing, so I began to announce my project openly. I made a point of visiting every shop in Toronto every month or so and bought every book I needed at my usual twenty percent discount. By this time everyone knew what I was doing, and prices had risen dramatically, but I was happy to pass on a share to my colleagues working on the twenty percent and usually content to add another ten percent on top. Of course, for really cheap books my profit would usually be everything under $50.00, my free limit (although, there were books I considered not proper at $50.00 and therefore I often shipped them to Ottawa for less).

While the dealers had radically raised prices, they still had to consider what they would do with a book that they priced high if I didn't take it, and generally no one got too greedy. After a few years on this project I had a good sense of scarcity, so that often I would buy titles by more interesting authors for stock, even if I had supplied them to the National Library already. So I built up a good stock of desirable Canadian issues of collected authors. I also began to get queries from foreign bibliographers seeking Canadian issues of their author's titles. Most of the queries I was able to accurately answer by this time, but a few times I would find a title that I had been confidently assuring bibliographers and collectors for years did not exist.

A few such embarrassing errors will instill caution, and a good thing too. Everybody who ever attempted bibliography knows that perfection is never going to occur; every bibliographer knows that within a week of publishing something they may have worked on for twenty years some bookseller is going to catalogue a book as "not in so and so." All bibliographers will presume after repeated comparisons of many copies that certain statements are exact, only to be later presented with some exception. That's why bibliographies get revised, even the greatest ones.

My biggest early lesson came from Jack London's *The Call of the Wild*, and I think it bears repeating for the lessons it teaches.

London must have been popular in Canada pretty early because almost all of his books had Canadian editions published by George N. Morang Ltd. Around 1910 Macmillan of Canada seems to have taken over Morang's stock and list. Morang had also published many Kipling titles, as well as many of the most desirable international authors in Canadian editions from the early years of the twentieth century. When Morang was bought out by Macmillan it disappeared from Canadian publishing.

Therein lies the mystery of Jack London's *The Call of the Wild*. Macmillan Canada, which began to publish in 1906, did an edition of *The Call of the Wild* in 1910 which is still pretty common, not surprising given London's popularity here. I had seen so many copies of the Morang issues of his earlier books without ever having seen a Morang edition of the original 1903 edition that I eventually concluded, after ten or fifteen years, that for some incomprehensible reason there had been no original Canadian edition of *The Call of the Wild* in 1903.

After time, I often stated this quite confidently. With all my experience there was no one to confute my theories—I was already the acknowledged expert in the field. But then one day, after about fifteen years of buying Canadian editions, I found in Pat McGahern's shop in Ottawa a Morang edition of *The Call of the Wild*, dated, not 1903, but 1905! It was in original printed wrappers, so I naturally assumed that this was the explanation for its great rarity, the wrappered issues, as one would expect by their more delicate format, being some ten or twenty times as scarce as the cloth ones. I bought it, sent it to Ottawa and promptly changed my story. A 1905 edition existed in paper covers and was very rare for that reason, I pontificated.

This worked very well for about six months. One day, while scouting another shop, I found the hardcover edition of the same 1905 date with exactly the same design as the paper issue. It was common for Morang to do both hardcover and wrappered issues of most of their books.

So surprised was I that I could have never seen a copy in over fifteen years of careful scouting that I immediately began qualifying everything I said about Canadian editions by prefacing my comments with "To the best of my knowledge." I still continue that wise practice.

But this is not the end of my London story.

After another five or ten years of stating that I knew for certain that the first Canadian edition of *The Call of the Wild* had been inexplicably published two years later than the first American edition, I found a Morang 1903 edition too. And in another few years I also came up with the 1903 wrappered issue. So, after some thirty-five years in all, logic again prevailed, and what should have been turned out to be exactly what *had* occurred.

Not only does this provide a cautionary note to making too-facile assumptions (thirty years is *nothing* in bibliography), but it also demonstrates the true rarity of many Canadian editions.

In the last two years I have found and quickly sold two Mark Twains, both so rare that neither BAL or Roper knew of them, one of which I had heard of in a manner that made me think it existed and the other which I had never seen or heard of. This happens enough to keep me looking and to keep me keen. Unfortunately the collector to whom I sold many of the Twain rarities, who very astutely agreed with my assessment of both their importance and increasing value, died a couple of years ago. The institution which gets his Canadian Twains will be very fortunate, for they will get the results, often in unique copies, of forty-five years of scouting.

Things went very well for several years and this project, like my earlier one for the University of Toronto, gave me enough certain profit scouting other stores that based on that sure profit from the Canadian editions I was able to indulge myself by buying other nice books from the dealers I visited, so they doubly benefitted by getting rid of their unsaleable Canadian editions and selling the visiting dealer other books as well.

But the real beauty of the project was my $50.00 limit, because Canadian editions, especially in small town stores, were often the books of obscure authors, popular in their time but unread and forgotten today. I often found them very cheaply. And while lots of them didn't justify my charging $50.00 for them, many did. So I was in the nice position that often the most obscure books were the cheapest and hence finding them was much more profitable than finding ones that I had to pay real money for.

But whereas my scouting efforts for the University of Toronto were seen as a great success by both parties, the National Library project ended in disaster, based on several common human failings, namely greed, spite, and envy.

For there was an exception to the general satisfaction my colleagues felt by my coming to their shops and buying, at good prices, what would otherwise have remained unsold and unnoticed. This exception resulted in a broken friendship, a near-legal mess with the National Library and waves of speculation and gossip throughout the Canadian trade for some years. As far as I could see dealers took sides based largely on their personal views of the participants.

As I said, I had made clear to my colleagues from the beginning that I had been granted exclusivity in my dealings with the National Library, and when I explained my system, the necessity of recording every title and the consequences of paying, say, $80.00 for a $100.00 book which would then ruin any chance of making the project feasible, they all understood this. Except for one person. To make the consequent debacle even worse, this one exception was my old friend and frequent drinking partner Steve

Temple, a bookseller who had his own business, but because of various economic setbacks had come to work for me, both part-time and, on occasion, full-time.

He, better than any other dealer, understood the necessity of exclusivity on this deal, because he had worked so closely with me on my project. The first clue—which I didn't get—was when he asked me if he could copy my list of Canadian editions—not the prices he quickly assured me—just the checklist of items supplied. Because I had a vague thought in the back of my mind that such a checklist might some day be a potential book—a checklist of foreign books published in Canada—I said no, something that I wouldn't usually have done. I am not normally secretive, and I am mostly too lazy to waste a lot of time trying to be smarter than others. And this has always worked for me. Just as I don't lie because I'm too lazy to remember my lies, by trusting people I don't have to concentrate on a lot of boring suspicion. If only one in ten people you deal with tries to cheat you, you still win nine of ten times. And you don't have to waste 90% of your time distrusting what people say. Most people will act decently, and I like to play using those odds. It takes up a lot of time being clever. I prefer to assume that people will act properly, and most of the time they will.

But one day the bad stuff started.

A man in a small town, an antique dealer who also dealt in books, bought the library of a man who had been an agent for one of the Canadian publishers who had been hugely involved in publishing foreign writers here. It was full of Canadian editions in fine condition, in dust wrappers. I found out when I was offered one very important volume by a major writer, the only copy seen before (or since) in the dust wrapper. I intended to visit this man to see the rest but I didn't drive then, while my soon to be ex-friend did. Temple went right out there within a day or so, returning with several boxes of Canadian editions, mostly very fine copies in dust wrapper. Chagrined at what was probably caused by my loose lips—and certainly my laziness in not going out there sooner—I waited for Temple to price them, whereupon I expected to pay the consequences for my laziness by having him get all the profit while I worked within my twenty percent discount. Many people seem to think that such a casual approach to business is an invitation to cheat me, but like others who prefer to assume the best in people, I am, when that trust is abused, pretty ruthless with those who mistake trust for stupidity.

But that didn't happen. One day, visiting Temple's store, chatting, I noticed on a hold shelf beside the counter a huge pile of dust-wrappered books which I knew were probably the new load of Canadian editions. There was a sheet of paper sticking out, in the manner dealers use when they quote somewhere—but where could he be quoting them, I wondered? I was the only customer, and like every other dealer he knew that I would buy them all without questioning. For individual authors there might be a customer, but not for an assorted lot. It looked as if Temple must be quoting them, but to whom? There was only me. When Steve went into his back room, my curiosity overwhelmed me and I pulled out the paper to be utterly stunned: "Dear _____, Here is the new batch of Canadian editions for your consideration."

He was quoting them to my customer. He had gone behind my back and approached my customer, selling that woman at the National Library the books which I had an exclusive agreement to supply them. No one knew better than Temple—for he had worked on this Canadians editions project for a very long time—the precise record-keeping necessary to keep the project feasible. I could now never confidently buy another Canadian edition for any sort of money for fear it would be a duplicate; my project was effectively ruined.

And this man was, I had thought, my friend. My friend? I had loaned him money innumerable times, paid his rent, run his business, sold it for him, given him my mailing list, and committed many acts of kindness—though not even considered kindness when done for a friend—and he had stabbed me in the back in this manner?

On the professional level he was breaking one of the strongest unwritten rules of the book trade—that information learned working for another dealer must never be used later, contrary to that dealer's interest. When I left Jerry Sherlock's employ I never would, and never did, approach any of his customers, not even to mail them a catalogue. This is standard procedure in the trade. If a customer I had known through him came into my shop that was both natural and okay, but one could not, nor ever would, seek out those customers.

I'd heard a few stories of assistants who, while working for a dealer, had tried to solicit the purchase of libraries from that dealer's customers for themselves, but this was the greatest *professional* betrayal (excepting cases of outright theft from the employer) that I had yet encountered (and it still is).

And, worse, when I came to think on it, were the implications and the consequences with which I would have to deal.

For Temple could not be unaware of what my reaction was certain to be when I learned of his iniquity. He had drunk with me for twenty years or so, he knew my character well and had he given it five minutes thought (I'm not sure he ever did) he must have known I would do exactly what I did. I left, returned to my store and phoned the woman at the National Library in Ottawa.

I vigorously pursued this with the woman (the replacement for my Edna O'Brien friend), who obfuscated and neither apologized nor even admitted she understood what I was talking about. Her attitude was very confusing because she had been present at many of my meetings with her boss, and she was fully aware of the way the program worked. Of course I knew by now that like all the others there she was a bureaucrat who knew nothing about books, and worse, that she probably didn't care.

I couldn't understand why she would act this way, so I phoned her boss, expecting him to fix things up. Though I was confused, I was beginning to see that something I was unaware of was going on, so I took the precaution of recording the call, as I often have as a record when things start to get dangerously complicated. In this call, an hour and a half in length, this man very adroitly managed to say nothing that could pin him down.

I have used this conversation countless times since as evidence of the bureaucrat at his worst. While I had spent all those years learning my trade, this man had spent thirty years learning never to say what he meant. Small businessmen get used to taking responsibility for their actions and even develop a certain pride in doing so, probably the main reason they come to despise the bureaucratic mind. While acting as though some confusion might exist which would easily be repaired, he never actually said that. Nor did he anywhere acknowledge as a given that a deal which had now been going on for seven or eight years, and which he had set up, and which had worked wonderfully, even existed. When I replayed the tape his obfuscation, worthy of a diplomat, just made it all even more confusing. Something was most definitely wrong, and I was not surprised when things escalated.

This conversation was followed shortly after by a lawyer's letter from the National Library containing thinly veiled but obvious threats, informing me that I should desist shipping them books without quoting, which told me that my deal was being arbitrarily rescinded. At first I believed that this was the basis of the whole fiasco. But, of course, this woman hadn't realized that by telling me to desist from shipping and billing automatically, she was admitting, in print, that the deal must have existed. This would have been pretty interesting to follow up on in court.

I could only surmise that she was taking over the whole department, didn't like the nature of the agreement I had with the man who was still her boss, and that she was exercising her prerogative with no regard for the interests of either me, the project, or more crucially the mandate of the National Library of Canada. I was furious and began preparing myself for what I thought would be a major fight with what was, for a bookseller, the most important institution in the country. Even the lawyer's letter didn't dissuade me. I've spent most of my life cutting off my nose to spite my face, and I was so offended that I was willing to take things wherever they might go. This incidentally is another of the unseen benefits of being a bookseller. People who run their own businesses will often take a certain pride in telling people who have offended them to screw off, but booksellers have an added advantage here: having never had much to begin with, they have little to lose by making a principled stand.

But while I never did figure out how Temple's resentment and malice and that female bureaucrat's inexplicable motives combined to ruin everything, I did find out what had motivated some of her reactions, and more importantly, why her boss betrayed me by not confirming that we had had an agreement, causing a worthy project to be destroyed when it had been so successful.

Confused by his inexplicable behaviour and preparing myself for a legal clash, which if nothing else would surely mean the end of all my business dealings with the major library in my country, I called an old friend in Ottawa who had long had extensive connections in that library and was also a student of the motivations which fuel all government society in Ottawa.

My friend knew the whole story, but when I recounted my confusion at the inexplicable response of the big boss who had made the deal my friend burst out laughing.

"It couldn't be simpler, Dave, you only know part of the story," he laughed. "You seem to think that it has something to do with the boss backing up his underling as a professional move. But the gossip here, and pretty widespread gossip it is too, is that their relationship is not solely professional, it's also personal."

Oh, Jesus Christ! Everything instantly fell into place, it all became clear—sickeningly clear.

Whatever her personal motives in rescinding the agreement I had made with him, whether because she simply didn't like me or wanted a clean slate in what was now her department, or even perhaps because Temple or another dealer had complained it was unfair (my own surmise), she was canceling everything. Of course, as a typical bureaucrat, neither knowing nor caring about books, she also seemed unaware or indifferent that her actions were ruining a system which had ensured that the National Library of Canada already held the greatest collection of Canadian editions in the world. This was, I guess, of no consequence to the kind of mind which gets its pleasure from power and its arbitrary use.

Her boss, now higher up the bureaucratic mountain, chose his personal interests over the interests of his employer, Canada, and backed her up.

I now found myself in a horrible ethical morass.

It became quite clear that, based on the evidence which I could easily provide, I would triumph in my proposed legal reaction to their actions. I could prove everything, and to do so would probably guarantee my winning. But almost certainly this would result in both those people losing their jobs, for to fight back would certainly mean that their dirty little secret would come out. It made everything clear, all the confusion evaporated, and I now understood all their actions.

But as I contemplated the implications if I reacted as I had intended, I knew that I wasn't up for it. I was still enormously angry; I felt betrayed and I had been prepared to relinquish a large percentage of my income by refusing to be pushed around by people I now despised. But I realized I wasn't about to stoop to that sort of petty reaction, no matter my rage. I despised them both as corrupt and demonstrably incompetent bureaucrats who put their personal interests before their professional mandate. But that was different from having them ruined for peccadilloes which were their moral problem and not mine. I wasn't about to lower myself to their level.

I withdrew from the fray completely. I dropped all of my legal preparations and withdrew from all professional contact with that library. I decided that their moral culpability was no reason for me to lose all the business that every Canadian bookseller does with our National Library. And more important to the country, it followed that their personal moral lapses were also not any reason for the Canadian National Library to lose my considerable talents in adding to our country's historical record.

I never spoke to either of those people again and have ever since refused all appraisal commissions from the library, though Debbie continues to deal with the National Library on our behalf.

We even continue to quote and sell them Canadian editions, although their despicable betrayal of their moral commitments obviated my obligation to offer them first refusal on any items found. I have always done that with all clients but I no longer felt that I had to give them first refusal any longer.

They lost my respect and they also lost the moral loyalty I have adopted towards all my clients. Now collectors and other libraries get first shot at the important rarities I scout out—the

National Library comes last. Not that it matters much now, for what is now merged into one huge bureaucratic morass called Library and Archives Canada buys nothing. They are collectively denying the moral imperative all sovereign nations have to preserve the written and oral record of their history. They are dissembling in the manner of all shadowy bureaucrats everywhere, and they are apparently engaged in sinister plots to ignore their mandate.

The current gossip informs us that they—they being our beloved government, in the form of these bureaucrats—are intent on breaking up the national repository of our history. Nobody seems to care, which tells me that they will probably be successful. When ten, twenty or fifty years down the road a scandal erupts and accusations of indifference and stupidity are leveled at the institution which should be acquiring and holding the artifacts of our history, you can be sure they will resort to the defensive mantras bureaucrats have always resorted to. "We were only doing what we were told to do. It's not our fault." If bureaucrats took their professional responsibilities as seriously as they take their perks we would have many fewer messes in the world.

I did not confront Temple—his actions had negated any conceivable explanation and, in fact, I didn't speak to him again for almost fifteen years.

Debbie put it all in the proper perspective when she pointed out early on that, whatever his motives, he had done it all for twenty percent of whatever he got by selling those books—for twenty percent of maybe a couple of thousand dollars he had permanently tarnished his professional reputation—at least with those who cared enough to learn the facts. And, of course, he had destroyed a friendship. I long ago gave up trying to fathom his motives.

So my Canadian editions project was ruined. Although I retain my complete record of what I supplied, there will now be many Canadian editions held there that aren't on my list. And should I continue to work on that proposed checklist of the foreign literary influence on Canada it will need extensive work.

And with Temple the ironies abound. Aside from the few thousand he made by his betrayal, he has cost himself many thousands of dollars since for I am famous for buying widely in the trade and since I started speaking to him again I have bought almost nothing from him—only books I needed to buy for my own collections or for important clients.

I have also amused myself—admittedly in a petty and spiteful manner—by never letting him buy a good book at any auction I've attended and by steering libraries offered to me to other dealers, when at one time I would have sent them to him.

But in spite of my abundant paybacks the continuing feelings of betrayal from that incident have caused me to remember the whole lengthy period of our friendship, both personal and professional, with a great sadness.

CHAPTER 14

Learning My Trade 2:
Auctions

M any people think that an auction, being conducted in
public, is wholly transparent and that each lot will reach
its appropriate price. I shall show you here how foolish such a
view is. Auctions are the most exciting way of buying books and
usually the most expensive. They are volatile and unpredictable,
and they can also be extremely dangerous.

Even after forty years attending them I still get nervous
when a coveted item approaches sale. No matter your experience or determination, an anxiety occurs which must be similar to those stories one hears about actors, even famous and
distinguished ones, who vomit before every live performance
in the theatre. I have worked out elaborate personal rituals over
the years both to minimize anxiety and to operate efficiently,
for myself and in pursuing the interests of my clients. One
often must make instant decisions and one must be prepared
to revise estimates on the spot, so a careful dealer must never
relax.

In my early days, Waddington's on Queen Street, an old established general auctioneer, had been purchased by Ron McLean,
one of several auctioneers who had learned their trade at the old
Ward-Price Gallery on College Street.

Every Wednesday and Saturday morning Waddington's had
estate sales where anything could appear. Nobody cared then
about books, and often one could buy a whole wall of books as
a single lot and usually quite cheaply. It was perfect for a used
bookseller, providing large lots of general books cheap. I went to
every sale and often did quite well.

One Saturday morning I had just bought two shelves of rather seedy-looking books when Richard Landon wandered into the rooms. Landon, not long then at the University of Toronto's rare book department, was already a serious private collector, regularly frequenting all the used bookstores and socializing a lot with much of the book trade.

That morning Landon looked at my two shelves of unappetizing-looking books and said with some disdain, "What did you have to pay for that pile of crap?"

"$18.00," I replied. "Why?"

He said, "You'll be lucky to get your money back from that junk. Why would you do that?"

A bit nettled, I made my first grievous auction error. "Because of this," I replied a bit testily, pulling off two thick quarto volumes lacking covers. They consisted of just the text blocks but they were in very nice condition otherwise, without the soiling generally to be found on books which have lacked their covers for many years.

Landon searched past the preliminaries to the title page of the first volume. The coverless book was an eighteenth-century edition of Johnson's *Dictionary*, dated 1775. It was some twenty years too late to be the first edition and besides, it had a Dublin imprint, which indicated it was probably a Dublin piracy, although I didn't know anything about the Dublin piracies then, or even that books could and often had been pirated.

"Oh," said Landon in a subdued voice, comprehension sinking in. In those days his favourite author, whom he quoted incessantly, was Samuel Johnson, and so enamored was he of Johnson and his world that he had even named his cat Hodge, after Johnson's pet. "Well, what do you expect to get for that?" he asked in an entirely different tone of voice, no doubt wishing he had got there ten minutes earlier.

I was caught—one of my earliest bookselling lessons about keeping my mouth shut. (I've had ten thousand others since then, none of which has ever sunk in, it seems.)

What could I do? It wasn't just that he was a friend, he was a librarian—in the rare book department of the largest university in Canada, which then was the only institutional client I had.

And it didn't take a lot of insight to be aware that his ambitions as a librarian were considerable. He was going to rise and I needed to rise with him.

I saw no way out. He knew what I had paid for the entire lot because of my big mouth and I didn't think it would be in my interest to come back to him later with a price of ten or twenty times what he knew I had paid for them.

I bit the bullet. "Okay, to you—right now—$36.00," I said reluctantly, doubling my investment. (Maybe Richard, I thought, will think that booksellers always only double their purchase price.)

"Okay," said Landon. "I'll pick it up when you get it back to the shop."

When he came to pick it up, he asked for an invoice, claiming lack of cash. Landon then took the book to Michael Wilcox, the great bookbinder who had recently quit his job gluing bird skeletons together at the Royal Ontario Museum to return to his first love. This was still some years before Wilcox began to do the design bindings for which he is now justly world-famous. The standard trade bindings Wilcox did then were lovely and technically perfect; I always buy them when I see them. And I've of course been beggaring myself for his design bindings ever since he started doing them at the behest of Roderick Brinckman of Monk Bretton Books, whose specialty was finely printed and bound books.

It turned out that the Johnson was the first Dublin edition in quarto and that it preceded the London quarto edition of the same year, making it the first quarto edition and, as Landon constantly liked to boast, worth a fair bit, especially now that they are housed in lovely Wilcox bindings.

However some two or three years later, sorting papers, I found Landon's invoice with no markings to indicate it had ever been paid. I called him.

"I just found the invoice for the Dublin Johnson. You never paid me."

Landon replied brusquely and firmly, "I always pay cash."

That has been his regular defense in the many instances when I have brought it up in the years since.

And I have been bringing it up periodically ever since—often at the Landon's dinner table with foreign dignitaries from the book world present. I've had a lot of fun doing this but I finally stopped when someone told me privately that Marie Korey, Richard's wife, had said she was so sick of hearing about it that she was going to pay me the $36.00 herself if I did it once more.

I guess I should admit here that all the evidence points to Landon's probable innocence. For $36.00 would have been a lot of money for me then, and it's unlikely that I wouldn't remember that it was owed. Once I suggested that we could rectify this unfortunate misunderstanding by Richard leaving the *Dictionary* to me in his will.

He replied, "I always pay cash."

My first serious auction was also at Waddington's, one of their rare early sales entirely devoted to books. They had acquired a very good library of Canadiana, which attracted all the collectors and dealers in eastern Canada.

I was then still apprenticing with Joseph Patrick, who specialized in Canadiana. I knew nothing about Canadiana and, in truth, very little about books at all. However my ignorance didn't matter because I didn't have any money anyway so I was hardly in a position to be competition for anyone. But in spite of my complete lack of any qualifications or money, I already had the instincts of a player and I wanted badly to participate and was determined that I would. The excitement generated by visiting dealers in the shop and talk of great rarities caused me to want to be involved as well. Most of the major dealers in Canadiana in Canada were in town for the sale.

I studied the books, not knowing which were the $10.00 books or which the $1,000.00 books. But I was hooked on the action, wondering how I could possibly compete.

I had been studying modern literature and learning how to ascertain what was, or might be, a first edition. I realized that my only hope of buying anything was to focus on what the other dealers ignored.

There were two titles I did know and which I ascertained were first editions. They were the three-volume first edition of Prescott's *Conquest of Mexico* (1843) and the two-volume first edition of *Conquest of Peru* (1847), both important historically and both of which were in stunning, almost new condition. I was too inexperienced to know then that this was very unusual. That period, from the 1830s to the 1870s, was a period of some of the ugliest book production ever, especially in America where these were published. The cloth used in America at that time was ugly and cheap. It chipped easily at the extremities, cracked at the hinges, and the gilt titling usually was so shoddy that titles regularly became tarnished or simply disappeared. And the paper, because of the reactions of chemicals in the still time-untested experiments of papermaking from wood chips, often turned dark brown, and worse, became so brittle that turning a page could cause the page to snap into pieces and crumble like a stale cracker.

Institutional libraries now find themselves needing to deal with these books, which are literally in danger of disintegrating at any handling whatsoever.

These two copies had none of these defects. In fact in the forty-some years since that auction, I've seen many copies of both those titles but never have I seen either in such fine condition. I guess they were included because they were technically Americana, even though they dealt with Central and South America. This is not so strange when one realizes that until after the American Revolution all books dealing with the Western Hemisphere were considered Americana, including books on Canada. Even after the revolution there were many books which legitimately were considered both Americana and Canadiana (and there still are), but Prescott, being an American writing on Central and South America, was collected as such.

I decided my only hope of participation was to try and buy them. I asked my boss Jerry Sherlock what I should do and what he thought. "I haven't a clue, Dave," he said, not even attempting to hide his indifference; he was too busy preparing for his own fights with his competitors for the prized Canadian rarities to care about a couple of books that weren't in his field. I was on my own.

And here, of course, is the lesson. None of the other dealers cared either, as I found out. Both books came up very early in the sale, luckily for me, because of the level of my anxiety.

Mexico came up and I can still feel the frozen, time-suspending terror I felt as the auctioneer said, "Now we have a set of Prescott's *Conquest of Mexico*. What am I offered? Let's start with $15.00 for the three volumes. Do I have fifteen?"

I timidly raised my hand—my first bid at a real auction! I was both terrified and exuberant—indeed the only difference between then and now is that I lacked any sense of what I was going to do next—I lacked any sense of determination, which is the real key to an auction.

No one else bid. Ron McLean, the owner, and chief auctioneer then at Waddington's and the best auctioneer I've ever dealt with, didn't fool around. He barely paused, then knocked it down to me. I was stunned, still shaking with excitement, but aware that I had another book right after it.

"Okay," said McLean. "Here's the sequel, *The Conquest of Peru*. How much am I offered? $10.00?"

I raised my hand again. Ten seconds later it was mine too. I remember nothing else of that auction. No doubt there were many great struggles for the desirable Canadiana, but I missed it all, savouring my great coup. I got them only because no one else bothered to consider them, not the last time I profited from the carelessness of others. After much research and considerable trepidation I priced *Mexico* at $75.00 and *Peru* at $45.00. After around ten years, by which time the prices had risen to around $350.00 and $250.00 respectively, they sold. In case ten years seems like a long time I should say that in those days, with neither the customers nor the knowledge of how to acquire them, that was not at all unusual. From that and many other similar purchases I learned another very important lesson; a good book, especially in fine condition, will always sell. I believe it is foolish to expect it to sell immediately and I never fall into the trap, common to many dealers, of thinking I have failed if I don't sell it the next day.

Of course a real businessman would point out—as my father, the banker, regularly delighted in doing—that any merchandise, even if you get it for free, which sits on a shelf in rented space for ten years is hardly a bargain, or even feasible for any *real* business.

That lesson, compounded some time later by a second lesson, caused me to formulate a system I have used ever since.

The second lesson occurred when I was much more experienced at auctions, but it was still a confirmation of the first. At Waddington's they would often put up the least desirable books early on, the principle being that bidders, especially dealers, will bid carelessly before they have spent serious money. The more they spend the more serious—and cautious—they become. Sitting there at this auction the first lot was a set of the eleventh edition of the *Encyclopedia Britannica* (1911-12), known as the Scholar's Edition, probably the best general encyclopedia ever done and still the only encyclopedia that serious booksellers buy for stock. Like everyone else, I had assumed that one of the many collectors or dealers present, knowing that, would pay around $300.00 to $400.00, its going price then. But it was knocked down for $30.00 because no one had the sense to bid, all of us ignoring it because we were concentrating on the exciting rarities awaiting us. But really we were making assumptions, presumably assumptions based on logic and common sense, but our error was in entertaining the notion that common sense had any part in the equation.

And that was the lesson. Don't assume that the obvious will occur. Don't assume that people, even dealers, will assess everything sensibly and act accordingly. Once, as we were packing up at the end of a book fair, I idly picked up a book from a neighbour's table. It was a good book on the Klondike which everyone knew was a $200.00 book. This man had priced it at $15.00. No one had bothered to look at the price during the entire fair since we all assumed that he too would be aware of its value. Same lesson. Ever since that day I have always used the system that those two incidents taught me, and I never deviate no matter how boring the material or how broke I may be. I look at every book and never reject a book, even the ones I'm not interested in, unless or until I have a satisfactory reason for doing so. There are books one can reject because of serious condition problems but even those need to be studied closely in case their intrinsic value or rarity could justify today's high cost of restoration. So I am always prepared. After viewing two to three hundred lots your memory will be faulty so I depend on my notes. Therefore, when a book reaches $200.00 and my note says $300.00 I will drop out if the bidder is a friend or a client, otherwise I go up to the limit as noted. I cross out any book I don't want at any price and, using my code, I note the minimum under which I will not allow anyone else to buy that lot.

All dealers have a code, used to provide themselves with details of purchase, etc. while hiding it from others. Many dealers enjoy attempting to break their colleague's codes. Sometimes such information can be helpful, but I think the real motivation is simply for the fun of it, like solving a puzzle.

These codes are usually formed from a ten-letter word with no letters duplicated—that informs a dealer what they paid for a book. It is usually accompanied by the date and the initials of the dealer they bought it from. This allows them to consider discounts or deals when they are sick of looking at a book.

I have two codes, one of which, after so many years, I can read as though it were the actual numbers. In fact, so deep is it imbedded in my brain I can actually add totals in code as easily as if it were the real numbers. This is a necessary defense and I do all my written business using it. And here's one reason why. Once, I was sitting behind a close friend, another bookseller at an important auction, and as this dealer turned around to say something I could see written beside the next item in their catalogue the notation "So and So [a very prominent London dealer] $15,000.00." He obviously had a commission from that dealer. What a slip, I thought. If that dealer hadn't been a close friend, and if that prestigious London dealer had been guilty of some perceived sin against me, even jealousy, it could have proved a very costly mistake for my friend and his London client.

Ward-Price, the old firm on College Street, held occasional book sales generally handled by a man called Lee Pritzger, who lived out around Hamilton and came in to run the sales.

Things would be bundled at Ward-Price sales and it was necessary to carefully count the books in any bundle before and after the sale, even though the lots were always tied together by string.

Once I bought a lot, its only desirable book a fine early T.S. Eliot. When I went to pick it up, the Eliot was missing, even though the lot was still securely tied together.

I told the man in charge "There's a T.S. Eliot title missing from my lot."

"How could that be?" he wondered.

"I don't know," I replied. "Maybe my lawyer might, though."

Off he went, returning a few minutes later, handing me the Eliot. "It must have slipped out of the lot," he said, carefully not looking at the still tightly tied bundle.

Yes, indeed. I heard quite a few instances of that curious "slipping out" of books from Ward-Price lots, escapes worthy of Houdini, one could say.

I attended many Waddington's auctions over the years. A very colourful part-time dealer, a school teacher named Robert Russell, had come to an arrangement with Waddington's and took to running their book sales.

With Russell in charge of the books, the sort of "slippage" found at Ward-Price took on a whole new meaning, culminating some years later when the publisher Charles Musson consigned what in a later magazine article he called a priceless collection of four thousand books formed by his grandfather, the original Charles Musson, and the whole collection slipped out of the bundle, so to speak. Some four thousand books, lost in this "slip-page," later appeared at Memorial University of Newfoundland, donated by Bob Russell who, coincidentally, had received an honourary degree from the university.

Even those of us who knew Russell well remained skeptical of Musson's accusations. Amongst other things, Musson claimed there were many first editions of Charles Dickens inscribed to the original Musson, who hadn't even founded his company until 1903, when Dickens had been dead thirty-three years.

Musson also claimed that the collection had resided at his cottage in some thirteen or fourteen wooden crates for some years. A curious way to deal with a priceless collection, some of us thought, storing it in a cottage, unheated for six to seven months of the year and infested by mice and other rodents. Not to mention that such crates might hold fifty to sixty books each at most—more would make them impossibly heavy—but certainly very many less books than Musson contended were stolen.

At an auction any number of things are going on of which you are completely oblivious. For instance, you, a stranger, will be getting checked out at the preview by dealers, trying to decide if you might be a threat to their interests. They were, also unbeknownst to you, watching you to see what items you looked at. If you looked more than fleetingly at anything which they believed to be in their territory, they took note.

Some people seem to think they can go to an auction and need only outbid a known dealer to get a bargain. Such people could be in for a rude surprise. For a hundred years or so, any outsider who entered, say, Sotheby's or Christie's in London thinking that way might leave with books for which they had paid three or four times the value, because the English book trade believed that auctions were their territory and they made any fool who didn't accept that pay very dearly.

Here is an example of what can happen if a dealer follows the old rule of always watching and always trying to figure out what's going on.

One evening I went with a couple of dealer friends up Bayview Avenue to a new auction which was small enough that you could easily preview it in the hour before the sale. While we were looking at the material I checked out the other viewers, as I always do. I noticed one man was meticulously examining every item with great concentration. It seemed strange to me that a man who I had never seen in any book-shop should be acting like a sophisticated connoisseur, so he kept my attention.

After the viewing my friends and I went out to eat before the sale and, it not being a significant sale, I relaxed and allowed myself a couple of drinks, something I would usually never do, for a lengthy sale demands intense concentration and instant decisions, sometimes involving real money. It is also unwise to place yourself in a position where you need a visit to the wash-room at an inconvenient time during the sale.

Back at the sale all of us were in a jolly mood, not really dangerous for pros in that kind of sale. My earlier focus of inter-est was seated in the row ahead of me so I was curious to see how he might conduct himself. At previews everybody is equally important. It is common to see people who looked at everything in an apparently knowledgeable manner who then bid on a few items but missed everything by dropping out at a very low level, thereby demonstrating their entire lack of understanding and any sense of the value of things.

At about the fourth lot in the sale the auctioneer said, "Now we come to the Canadian whaling log and drawings."

The whaling log—what whaling log? I hadn't seen any whaling stuff, nor any manuscript. As the floorman lifted a large bundle, string-tied, I turned to the colleague beside me.

"What's the whaling thing?" I said, a bit confused. "I didn't see that."

"I don't know, I didn't see it either," he replied.

The dealer on the other side of me shrugged, "Me neither. I must have missed it too."

Suspicious.

The bidding began and who should start bidding but my strange, over-attentive gentleman of earlier. That son-of-a-bitch, I thought. He hid it under the table. I'm going to buy that, I thought, whatever it goes for. I started bidding too. When the only other bidder, that unknown gentleman, finally dropped out, it was mine. I think it went for $200.00, not a fortune then, but not a small amount either.

"What was so good about that?" one of my friends asked.

"I don't know," I replied. "I had a hunch. I'll find out later whether I was smart or stupid."

Examining it the next day, I found it was a hand-written diary/log of a seaman from Quebec who had shipped out on a New England whaler in the seventies of the nineteenth century. It was incomplete but substantial, including quite a few drawings in a competent hand of ships and scenes of whaling.

It turned out that the only Canadian connection was that the man had been from Quebec and shipped out from there. I shopped it around to some Canadian institutions first, but no one wanted it. So I raised the price to reward myself for my cleverness and nerve and sold it to one of the many New England institutions who collect whaling history.

I was very pleased with myself and secretly thanked the two or three drinks I had had, which no doubt contributed to my sense of adventure and to the nerve to follow my hunch.

I got, if I remember, $4,000.00 for having the confidence to trust my instincts. And so I should have, for I could just as easily have lost my investment.

And, of course, I never again saw that mysterious unknown man who thought he could outsmart the pros by hiding something under the table. But ever since I have paid as much attention to the people at the previews as I have to the material.

So if you think auctions are logical and straightforward you should think about that story before you venture into unknown territory. Why do you think it is that knowledgeable librarians or collectors never bid for themselves at auctions? They always hire a dealer at the usual 10% commission, which must be one of the great bargains in all bookselling.

One of the most relevant of such auction anecdotes I know was told me by Justin Schiller, the acknowledged pre-eminent children's book dealer of the world.

Two copies of the true first edition of *Alice in Wonderland* came up in Paris—the 1865 printing which so dissatisfied Lewis Carroll because of the inferior printing of Tenniel's illustrations that he had suppressed it. His publisher had withdrawn the entire edition, excepting the very few copies sent out before publication. They sent the whole edition to America, where it was issued with a new title page as the first American edition. So rare is the real first edition (there are twenty-two recorded copies of the 1865 Alice, of which only five were then still in private hands) that the new, 1866 printing is generally referred to as the first edition, the true first edition being almost unobtainable.

Two copies of the 1865 *Alice*, as it is generally referred to amongst the cognoscenti, came up at a sale in Paris run by Drouot, the major Parisian auction house.

There are so many bizarre details in this anecdote I hardly know where to start. Both these copies were extraordinary.

One of the copies of *Alice* had ten of the original Tenniel drawings tipped in and was then believed to be Carroll's own copy since it had markings in it in the purple ink Carroll habitually used. The other copy was inscribed by Carroll to Dinah Mulock Craik, the Victorian novelist who wrote *John Halifax, Gentleman*, and it was rendered even more important because her husband, a partner in Macmillan, was Carroll's editor. Not only two copies of great rarity, but both copies enhanced by stunning associations.

Both copies were together as the last lot in a sale which mostly contained very early and important books in other fields.

These Carroll books had been purchased by the great dealer Dr. Rosenbach and sold to a collector named Eldridge Johnson. How Johnson handled these priceless treasures is so amusing and eccentric that I cannot resist recounting it. Johnson would travel with them on his yacht, carried in a solander case and he would place them in a special waterproof safe he had anchored in his stateroom. If ever the ship were to sink a huge buoy attached to the safe with a long thick rope would rise to the surface. On the buoy, in bright red letters, was painted "ALICE," so that the world could locate the safe and rescue these priceless treasures. The Alices would be saved even if the humans weren't. Who said collectors are eccentric?

Justin wanted these badly, one of them for his personal collection. But how to deal with the competition? He learned through a colleague that his biggest competitor was likely to be John Fleming, a prominent New York dealer who had worked for Rosenbach and wanted to buy them for the sentimental connection. Rosenbach had, in fact, bought them twice at auction over the years.

Justin very cleverly approached Fleming, who agreed to act for him—a brilliant ploy—thereby eliminating the competition at the mere cost of a 10% commission.

And then it got more bizarre.

It is said that a private offer was made before the sale of $250,000.00 for the two Carrolls but that the French auctioneers made an exchange mistake and the catalogue estimate was shown as 250,000 francs (then between 4 or 5 new francs to the dollar.) It was a long sale and the auctioneer must have been weary, wanting it over. He announced the last lot and started it at two hundred and twenty thousand francs. Fleming raised his hand and the auctioneer banged down his hammer instantly and departed. Justin got both books for well under one-third of what he had been prepared to bid.

But more important to a dealer is the lesson which can be learned from wrestling with such a dilemma, and I have factored the implications into many of my own business strategies since. "If you can't beat'em, join them," goes the old adage. For a bookseller, revise that to, "If you can't beat'em, have them join you: hire them."

While bidding for rare items at auctions generates its own special excitement, this excitement becomes both more intensive and hence more dangerous when personal interests play a part in the circumstances. Besides things a dealer may want for his personal collection, emotional ties to an important client or an institution which one cares deeply about magnify the emotional intensity.

I have known several librarians who acted as though the institutional library they managed was their own personal library. And I believe that during their tenure it *is* their library. Dealers often have similar emotional attachments with institutions that go far deeper than mere commerce would suggest. A dealer will often go to great extremes to be part of the enhancement of collections they care deeply about.

Such was the case in both of the following anecdotes, as they both concern institutional collections which I have long served.

It was simple enough when it started. A catalogue from Waddington's, the auctioneers, which on perusal contained some books of interest, the most compelling being a copy of L.M. Montgomery's rare book of poems, *The Watchman*. This is a very scarce book, although not nearly as scarce as *Anne of Green Gables,* which is not only the most desirable Montgomery title but the rarest of her books. But the copy of *The Watchman* to be auctioned was a presentation copy, inscribed by Montgomery to Frede MacFarlane, her cousin and her closest friend. The inscription read "To Frede, with the author's love, Xmas 1916." A further inscription to someone else, in a later year, was explained by Frede having died. The auctioneer suggested that Montgomery, having sorted the effects of her cousin when she died, had retrieved the book and inscribed it to other friends later on. That makes sense and helps to explain why many authors never have copies of their own books, especially the earlier ones done in smaller editions, because they are constantly giving them to friends or admirers (or maybe lending them, which to most people is the same thing as giving).

Anyway, the auctioneer's estimated sale price was $1,600.00— $1,800.00. Fat chance, I thought, for I knew that it was worth thousands with a provenance like that. But I didn't do more than make a mental note because while I had many names in my customer-want files for Montgomery, they were almost all young women, often red-haired young women, in fact, who had limited means, and while their passion for Anne was usually such that they would scrimp and save and while I have always had a policy of making good books available to the young on very extended

David Mason

terms, this was going to be too much for any young person, so I didn't have anyone to phone.

But a couple of days later I had a call from Elizabeth DeBlois at the L.M. Montgomery Institute at the University of Prince Edward Island. They had received a notice from Waddington's and wanted to know what I thought about the auctioneer's $1,600.00 to $1,800.00 estimate. I told her what I thought it was worth, which was around $7,000.00, and told her that if she could find a donor to buy it for the Institute, I would act for them for a token commission, as I took an interest in the university and I wanted to help them if I could. But I really didn't expect that they would find anyone who would see the historical importance of such a thing, much less the importance of returning it to its original home in PEI.

One of the greatest frustrations for people like me who devote their lives to books is the inability of most people to see their significance in the same way we booksellers do. So it never occurred to me that she would find an Islander who could not only see things in the right perspective, but would also dip into his own pocket to the extent needed to bring the book home. Imagine my astonishment when Elizabeth called me back a couple of days later. We have someone who wants to buy us the book, she told me. I was shocked. I knew it couldn't be the university, as they didn't have any money; neither do most Canadian institutions these days. Did you tell your donor what I said about the price? "Yes!" she replied. "He's willing to pay 'X amount'." It was over double my estimate of value. Now I was truly surprised, and even stunned. That meant their donor was someone who could not only afford such a gesture but who, more importantly, understood a lot more about the way things work in auctions than I would have expected.

Immediately I knew a couple of things were probable. Besides the obvious fact that our man or woman had money, whomever it was understood that if you really want something it is usually smart to be ready to pay considerably more than an assessed value. There are few second chances in collecting, especially for unique items like that one. Not long ago Debbie, my partner, and I did a large appraisal in Pittsburgh for the University of Notre Dame. We submitted our formal appraisal and with it enclosed a private letter advising the librarian that in my opinion he should disregard the value I put on the collection, which was a lot of money, and pay whatever was necessary: it was too important to miss. I felt the same way about this copy of *The Watchman*.

As a dealer, one of my professional obligations is to tell clients what I believe something is 'worth', an arbitrary term at the best of times but especially so at an auction because at auctions a lot more factors, mostly human ones, come into play than can be fit into conventional expectations.

But if I am asked my opinion of what should be done after a value is estimated, even a speculative one, a whole different set of factors must be brought into play. Firstly, who else wants it? How badly do they want it? What can they afford? On the personal level I have to ask: Will my competition be a friend? A client? A colleague? Perhaps a colleague who doesn't like me or one who bears malice for some previous sin of mine either real or imagined? And within these categories there are subcategories upon subcategories. It is the job of the dealer to take all of these considerations into account and juggle them with a hundred other factors, most of them so subtle that they are not even perceived by outsiders.

One of the great bargains I know of in all collecting is what clients get for the usual fee of ten percent when they hire a dealer to act for them. When I am finished here, I hope you will understand the equation a little better.

On the night of the auction, off I went with all the jaunty confidence of someone who bears a huge bid with which to whip his detested adversaries, pummelling them into submission and into a properly respectful attitude to their superiors, namely myself.

I had calculated all my competition among the trade: Who would have a client? Who would be smart enough to assess the book's real potential value? What dealers might have formed a syndicate to share the book's huge cost of ownership? And, most importantly, how would all of these people react when they knew that I was their opponent? Anyone who doesn't understand the extent to which such human emotions determine events at an auction should take heed.

By the time I got to the auction, paranoia had intervened, as it often does in uncertain situations. In that sense, auctions are like a poker game: you may think your hand too good to be beaten but most hands can be beaten, and once a suspicion enters the mind paranoia tends to follow. For instance, a dealer in Boston currently has in stock a first edition of *Anne of Green Gables*. Admittedly this is a truly rare book but this man is asking $65,000.00 (Cdn), far more than I or anyone I know thinks it could be worth. But the owner is a long-established dealer and he's not a fool; gossip has it that he paid $40,000.00 (Cdn), and so obviously he believes it's worth that. And who knows, he might get it. In fact, he probably will, sooner or later.

Either way, a price like that will affect the whole *Anne* market. So I found myself getting nervous. Maybe there was a syndicate of American dealers who, based on the Boston *Anne* price, would consider a Montgomery presentation copy worth much more than my bid. It didn't take long for that to become a certainty in my mind and I found myself believing that my bid, not long ago a certain success, was ludicrously inadequate. Such is paranoia.

Now, I have my own favourite place where I like to sit at Waddington's and I always go early to be sure I get my seat. Just over halfway towards the back of the auction room there is a pillar and I like to sit just in front of it on the aisle. This allows me to observe all my competition, mostly dealers who think it's smart to sit up front so they can be seen, and at the same time it hides me and the fact that I am bidding from those behind me. It works pretty well. So much so that I have always considered that those dealers who like to display their assumed brilliance front and centre in the first row are really just displaying their vanity.

But as I approached my accustomed seat, all the while scanning the assembled crowd, checking the competition, I saw that it and the adjoining seat were occupied by two women, one young and the other older, both impeccably dressed, and both exhibiting the unmistakable signs of wealth.

Having been properly educated about how one discerns the signs of wealth in women, which is, I'm told, by their hair and their shoes, even I could see that these two women easily passed the test. They were both regal and I guessed that they were probably a mother and a daughter. Then came the blow. A young man, one of those running the auction, came up to them and handed them a bunch of Xerox copies from a magazine, saying, in a very deferential tone, "Here's the article that I told you about. Good luck."

Naturally, I peeked over their shoulders to see what the article was; after all, that's part of my job. Its title read "Collecting L.M. Montgomery." I knew the article and I knew the magazine it came from and that, combined with the extremely courteous demeanour of the auctioneer, told me that I was in trouble. Deep trouble.

I knew at once that they were my real competition. Now there are two distinct factors that a professional dealer fears most at an auction: unlimited money and ignorance of the way the marketplace works. Combine them both and you have the dealer's worst terror. For unlimited wealth dismisses competition and ignorance fails to recognize danger and therefore can't be intimidated. I went and sat behind them, all fear of other booksellers evaporating in the face of this unknown threat.

While I was sitting there trying to figure out what to do, a long-time colleague approached. "Are you going to be bidding on the Montgomery?" he inquired, as casually as he could. "I might," I replied. "I don't think it will go for more than $4,000.00, do you?" he said, thereby giving me free information. I presumed he had a bid of $4,000.00 and I was pretty sure I even knew the American dealer friends of his who would be the real bankrollers. Such a transparent slip would have been welcome under normal circumstances but my new discovery had already rendered his competition irrelevant. For now I had serious adversaries, ones with perfect hairdos.

As I sat behind my unknown adversaries I realized this problem would need some radical action. There was no use sitting behind them to see what they might do. I knew what they were going to do. They were going to steal my prize. There was only one thing to do, I thought: I must bluff them. I got up and moved right into the row in front of them. I sat right in front of the younger woman (maybe she wasn't the daughter, maybe she was the special executive assistant, but I guessed that she would be doing the bidding). As I sat down, I casually glanced back. The older lady smiled at me in a friendly and courteous fashion. I looked through her blankly, feeling rather ashamed of my deliberate rudeness, and returned to staring straight ahead.

When the auction started, luckily there were a couple of items early on which I needed, so I bought them brusquely, looking neither left nor right, staring straight ahead as if I didn't give a damn who was bidding against me or what I paid. I got them both but I was really only concerned whether my competition had noticed.

Then *The Watchman* came up. The auctioneer started at $400.00 to $500.00 and the room exploded with bids from everywhere, while I sat back watching to see where the competition was.

Sure enough, the younger woman started bidding. I was watching her with the eyes in the back of my head that I keep for such occasions and I waited until they got to around $3,000.00. Then I entered the fray. I raised and lowered my pencil in an imperious fashion, firmly and abruptly, looking only at the auctioneer. Waddington's is not a country auction. There are no lengthy waits while they try to coax more bids; it goes very quickly and one must be alert. But the auctioneer knows me and he is a very good auctioneer, so I knew that once I started he would consider me bidding unless I indicated to him by gesture or eye movement that I was done.

At $4,200.00, one bid over what I had guessed was my dealer friend's limit, he dropped out, thereby confirming his lack of cunning, and only the younger woman and I were left. Around $5,000.00 she got a bit nervous so I turned up the heat some, bidding instantly as soon as she had raised her hand, no hesitation, as though I had already won the prize and she should stop wasting everybody's time. She began to falter, taking longer and longer to decide if she should try another bid. Each time she did I struck back ruthlessly, trying to emulate how I thought the Emperor Nero would look when he was condemning some wretch to be thrown to the lions. Finally, at $6,000.00 she yielded and the prize was mine. A murmur spread through the crowd, a fitting approval I thought of my cleverness and cunning. A few moments later the two women left, and as they did the younger one approached me and handed me a note. When I had a blank stretch in the auction I read it.

"Hi," it said. "You successfully bid on L.M. Montgomery's book. I am Melanie Campbell Gibson, a distant cousin [of L.M. Montgomery she meant]. I would be interested in knowing who you are or who you represent. Sorry to disturb you during the bidding. If you would call me, I would really appreciate it. Thank you." It was signed Melanie and included her phone number.

The next morning back in my store I called Elizabeth DeBlois and recounted my tale of triumph and told her that the book was now theirs and with the buyer's premium applied by the auctioneer and my token commission, at just about the price that I had originally estimated it to be worth. I was enormously pleased with myself. Then I phoned Melanie Campbell Gibson. She sounded friendly and charming and not at all miffed after I told her who I had bought the book for. She told me she was a Campbell from Park Corner and had wanted it for sentimental reasons. We traded Island gossip for a bit, establishing in the traditional manner how we both fit into the scheme of things down there. (My own connection to the island is too complicated to go into here: it is sufficient to say for now that I hold an honourary doctorate from the university, to whom I donated my substantial collection on the province.) I told her the book was already on its way to the Island, and she seemed relieved that at least it wasn't going to Japan or somewhere faraway. Then she said, "You know, my husband gave me hell. 'How could you let that guy beat you out?' he said. But the truth is you scared me," she said. "You looked like you weren't going to allow anyone to have that book, so I thought I had no chance."

"Well," I replied, "because you sound so nice, I'm going to tell you the story. You were supposed to be scared. Everything

I did was calculated to intimidate you, that's why I sat in front of you and that's why I bid that way. It was all for your benefit. I knew you were my competition and I knew I needed to make you feel you had no chance. And while we're at it, would you be kind enough to apologize to your mother for my rudeness. I did that on purpose too. It was part of the strategy."

She roared with laughter. She was delighted. The book was not hers but at least it was going back to where it should be and I think she was not displeased to be part of such a nice story. "How did you know I was your competition?" she asked. I would have preferred for that to remain a mystery but I told her the truth about that as well, lest she think my friend in the auction house might somehow be in collusion with me. And I think she realized that if she ever ventures into such unknown territory again she should use her new knowledge to hire a professional as her guide.

Any auction, indeed any interplay between dealers in general, will contain elements of envy and spite over perceived advantages or old grudges.

No outsider can understand, even partially, most of these factors. Obscure reasons can be in play: the other bidder, another dealer, could be his sworn enemy and he may have decided that his despised opponent will not buy that book no matter the cost. Vanity and malice are emotions which will defeat common sense every time.

The story of my own favourite auction triumph gets complicated because it operates on several of those levels. The auction I refer to here, with the attendant subtleties, included a rivalry between two dealers who had once been friends but no longer were by the time of the auction. It also includes one of the greatest examples in my experience of the kind of cooperation between a dealer and a librarian which can occur when both parties are operating in an area where they understand each other and each carries in regard to the other a professional respect and trust.

On viewing the offerings in the preview a few days before the sale I found a copy of Robert Service's rare first book *Songs of a Sourdough*. The copy offered was bound in plain paper wrappers instead of the cloth it was issued in, making it appear to be a book missing its covers, which had had brown wrapping paper pasted on. It had come from the estate of Fay Fenton, a journalist who had lived in the Klondike, and it was immediately obvious to me that it was a proof copy and probably unique. It made sense to assume that she would have known Service and that he had undoubtedly given it to her. Service's first book, for which he had paid the printing costs, at least for the first one hundred copies, was already a legendary rarity, selling even then for $2,000.00 or so.

Like many another hopeful scout, I had always been looking for it. For many years every time I went into the Old Favorites Bookshop, I went first to "S" in the Canadian poetry section hoping that one day it would be sleeping there, waiting for the handsome prince to come and wake it from its slumber. One day I walked in and there it was—priced $10.00—another example of why scouting is so exciting. It was a fine copy and I sold it for $2,500.00 the next day.

The people then in charge of Waddington's book sales were a little short on experience and they had not realized that it was a proof copy and had it described as "in plain wrappers," and had estimated it in the catalogue as selling in the $100.00 to $200.00 range. I knew it was worth very much more than that and left hoping that other dealers might go past it without seeing it, or if they did see it, would also be too inexperienced to know its importance. I knew that was unlikely, but....

I thought about it for some time and arrived at what I considered a proper retail value—$30,000.00 to $35,000.00.

But, unfortunately, I knew who would be very unlikely to miss it—my ex-friend Steven Temple. Still deeply hurt and smarting from his actions over the Canadian editions debacle, I was determined that he would not get it. But in spite of my continuing anger I knew he was far too good a bookseller not to know exactly what it was and what its value should be. His specialty at the time was Canadian Literature, and I had no doubt that he would be my most dangerous adversary.

I knew that my anger towards Temple was both childish and unbecoming but it was still there and my whole strategy was influenced by those feelings.

I figured it would take around $10,000.00 to buy it if Temple saw it, and I figured he would try to raise that amount, maybe by borrowing, or maybe by taking on a partner.

Given the threat from the competition and my financial state I wondered if I should contact Richard Landon and work on commission for the University of Toronto. If I did that and he commissioned me I would get only a ten percent commission for my trouble. But I had recently done that for a very scarce early Canadian literary title which was about a $1,000.00 book. Not caring much, but my still-hurt feelings demanding that I not let Temple get it because of his iniquities, I had mentioned it to Richard and got his commission, but it did not turn out well for me since Temple didn't attend the auction and I had no knowledgeable competition at all. I bought the book for the University of Toronto at $90.00, making a profit of only $9.00 instead of the $900.00 or so I should have made. So with the Service it could work both ways. My cowardice could do me in as easily as my spite.

Checking my credit line I found I had a $15,000.00 limit, still unused, which was about exactly what I felt would have to be my uppermost limit if I bought the book on spec. So it would take all of my available resources of credit, an uncomfortable situation. Even though I firmly believed it was a $30,000.00—$35,000.00 book, any book in that range becomes problematic as any such price demands the resources to pay it. And, of course, when books get up in that price range customers are limited; one might sit on such a book for several years before a knowledgeable collector appears.

Two days before the sale I decided that I was too close to the edge and contacted Landon. By this time I was far more concerned with simply getting the book as opposed to any potential profit. The problem was that Landon was in England. I knew he usually stayed in London with Ian Willison, a retired librarian at the British Museum, but they didn't have Ian's phone number at the Fisher. On a hunch I phoned Marie Korey's assistant at Massey College to find that Marie had left Ian's number for any emergency. I phoned. It was evening there and Ian was home alone. He informed me that Richard and Marie were in the Lake district and that he expected them the next day. I explained my dilemma; a unique format of the first book of a very important Canadian writer (before you dismiss Service as a writer of doggerel you would do well to remember the poetry of Kipling). As we spoke Ian became more and more excited himself. My God, I thought, a real librarian, who actually cares about books and understands their importance! I hadn't yet met Ian. The next year when I did it was at the Landon's dinner table and I could see instantly that he was indeed that wonderful rarity, a real librarian who was a real bookman. To compound my pleasure at meeting him, he had known one of my youthful intellectual heroes, Colin Wilson, when they were both young and Wilson was writing *The Outsider* in the reading room of the British Museum.

We left it that he would have Richard call me as soon as he arrived. The next morning, the day of the sale, Richard did call. I explained the situation to him and said we couldn't count on others making the same mistake that Waddington's staff had. "What do you think it will go for?" Richard asked.

"I think it should go $10,000.00-$12,000.00," I said.

"Okay," he said. "I'll go that high."

A pause. I knew I had to say more.

"Listen, Richard, if it goes for $12,000.00 or less it's yours. But I have to tell you if it goes higher I'm going to go on for myself. I want that book."

Another pause. "What do you think it's worth, Dave?"

"I think it's a $30,000.00 to $35,000.00 book," I replied. "And I think I can sell it for that pretty easily. And I'm going to buy it if you don't."

A longer pause.

"Okay Dave. I don't have any money [by which he meant that his budget was exhausted]. Just buy the book. I'll get the money somehow."

I had an unlimited bid, every dealer's dream. This is what can happen when a system of trust exists between two knowledgeable people, a trust which had developed over many years.

An unlimited bid—almost unheard of. An unlimited bid contains unlimited power in its essence, a wonderful feeling. Of course, I didn't really have an unlimited bid, as both Landon and I understood—without it needing to be said. He was trusting to my professional expertise. If some unknown fool had crazy ambitions I was expected to realize that and desist if necessary. Still, up to $25,000.00 or so I was free to act. We had both understood this without any need to state it.

When I entered the saleroom that night it was full. I surveyed the crowd, noting several western dealers whom I knew would covet it too, and of course the entire eastern trade was there including the one I saw as my real competition: Temple. I felt an almost benign affection for the lot of them. Poor guys, I thought magnanimously. Their dreams of glory so soon to be shattered. It was sad.

I looked, as I always do, for a spot where I could observe my presumed probable competitors without being seen myself. I sat two rows back and on the other side from Temple. The two most dangerous western dealers who were also plainly in view— including their hands, which you need to monitor closely, since they are used not only to bid but give off the most telling indications of intention.

The Service came up very early. Ron McLean, a very astute man and the best auctioneer I've ever encountered (his son Duncan is not far behind him), announced the lot number, adding in a manner he often adopted—where he pretended to be dumb—that someone had told him that the next item might be unique.

"What do I know?" he asked with a shrug. "It's estimated at $100.00—$200.00," he said slyly, "so in case that unique stuff is true, I guess I'll start at $200.00. Do I have $200.00?" He knew very well what he knew and I'm sure he expected exactly what happened to happen.

The room erupted, arms in the air everywhere, McLean pulling in bids as fast as he could call them, the place chaos. I didn't bid; I watched. Sure enough, the west was bidding frantically. Then Temple raised his hand and kept it up imperiously, the gesture presumably intended to tell all of us that it was futile to thwart him, but telling me that he had indeed obtained money, a loan or a partner or both. The bidding died down in the $3,000.00 to $4,000.00 range—as always, an indicator of lack of imagination. I entered at around $4,000.00. There was only Temple, his arm still pompously in the air, and a couple of others. By $5,000.00 it was just me and Temple. He couldn't see who he was bidding against, but at $7,000.00 he started to get nervous—this wasn't going the way he'd planned. At $8,000.00 he started lowering his arm, then it went up again, then down, then up again—but each time more hesitantly on the up part. McLean watched us both intently, back and forth, a small smile on his face, continuing now in $500.00 increments.

Down came Temple's arm, a look of intense frustration on his face; a pause, up again, one more try, the hope born of desperation. I bid instantly every time, hammering it home. Finally at $10,000.00 Temple was at his limit and showed it. After a few seconds he made his last desperate move, one more bid, hoping his opponent's level was also $10,000.00. I raised my pencil one last time and Temple slumped in his seat, defeated. It was mine at $11,000.00!

There was silence for a moment and then the entire room erupted in loud applause. I had always believed such applause at an auction to be vulgar and ludicrous. Imagine cheering just because some fool spends a lot of money?

But, curiously, this time I did finally see the sense in that just acknowledgement of the victor's superiority. In this case it clearly wasn't the money spent they were applauding; it was my cleverness and courage they were celebrating. I positively basked in it. Then Ron McLean joined the game. A born actor, as are all great auctioneers and great salesmen of all sorts, he knew how to play a crowd. He knew how to turn any result to his advantage, to create a feeling that anyone could do it.

"That's David Mason who bought that," he announced. "I can remember when he would come in here as a kid to buy a wall full of books for $10.00 or $20.00. Who would have thought then that he'd be spending $11,000.00 for a single book today?"

Ron was still playing the room. He was telling them all that they too could be applauded. You too can be world famous here tonight, all you have to do is stick your arm up and keep it up and we will cheer for you too.

And so, the University of Toronto got a unique copy of the most famous book of poetry ever published in Canada. But I got the glory—and this story.

CHAPTER 15

Learning My Trade 3:
The Art of Appraising

The appraisal of personal archives is an art, not a science.

It is my intention that the following anecdotal accounts demonstrate not only my increasing expertise as an antiquarian bookseller, but also my increasing sophistication in the understanding of the importance of history and tradition. I also hope to demonstrate the incredible importance of personal papers as sources in the study of human history.

Of all my activities as a bookseller, archival appraisals have taught me more about the importance of tradition and continuity than anything else. That's why I now refer to myself as essentially conservative.

The appraisal of books is very different from the appraisals of papers. We are required to appraise books at what the government refers to as "fair market value"—the price that demands a willing buyer and a willing seller, both of them prudent, knowledgeable and in possession of all relevant facts. I will leave books for the moment and dwell on papers, for it was through the appraising of papers that I learned much of what I know about archives and formed the habit of looking at everything, books or paper, from the perspective of what they contribute to our understanding of humanity's historical record.

Appraisals began when our government—in a rare display of common sense—decided that people who owned significant treasures ought to be encouraged to donate such things to the country. This encouragement mainly occurred through the issuing of tax receipts so that donors could be financially compensated when they considered our common heritage and left their valuable artifacts to the nation. No doubt this started with fine art and historical objects, but by the late 1960s, with the flood of money the government began to bestow on universities to provide them with the capacity to deal with the oncoming baby-boom generation, it had spread to education, literature and politics.

This government largesse initiated much spending, a lot of it pretty stupid. One university, which I won't name, purchased the entire stock of two different bookstores. One was a Canadian store, and the proprietor had been dead for several years, which meant over the years scouts had plucked the best of his stock. The other was a large American shop whose shelves, emptied after that sale, were filled again the next day from the company's warehouse. The university was concerned with quantity, not quality. The duplicates of nineteenth-century American fiction alone, filtering back into the Canadian trade for years, were priced at $1.00 a book, and still no one wanted them except me. I built up a large stock of nineteenth-century American fiction that still sells regularly, and not at $1.00 a book either. This was a continuation of my early poverty-induced system of concentrating on what others ignored. It's still paying off. A further point arises here: it was this huge accumulation of unwanted American fiction from which I learned how to properly collate a book. In those days they were just rounding out the publication of Blanck's *Bibliography of American Literature* (Yale University Press, 1965–69). I used this bibliography to teach myself the collation of books, and it was a very painful process. A leaf where it shouldn't be, or not where it was called for, tortured me for months until, as always with my learning process, one day everything seemed to fall into place and become clear. Another point also became clear: the literature of any country is what endures because of its intrinsic value as literature. That many writers in BAL are unknown to the general public does not lessen their contribution. I tell my writer friends, "If you're good, you'll be found someday in BCL (the not-yet-completed *Bibliography of Canadian Literature*) even if ninety-nine percent of the world has forgotten you." Though I must admit I've yet to meet a writer who thought this just compensation. At least, I've never seen one smile happily when I say it.

Buying entire bookstores is foolish. Any knowledgeable bookseller could point out that eighty to ninety percent of the stock of an old, long-established bookstore will be dead stock—fillers—and of little value. Still, some years later a president of that university told me how proud he was of the librarian who had so astutely thrown away probably many tens of thousands of dollars on what was essentially junk. These universities had needed instant libraries, which is what had led to such excess. This also illustrates a common delusion held by some librarians, that they could simply go out there with no training and do what a bookseller spends a lifetime doing: buying wisely. Any competent bookseller could have earned himself a decent yearly wage supplying good books to these libraries and still saved those institutions money. People who think that professional training counts for nothing set themselves up for the sort of opportunists who are everywhere in society, waiting and watching for such fools.

Curiously, among private collectors the occupation most susceptible to this delusion is made up of medical people. Doctors, for some reason, seem to think that just because they have mastered the art of healing humanity they can master the intricacies of finance and business in all its forms and compete with people who do it for a living. There's no mark like the mark inside. Still, doctors, the best ones that is, whose view of life has been initiated and then fuelled by not just their experience but their study of man, are easily the most congenial of collectors. For a man who tempers his experience of misery and death with philosophy and learning becomes even more civilized. The best example of this axiom I've seen is Sir William Osler.

The catalogue of Sir William Osler's great collection on the history of medicine not only unmistakably conveys Osler's greatness, but also his humanity. And it is wonderful reading too. Meant to be his annotated record of his collection, it can, in fact, be read as a commentary on man's struggle against the darkness of ignorance and prejudice. I often pick it up at times when I suffer from doubt or despair and find that it rejuvenates my sense of purpose and my pride in the accomplishments of humanity.

These university spending sprees also included purchases of writers' papers, but then the money ran out. Universities continued to want writers' archives, but they no longer had the money to buy them. Writers, already painfully aware of their probably lifelong struggle to survive—at least until they wrote the great Canadian novel—found that they couldn't sell their papers, so they had to be content with accepting tax receipts in the forlorn hope that they might earn enough in that year to at least not pay taxes on their pitiful earnings. In case anyone might think I am merely trying to be funny, let me say that I have seen the financial records of many, many writers in my years of appraisal work, and the financial return for all that talent and effort is often appalling. To see the six-month royalty statement of a serious writer for a book after its initial surge has run its course, where the cheque wouldn't buy a meal in a decent restaurant, is not uncommon. I, at least, find this depressing. And if it's depressing for an appraiser, imagine how the writer must feel. Years of suffering over a work of art and still needing real jobs like teaching or journalism to feed their families. The more I've seen, the more I have come to respect the French, who understand that a nation's culture is as important as any other aspect of the nation's well-being and support their artists accordingly.

We do have the Canada Council for the Arts, which tries to help, but a recent article by Canadian poet and polemicist David Solway lists—in dollar amounts—the writers who seem to have benefited most by the largesse of this system, and it clearly shows that, as usual, the benefits accrue to those who are most adept at exploiting the system and not necessarily to those who are the most deserving writers.

Solway's piece in *Books in Canada* (itself now defunct—along with several other Canadian magazines and reviews—again, because of the withdrawal of government support) lists actual numbers of grants and the actual dollar amounts of these grants, citing recipient writers whom the average Canadian would never have heard of. Writers, I should add, that many other writers must have been appalled to learn had received so much public funding.

Canadians, it seems, like other unimaginative drones, don't assign any importance to what they can't see. Give us some more highways or honeycomb apartment blocks. Give us the security to have comfortable existences, but who cares about the soul of a country. Not most of us; not, at least, until events necessitate vision and courage. And then all too often we learn we have failed to instil character in our nation.

That's why I have a policy of being as generous to imaginative writers as I can justify—justify to myself I mean, not the government—short of setting myself up for prison. I work on the assumption that our writers *are* our collective imagination, providing us with our dreams as a people; they are often not only our consciousness but our conscience. They deserve our respect, and more, they deserve to be compensated according to their contributions to our culture. Our writers provide all of us with our dreams, and with the fuel that provides a sense of purpose as both a nation and as individuals.

Writers should be lionized, and in some societies in the past they were. There have been times and places where writers enjoyed the acclaim that Hollywood celebrities and rock stars enjoy today. But the days when people lined up at bookshops to get the latest installment of a Dickens or a Scott novel seem to be gone, which means that our collective consciousness is now provided by the appallingly trite pap we are offered on television and in most movies.

By law I am supposed to appraise on the basis of a willing buyer and a willing seller. My interpretation of that law is that I may act as if any institution that accepts a writer's archive as a donation, with all the financial consequences that acceptance denotes—arranging and cataloguing are very time-consuming—deserves to have it appraised as though it would have paid real money for the archive had the government had enough vision to provide proper funding.

So, I decide what the writer should receive and my reports reflect this amount.

I have had people tell me that my figures are absurd.

"No one would ever pay that for that hack's detritus," I am told.

My response is, "Well, that is what a civilized people would pay for an archive of that importance." If you or the government do not agree, that's your problem, not mine. I'm not responsible for either your own or the government's cultural deficiencies. My job is to assess real cultural value. In this sense Canadian authors actually have an edge over their American colleagues. American law does not allow writers to donate their papers for a tax receipt, so they are forced to sell them. At least Canada has had some small amount of foresight, because the writers who are considered to be in the second or third level by today's standards, which are quite different than posterity's, can at least have their papers safely protected in an institution while we await time's eventual verdict.

With the paucity of government funding in most places, writers and therefore most national cultures suffer. We also owe a greater cultural debt to the small number of truly imaginative librarians and archivists than most people would imagine. The archive of a writer of even Norman Mailer's stature was on the market for a long time—maybe ten or fifteen years—before some persistent custodian could convince his bosses at some university that paying two and a half million was not only feasible but probably, eventually, also a bargain.

Any bookseller who has been around for as long as I have could make a list of a hundred or more authors who were ignored in their own time and whose books now command startling prices in the marketplace. I paid £100 for the first copy of Joyce's *Ulysses* I ever bought, around forty years ago. I ordered it from a catalogue and even then I was astounded to get it. Today the latest prices asked for it on AbeBooks are between $75,000.00 and $150,000.00.

Time changes society's views.

No bookseller or librarian can forget the infamous librarian at Princeton who turned down the papers of F. Scott Fitzgerald, stating: "We are not a charity. We are not going to buy the papers of some second-rate Midwest hack, just because he happened to have been lucky enough to have attended Princeton—unfortunately for Princeton."

The Fitzgerald papers eventually did sell to Princeton for $2,500.00. The most recent fine copy in dust jacket of *The Great Gatsby* I saw was being offered for $125,000.00. What would the manuscript of that book, included in that piratical purchase, bring at auction today? Several million dollars?

David Mason

The U.S. government shows little imagination by refusing to allow American writers to donate their archives for tax relief. In these times this means that libraries will not have the funds to purchase the papers of writers who are considered lower in rank, thereby depriving the country of parts of its literary heritage.

Sometimes the content of a writer's archive will arouse emotion, stunning one into a reverent silence. Am I to consider what some unimaginative bureaucrat might think is a fitting amount of compensation? Not likely. I trust my instincts, honed now by many years' experience and reflection. I give them an amount that any civilized nation should be prepared to pay. If someone in the government disagrees with my assessment, I simply assume that it reflects their lack of civilization—not mine.

While much experience is needed, the appraising of archives can be learned. Most Canadian dealers of my age had to learn it themselves; the lucky ones are those who had an older dealer to guide them. For what is, in essence, intellectual property, there had to be some mechanisms developed in order to assign value to the donated archives of writers. It was logical for book dealers to be called in, since we already dealt in letters and manuscript material in smaller amounts and, more pertinently, we already had much experience in the mechanics of measuring relative value based on importance. These skills had only to be extended to cover an entire creative output.

A writer's archive will reflect the writer's research, creative focus, intent and, not least, the writer's character. We, both dealers and the institutional custodians we work with, have to teach ourselves the techniques. Now we dealers teach one another, often while we work. While study of the writer, the importance of the writer's work and its perceived position in the literary hierarchy are all measured, other factors must also be considered. Some can be found in the archive itself while others are based on the appraiser's knowledge of the author's private life, often drawn from gossip—sometimes unkind and malicious gossip.

My own personal system with an archive always begins with the individual's correspondence. By starting with these I am introduced to the full range of the person's activities, both public and, to me more important, private. But, most crucial, it is in the correspondence where one meets the personality, which, to my mind, is the key to assessing everything. That doesn't mean I'm trying to find out if the author in question is a nice person. If we had to exclude the work of all the miserable sons-of-bitches, the despicable creeps, mean-spirited fanatics, or the near-insane we would have to relinquish a good part of our literature. What are the admirers of such people as Ezra Pound, Louis-Ferdinand Céline, or my own beloved Knut Hamsun to do with the records of these geniuses' flirtations with the Nazis? Or that huge number of writers who either joined the Communist Party or at least admired Stalin? The usual moral lines don't always work with art. For that matter, they don't always work with life either.

This brings me to a serious point that I should make. Very early on I realized that, having access to what constitutes a person's personal life, I had to follow the same professional obligations that a doctor or lawyer must, especially in the matter of discretion. Since I am widely known as an inveterate gossip, some—including one widely known national columnist, himself a renowned gossip—have questioned my integrity. This man wrote a column about me once where he quoted my standard line, which is that I forget everything I've seen by the next day. He derided this explanation, not because I'd ever revealed anything to him that I shouldn't have but maybe because of his chagrin that I hadn't.

It was not until I'd been doing appraisals for many years that I started to notice a certain pattern. I found that certain things that I had come across in archives stuck in my mind, and would often surface many years after I had conducted the appraisal. The significance of this discovery was that there was no discernible reason why I should remember those details from what were often immense and very rich archives. Obviously, they must be things that had touched me on some deep level, and they came back in moments relevant to what they had touched on. When I noticed this phenomenon I began making notes on things I discovered in papers, and I often repeat them if they do not have to do with personal and private matters.

When I relate such things I sometimes alter details and always relate them without attribution if the subject is still alive. Some donors, of course, restrict parts of their archives until after a death or for longer—those archives I never discuss in any manner. Most of these archives are open to any scholar anyway, so I do not trespass by making notes.

Whether literary, political, scientific or simply reflective of social history, an archive is raw history—history not yet sifted by scholars with the pattern of a thesis or history resulting. Some archives contain material that moves one deeply, and some are boring. Politicians are easily the most boring—all those photos of rubber-chicken lunches with Korean trade delegations need to be endured, not assessed.

The single most boring archive I ever appraised was the papers of a Premier of Ontario; the single most disappointing was the archive of Keith Davey, widely known as the consummate back-room fixer. As I approached that one, I thought that I would finally be privy to the real back-room deals that fuel the politics of the country. I was wrong, of course. The whole essence of what really goes on behind the scenes never gets written down. Politicians must have learned that from the bureaucratic masters who really run every country. The essentials of protecting your back: never write something down. Never even say it.

I once recorded a conversation I had with a bureaucrat with whom I was having a dispute, after he promised something verbally and then shamelessly broke his word. In a conversation that went on for an hour and a half, he adroitly managed to avoid making a single concrete statement. He was masterful in his obfuscation. That wonderful quote from John Gregory Dunne, "Hello, he lied," came from this type of person. Every once in a while, when I despair a bit about never having made much money, I replay parts of this conversation. It shows me that at least I didn't sell my soul for a pension.

One political archive I did want to appraise was Pierre Trudeau's. I was asked to do it but I wouldn't agree to the ludicrous system the authorities demanded for such appraisals. This needs a bit of background. When the original laws relating to gifts-in-kind were formulated, the government—in its normal bureaucratic stupidity—set up a system of forming an official board called the National Archival Appraisal Board (NAAB). This board consisted of an historian, an archivist and a bookseller who would travel together to institutions where they would value donations by consensus. Perhaps this appears sensible; it did to the government, and these boards have been operating for many years now. Indeed, the gossip I hear lately states that the same sinister back-room strategists are attempting to make the use of such boards mandatory throughout all the institutions in the country. Of course every bookseller and good librarian knows just how stupid this idea is, even those many colleagues of mine who serve on these ludicrously compromised boards.

Richard Landon of the University of Toronto wouldn't allow them in his library. The only time I know of them being in the Thomas Fisher Rare Book Library was when the government ordered it after questioning an appraisal done by Robert

Wright and me, which they didn't believe was worth the near half-million figure we came up with. Wright and I had spent three days assessing this archive; NAAB spent two hours deciding it was worth around $75,000.00. In the ensuing fuss I got quite angry. I wrote to the head of the Cultural Property Board demanding to know how they dared question my competence when they had no one on their board competent enough to judge my work (they had no bookseller on their board, nor had they had for several years). They appointed a special person to submit a report. In case you think you're hearing sour grapes, they hired a man who had been the rare books librarian of the National Library of Canada and, previous to that, an antiquarian bookseller. This man's report completely vindicated our opinion, and our original appraisal was reinstated. If you're thinking this demonstrates something about government in general, you're right. And the lesson, in case you missed it, is this: the bureaucrat rules. In government, stupidity will always trump expertise. Experts: $500,000.00; bureaucrats: $75,000.00—think about that.

That's what they wanted me to work with on the Trudeau papers and, of course, I refused. Jerry Sherlock worked on one of these boards in the very early days and he told me he wasted untold hours trying to explain to the historian and the archivist he was working with that the papers under consideration were worth ten times what they thought adequate. Jerry knew the marketplace. These people, completely lacking in any such experience, had no means to even guess what things might sell for—how could they? They'd never bought or sold anything. But it didn't stop them from guessing. Faced in their own fields with such ignorance from an outsider they would have no doubt been enraged. But, to quote Schiller, "Against fools, even the Gods are helpless."

The government's logic, put to me in the Trudeau case, was that the archivist and the historian would be able to point out to me the archival and historical importance of the material. This could be logical only to a bureaucrat, and my response was appropriate to such a ludicrous view. All my training as a bookseller, over forty years, consists in being able to recognize the historical significance of everything I look at. Since booksellers buy their material and pay hard cash for it, if that sense wasn't well honed, we wouldn't survive. I pointed this out to the bureaucrat pretty bluntly. If I need the help of anybody to ascertain the historical value of what I'm assessing, I shouldn't be hired in the first place. They hire me precisely for that reason: my ability to make an assessment of value.

I read much history and have great respect for those professional historians who, with their extensive training and experience, dredge through the morass of an archive and assemble a coherent thesis. I work closely with several archivists and I have come to have enormous respect for their ability to take a huge mass of paper, often simply thrown with incredible disarray into boxes, and arrange it into a comprehensive, workable archive so that historians can locate the essence of their books. Even after forty years of working with these people and discussing their work with them, I still don't understand the skills that allow them to make order out of such chaos.

Like all highly developed skills, theirs remain incomprehensible to outsiders. But these people, both historians and archivists, know nothing, nor should they be expected to, about the marketplace in which I operate. How could they?

Anyway, I missed Trudeau, although I have seen enough evidence of his intellect in the papers of others. He corresponded with several of Canada's prominent public intellectuals whose archives I've appraised, which in itself is an indication of his importance. But I'm still a bit chagrined. If any Canadian statesman since Macdonald had the guts to say what he believed, it was Trudeau. Maybe he actually wrote some of it down, too.

This may be the place to point out that this is precisely why original archival material is so important to our history and why the government wisely (for a change) allows compensation for the donors—for their contributions to the historical record.

Of all the appraisals I have done the first two are, if not the most important, still the most significant to me, and remain the ones that are most clearly embedded in my memory. I guess they are there in the same manner, and for the same reasons, that our earliest experiences of love are also the most ineradicable. I can't remember which of these two came first, but it hardly matters. They were both done for the University of Toronto. The librarians I worked with then weren't any more sophisticated than us dealers. I think we all educated ourselves as we went, learning through experience.

The truth is that we both—librarians and booksellers together—had to educate ourselves not just in evaluating content, but also in terms of technique. We learned on the job, and in retrospect I think that we did a pretty good job of it. I can't remember a single instance when we shortchanged a donor, although I do remember several occasions when I thought I was using the usual profession caution when I didn't really have enough experience to make proper comparisons.

My first two appraisals were of the papers of Mark Gayn, the long-time foreign correspondent for the *Toronto Star,* and James Mavor, Professor of Economics at the University of Toronto, a member of the Scottish-Celtic revival at the turn of the twentieth century, a friend of Tolstoy and, not least, the father of Dora Mavor Moore and grandfather of Mavor Moore, a family which has contributed so much to Canadian theatre. It was James Mavor, through his personal friendship with Tolstoy, who was instrumental in arranging to bring the Doukhobors to Canada as immigrants because of their religious persecution under the Czar.

I'll start with the Gayn appraisal because that experience illustrates the sort of chaotic state that typifies the beginnings for me.

I entered the reading room of the Fisher Library one day to find all of the tables covered by some hundred and sixty or so cartons. This was the way Gayn's widow had sent his archives: large cartons, each labelled with the subject of the carton noted on top. Such an appraisal today, when all of us, both archivists and dealers, are so much more sophisticated, might need a year or two of work on the part of the archivists and perhaps a week's worth of work on the part of the dealers. But those were different times.

I looked at this enormous mass together with Richard Landon. "We need a figure and it needs to be a fair figure. But the truth is, Dave, what Gayn's wife really wants is for this archive to be accessible to future scholars. I don't think she gives a damn about the money." Today we call such appraisals "ballpark appraisals," and there are still occasions when an educated guess, needed quickly, is acceptable for various reasons. Had I known then what I do now I might have insisted that they properly catalogue everything so that I could spend a week or so immersed in this incredible treasure trove. But we didn't have the time, nor had I delved deep enough to realize what I would be missing. But somehow I already seemed to have had the proper instincts. I quickly realized that in spite of the incredible breadth of Gayn's activities, what would indicate its true importance would be its depth, its richness.

It was obvious that if I skimmed the material I would miss much of its importance, but a proper appraisal of that much material in

David Mason

its unsorted state would take months. So I invented my own system out of necessity. I looked at every box, noting subject contents, and made notes on the whole mass. Gayn had travelled everywhere for the *Toronto Star* and, earlier, several American newspapers. He had both experienced and written about most of the major international events of his time, as my examination of the box labels showed. Googling him recently, I find him described by the FBI as a Russian spy. One assumes, given his antecedents and the time, that he may well have been. Now that the political history of the twentieth century is being placed in its proper historical context, we know that many people, not all traitors or curs, could be justly accused of the same. In the thirties, when almost the entire intelligentsia was appalled by the rise of fascism and the Nazis, those same people had an almost mystical regard for the promises of socialism, which caused many of them to join the Party or at least sympathize with what they considered the "Great Experiment" in Russia. Maybe Gayn, of Russian descent, was simply one of the many who offered their allegiances to the ideals of equality and brotherhood by serving Russia and therefore Stalin, resulting in a tyranny of equal depth, if not exact form, to that of Hitler and his thugs. A lot of people seemed to have relinquished their reason to those ideologies, and maybe Gayn was another of them. Or maybe, more logically, he still had relatives in Russia and chose to give in to the threats we now know the Soviets regularly used.

Anyway, we worked out a system which we sometimes still use today to reach a "ballpark figure." That is, we estimate by examining superficially and extrapolating. What I did with the Gayn archive was examine all the boxes that were labelled by subject area, and then chose two distinct subjects to look at in depth.

The boxes were standard packing boxes of some size, mostly two to three feet deep, so there was a lot to look at. I felt that would give me a proper sense of the richness of the archive and

278

that I would then be able to extrapolate from what I learned in those two areas onto the entire mass. And it worked, too. To be frank, I remain, all these years later, astounded at the prescience I had then to arrive at what seems to me to be a brilliant system. Indeed, it makes me marvel once again how such an obviously brilliant innovator has never made a living above the official poverty level. I guess it's all those books I've bought.

The Gayn archive was stupendous. I believe I undervalued it, although I don't remember what I appraised it at. I remember a high appraisal, around $200,000.00—but today, with forty years experience behind me, I would value it much higher.

Gayn was born in China. His parents were Russian Jews who had escaped, probably after one pogrom too many, and eventually made their way to the promised land, America, where, with a new anglicized name their son became a journalist. He was the foreign correspondent for the *Toronto Star* for many years, writing about world events for as long as I could remember.

Gayn was one of *my* people, a hoarder. He never threw away anything; it was all there. Since I assessed only the two chosen areas, I still wonder periodically what historical treasures I missed. For many years I have toyed with the idea that when I retire one of my personal projects will be to spend some time, maybe a lot of time, exploring the intricacies of twentieth-century history through a study of the Gayn archive. But, of course, booksellers don't retire; my current resolution is to force myself to make time. I still hope to do so.

I thought it would be an interesting tactic to choose boxes based on my ignorance. Meaning that if I chose areas where my reading hadn't taken me I might be better able to assess research value based on what I learned. Of course the opposite argument could be just as valid. Had I chosen areas I did know reasonably well from my reading, I might be in a better position to assess what was lacking or erroneous. But I think I did take the best course, because I still have vivid memories of what I learned.

I chose two areas of which I barely had any even superficial knowledge. They were the Japanese post-war war crimes tribunals, and the Greek near-civil war/revolution of the late forties, when the Communists tried to take over. Like many another I had read considerably about the Nuremberg Trials, but I knew nothing about the Allied treatment of Japanese war criminals. What a history lesson.

It turns out Gayn was an obsessive. It seems he wrote his wife a letter every day of his life, often three or four pages long on 8 ½" x 14" paper, single-spaced, and kept an onion-skin copy of each one. I still remember vividly how the first one I read began. Gayn is flying to Japan and tells his wife that he is sitting strapped into his seat on an old DC-3 because of the turbulence, with his typewriter strapped on his knees with his belt. He tells her that everyone but him is deathly airsick, the stench of their incessant vomiting only bearable because his intent to tell her everything allows him to ignore it.

He goes on, recounting all sorts of salacious gossip, mostly sexual, about the American generals and diplomats involved in the Pacific War and its aftermath. He passes on all the nicknames that the U.S. servicemen had affectionately bestowed on their commanders, from Eisenhower and MacArthur on down, almost all of them relating to their personal traits and most of them entertaining outrageous sexual insults. It reminded me of my readings in ancient history, when Roman generals (Caesar especially) would exhort their troops before battle by insulting them with sexual taunts designed, usually successfully, to instill the emotional connections which made men then, and it seems now, love their commanders enough to be willing to die for them.

Reading history gives perspective. I write from a distance of forty years, yet I still retain the impressions from those letters.

Here are some of them: Japan was devastated, flattened before its surrender, not just Hiroshima and Nagasaki but every city of any strategic significance. Cities built of wood and paper were devastated by incendiary bombing, leaving almost nothing. The poverty and want were horrendous. Gayn relates going to an open market where old Japanese women would be sitting cross-legged with the wares they hoped to sell on a handkerchief in front of them, things like a bent nail, a cracked glass blackened by some incendiary bomb, an empty tin can, bent and filthy. These people were starving and desperate; as always, the ordinary people paid for the sins of their so-called betters, their leaders. And we get all the dirty gossip of the war crimes trials, different from Nuremberg only in detail, not essence.

As I said, Gayn had the true historian's eye for detail, and the bonus was that I found, every time, three versions of his dispatches to the *Toronto Star*. First one would encounter his observations in the copy he sent his wife, full of incredible detail, and his own horrified opinions. Then would come his actual dispatch to the *Star*, usually only half the size of his wife's version. Then would come the third version, which the *Star* published, usually around half of that. Therefore one initially gets a fully salacious version and, lastly, the version a major newspaper saw fit to print.

Incredibly, Gayn had also been on the beginnings of Mao's long march. There was a movie, grainy and jerky, that showed the beginning of the march and the caves bored into hills from which it all originated. This was the first time I was ever paid, and well, to watch a movie. Not easy—to be forced to endure a fascinating historical experience, just because it's one's job, and to be paid for experiences that one clearly remembers with enormous pleasure forty years later.

I opened one envelope that contained quite a few gruesome original photographs from the time of the Japanese attempt to conquer China. The photos show Japanese soldiers decapitating Chinese captives, complete with severed heads strewn everywhere, and including a photo of a just-severed head still suspended in the air. I remember thinking, "I bet the Japanese regret that some bystander snapped these disgusting and revealing records of such barbarity." Some fifteen years later I discovered how wrong that supposition was. It turns out that the Japanese themselves had taken and then distributed these photos, their intent being to terrorize the Chinese who, in 1935, they were intent on conquering. They wanted to terrorize the Chinese by demonstrating the consequences of resistance to Japanese superiority.

I bet it worked, too. It certainly did with me.

There were also examples of Japanese World War II propaganda, mostly sexual in nature, which the Japanese dropped from airplanes into the hands of the Australians fighting them in the jungles. There would be overlaid cards, folded so that one scene would show, and then when you pulled the ends, opening the card to double the length, a very different scene unfolded. The one I best remember showed, on one side, a smiling attractive woman and on the other a laughing soldier with the easily recognizable American helmet of the times. When the card was pulled out it revealed that the woman was on her hands and knees and the American soldier was entering her from behind. The text, also revealed by the unfolding, said, in typical Japanese-English, "Australians. This is what the American soldiers are doing to your women in Australia while you conduct your futile struggle with us, the Japanese liberators, here in the jungles of Burma. Go home. Rescue your women from these American barbarians." If these were not the exact words—my memory is not what it once was—they certainly capture the essence of the card's message. The pictures were very precise.

The Greek records were similar. The Machiavellian politics of that area in that time are masterfully conveyed today in the magnificent historical "spy thrillers" of Alan Furst, a man who, like Eric Ambler before him, has the talent to make you feel you are actually present at histories unfolding. Mark Gayn prepared me for those historical novels. Furst doesn't miss a nuance, as my recollection of Gayn's facts clearly proves.

The Mavor archive was different in content but not in emotional force. That appraisal was also huge, but it had already been properly sorted and catalogued when I was confronted with it.

Mavor, a participant in the literary Scottish-Celtic revival of the late nineteenth and early twentieth centuries, had been hired as a Professor of Economics by the University of Toronto, thereby conferring on Canada the cultural benefits continued by his more famous descendants. I seem to remember that I spent three or four days immersed in his incredible archive. One day, after Richard Landon and I had returned from one of our lunches, where I had had two or three glasses of wine, the first letter I picked up was from Prince Peter Kropotkin, the eminent anarchist, to his friend Mavor:

"My friend I have to inform you that yesterday died our old mutual friend, Tolstoy."

Wouldn't you cry too? Faced with such raw history? Especially after two or three drinks?

In a perhaps unseemly display of emotion I blatantly appraised that letter at $750.00 and then later, sober, worried for some time that someone might demand a justification for such an outrageous estimate. Today I would, without any hesitation, appraise it at $15,000.00 to $20,000.00, maybe more if I had time to think on it. That would also perhaps be my first personal temptation. Who would miss it, I thought, among such riches? But my 1960s experimentation with drugs paid off here. I already knew that the first one only seems innocent. It isn't.

The Mavor appraisal contained history in its most raw form: literary, social and political, with correspondence from every type of intellectual involved in the period of the Celtic revival and the political movements of the time. But one of its components so affected me that forty years later it still resonates. Since it also demonstrates the effect of primary archival material on history, I offer it as a good example of how important the evidence found in an archive can be.

I have read many accounts and memoirs of the horrible carnage of the First World War, but no book I have ever read conveys the real horror of that insanity so well as what Mavor's papers contained. There were several boxes of letters, all black-edged in the fashion of the time, all from the parents of students who had been killed in action. I guess Mavor had sent a letter of condolence to the parents of his students who had appeared on the casualty lists. These black-edged letters were their answers. The sheer number of them was overwhelming. One professor, in one university, in a smallish city in a far outpost of the Empire, yet it seemed like he had lost hundreds of his students. It was shocking in a manner that no mere recounting of numbers could be. And to compound these emotionally devastating numbers were the sentiments expressed by the parents in reply. Letter after letter said essentially the same thing. "Dear Professor. Thank you for your sympathy at the loss of our Billy. We only regret that we had only one son to sacrifice for the good of our great Empire."

Letter after letter expressed these sympathies.

I have never been able to forget these sheer numbers—two or three boxes of such letters—and these poor people who lost their only son at eighteen or nineteen and could regret only that they hadn't more kids to offer up for slaughter, for the good of "the Empire." I've never read another word on that war without feeling the impact of these simple handwritten notes from ordinary people. This is pure history in its essence.

In the end I appraised so much material, for every generation of the Mavor and Moore families, and I became so familiar with their history, that I would joke with Mavor Moore that he should adopt me into the family.

At an early stage Mavor took me up to Dora Mavor Moore's home to look at her books, which were going to the University of Toronto. She was quite elderly then, and all I remember was a tiny woman with huge luminous eyes, which actually glowed with warmth, curiosity and enthusiasm. Her apartment was jammed full of memorabilia, artifacts, plaques, signed photos of actors and actresses, Canadian and foreign testimony of her long and illustrious life and contributions to the Canadian theatre world. I liked her enormously. How couldn't I? She obviously shared my own character trait (thought by some, especially my partner, Debbie, to not be a trait but a defect, if not an incurable aberration) of hoarding sentimental curiosities. It was difficult to even navigate the apartment, there were so many mementos, but how could there not have been after such a long life full of accomplishments? Mavor also delighted in her—his adoration was obvious. He was also pretty good at navigating all the hazards of the apartment; he knew when to dodge and where to tuck in his elbows.

Mavor was then married to Phyllis Grosskurth (known as Pat to her friends), the justly acclaimed biographer of Symonds, Byron and psychologists such as Melanie Klein. Pat was a very beautiful woman, and she was one tough lady, too. Her maiden name had been Langstaff. I even appraised Pat's grandfather's papers. Her grandfather had been a doctor, and in his time he delivered most of the babies within a fifty-mile radius of what was then Langstaff (now swallowed by Richmond Hill, leaving only Langstaff Road as a memorial). I still remember many accounts of him hitching up the horses to his sleigh to travel untold miles in the middle of the night to deliver yet another baby. And I remember the many unpaid bills for those deliveries I found, still in his papers at his death. People may have promised anything to have a doctor travel miles on a sled to deliver a child, but they seemed to resent paying for it when the danger was past.

One day at the University of Toronto Richard Landon set in front of me a small pile of handwritten letters, all written on the cheap lined paper, now browned, of the sort that we all remember from our school exercise books. They were all in the childish hand of a young girl and were addressed to her mother; they were written from the Bahamas.

The young girl was Elizabeth Hughes, the daughter of President Warren Harding's Secretary of State, Charles Evans Hughes. She was a diabetic. Hughes had apparently heard of a Canadian doctor who had discovered a new medicine that might stave off the inevitable early death that then claimed all those born with diabetes. The doctor's name was Frederick Banting. I'm sure Hughes used all his pull and connections to get Banting to treat his daughter; but then again, what father wouldn't?

These letters, all written to the girl's mother, contained no background or indication of their importance to medical science.

At first the letters were ordinary, mundane even, pretty much like any letter that parents get from an eleven-year-old kid away at summer camp. The girl was so young that her hand was still completely neat and legible, having not yet evolved into the distinctive style that comes when the personality develops. There were long sentences about events lacking any interesting detail— simple accounts of mundane activity. The earliest ones read like that, except when she mentions how nice the doctors were to her, especially Dr. Banting.

Then you start to notice curious distinctions. She informs her mother that she managed to eat almost half a bowl of porridge that morning, as though it were some sort of triumph. Then she tells her mother that she is very excited—she thinks she has gained half a pound in the last week.

I decided I needed better background; I asked for a copy of Michael Bliss's book on Banting. I checked her name and her father's in the index and then turned to the section of pictures. The letters so far reflected any ordinary eleven-year-old girl. When I looked at Bliss's account and the pictures I was stunned. The pictures and description of her physical state are horrendous. She is skin and bones, she weighs a fraction of what a girl her age should, she has almost no hair, her dress hangs like a sack. It is hard not to conclude that it is a stick puppet we are seeing.

It is hard to imagine that she can be alive; in fact, she should be dead—she was in the later stages of diabetes when her father found Banting. But things became better.

In succeeding letters she informs her mother that she was right—she is gaining weight. Only an occasional reference to her physical appearance is mentioned. Of course she is, like all young girls on the cusp of puberty, obsessed with her appearance. She is not going to tell anyone, even her mother, that she looks like a hairless scarecrow. I'm sure that's the source of her delight as she recounts how she managed to eat two more spoons of porridge today than she did yesterday.

I had to stop; I was tearing up so much I couldn't read. I regained my poise and continued.

"Mother, you won't believe it—I've gained two pounds."

These letters were the personal account of one of the first children saved by Banting and Best's discovery of insulin. I was looking at a first-person account, maybe the first one, of a very important medical discovery, which has since saved countless lives.

I read all the letters, twenty or so, on their fragile, browned paper and decided that they should be worth $50,000.00. Now fifteen or twenty years later I wish I'd had the courage to appraise them at $100,000.00.

How the University of Toronto library came to have the letters should be mentioned, for it illustrates how scholars discover and use archives such as these. When Bliss was working on his Banting book, knowing that Elizabeth Hughes had survived and married, he tracked down her son and wrote him to inquire how long his mother had lived after insulin saved her life. Imagine his suprise when Elizabeth Hughes answered the letter herself. She was still alive! Bliss travelled to visit her in order to incorporate her story into his history of this discovery. When Elizabeth Hughes died a few years later, after a long life, her children sent, and later gifted, the letters to the University of Toronto.

Booksellers, scholars and archivists love stories like this, which indicate what we all believe is our primary function: to save the records of the past so history can be properly written.

Some time after, I was with Richard Landon exploring some things in the deepest basement level of the Fisher Library. (I usually refer to those basements, where I often work, as "The Dungeons," intending to convey to the librarians that I am labouring in sub-human conditions, a pitiable situation for which I am obviously not being properly compensated.) Suddenly Richard said, "You might like to see this," handing me a small, fuzzy, hinged case. I opened it. Within was a large, gold-embossed medal attached to a blue ribbon. I lifted it out.

"That," said Richard, "is Banting's Nobel Prize medal. Banting's family donated it here with his papers." I turned my head so that Richard wouldn't see how this affected me.

This is an award that means something; this is real, uncontaminated by the current plethora of awards for everything. The Nobel Prizes for literature and peace, awarded more for political reasons than merit, are now as contaminated by excessive and inappropriate recipients as are most other prizes. But the scientific ones are still awarded for true and important contributions to the sum of human achievement. When confronted with one it is impossible to remain cynical; certainly this is the case when I recall those photos of that little girl on the edge of extinction. Such experiences invoke in me what must be the same emotion that religious icons and symbols invoke in believers.

The most beautiful archive I have appraised was probably that of Robertson Davies. With his, one first found neat notes, then a handwritten manuscript, then a typed version with Davies' neat corrections in red ink, then another typescript with less correcting, still in red ink, then the finished version. A researcher can follow Davies' entire creative process, and very clearly, too, since Davies wrote in a lovely, almost Gothic hand.

I remember coming across one small notebook page that in a sentence or two gave the outline of *Fifth Business*. There, on a tiny piece of paper, one sees the seed of Davies' most important work.

Surely the most fascinating literary archive would have to be Leonard Cohen's. Cohen is either a compulsive hoarder or has always been very conscious of his eventual place in our letters, because he seems to have kept everything.

I like to play a game during appraisals, where I select a piece that I would take away with me at the end, if I could, as a "door prize." I do the same at art exhibitions, choosing what in a just world would be my reward for my impeccable taste. With Cohen, I enlisted the other appraiser to play my game as well. Value should have demanded we chose the three or four restaurant napkins containing versions of the words for his famous song "Suzanne," written in magic marker and probably composed in a bar, showing the creation of that haunting ballad in its formative stages.

But curiously both of us chose the same item as our senti-mental favourite. In Ira Nadel's biography we read of Cohen as a young teenager sending away for a booklet on how to hypnotize people, as advertised in the back of a magazine. Nadel recounts how Cohen studied that pamphlet and then successfully hyp-notized the maid in his family home, inducing his subject to undress for him. As he marvelled at his astounding success and the displayed reward for his feat, he heard the door slam as his mother returned. He had to frantically try and bring the maid out of the hypnotic state so that he could evade his mother's ret-ribution if she found them.

When I read that account in the biography I thought that it surely must be fanciful. But then I opened a file and found a pamphlet with lurid covers, a common sales device in those times. It was titled *25 Lessons in Hypnotism: How to Become an Expert Operator*. Signed in ink on the upper corner: "Leonard Cohen." It was instantly my choice as the sentimental plum of that archive. I'm still not sure I believe he actually got her to undress. Whatever the truth of the matter, I guess Cohen donated the pamphlet because he no longer needs a book to hypnotize women into undressing for him.

Appraising archives has taught me far more about life and its complexities than it ever taught me about the value of objects. I now always approach archives with an open mind and a certain reverence. I know that however slight an archive might be, I am going to see life in its most raw, basic form. For that is what an archive is: history in the raw, history's essence.

CHAPTER 16

Private Collectors

G eorge Orwell once said, "People go into most stores to buy something. They go into used bookstores to make nuisances of themselves."

I said somewhere else once that my customers had provided me with most of my education and with many of my closest friends, and I was not exaggerating. In the somewhat schizophrenic world of bookselling I often have conversations on a dozen different topics or disciplines in any given day, covering the entire range of human thought and activity. It is also very common to have a conversation with a man so immersed in the arcane details of his subject that he has lost all sense of balance, so you are subjected to harangues where you haven't any basic knowledge about the subject and therefore hardly any basis to comprehend what's being said.

Conversations with such people are never conversations, they are lectures and often one understands nothing of what the man says, so obscure is the subject and so overwhelming his depth of knowledge. Nor could one ask a question without being subjected to even greater excess, so one learns to smile and nod until the torrent runs dry.

But a dealer's education comes from his customers. On any given day, I might see my collector of Lewis Carroll, Joe Brabant, whose specialty was anything and everything related to the Mad Hatter. Who might be followed by Stillman Drake, a collector of works of early science, especially the world of Galileo. Which could lead to the Inquisition, modern firsts, history and maybe current book buying practices in Italy. Then maybe a discussion

David Mason

of medieval church structures with a farmer, his hands indelibly tattooed with cuts full of dirt from a lifetime in his fields, who knew more about the middle ages than any Professor I have ever met. Or Bert Kenny, a still-active and passionate member of the Communist Party, full of anecdotes of RCMP persecution of the travelling labour agitators on the freight trains going across the prairies in the '30s, and a man whose inability to question the party line caused him to lose a few more friends every time the Russians committed another atrocity. Until finally, with Hungary and Afghanistan, he had none left except the book-sellers who had learned, early on, never to discuss current affairs with him. Bert was sure that both Marty and I were sympathetic to communism because I had formed a huge personal collection on the Spanish Civil War—now in the University of Toronto—and because there is a photo of Marty at ten years old playing in The Finnish Workers Party marching band in an historical book on Spadina Avenue. Neither Marty or I disabused him of that notion, as it was easier not to. He died in his nineties unrepentant and left the greatest collection ever formed on the history and the struggle for social justice in Canada, also now at the University of Toronto. Aside from his political observations he had an encyclopedic knowledge of William Morris and his world, especially his printing activities. His friends in the book-trade were secretly relieved that he died before the collapse of the Soviet Union, sparing him the devastation of seeing his lifelong dream, no matter how misguided, crumble in the face of history and logic.

Or John Slater, the Professor of Philosophy who built the greatest collection of Bertrand Russell's books in the world, but refused to enhance the value with manuscript material because of his fervent belief that original material had to be in public insti-tutions so scholars could have access to it. When he ran out of

Russell to buy he focused his now uncontrollable passion on the entire field of modern philosophy (from about 1850 to the present). This collection was also gifted to the University of Toronto and, complemented by the collection of early philosophy in primary editions formed by Michael Walsh, a Toronto investment banker, constitutes what I believe is probably the greatest philosophy collection in the world. Those who belittle private collectors as befuddled eccentrics should examine such collections in every important institution in the world and they might learn something about the unparalleled importance of the private collector to the pursuit and retention of the historical printed record. No librarian in charge of a large institutional collection could hope to cover areas like these to the depth and with the persistence that a passionate collector brings to the chase. Their dedication unfortunately is neither understood nor lauded; indeed, often their own families consider them demented.

Or Edwin Harris, an obstreperous and opinionated Yorkshireman, who bullied us booksellers, demanding instant attention along with a cup of tea, driving us all to distraction, but who was much missed when he died. A tiny man who loved the old folio editions of the great classics, he was so small that when he read one of these folios in his chair the book entirely hid him from view. His familiarity with Camden's *Britannia*, or Plutarch, or John Evelyn was matched by his incessant rereading of the entire output of E. Phillips Oppenheim, H. Rider Haggard, and Edgar Wallace.

Or the man who drove for two days through a blinding snowstorm from a Midwest state to Toronto to pick up a rare early photography book, John Thomson's *Illustrations of China and Its People* (London, 1873-74, four volumes) I'd found for him—admittedly I had grossly undervalued it—selling it to him for $400.00. The most recent auction price I've seen is for a set described as "worn" and with volume one in the second edition, a set which sold in 2005 for \$14,000.00. The man was too frightened to drive home until the storm ended, fearing for the book's safety, not his own.

And those are my respectable customers.

I'm not even going to get into the true eccentrics, like the man who made the papers a few years back when his own brother turned him in for filling his widowed mother's house with books and pamphlets and millions of newspaper clippings on the Titanic. The fire department and the city issued injunctions, and even though one passionate bookseller went to his defense, his collection was legally put on the street, where it was destroyed. An eccentric no doubt, but the annals of the book trade contain countless anecdotes of people, no less crazy, who formed magnificent collections of immeasurable importance to our civilization which now rest in major institutions.

The first lot of books I bought privately was from Allan Fleming, the designer whose work is still visible in such things as the design of the famous CN logo. Allan told me once that the idea for that brilliant logo came to him in an airplane circling New York, an idea which he sketched on a napkin as they waited their turn to land at LaGuardia. He also designed the Ontario Hydro logo, amongst many other things. After a very successful career in advertising he became the designer for the University of Toronto Press, where I expect his influence is still felt.

Allan was a passionate collector whose main focus was finely produced books, exemplified in his case by his wonderful collection of the Nonesuch Press. I once spent an evening with Allan and his wife studying his collection, where, as always happens with focused collectors, I learned a great deal about the Nonesuch Press and fine printing and design in general. Ever since I've retained a great affection for the Nonesuch output and

I never buy or see one without remembering Allan and his great gentleness and his civilized generosity with his knowledge.

We had a regular customer once, the rejected, disowned son of a prominent Toronto family, the Langstaffs. As a young man, many years earlier, John had had some kind of mental breakdown, leaving him a filthy, unshaven street person, befuddled and usually nervously distraught.

He got a disability cheque from the government every month, and perhaps a subsidy from his family. We found out eventually that his money was regulated by an arrangement whereby his landlord got the cheque, took his rent and then doled out money to John. Otherwise, like a child oblivious to consequences, John would have spent everything on books immediately. And spend it all on books or sheet music, which a few days later he would bring back to sell. I never heard any evidence that he still played the piano, so I assumed he read the sheet music in the same manner one reads a book.

But the trouble was that what he returned after use would be filthy, often ruined, and most dealers would finally only sell him books of little value, that didn't matter much. His clothes were the same. Someone was obviously dressing him, usually in donated cast-offs, sometimes completely inappropriate—checkered pants six inches too short, with jackets that had different checks, horrible. In fact he looked just like Al Purdy did, except that Al actually *liked* his outfits. John was completely indifferent to how he looked. John's new monthly outfit would quickly deteriorate, becoming grubby, then filthy. In his urgent search for his current author he didn't even notice. Once he came in carrying the fat Penguin edition of Gibbon's *Decline and Fall of the Roman Empire* and I said, "Well, John, you're reading Gibbon."

"Oh," he replied. "I've already read it, but the edition I read didn't have an index and this edition does. So I'm rereading it."

As someone who has started Gibbon and bogged down many times in the face of its sheer bulk I was properly impressed. He'd read Gibbon twice and all I've ever done is dip in, start again, only to bog down again and give up. And now I'm too old to kid myself that I will finish it before I die.

John, when on one of his compulsive missions to find a book he needed, would drive us nuts for months, demanding copies of obscure books which no one ever reads anymore. Once found and read, another book would be sought, but always obsessively and urgently—it was life or death to John. It was standard practice for John to come into every store on Queen Street West (there were then maybe twenty of them) every day, sometimes twice a day if he'd forgotten he'd asked for a particular book that morning. When told that we still hadn't found one he would grimace with disappointment, his pain obvious.

During one period it was Lesage's 1715 novel *Gil Blas*, which one assumes is not much read anymore except by period specialists in French literature. But John wanted desperately to read it. I had only a fancy illustrated edition done by the Limited Editions Club, which naturally I couldn't sell him, not because of the $150.00 price tag, which to him would be irrelevant, but because I couldn't be a party to him destroying such a handsome book.

One day I had a call from a bookseller up the street. "I just bought a copy of the Limited Editions Club version of *Gil Blas* from Crazy John which seems to have your writing in it," he said. "Did you sell it to him or did he steal it?"

"He stole it," I said, and went up the street to buy it back.

When John next appeared I confronted him. He was properly abject, but I could see not really repentant. "I had to read it, don't you see? And you wouldn't sell it to me," he offered as an excuse for this theft, a self-evident explanation to him. Although I could hardly admit it, I secretly agreed with him.

So John was banned; in fact as word went around he was banned from every bookshop in Toronto. But after he paid me back the amount I had to pay my colleague, I lifted the ban and so did my colleagues. (It took him a couple of months to repay me; he didn't care about the money, but I guess it was painful to pay for a book he'd already read and he needed to keep some money for books he hadn't yet read. I suspect that all of us secretly admired someone who wanted to read *Gil Blas* so much they would steal it to do so.)

Later on, Debbie would sometimes eject John instantly, as he tried to enter, chasing him down the stairs as he cried out, in a futile effort to placate her. "God bless you, you're a wonderful person. God bless you. You're a fine Christian woman," he would yell as he ran.

This was because John started having problems with urinary control and he would sometimes leave puddles on the floor, where he had been standing. Especially when Debbie appeared, because she always aroused anxiety.

"You're too soft, Mason," she would rail at me. "Stealing *Gil Blas* is one thing, but I won't have that filthy bum peeing on my floor. Out he goes! I don't care if he *has* read Gibbon twice."

As I said, John's family was an old Toronto family which had had a town, Langstaff, named after it. [His sister was Phyllis Grosskurth, who I mentioned in the last chapter]. John and Pat had been long estranged. Pat is a scholar with an international reputation for several biographies and the possessor of one of the finest minds I've encountered, ever. I've appraised her papers for years, so I have seen evidence not usually available to outsiders. One of her books, *Melanie Klein: Her World and Her*

Work (1986), aroused such controversy that she was attacked viciously in the pages of the *New Yorker*. She devastated her critics in her replies; and I've seen the whole evidence. Once, a few years ago, she was brought as a guest to a lunch club of which I'm a member. We sat together over coffee and the couple of glasses of wine I'd had gave me the courage to think it might be okay to mention John. She had recently published a memoir and, reading it, I had learned both that John was dead and that his real name had been Gary. This discovery saddened me so much I never could finish her memoir. Sadly, it's not uncommon for booksellers not to know their long-time customers have died. It's usually only when one remembers that they haven't been in for a year or so that the logical conclusion is arrived at. Lack of money won't dissuade a true book person; only death will.

"I knew your brother," I told her. We had a lengthy, intense conversation, which a couple of times brought her to tears.

"You mean he went into all the bookstores regularly," she asked, her disbelief making her astonished.

"Yes, we all knew him well. Liked him too. Admired him in fact, except some people didn't like it when he peed on the floor."

She couldn't believe it.

"But David, what about his violence? His insane rages, that's why we had to disown him, hospitalize him."

"We saw no violence, not a trace," I replied. "In fact, a harsh word would reduce John to tears."

This brought tears too. I felt badly, but I sensed that she was comforted that, although clearly hopeless, John was held in affectionate regard by all the booksellers.

Another of the unforeseen benefits of being a bookseller is that one becomes less judgmental, or at least one becomes judgmental in a different way. Our feelings for those people who don't read books, for whatever reasons, range from pity to contempt, but a passionate lover of books will be forgiven much. The booksellers didn't care that John was an unshaven dishevelled addled bum—he loved books. So he was accepted (except for peeing on the floor), and generally treated with patience and affection.

But let us now look at the other extreme.

Joe Brabant was a customer for my entire career but only a friend for the last twenty-five years of it, due to, I guess, another of those weird conventions which make the book world so eccentric and delightful.

From the first month or so I was open, Joe would come in when he was in town. He was a lawyer, the House Counsellor for *Sun Life*, whose head office was in Montreal then. He travelled for *Sun Life* regularly to Toronto, but also to most of the important cities in the world.

This was perfect for a book collector, for it meant that he could put in his day's work in London or Prague or Cairo and in the evenings he could visit those cities' bookstores in search of his real passion, in this case anything relating to Lewis Carroll. I suspect that Joe was famous in the book trade worldwide due to his persistence. As I later learned, Joe had decided early on that, due to the almost endless supply of reprints of Alice-related books and advertising material incorporating Alice and her friends, he should primarily focus on only one aspect of Carroll/Dodgson's activities: he chose the Mad Hatter, which after Joe and I became friends I came to believe was more appropriate than it first seemed. Always impeccably dressed, as befits a lawyer in an important position, in the beginning Joe was always quite formal. He would enter the shop and greet me in the same manner every time. "Good day, Mr. Mason, do you have anything for me today?"

"Hi, Mr. Brabant," I would reply and either go get whatever was on the hold shelf to show him or tell him, "No, I've got nothing this trip."

This went on for many years, during which time Joe endeared himself to me by his impeccable behaviour, especially when he acted against his own interests.

I sold him a fair bit since he bought every illustrated *Alice*, indeed anything which he didn't have. Some years later when primary Carroll material, inscribed books and such, reached startling levels, Joe would get angry when I would bring some great Carroll item to his attention from a catalogue, an item which might be priced at $15,000.00 or $20,000.00.

"I wouldn't pay that even if I could," he would fulminate.

It wasn't that Joe was cheap, he always bought what he needed without questioning the price, he just believed those prices were ludicrous and he refused to break his principles.

Joe endeared himself to me early on through the following incident. I had acquired, without fully understanding its scarcity—the biggest pitfall for the inexperienced dealer—a great Carroll rarity, the true first edition of *The Game of Logic*, one of Carroll's mathematical games. First issued in 1886 it had suffered Carroll's displeasure for technical reasons, as had the first *Alice*, and had been suppressed. No more than fifty copies of *The Game* were printed before it was suppressed, and their rarity was compounded by the fact that a small packet of markers—to play the game—had been issued, loosely inserted in the book, and were often missing in the few copies which remained.

I happened on quite a fine copy of the 1886 edition, and with the markers still present. After extensive research, which really only demonstrated that it was so rare I was on my own with price, I put $200.00 on it and set it aside to show Joe on his next visit.

When he came in next he looked at it and told me he had it. This is when he showed his character.

"That's a very scarce book, Mr. Mason. I must tell you that I bought my copy from Scribner's in New York over ten years ago. My copy is not nearly as nice as this one and I paid then $300.00 American. I think your copy is much too cheap."

I was shocked.

I was operating, as I still do, on the strict principle that to the one who has the knowledge should go the profit. Painful as it was to me, it was obvious that he should take the fine copy and sell his own copy for considerably more than I was asking, thereby getting a much better copy and making a profit as well.

I told him that—which, of course he knew—but he refused anyway. This was improper, contrary to the unwritten code of collecting. It's all very well to be kind to a neophyte but a collector shouldn't allow that to influence his opportunity to upgrade his collection.

But Joe refused. There could be no rational explanation for such behaviour on the part of a collector (and in forty-five years I've never seen any other collector do this). It could only mean that he refused to profit by the ignorance of a neophyte.

I never forgot that fine gesture and Joe profited considerably in the end from his class.

Incidentally, I sold *The Game of Logic* the next day for $1,000.00 to a colleague in California. But in spite of that enormous profit I still feel badly. Joe deserved that book and he should have taken it.

Joe had so much Carroll material that in the later years most of what he would find waiting for him to examine was ephemera. Debbie and I would go to considerable trouble to collect advertisements relating to Carroll (the Mad Hatter still gets used very often in sales brochures and such).

Once Debbie told Joe that she had seen a huge poster with Alice and the Mad Hatter in a bus shelter. The next day Joe was at the TTC offices getting one.

Another time, in her bank, an account promotion was using a large kiosk-type structure, covered with cut-out illustrations of Alice and her crew to solicit accounts. I wondered what the bank manager must have thought when this distinguished man made an appointment with him, not to open an account but to try and buy two of those kiosks. He got them, too.

For the kinds of ephemeral pieces we found, I could have asked, and Joe would have been happy to pay, $5.00 or $10.00 each. But instead I took to giving them to him. It made me feel good and he always graciously accepted.

After some years of this *Sun Life* moved their head office to Toronto in 1979, during another of the Quebec separatists' threats to split the country, and Joe chose to move with them.

Then I would see him every week, always at opening on Saturday mornings. The only difference was that he would be dressed on Saturday in a ratty old tweed jacket and turtleneck sweater instead of the impeccable business attire we were used to.

But the ritual was the same. "Good morning, Mr. Mason. Anything for me today?"

"Sorry Mr. Brabant, nothing this week," or I'd hand him some magazine with an Alice ad. And then, "Well, see you next week," and he'd leave.

I had, of course, had a few conversations in passing with Joe, some where he had dropped interesting tidbits into the conversation on political and other subjects, such as a casual comment once that he and Pierre Trudeau were members of the same club in Montreal and he didn't much care for him.

One day I decided this was silly. I'd known the man some fifteen years or so, liked him a lot, but I'd never had any sort of personal conversation with him. The next Saturday as we went through the regular ritual I simply didn't let it go. I just started talking, questioning him about Trudeau and the politics of the country. At first he was a bit disconcerted—I was contravening our usual ritual—but he quickly opened up. The next Saturday I asked if he'd like to stay for a coffee. He would, and sat down and chatted with Reg Innell and me for over an hour. Like so many book collectors, he was lonely in the bookish sense, he had no friends who collected, except for the large Lewis Carroll Society, which flourished worldwide, and when he was given an opportunity to chat with the other book collectors who came in on Saturdays he loved it.

And he went from a man who said little to someone who had lots to say when he was in bookish company. He would enter every Saturday at 10 AM, offering to pay or to go for the coffee, and sit for a couple of hours. I got to know Joe pretty well on those Saturday mornings, and some of what I learned was extremely helpful in what occurred later.

Joe, lawyer though he was, hated two things vehemently—politicians and lawyers. He was a man of rigid principles, as my anecdote of him refusing a $500.00 or a $1,000.00 profit showed, and that was why he hated politicians; his distrust of politicians was visceral.

Of unimpeachable character himself I guess he came to despise lawyers because he had seen too many examples of lawyers who lacked his integrity.

There was a group of collectors then who formed a little group for discussion of book matters and they began meeting every month or so for coffee and talk, often dropping into the store afterwards. Like most book groups it was a disparate lot, the only common thread being the love of books and talking about them. Aside from Joe, there were people like the aforementioned

John Slater, the philosophy professor who built the magnificent Bertrand Russell and modern philosophy collections, and Michael Walsh, the investment banker who built a collection that complemented it. Both these collections are now housed in the Thomas Fisher Library at the University of Toronto. And my friend Reg Innell, a well-known photographer at the *Toronto Star*, who had met and photographed every major literary and show business personage who passed through Toronto.

And Brian Kennedy, who originally came in seeking Margaret Atwood first editions as gifts for his wife. He and I had long chats and he got interested in collecting himself. After a bit, I started loaning him books on books and this became a regular occurrence until one day he returned several and when I asked if he wanted some new ones, he said, "No, I've read enough, I'm going to start collecting. In fact I've decided to collect Thomas Hardy. And as I've learned from these books and your talk, I'm only going to buy books in original cloth and in fine condition."

I offered him another lesson on the spot. Just a couple of days earlier I had received the latest catalogue from Sumner & Stillman, who specialize in nineteenth-and early twentieth-century literature and have, for many years, issued what I consider to be amongst the most interesting and best-researched catalogues anywhere in those areas, catalogues from which I quite often treat myself to a personal book for my own library. This particular catalogue contained the three-volume first edition of Hardy's *The Woodlanders,* in what they called very fine original cloth. I knew their style very well and I knew that meant the book would be like new.

I showed Brian the catalogue entry, explaining that it was a pretty good example of what he would face if he insisted on really fine condition.

This copy was priced at $3,000.00 US and I told Brian that a normal copy, in nice original cloth, would range from around $1,250.00 to $1,750.00.

"This is what you'll be faced with if you insist on very fine condition, Brian," I lectured. "This copy is double or more the normal and I can assure you, for what it is, it's not overpriced."

Brian looked at it for a moment while I waited for him to absorb this lesson and demur. Then he said, "I'd like to buy that. Can you get it for me?"

As befits a very good lawyer, and Brian is, he had carefully prepared, considering all the details, and once he'd decided he acted decisively.

He's been my lawyer ever since.

When I got over my momentary shock I phoned Sumner & Stillman and secured the book. A few days later the book arrived. I didn't open the package but waited for Brian to come in so he could experience the pleasure and anxiety of unpacking his first major purchase. As I knew it would be, it was a lovely copy, in about new condition. (As I've said elsewhere, proper dealers never used the term mint, even if it is.)

I felt constrained to give Brian, a Brian properly delighted with his first three-decker, yet another lecture.

"Brian you'd better start lowering your standards of condition right now. If you insist on only this sort of condition you may never be able to buy another nineteenth-century book."

I could see that Brian didn't think that would be true, and in fact it led to several errors over the next few years where he erred in the opposite manner to most new collectors.

Most beginners make the error of buying desired books in less than proper condition, ignoring defects, deciding that they are of no importance, lulled perhaps by a cheaper price or certain that they can live with obvious defects.

Another of my caveats for collectors when I'm trying to help them decide if they can live with a defect in a book is often stated like this: "Look at it this way. If you don't like this stain, or tear or whatever now, it won't get better. Everytime you go into your library that defect will leap off the shelf and hit you in the face. Decide, before you buy, what you can live with and if you're not yet sure, do it only with cheap books, until you learn this lesson."

Brian held to his unrealistic standards for several years, which resulted in him missing several books I expect he now regrets not buying. We offered him a fine first of *The Trumpet Major*, which was rebound in a lovely half-morocco binding, which he refused because it was rebound. I think he has regretted it ever since. Debbie, who also loves Hardy and has a few nice ones, deeply regrets that she didn't buy it when Brian turned it down.

Now neither of them own a copy and it is now worth double or triple what we sold that copy for. It remains a painful regret for both of them.

But back to Joe Brabant.

Once Joe invited Debbie and me up to view his collection. He lived in a sumptuous apartment on St. Clair, his window overlooking the remains of one of the oldest cemeteries in Toronto, seemingly a rather macabre situation, but to my mind quite appropriate for book people like us who live in the past anyway. The crumbling and tilted gravestones seemed to emphasize our antiquarianism.

It was quite a spectacle. Except for his books Joe was a minimalist. There was a large eighteenth-century desk in the living room, French I would guess, and obviously quite valuable, with a matching chair, a very nondescript, almost shabby chesterfield, an early wooden bed that, I think, was probably French-Canadian and probably seventeenth-century, and worth I would guess even more than the desk—and nothing else. Just bookshelves, lining every wall, and all filled with Alice and her cast of characters. On the bed was a shabby, worn quilt, also quite old, perhaps some family heirloom. It was obvious Joe didn't care about most things, except his books. Just as he was unimpressed by important people, he seemed indifferent to decor. Of course he could only get away with this because he never married.

The collection was stunning. Row after row of the familiar red and gold Alices, in every printing, all the early editions. And thousands of illustrated reprints. We had seen nothing like it in scope or size. Justin Schiller called it somewhere the second greatest collection in private hands in the world. This is high praise, for Carroll is much collected.

Joe had always told us that his collection was willed to Carroll's own college, Christ Church, Oxford, where the author was a professor under his real name, Charles Lutwidge Dodgson. In an interesting aside I once called Joe to inform him that I had received a catalogue from a dealer I didn't know which contained an Alice title inscribed and signed as Charles Lutwidge Dodgson. It wasn't cheap, but neither was it outrageous. Joe's immediate reaction was, "That's a forgery. Carroll never used his real name when he signed or inscribed any of what he considered his 'non-professional' books, *Alice* and the others. There is no known copy of any 'Lewis Carroll' book signed as Dodgson."

I learned a lesson there and discreetly sent a postcard to that dealer, in case he was an honest man who also didn't know that.

One day Joe came in, quite upset. "I'm changing my will, David. I'm not giving my collection to Oxford."

After such certainty, over so many years, I could hardly believe it.

"Why, Joe? What happened?" I asked.

"I've just been in Oxford. The librarian took me into the basements to show me something in the Carroll Collection and I saw a room with stacks of cartons piled in a corner.

"When I asked him what was in those cartons, he told me he didn't know. It was just a bunch of stuff Carroll's family had given them after Carroll's death in 1898.

"In all those years no one had even bothered to look inside them, never mind treating them properly in spite of the obvious importance they must have. They're not going to do that with my collection."

I guess I should have added bureaucrats to Joe's earlier hate list. He didn't trust them either, as I found out soon enough.

I already knew that Joe meant what he said, so when he followed that by asking me what I thought he should do I knew he had made up his mind. He had graduated from McGill so it was his first thought, but I began right then my campaign for what I considered the most appropriate place in Canada, the Osborne Collection in the Toronto Public Library, one of the greatest if not the greatest collection of children's books in the world. That collection came about in a curious manner.

Edgar Osborne, I was told, had been in charge in Britain during the Second World War with the responsibility of handling the books that citizens donated to be pulped for paper needed for the war effort, another form of those scrap drives where people were urged to hand in scrap metal which could be converted into weapons. Osborne loved children's books and searched through these donations and rescued many important early children's books.

After the war, visiting Toronto, he had been so impressed by the Toronto Public Library that he donated his whole collection here. It resides now on its own floor in the College Street branch of the TPL with the magnificent sculptured griffins, modelled on Maurice Sendak's drawings, who guard the portals. It is a library very close to my heart because of the immeasurable debt I owe to the TPL children's librarians in their northern St. Clements branch, who guided me as a very young child in my reading and started me on the path I'm following still.

A few years back I gave them the first major collection I have donated, my Thornton W. Burgess collection, my earliest favourite author. I told Leslie McGrath, the current custodian, about my reverence for those unknown librarians who so influenced me all those years ago, and one day she gave me a photograph of a woman who was the head of that branch then.

"But Leslie," I said, "She was the head. I wouldn't have met her."

"Yes, you would," said Leslie. "All the librarians then did everything."

So this picture hangs in a place of honour in my shop. But the truth is whether that librarian did or didn't ever help me choose a book is irrelevant to me now. I much prefer the idea that I owe my life's greatest focus to *all* librarians.

I continue to refer to those anonymous women as the "Unknown Librarians," those people who gave, no doubt not even aware what they were really giving, the incomparable gift of civilization to some timid, shy kid whose imagination they fed with the glory of what being human means.

Like the unknown soldier, the unknown librarian, in following her vocation, gave humanity some of its greatest gifts.

It's probably impossible not to sound trite or pathetically over-sentimental when saying such things, so I won't try not to.

Joe was also involved in another group which met every month. This group was made up of George Walker, the talented wood-engraver, and Bill Poole, who owned and ran the

Poole Hall Press in Grimsby, another member of those groups of seemingly crazed people who still print beautiful books by hand, usually for no other reason than their passion for fine printing.

These people are possibly even crazier than book collectors because they often devote their entire lives and most of their incomes to this pursuit in spite of the fact that the rest of the world, if it even knows, doesn't care.

These three men met regularly as they printed very small editions of Carroll's books, with Joe doing the editorial work on the text, George Walker providing the woodcut illustrations and Bill Poole doing the printing. The editions they eventually issued after many years of monthly consultations were done in very small runs and are rarely seen in the marketplace. And while I'm certain profit had nothing to do with the motivations of any of them, when one appears it brings pretty high prices.

It took many years to finish these books and Joe took enormous pleasure in the collaboration.

Anyway, I worked on Joe for a couple of years and it was finally decided that the Osborne would be the recipient of his life's passion.

But then one day that plan too imploded, this time due to the actions of the head of the Toronto Public Library. This woman had already displayed her lack of credentials as a real custodian of such things by letting it be known that she expected to be considered not a librarian but the "CEO" of the library system.

If such pathetic snobbery hadn't been enough, she then announced that the library would place the entire Osborne collection in "storage" while a new building was constructed. Simultaneously the library board, which along with her was made up of various appointed people, discussed selling the Osborne collection.

This seems to have been initiated by James Lorimer, who had briefly flourished in the sixties and seventies as a publisher of various left wing anti-establishment books which he no doubt considered to be radical but which were really doctrinally socialist in design, and to my mind evinced the sort of totalitarian fascism which is our real enemy.

Lorimer apparently considered research collections such as the Osborne and the enormously important Arthur Conan Doyle Collection, also held by TPL—one of the prime centres in the world for that delightful, if somewhat eccentric group of Sherlock Holmes aficionados known as the Baker Street Irregulars—as frivolous and elitist. That two such magnificent collections, both justly world-famous, could be so misunderstood is to me indicative of a type who are the same as those Taliban fanatics who blew up the ancient Buddhist statues in Afghanistan. All civilized people have an obligation to fight such barbarians.

Apparently Lorimer thought the collection should be sold, with the proceeds being used to provide such things as language tapes (in Estonian or Bulgarian) for branch libraries, so "the people" could be served by practical, useful services. Lorimer, who I'm not surprised to find out came from independent wealth, seems not to understand that the historical collections of major public libraries in cities and countries are exactly the same as museums. Their function is to preserve physical artifacts, in this case printed artifacts, so posterity can have the ability to study its history.

This all happened twenty years ago and I've been hoping ever since to meet Lorimer at some social function so that I can properly insult him for his ignorant barbarity. So far I haven't, but someday I hope to get a chance.

Luckily, the Osborne Collection has a very extensive worldwide group, officially known as The Friends of the Osborne

Collection, which contains many people who both despise such ignorance and are not shy about fighting it, so this abysmal proposal got nowhere. But it certainly taught me the importance of such groups. People who care about things that most of the world is indifferent to must organize themselves for precisely such ignorant assaults on reason.

Anyway, this combined display of snobbery and ignorance by people who should have known better proved the final straw for Joe.

"They'll pack my collection in a basement somewhere, David. I know it. And it'll never come out. It'll rot in some basement. They're not having my collection."

I knew he meant it.

So I started the process again, and this time the recipient of choice was the University of Toronto. But there was a problem there. Joe didn't like something about the University of Toronto because of an earlier incident.

Discussions continued for over a year, and in the end I was forced to pretty much tell him that if the University of Toronto wasn't going to get his Carroll collection he'd have to return once again to Oxford. In the end Joe had things decided for him. One day he came into the store, sat himself down and said, "David, you can call your friend at the University of Toronto. I've just been to my doctor. I'm riddled with cancer. He's given me six months or less."

So the arrangements began. Richard Landon hired Justin Schiller, the children's dealer who had sold Joe much of the rare and expensive material, and I did the appraisal with Justin.

I was pretty much out of my depth, never having seen much less handled much of that sort of material. What Justin and I did in two days probably would have taken me two weeks or a month to properly research.

Justin would pick up a book and say, "What did you pay for this, Joe? I seem to remember $8,000.00, yes?"

"Yes," Joe would reply. "That would be around fifteen years ago."

"Well," Justin would say, studying the book or the photograph or the letter, "I think we'd better say $50,000.00 for that now." And we would write it down.

Book after book, inscribed to important people or with original illustrations tipped in, would be $40,000.00, $75,000.00, or more. In the end one small section, maybe eight feet tall and four feet wide, added up to $1,000,000.00—I was astounded both at the richness of the material and at Justin's sense of value.

Then Justin went home and Debbie and I appraised the rest of the packed apartment after Joe died. That took two or three days and came to another million.

When we thought we were close to done, we thought we'd better just check the closets in case Joe had put any posters or things in them.

He had indeed. What he hadn't put in his closets was clothes. A couple of his business suits, the ratty tweed jacket he almost always wore after he retired, that was all; the rest was stuffed with more Carroll material—including the two huge kiosks he'd bought from the bank after Debbie's tip.

It was astonishing—the closets had $100,000.00's worth of posters, pictures, and bulky paraphernalia in them. It was obvious that, had Joe lived, he would have needed more space very soon. There were no more clothes to get rid of and only three pieces of furniture.

As the appraisal of a major collection always does, handling every item in Joe's collection both taught me a lot and demonstrated clearly what a single passionate collector can accomplish on his own. But it still took a lifetime. And I'm sure that he loved every minute of it.

The University of Toronto issued an exhibition catalogue of Joe's gift. In the introduction Richard Landon called it the single largest gift they'd ever received to that time.

Joe, in his time in Toronto, made a large number of friends in the book community at large and his many friends still miss him greatly.

Since collectors also love to boast of their sleepers—except, of course, to the dealers they bought them from—I have heard quite a few stories of their triumphs as well. But my favourite and the one which I think illustrates not just the principle of the educated eye but the historical principle of rescuing the past in a lowly used bookstore, concerns one of the greatest collectors I have known, Stillman Drake.

Stillman Drake, when I met him, was a professor of the History of Science at the University of Toronto. Earlier he had been an investment banker in San Francisco and an old friend of Jake Zeitlin's, with whom he had spent considerable time scouting Europe, mostly Italy, for early science books. Stillman was a born teacher. He certainly taught me many things in every conversation I had with him. Without ever talking down to people he seemed to always be imparting knowledge, usually the arcane anecdotal details which make all history so fascinating.

He seemed to assume that his listener also knew basic scientific things—which, in my case, I often didn't—but by the end of the conversation you often had an understanding you hadn't had when he began.

Stillman would come in often because I was around the corner from the post office which he visited a couple of times a week. As I have mentioned more than once, he had an important collection on the history of science, centered on Galileo. I was told that he was considered one of the two foremost authorities on Galileo and his times in the world. He had placed his collections on deposit in the University of Toronto and every year we would appraise another lot as needed for his taxes. I believe the university also bought a portion of it outright every year too.

After it was all absorbed, Richard Landon offered me the residue, the duplicates—which I'm still selling. One of Stillman's credos which he could and did justify was that an early science book which had defects like a missing plate or page should still be purchased, for he had concluded in his early years that a defective copy was preferable to no copy at all, and he began when the collecting of early science books was in its infancy so it was a largely unexplored area. Hence, that most important of book collecting principles, scarcity, was still largely unknown. Occasionally we get orders for books with his bookplate in them and I often presume it's other scientists who just want to own a book from Stillman's library. I have a few of his books myself in what I call my "sentimental collection," books from the libraries of book friends or famous dealers or collectors. Such a collection, foolish and pointless to anyone but the person who collects it, affords me much pleasure, reminding me of people who went before me. It also reminds us that we don't really own these books; rather, we are only their temporary guardians, privileged to hold them safely until another generation can absorb their contents and treasure their beauty.

Some years ago a group of Toronto bookmen formed a club where we met once a month and someone would give a talk. We called ourselves The Amtmann Circle, after Bernard Amtmann, who had attempted several times to organize such groups, his last effort being The Erasmus Circle.

The first talk was given by Stillman, wherein he spoke very amusingly of various rules he had formed in his long life of collecting, illustrated by examples and very shrewd comments. When he gave the talk it was an enormous success. I considered it amusing but ephemeral, perfect for a pleasurable social evening, but not very deep in content. With time I proved myself wrong, very wrong.

Some years later after I had read the pamphlet several times, the Amtmann Circle imploded and we offered the remaining copies of our publications to members at $5.00 each. This was about the cost of printing them, for we had done them properly, often at the Coach House Press, and they were finely printed and quite attractive. I bought about fifty of them in the same manner I had been buying remainders for years, for eventual resale at what I figured would be a fair profit. But this is how I came to discover how superficial my original opinion of its content had been.

One thing every serious dealer does is constantly instruct his clients. The smart dealer learns quickly that the sophisticated client is much easier to sell a fine and important book to and it is therefore in his interest to educate his clients. A good book needs no sales pitch to a sophisticated collector—it will sell itself to the man who knows what it is and its importance.

I found, especially with newish clients, that I was constantly quoting Stillman's "slight" talk. Time after time the seemingly simple advice he had given would afford a perfect example of what collectors should do in similar situations. Indeed so enthusiastic would I become in quoting his remarks, working myself into a state of excessive enthusiasm, that I found myself impulsively giving them a copy, wanting to both share the knowledge and my pleasure in his wisdom.

In this talk Stillman recounted, along with his brilliant conclusions about how to collect books, what he considered the discovery which was his most important contribution to scholarship in his long career. For me it remains one of the most remarkable examples of the importance of the book collector to scholarship I have ever heard.

Browsing in the Holmes Book Company in San Francisco one day Stillman came across a book called *A Treatise on Language, or the Relation Which Words Bear to Things*, published by the author in New York in 1836. On investigation Stillman came to believe that this obscure self-published book by an unknown man—a banker in Utica, New York—was perhaps the most important contribution to philosophy by an American, including even William James.

It was a treatise on semantics but was published a century before that subject even became generally recognized. Two things seem important to me here: that it was discovered in a used bookshop, not offered to him by a rare book dealer, and, more crucially, his appreciation of it was as perfect a case as one could find of the educated instinct in operation.

The average person, even the average dealer—and possibly even the specialist science dealer searching for known authors and titles—would have passed right over it. Without taking the time to examine it closely or without the scientific knowledge to understand its significance it had already rested in obscurity and its author in anonymity for a hundred years till Stillman happened on it.

Stillman Drake went on to assemble a collection of all this man's books and pamphlets. His name was Alexander Bryan Johnson, and thanks to Stillman all of Johnson's books are back in print—his status assured—mostly bearing introductions by Stillman, and his great contributions are now part of the historical record.

So we find a scholar, browsing through a grubby disordered used bookstore, who has added to the sum of scientific knowledge, but only because the right sensibility encountered a key book and had all the necessary equipment to realize what it was.

Every dealer has hundreds of anecdotal stories about the serendipity offered by browsing in used bookshops, but this remains my favourite example of the scholarly rewards which can ensue.

Chapter 17

Employees

After all these years it's hard to even remember all the employees I've had. A curious contradiction of the book trade is the fact that no matter how poor a dealer may be, he must have employees, almost from the first, if for no other reason than that he would otherwise have no life at all outside the store. So poor was I when I started that my infant son would mind the shop beside me, sitting in a sloped children's holder, observing the eccentric habitués, while my wife worked a part-time job to help pay the bills. Then, at home after work, along with her usual home duties she also did the invoicing and typed the catalogues while I manned the shop until the last customer left, sometimes very late. It all seemed quite natural at the time, even fun, for we were working for ourselves; we felt we were creating our own future.

Many beginning dealers, having no money, only time, stay open long hours, often 9 AM to midnight, seven days a week. Even living over the store it doesn't take long to discover this kind of life is impossible to sustain, so a young dealer finds himself an employee, paying minimum wage or slightly above it. This person ends up earning a wage that the owner can't count on earning himself.

These early poverty-induced lessons served me well in many areas as I was constantly trying to figure ways to increase sales with the only means I had at my disposal: new ideas. But there was no escape from time.

Recently I found my earliest ledger, which revealed that I was almost a year in business before my gross sales for the month

reached $1,000.00. That's gross sales, all of which had to pay the $300.00 rent, replace stock, and feed my family. Still, gross sales in those days were actually net sales, for no new business at that level needs to contemplate such ordinary concerns as taxes. The normal advice from older dealers to newcomers then (and maybe now) was to not even submit a tax form until you had been in business for at least five years. This had nothing to do with honesty but was simple common sense. When you consider that it would be at least that long before any actual profit would be possible, it was thought that it was better to be under the radar with any government agency. Actually, that still holds. It's no accident that all small businessmen distrust and avoid bureaucrats. One learns very early that these people live by their own rules; they don't care, probably can't even understand, that a new business which has a $25.00 or $50.00 fee or penalty imposed may result in a family poorly fed. One comes to avoid all contact with government, which I still do. I am responsible for everything I do. Why would I want to have to reason with someone who takes no responsibility for their actions, having a barrier of inflexible rules to protect them from needing to consider the consequences of their legalities? One comes to despise even the attitude of such people. But curiously, after a few years of always paying for your mistakes one comes to take an inordinate pride in doing so, even getting to the stage of not envying the affluence of such cosseted bureaucrats compared to your own financial straits, when you see what their security really costs them.

On the whole I've been pretty lucky in the employees I've had, or maybe it's just that I've mercifully blanked out the unfortunate memories of the few failures.

Question the prominent booksellers of today and you will find an intricate web of associations leading back to the major dealers of the previous generation; that is how learning and tradition passes on in the book trade.

Of all the booksellers who worked for me before starting their own businesses, and there are now a few of them, my favourite is Yvonne Knight, the proprietor of St. Nicholas Books. St. Nicholas specialized only in children's books. Yvonne retired and St. Nicholas is defunct so some of you may not know of it. I'd like to tell you how St. Nicholas came to be. Yvonne came to work for me around 1971 and was my first full-time employee. I encouraged her to specialize in children's books, a part of my stock that I had been consciously building up for a long time.

My store then was in a converted house on Church St., and adjoining the entrance to the washroom was a small alcove which I had shelved, leaving only a narrow aisle for access to the washroom. When shelved this space was hardly larger than a closet, and that's where we put the children's books. Yvonne had started working for me in April or May. In January of the following year she came to me and told me she had to return all the money I had paid her for the entire previous year, some six or eight months. It turns out that her husband, who is a doctor, had been told by his accountant that her having a job was going to mess up his tax return so badly that it would cost him more than her total earnings. To avoid that mess he told her to return all her pay.

I didn't know how to respond to that, except I knew I couldn't allow her to work for nothing—even though she said she'd be happy to do so. I finally thought of a solution. Which was, that I gave her all my children's books and the space they were in. She had an instant business. We thereafter referred to her first shop, beside my washroom, as the world's smallest bookstore, contrasting it deliberately to the World's Biggest Bookstore in downtown Toronto. I continued to buy children's books and paid her with them, which suited us both. She ran her little shop while still working for me for a few years, until its size became impossible, about the same time she felt ready to become entirely independent. She moved her business into the third floor of her home where it went from being the smallest bookstore in the world to certainly the loveliest children's bookshop in Canada.

Yvonne and I remained close friends—we shared booths at international book fairs several times and some of my best kid's books came from her. Yvonne sold her books too cheaply and she also over-described—to over-describe means that a dealer notes all defects with such detail that it often results in a book's condition sounding way worse than it is. Which means that if you ordered a book from her that she had described as good you would be delighted because it would invariably be in fine condition. Obviously her customers loved her and she sold a very high percentage from her catalogues.

After she left my store I would only see her stock when I visited, when she issued a catalogue, or at book fairs. This often resulted in my buying some of my best children's books from her without even needing to leave my booth at a fair. Once, at a Los Angeles fair, she had mounted a lovely display in our shared glass display case. As soon as I saw it I wanted to buy over half the books in it, but especially a very ornate set of tiny nineteenth-century children's books in a special wooden bookcase. It was beautiful and, as usual, too cheap. I wanted the set badly but Yvonne asked me not to buy anything until the fair had opened, because she didn't want to ruin her display. Out of deference I agreed, but later, still before opening, a dealer I quite disliked, a guy who had a reputation as a vulgar bully with his colleagues, came up and tried to buy the books. It looked like being accommodating to Yvonne meant I would lose my treasure. But he wanted 20% off, which luckily gave me an out. In those days the standard discount was just 10%, which means he was being pushy again. Yvonne wasn't in the booth and I told him he'd have to come back and ask her. When he left I promptly took the set out of the case and hid it. When I told Yvonne why, she wasn't angry because she didn't like this man either. I paid her the full price and then had the pleasure of telling the pushy bully, when he came back, that it had sold. I didn't tell him it had been sold to me. I just told him it had been sold to a dealer who didn't try to beat her down. But, sure enough, this guy was so dumb that he didn't even get the point of my insult. I still have this set and it's still beautiful.

Another anecdote is more painful. Visiting some recent friends and clients once in their home I saw one of the great rarities in Canadian literature, a first edition of *Anne of Green Gables*. After expressing surprise that they had such a rare book, I asked if they could tell me where they got it and how much they had paid. They told me that they had bought it from Yvonne Knight for $400.00. $400.00! I almost cried. Even then that was grossly underpriced; Yvonne simply hadn't thought to mention it to me, so I had missed it. Which is as good as an example as you'll ever hear as to why it's a good idea to visit used bookstores regularly. Some years later, I bought it off my friends—for a bit more than $400.00; in fact I paid them $9,000.00 for it, and sold it for $10,000.00 the same day. If you'd like to have a more detailed account about that you will find the whole story in an essay on my website entitled "Anne's Adventures on Her Way Home."

Aside from Steve Temple's periodic stretches working for me when he was in financial trouble, two of the best booksellers now active in Canada worked for me in their early years: Robert Wright, and Debra Dearlove, who still does.

Some time after Wright left to go on his own I also hired Janet Fetherling (previously Inksetter, and now Inksetter again).

After a couple of years Janet Fetherling came to me one day and told me she had bought a bookstore, Annex Books, and would be leaving. The old syndrome again—if they're any good they will want to go out on their own. I could only be gracious and wish her well but I was pretty sick of hiring people, spending an intensive couple of years teaching and training them, only to lose them.

Of course much worse were the ones who, after all that effort, didn't work out.

This time I resolved to try and be a real businessman and conduct proper interviews and consider carefully all applicants before I hired one. I began to question friends and clients who had done extensive hiring on how to do this. One librarian friend, David Kotin, in the upper levels of the Toronto Public Library, depressed me by saying it was all a crapshoot.

"The best employee I ever hired, Dave, had the worst qualifications and the worst mistake I ever made had two or three degrees."

This made me even more depressed. To make matters worse, I was living in my store then, having had an abrupt parting with the woman I'd been living with, so I had no home, no lady, now no employee and worse, I couldn't even type.

One Saturday I started chatting with an occasional customer, Debra Dearlove, and on telling her my problems she responded, "Why don't you hire me?"

Turns out she had worked in insurance, hadn't liked it and returned to York to do postgraduate work, but discovered that she didn't care for the upper levels of university life and was dropping out.

In spite of all my newly mustered intentions, I trusted my instincts and offered her the job. I doubt that those proper methods would have worked anyway. Every dealer I've ever spoken to hires in the same manner I did, just as most of them entered the trade by happenstance as well. Whenever you read a bookseller's biographical note or question him, almost everyone in the trade seemed to enter it by accident. I've heard variations of the same story countless times since I read it in David Randall's *Dukedom Large Enough* (New York, 1969) and the similarities are a bit eerie. A university student, usually an English major (although there have been engineers, pre-meds, etc.) finds himself spending more time in the library or in bookstores than at lectures, finding the attraction to books irresistible till he finally finds himself both hoarding and scouting. At first thinking it was merely a sort of new hobby, then becoming increasingly involved, until his preoccupation with books becomes an addiction and the fascination transfers itself into an all-consuming compulsion, and another bookseller is born. There are many variations of this theme, my own case being one, starting at fifteen, but not realizing my vocation till I was thirty. But all those years of travelling, reading, talking, I now see, were preparation for what was my certain destiny from the age of four or five or whenever it was that I first learned to see order in the hieroglyphics of our language. The clues can always be found if one looks.

How could someone who believes in his heart that he was born knowing how to read have become anything else but a life-long lover of books?

I hired her on the spot and she is still here twenty-five years later—in fact, pretty much running things now. It was later before I realized that working in my bookstore was dangerous in an entirely new way for both of us. By that time it was too late. I was truly seduced, and I still am.

For, within a few months, life took over and I broke the first rule of business, which is, of course, never mess with your employees. We began seeing each other on a personal level as well. Her father, who himself had owned and run a company, put it succinctly when he was told of the complication: "Well it's not like she'll lose a job that's paying her any money." He'd already learned a few things about the book business.

Debbie was a natural. Already a collector of the work of George Gissing, she understood the essence of the collecting instinct, which quickly translated into her becoming first a natural bookseller, then a very good one. Friends enjoy kidding me over this. "So, David, you finally got a perfect employee and you think marrying her will keep her from leaving. This time if she leaves you'll lose everything." (Actually, it's most often Debbie herself who points this out to me, and the most chilling part is that it's true.)

Merging our personal and professional lives wasn't easy in the beginning for obvious reasons. It wasn't just that I was the boss, it was that I knew things she didn't (I still do, although she might not admit this). In other words, I had the obvious advantage of always being right, inevitable and proper in a teaching and boss/ employee situation, but neither desirable nor even possible in a personal one.

That we pulled it off and are still doing so twenty-five years later says something about us, I think. These days I make up for my early vulgar crassness of always being right by now always being clearly wrong. I'm still not sure if we need another twenty-five years to even the slate so that we'll simply be equals.

But in spite of joking and the pointed comments of our friends, it has worked—so much so that I must admit I couldn't run things without her. It is a demonstrable truism in the book trade that partnerships don't work and invariably fail, often disastrously. But it seems that those forged in marriage or personal bonds can and do.

I have often been thankful for whatever instinct caused me to refuse Jerry Sherlock's offer of a partnership before I went on my own, for I now realize that our friendship might not have survived. It's one thing to find a person's eccentricities amusing when they cost you nothing, but when ludicrous business practices take the food from one's family's mouth, so to speak, they are less so.

Debbie and I compliment each other well in the business— almost like good cop, bad cop (naturally, I am the good cop, although she would contend I'm really a fool and a sucker)—and with the great gift that we both share in everything, our near constant verbal bickering seems to evaporate almost instantly, leaving the air clean of resentment and anger.

This is no small thing, for as every person who has grappled with the obsessions of addiction knows, resentment is one of the most insidious and destructive of all human traits.

All this means that I have also solved the great dilemma facing all older booksellers—what will happen to the business when the founder dies. I have now seen many, many cases where book businesses simply evaporated after the owner died. Warren Howell took over after the death of his father and it is said he was a much better bookseller than his father had been, but on his death John Howell Books was liquidated. Jake Zeitlin tried elaborate schemes for many years where he would hire the sons of his wealthy clients, the idea being that Jake would teach the young man the business then sell it to the father, establishing the continuance of his business. Jonathan Hill was supposed to do this, I believe, but instead set up in his own business, perhaps motivated in the same way I was when I turned down Jerry Sherlock's offer of a partnership. When Jake died, Zeitlin and Ver Brugge disappeared as well. This saddens me but it affords yet another example of what I have come to believe is a necessary consequence of being a bookseller. It offers fuel for the philosophic position which I believe is an inevitable consequence of being a bookseller: seeing in everyday mundane occurrences philosophical implications far more profound than those afforded in normal occupations. And why would that surprise? How can one, after a lifetime immersed in records of human history, the noble and the foolish, think otherwise?

A bookseller comes to see how important tradition and continuity really are. And all small businessmen come to know that all actions cause reactions and that there are consequences to everything one does. Trite, no doubt, but true for all that, and inescapable. It's a good lesson to learn.

Bookselling is a vocation, not a job, and the numerous cases we see of dynasties are almost all in Britain, where up till recently a young man, having to choose between his father's bookshop or the factory, would sensibly become a bookseller. Some of those people became very good booksellers too. I don't know what that means.

The other exception would be the old Jewish dynastic booksellers, where such people as Barney Rosenthal can point to four or five generations of booksellers in both branches of his family and relations all over the world in the trade, scattered by marriages within the tribe, and later by the Nazis.

So, usually, the business dies with the bookseller. Debbie being twenty years younger than me will carry on. My son, like most of his generation, is more interested in movies than in books.

She will inherit a large and wonderful stock, the best in Canada I believe. I like to tell her that that was a small price to pay for relinquishing her virtue, but seemingly she doesn't agree, having taken in the last few months to dramatically proclaiming that I have ruined her life, she having sacrificed her best years to a world so corrupt that only a diminishing few treasure books any longer. She seems certain that the book itself will die about the same time I do, leaving her with massive overheads to house books that no one wants.

I hope that's not true.

If Yvonne Knight was my favourite employee, Reg Innell has been beyond any doubt the most singular. Like me a lifelong reader and amasser of books, I knew Reg as a collector and customer for twenty-five years before he came to work with me.

Reg Innell is an Englishman in the mold of Edwin Harris— both were opinionated free-thinkers (for this type of Englishman that means an aggressive atheist), lifelong socialists and ever ready to take offense at any perceived challenge to any of their assertions. These were the sort of Englishmen who refused to bow to Hitler when most of the rest of the world had counted them out. This moral certainty in the rightness of their opinions may have saved western civilization, but it also tends to make them difficult to deal with on the personal level.

Reg worked his whole career for the *Toronto Star*, where he was a bit of a legend.

Debbie and I attended the party at the *Star* when Reg retired and were not surprised when every single speaker recounted stories of scenes Reg had caused, usually in the parking lot, when some hapless innocent made the error of parking in restricted spaces. The favourite at the retirement party seemed to be the time he called the police on some man only to find that the man was parked in Reg's spot because he was catering a party in Beland Honderich's office and had hot food. Prestige and position meant nothing to an aroused Reg.

His greatest public fame came when he accompanied Pierre Trudeau on his trip to China.

Reg, who has a bushy beard, had taken to wearing a tiny peaked Mao cap, which indeed gave him a startling resemblance to Karl Marx. At the welcoming ceremony for the Canadian Prime Minister, Zhou Enlai, Mao's second in command, noticed Reg in the front rank of photographers, and exclaiming, "That man looks just like

Karl Marx!" He came over to Reg and chatted, and then posed for pictures with him, which appeared in newspapers all over the world. A smug, smiling Reg Innell and a delighted Zhou Enlai upstaged Trudeau and adorned the front page of the *Star*. Reg, never overburdened with modesty, considered it only his due.

As a bachelor, Reg lived in a basement apartment in Yorkville, the only window completely covered by a blow-up of one of his photos of the Beatles from their first Toronto concert. Reg claimed this was a very effective attraction for the young women who frequented Yorkville in those days. He also boasts of providing free publicity photos for one of the young female singers who started in the Yorkville coffee houses in the sixties—Joni Mitchell.

As the assignment photo editor at the *Star,* he invariably assigned himself to meet whichever visiting celebrity interested him. He invariably met the literary ones, and I have been slowly acquiring some of those photos by a combination of flattery, whining, and even payment over the years. Reg usually refuses to sell his work in spite of the endless queries I receive regularly from people who see the portraits I have hanging in the shop of Auden, Leonard Cohen, Aldous Huxley, and John Fowles. Once, when Jake Zeitlin was visiting Toronto, he came in with Stillman Drake and seeing the one of Huxley (whom he knew well) acknowledged that it was the finest photographic portrait of Huxley he'd ever seen. When Jake turned eighty I managed to wheedle a copy of that photo from Reg and presented it to Jake. Jake loved it. I never told him of the humiliation and shameless begging I had to stoop to to get Reg to part with it.

Reg often made life difficult for booksellers too. He would become quite angry with booksellers who were as much as five minutes late in opening their stores, especially the hapless Norm Hart, who was habitually late opening, as was Joyce Blair at Abelard.

The rest of us became quite sick of Reg's impassioned lectures on the iniquities of people who posted shop hours but didn't keep them precisely. Reg's wife and daughter refused to even enter public stores with Reg because any lapse in decorum would arouse his acute sense of propriety and he would demand to see the manager, whom he would then berate about proper business practices, grossly embarrassing Reg's womenfolk.

In spite of Reg's difficult personality he and I became close friends, and when he retired from the *Star* he came to work with me, running the store himself on Sundays and with me on Saturdays. We continued also, until his recent health problems, to go on scouting trips together. Reg has a wonderful library which he refers to as a "workingman's" library, by which he means not that it reflects the working classes but that it was built by a workingman on a workingman's salary. A good loyal socialist workingman, too, and no one was ever allowed to forget it.

Reg's original great love was Shelley, more for his personality, I have always believed, than his poetry—by which I mean it was Shelley's defiant atheism which Reg loved most. Whenever some hapless young man, enamored of Reg's lovely daughter, would come courting he would be greeted at the door by a scowling Reg who would first demand to know if the young man was a believer.

But Reg's interests were much deeper than that. His obsession with Shelley was gradually transferred to Hazlitt, the essayist. It has never been necessary for me to seriously immerse myself in Hazlitt because Reg has bombarded me with countless quotations (these days mailed in letters, for, like me, he disdains that ubiquitous upstart, the computer). But several shared passions—Clarence Darrow, T.E. Lawrence, George Orwell and Mark Twain amongst others—indicates some shared heroes and probably hints at why we became such close friends. His passion for William Morris is also deep, although it is more attuned to the philosophy—he never had the money to indulge himself by buying the Kelmscott Press editions. No doubt he could have in the early years, but he probably felt his other passions would suffer if he did.

But Reg's greatest passion is arguably for one book, Robert Burton's *Anatomy of Melancholy*. If Reg has a favourite book it would have to be that one. It became a great joke in our shop that no matter what book some innocent seeker might inquire after, within five minutes Reg would be passionately selling them one of the many editions of Burton's *Melancholy*. We found it almost impossible to keep it in stock due to Reg's belief that his mandate in life is to save the world by introducing the young to Burton's genius. Burton and good old-fashioned English socialism would be our salvation, if only we could see it.

His colleagues at the *Star* had many stories of his outrageous behaviour, but I have thousands; like the very famous Hollywood star who, posing for Reg, said, "I think I'll take this pose," only to be curtly ordered by Reg to shut up. "You may be some big deal in those movies," he said, "but here I'm the professional. You'll do what I tell you and you'll pose as I tell you to, or there'll be no bloody picture for you." She obeyed (I think it was Jane Fonda, but it might have been Audrey Hepburn). Reg did, and does, swell with pleasure whenever someone describes him as an outrageous curmudgeon.

I have literally hundreds of anecdotes about my old friend— my favourite scouting one having nothing to do about books.

One day some years ago Reg and I headed down to Hamilton to do the bookstores. Half-way there Reg exclaimed, "Bloody hell, we're almost out of gas," turning into the first gas station.

"It's some sort of bleeding self-serve place," he said, outraged. "I never use those, I need someone to do it. Do you know how to load it up?" he said apprehensively.

I didn't drive then, and I was equally ignorant. "No, I don't, Reg. But we're grown men, surely we can figure it out. I see women doing it all the time," I said confidently.

We formed a plan. Reg would put the nozzle in (surely all that experience, what with the Beatle's photo in his Yorkville window, would have taught him that), and I would monitor the panel so we would know when to stop. It seemed to be sensible.

Reg opened all the little caps, inserted the nozzle, then said, "Okay, it's a go."

I pressed the lever, my back to the car while I watched the dials.

The panel numbers began to rotate when Reg bellowed, "Bloody hell! Outrageous!"

I turned. Gasoline was spraying out all over Reg. He was wearing a good camel hair topcoat and by the time I turned he was already completely soaked in gasoline: his coat, face, hair, beard. He had not pushed the nozzle past the small protective cover of the tank, instead placing it up against the plate and almost half a gallon of gas sprayed him before he had the sense to yell so I would release my grip on the pump. He was deeply affronted and even more so when I couldn't control my laughter.

But he calmed down and the gas, which had looked like it had destroyed his expensive coat ("Serves you right," I couldn't help saying. "Who ever heard of a socialist in a camel-hair coat?") finally evaporated, leaving only the odor.

We continued to Hamilton. In the first bookstore we entered the stench of gasoline first frightened, then confused the owner. When we explained, he promptly ordered all his other customers to put out their cigarettes (this anecdote occurred in more civil times). "There's important books and stuff here," he stated. "We don't want to be burning down the bookstore, do we?" As a good bookseller he was more concerned about his books than he was about Reg and me.

In another store we were almost kicked out. The proprietor thought we were rummies who must be sniffing something. We explained, but only my business card saved us from expulsion. We were looking at shelves in the rear of the store when a man entered, sniffed and started yelling, "I smell gas. Fire! Fire! It's going to explode. Call 9-1-1! Get out!"

The proprietor calmed him.

"It's okay. It's only those two guys over there." The man ran out anyway.

So, what you have here are two modern men, their homes bulging with books, the records of man's triumph over nature and ignorance and stupidity, who can't even manage between them to fill the gas tank of an automobile.

Just as with the regular customers, bookstore employees tend to become friends, and when they go out on their own, equals, valued colleagues.

Reading Sheila Markham's wonderful *A Book of Booksellers* one sees clearly the incredible network of apprenticeships, a clear indication of how intertwined the history and the workings of the book trade are and always have been.

It also demonstrates the serendipitous manner in which so many booksellers found their vocation.

One of Markham's interviews, which missed the cut for the book, contains perhaps my favourite description of how so many dealers have entered the trade.

It is with a bookseller I don't know named Fern Poel, and begins: "I'm just like any other misfit in the trade. At some point you become unemployable and end up going into your hobby."

Amen.

CHAPTER 18

Crooks and Cranks

The book business has always sheltered many eccentric people of Honsberger's sort.

Though perhaps it's not that bookselling attracts the crazies so much as it is that long-term bookselling makes otherwise sane people crazy. I use crazy here because most booksellers don't fit my personal definition of eccentric. If you are rich, you can pass as eccentric; if you're poor, you will be viewed as crazy. Whatever the definition used there are lots of noticeably strange people in the book trade, one of its more endearing aspects. My own opinion is the more the merrier.

Booksellers are often loners; bookish loners, with strong opinions and usually very independent characters, and as they get older, often very cranky ones.

There's something about spending many years starving to death, offering the great works of civilization to people who don't give a damn—while the friends one started out with become affluent or at the very least secure—to make a man take refuge in his own view of his social importance. There's a great sense of freedom which comes with having nothing to lose, and when you mix that with having read thousands of books, by and about the innovators, rebels, and misfits of every sort and the geniuses who have left us so many stunning examples of creativity, moral courage, and obstinate defiance, it's not surprising that the result will often be a cranky eccentric who doesn't really care if you buy a book or not.

I was once in a bookstore in New York on the day before the New York fair, a shop which gradually filled up with visiting booksellers wanting to buy books. It was early morning, pouring rain outside, and the two elderly proprietors were viewing the hoard of hungry scouts with increasing suspicion and truculence.

One whole wall was covered with a clear plastic drape, protecting their latest catalogue—just being printed we were informed. The old men in charge didn't like all this activity, we could tell: dealers greeting old friends loudly, water dripping from the new arrivals, the anticipation of great buys causing a lot of boisterous enthusiasm. We waited to see which of us would have the temerity to ask to explore the stock behind the plastic curtain. A friend of mine saw on the proprietor's desk the very scarce and very desirable five-volume catalogue of the George Arents Collection on Tobacco now in the New York Public Library.

"Is that for sale?" he courteously inquired of the old man who was eyeing him suspiciously.

"This is a bookstore isn't it?" the crusty proprietor replied.

Even more politely my friend inquired, "May I ask how much it is?"

"It's $450.00," the proprietor barked, glaring at my friend.

"I'm a bookseller, you know," my friend said gently, knowing the proprietors were aware that everyone in the store was a bookseller, but stating that just so there would be no doubt that he expected the customary trade discount.

"It'll be 20%," the man said, now noticeably angry.

"I'll take it," said my friend.

The owner softened a bit, but not much. A nice sale assured, my friend, feeling he had established his credentials as a serious man, notched things up.

"Could I take a look under the plastic, at the new catalogue?" he essayed tentatively.

"No," said the old man bluntly. "And in fact we're closing now—for lunch. You'll all have to leave." It was about 10 AM.

And with that he threw us all out into the downpour, around fifteen dealers, hungry for books and with our bank accounts still full of money. Many potential sales lost, but they didn't care. No noisy, snotty young punks were going to get away with such pushy tactics in *their* store. There was no way they were going to let us get away with giving them $20,000.00 or $30,000.00. My friend paid for the Arents (he sold it an hour later to another colleague for $750.00) and we slunk out. We all knew better than to protest at such arbitrary craziness; there was probably not a one of us who hadn't done a similar thing for equally stupid reasons, defying normal economic sense, although certainly not with quite those financial consequences. We'll sell the books to someone else sooner or later, they no doubt felt. We didn't starve for fifty years to put up with those smart-alecky punks now that it no longer matters.

And this sort of behaviour is not uncommon either, perhaps another of the many reasons booksellers die broke.

From Barry Young—my first employer, selling new books, who, "on principle," would spend all day in court fighting $2.00 parking tickets while he paid me $3.00 an hour to mind his shop—to Norm Hart, who drove the owner of Acadia, Asher Joram, near-crazy by ignoring the posted hours of 10 AM to 6 PM, arriving later every day until *his* personal hours were from around 4 PM until midnight or so—bookstore owners are often as eccentric as their scouts and customers. Once Norm was found in the shop at opening but only because late the previous night, reaching for a book on a shelf in a narrow back hallway, he'd pulled the entire shelf off the wall, burying himself in books. Pinned to the floor by the shelf but entirely unhurt, Norm spent the whole night there, the shop lit up, the door unlocked, his only complaint that he was buried in books but couldn't read one because of the weight pinning him. Naturally, no one bothered to enter the unlocked store the entire night, for even burglars know the futility of bothering to rob a used bookstore.

Norm also had formed the habit of falling madly in love with his female customers and would give his latest obsession huge discounts, which naturally infuriated Asher.

Norm had a tiny locked room in the basement of Acadia where he kept treasures while he "checked them out." Since he was far too lazy to actually do any research, this usually meant that things would sit in the locked room for years, until he got sick of looking at them. When he finally did price an item which he had believed to be rare, it might still be very cheap, since his lazy obstinacy ensured that he had learned nothing new in so long that his feel for things was hopelessly out of date.

That's what happened with the legendary pamphlet. One day he showed a pamphlet to Jerry Sherlock, an eight page delicate paper sheaf with a crude woodcut engraving on the cover, the author using a pseudonym. It was dated Toronto, 1852. He, of course, was showing it to Jerry in hopes that Jerry would tell him what it was and perhaps price it for him. Naturally, Jerry wasn't about to succumb to this ploy; he wanted to have it and he knew if he said too much Norm would put an impossible price on it, just to show Jerry he wasn't a fool. "This must be very rare, Jerry. I've never seen it. Have you?" said Norm, fishing.

"No, I haven't, Norm. What do you want for it?" Jerry replied.

"Oh, I'm checking it out. I don't know yet."

"Well, when you price it can I have first refusal?" said Jerry, giving nothing away.

Jerry knew Norm's eccentricities and he knew he had to be careful. If he showed too much interest the price would escalate. Jerry knew that it had to be quite valuable. 1852 for a humourous pamphlet with a woodcut was pretty early for Toronto.

The city was then eighteen years old and almost anything from that early date, especially such a delicate production, would be rare and valuable. Jerry did his own homework, but discovered only one thing. Completely unknown to every bibliography and history, it was unrecorded, a bookseller's dream. Unrecorded means that the price is limited only by the dealer's imagination.

A humourous political satire with a woodcut illustration and published under a pseudonym. It could have been written by some later famous person or could libel some prominent citizen, making it valuable on several levels.

Jerry would, every two months or so (more often might give Norm a clue), go to Acadia and casually inquire, in passing, if Norm had priced the pamphlet yet.

"Still checking, Jerry," would answer Norm.

Jerry was forced to bite his tongue—he knew all the checking in the world was not going to result in anything, and the pamphlet's value had by now risen to quite a level in his head.

After a year of this Jerry lost patience with Norm's bull-headedness and took a chance.

"Norm, forget it. You won't find a price for it. I'll give you $100.00 for it right now."

Norm was shocked, as $100.00 was a lot of money then, the equivalent of $2,000.00 or $3,000.00 today.

"Okay, I'll sell it to you for that. Come on."

They went to the basement, Norm unlocked the secret room and then the locked drawer, and there was what remained of the rare pamphlet—a few pitiful scraps of paper, chewed to pieces. The mice had eaten it.

Jerry told me that he almost cried. An artifact of early Toronto history, hitherto unseen and unknown and now destroyed by mice and by Norm Hart's obstinacy.

David Mason

And it's still unknown—no other copy having appeared in the fifty years since.

Norm's eccentricities were exacerbated by some kind of combined neatness/cleanliness compulsion. He'd spend hours spraying and wiping every paperback and dust jacket with Windex. Once I was there when someone accidentally spilled some coffee on the floor and Norm without even interrupting what he was saying got down on his knees with Windex and paper towels and scrubbed the floor. But his most irritating compulsions severely damaged books. He had the habit of taking any dust jacket which had any wear and clipping off the flap with the book's description, which he would then staple to the free endpaper, rendering first editions enormously less valuable because he'd destroyed the dust jacket and made permanent holes in the endpaper. And worse, he would clip off the corners of the endpapers, claiming the corner was soiled from too much rubbing-out of the penciled price. All these practices enraged those of us who dealt in modern firsts because it made those books seriously defective to a collector, and I would regularly threaten to complain to the ABAC about his depredations.

"They'll fine you, Norm. They'll throw you out for destroying books," I would tell him. This was, of course, a bluff, but Norm didn't care.

"The corners were soiled, Dave. You modern first guys are all nuts," he would reply. "Those books aren't worth your crazy prices anyway."

Finally, after many years of subjecting Asher to his eccentricities, Norm insisted on vacuuming the floor one day with a dozen or so customers waiting vainly to pay for books. Asher remonstrated with him and Norm quit on the spot, stomping out indignantly. Naturally, he returned to work the next day, pretending that nothing had occurred. But Asher had been waiting some years for just such a stroke of luck as this—for he was far too soft a man to fire Norm—and he refused to capitulate. He paid Norm off handsomely and Norm was forced to do what he had been threatening to do for years and open his own shop.

He was a good bookman but he chose a location which could hardly be found without a map, and that combined with his never showing up till four or five hours after his posted hours did him in.

His real weakness, though, was the horses, and that combined with his other eccentricities finally finished him. Norm was one of three people I've known who seriously contended that they could consistently win at the races, even though any sane person will tell you that Mario Puzo was right on the nose (pun intended) when he said that he didn't bet the horses because they were "Noble, lovable, and true, but controlled by men not so noble."

Norm spent his life waiting for his horse to win and died one step above the Sally Ann hostel. Of the other two believers, one was a schizophrenic and the other, a fairly well-known writer who suffered a few apparent criminal attacks, which always seemed to me to hint at the sort of things which happen to people who have borrowed money from the mob.

I believe Asher "loaned" Norm a considerable amount of money in later years. All the rest of us dealers loaned him money too, on the principle that after he owed us all $200.00 or $300.00 each, he would be too embarrassed to come around, and that's what happened. Somehow he lasted another few years, ending up living in a room above a strip bar where he would, I'm told, spend his days with a single beer, hopelessly in love with all the *artistes*.

Any account of the antiquarian book trade must deal with the subject of theft, a serious problem for all used booksellers.

But unlike what you might expect, the greatest problem is not what is stolen from us, but the books we are offered by thieves, who have stolen from our colleagues or from new bookstores.

There are various classes of thieves with which the antiquarian bookseller must contend. With many of the bookshops on Queen Street in its heyday, both new and used, the easiest ones to catch were the drunks and street hustlers who would steal from one bookstore and walk along the street to sell their loot to the next bookseller on the row. This is relatively easy to deal with, for when a ratty looking drunk or a near-illiterate brings in a pile of nice books it's not hard to figure out that something is wrong.

These street people conclude quickly that stealing is pretty easy. Part of the ethos of antiquarian bookselling dictates that we do not follow people around spying on them. Nor do we mount those convex mirrors or cameras, another result of our conviction that we have a more serious destiny, seeing ourselves as purveyors of civilization. Many dealers, and I am one of them, decided years ago that we would prefer to suffer the odd loss rather than lower ourselves to such a level.

The most dangerous thieves are the ones who steal because they want to own the book. Against them we are near powerless, unless we catch them in the act. Or unless some crisis causes them to try and sell their stolen books.

Something of that will be obvious in the following anecdote.

One day Steve Temple called. "I've been buying some books from so and so," he said, naming a young guy who was well-known to the Toronto trade, a frequent visitor who, like any young person who demonstrates enthusiasm, we had all spent a fair bit of time with, teaching and guiding. He bought regularly but carefully. He was a paramedic, so it wasn't so much that he was poor; his caution in buying was, it seemed, based on the natural caution that any intelligent neophyte uses while learning. That's why dealers spend so much time talking to such people. We see one of our primary tasks as educational, assuming our rewards will come later, commensurate with the increased sophistication that we help to instill.

"He's having a divorce and needs to raise some money," Temple said. "He's just offered me some books of a sort that he never showed any interest in. There's an early book on Angling in the last lot and when I looked in the back [many dealers code their costs on the last blank leaf] the code was in your handwriting. Did he ever ask you about fishing?"

I should add here that another of the ways we catch thieves is through their cover stories. Dealers in the same area become proficient in recognizing their colleague's handwriting. So when someone tells you that he inherited his grandfather's library (almost always another of the giveaways that the books are stolen) and one sees that the handwriting on the blank pages is that of a friend or colleague, suspicion is immediate.

"No," I said. "I'll check."

I checked, and found that the book had not been sold. I went over to Temple's and we examined the books. Others had marks in my hand and in those of several other dealers. Some might have been purchased but too many didn't fit his known interests. We reluctantly decided we had a thief on our hands. We were very upset. He was a nice guy, an enthusiast who we had, as usual, decided was one of the good ones and left pretty much alone in our shops.

He came to my store often on Sundays, and when I questioned Reg Innell, who ran my shop on Sundays, he recalled the seeming-coincidence that often our young friend would choose to leave the moment Reg was called to answer the telephone. It became apparent that our young man was a thief, and calls to several other dealers in town confirmed our suspicions.

Temple stopped payment on the cheque for the last lot purchased and phoned our culprit. He told him that a glitch at the bank had caused the stop-payment, and that if he came in the next day at 4:30 PM he would replace the cheque.

The next day the guy entered Temple's in his paramedic's uniform with his ambulance parked outside to be greeted by seven or eight dealers and two detectives from the Toronto Police force. Confronted, he confessed immediately, all the dealers watching in a silent contempt mixed with a certain sadness at this disturbing betrayal of our trust. Catching a thief whom you had thought to be a friend causes pain, similar to the destroying of trust which results from betrayal in friendship or marriage. As the police led him out in handcuffs he turned to us and in one of the most bizarre justifications I ever expect to hear said, "I just want you all to know—I only ever stole books."

What an incredible thing to say to an audience of booksellers! Did he mean that stealing only books meant he wasn't a thief? I'm still trying to figure that one out.

Off he went and the clean-up commenced. Of course, he lost his job since he now couldn't be bonded. We had several meetings with the Toronto police officers, who acted in a marvellous fashion, way beyond their legal mandate. What really impressed us was that, unlike in the past, they didn't dismiss book theft as though it was simple shoplifting; they understood that it was a serious problem, and a cultural problem which was becoming international.

More amusing was how our books were returned.

One of the detectives called one day to say they had all our books at 52 Division and we could come and claim what was ours. There had been a liaison with the police in Cape Breton, where our thief was from and had returned after his conviction, and where his ex-wife lived. All the books in her home had also been seized and they were shipped to the police here. It happened to be a holiday, so Debbie and I went up to 52 Division where we were shown several separate piles of books (we estimated there was $50,000.00 to $75,000.00 worth of books from the stocks of most of the Toronto dealers in those piles).

The detective explained that the thief, seeking to make amends or at least to mitigate his sentence, had separated them into piles denoting the separate stores he had stolen them from. We started to look through our designated pile.

"That's not ours," said Deb, "it's Temple's."

"Nor that," said I of the next one, "that's Acadia." And so on… "That's Gail Wilson's, that's About Books." We knew our colleagues' handwriting—one of the reasons we caught so many thieves.

We looked at Temple's pile—it contained several of our books, Debbie said to the cops. "This is a mess. You'd better bring in all the other dealers so we can sort this out."

"Oh no," said the detective, "we never do that. We used to do that with jewelry robberies, but we'd have ten jewelers in here all claiming that every piece of jewelry was theirs."

That won't happen, we assured him. He was clearly skeptical, but finally, reluctantly, he agreed. Within an hour there were ten dealers there sorting the piles. "That's not mine—I think it's yours," one would say, handing a book to another dealer. "Well, I think that's your writing," said another, passing another book from his pile to another dealer.

Within an hour we had all new piles, entirely different from the thief's sorting. Obviously he didn't remember what he'd stolen from whom. By this time we were encircled by an audience of about fifteen to twenty cops, all of whom were astounded that we were consistently rejecting valuable books saying they weren't ours. They could hardly believe it.

Even more amusing was their consternation when, at the end, there was a fairly large pile of books that none of us had claimed. Maybe they were legitimately owned by our thief, but nobody was claiming what wasn't theirs. The cops seemed quite impressed that none of us wanted to claim books which weren't ours. We all took great pleasure in so impressing them.

We suggested that they bring in other missing dealers who might be the owners. I believe that what was left over was subsequently auctioned at one of the periodic police sales.

There was a further addendum to this incident. Naturally, we circulated details of the thief throughout the entire Canadian trade, especially in Nova Scotia, where he was from. About eight months later I happened to be in Halifax visiting my son, who lived there, and as part of my duties I was trying to properly describe our thief to our colleagues there, in case he still thought his methods of collecting acceptable. Several thought they might know him, but were naturally being cautious, not wanting to condemn the wrong man. On a Saturday morning I was in Schooner Books trying to describe our thief to John Townsend and his assistant when who should I see through the front window walking up the path to Schooner's door but the thief.

"Well," I said, "forget my description. He's coming in the door right now."

The door opened, he came in, greeted John and his assistant warmly, and then saw me sitting there, gazing at him. He turned white, quickly turned and pretended to examine a bookshelf behind him. After a few seconds we continued our conversation. A couple of minutes later he quietly slunk out. For a couple of years after that I would monitor him whenever I spoke to Townsend, but of course he had not been seen again in any bookstore in eastern Canada.

It's a little sad—he really did love books. His mistake was in concluding that our casual trust was stupid and careless. He didn't realize that our treatment of him was based on our concept that we are civilized people. We take great pride in this system of assuming people are civilized until they give us reason to believe otherwise. And, sadly, what he also didn't realize was that like many people who like to confer trust on all we are ruthless when that trust is violated.

Jerry Sherlock was involved in a incident with stolen books during the time I worked for him. I don't believe that there has been a better example in my experience concerning the problems raised by theft.

The hardest thieves to catch are the ones who are intelligent and have a feasible cover story. One day at Joseph Patrick Books a young man introduced himself as a salesman who travelled throughout Ontario selling his employer's goods. Often, being early for appointments and being a history buff, he would explore the small towns he went to for used bookstores and Goodwill shops. His own interest, he said, was Ontario local history. Of the first lot he brought in Jerry bought about a third, and then spent some time as dealers do with a potential good scout explaining why he couldn't buy the rejects—too common, not very good, etc. etc. He was educating, as good dealers always do, both customers and scouts being easier to deal with when they become sophisticated. And the time spent coaching is part of the mandate of the truly professional dealer.

The next lot the young man brought in contained a higher percentage of decent books, and Jerry bought half of them and continued with the teaching. But by the third or fourth lot 80-90% of the books were desirable ones. Jerry became suspicious.

"Nobody learns that fast, Dave. And nobody finds books that good by chance in some small-town Goodwill," he said. (That was certainly true for me; I didn't know which Canadian books were ordinary or desirable myself after months working for Jerry.)

His suspicions aroused, Jerry started examining all the books he had bought.

He found a good Ontario history book with the signature on the title of Andrew Hunter, a local historian who had written the best history of Simcoe county, indicating it had been his copy. Jerry started making calls to find out what had happened to Hunter's library after his death. Eventually we ascertained that Hunter had willed it to the Ontario Historical Society. Jerry phoned there.

Yes, they had received his library, but they couldn't identify his books because apparently they didn't have their books catalogued. Jerry mentioned the young scout's name. There was silence on the other end.

"He works for us part-time. But surely he can't be stealing. He's such a nice young man. In fact, his father is a Protestant minister and also a member of the Ontario Legislature, a Minister in that government, in fact."

"You'd better send someone down here to look at the books," replied Jerry, now certain we had caught a thief.

Jerry and I spent the whole day going through the stock trying to reassemble all the books bought. In spite of the trouble, we were pleased with ourselves. We had caught on, in spite of his clever front, done the detective work ourselves and stopped a dangerous thief fairly early.

The next day a delegation from the Ontario Historical Society appeared, three elderly men.

I was first astounded, then enraged, by their behaviour. They treated Jerry with barely concealed contempt. It was obvious that they considered him on a level with a criminal himself. These old fools, no doubt retired or amateur historians, seemed unable to comprehend that Jerry had saved their books and had done it all himself. If he wasn't completely honest and very smart these thefts would have continued indefinitely, but they acted as though he were himself implicated.

I was furious, but when I said something to Jerry afterwards he just shrugged. "They can't help it, Dave. They have to blame someone and they don't want to blame themselves for not cataloguing their books or protecting them properly. So they make me the scapegoat for their lapses. And they're probably all friends of the guy's father, anyway."

Jerry was always saying things like that. Someone would commit some particularly despicable act and Jerry would say, "They can't help it, Dave. They weren't lucky enough to have a proper upbringing like we had." Jerry said that a lot; he believed that parents were responsible for the moral education of their children, something which he and his wife took very seriously. I have spent some forty-odd years being amazed by Jerry. One of the greatest ironies to me is that most of Jerry's brothers were priests— one of them a bishop—and his two sisters were very active in lay capacities in the church. But Jerry, who often joked that he was considered in his family to be the classic non-achiever—in ordinary terms, a loser—remains the single most Christian Christian I have ever met.

The young man was arrested, confessed and received a suspended sentence, a very common treatment for book thieves then—and now, even though thousands of dollars worth of books were involved. But I learned another of those important lessons which all booksellers need to learn early. We must protect our own reputations; it will be assumed by many that we welcome the opportunity to buy stolen books. I learned to be always suspicious, to check out people who offer good books, and to ask subtle questions to entrap the nefarious.

We had a collector in Toronto, a man called Darwin Yarish. He was very passionate about books, having formed a very important collection relating to Walt Whitman, and another on Irish literature, and had been one of my earliest customers, one of the very few long-term ones from my Gerrard Street days. Darwin was very intense about books. I had had a problem with him early on because his job as some sort of technician in the University of Toronto library didn't pay a lot and he wanted all my best books. Like many of my young customers Darwin got to pay off his purchases over time, so much a month, which he always did. But my problem arose when he wanted to buy the three best books I owned, not hugely valuable then, but still, the only three really good books I owned, and in the context of those years worth a not insignificant amount.

"Darwin, I can't let you take them all, it will take you three years to pay for them; in the meantime I don't have the books and I don't have the money. I'm too small to let my best things go out of circulation and with no money to replace them. I'm too small and it's not fair. You'll have to buy each one after you've paid off the last one, if they are still here."

Darwin was angry. He acted like I was being unreasonable, a warning sign that I was dealing with a man whose lust for books was barely under control, if it ever had been.

Sometime after that I was having a drink with a librarian friend, Beth Miller, then the special collections librarian at the University of Western Ontario. I must have recounted that amusing anecdote and I must have mentioned his name, because a few days later I got a letter from Beth, an indication of how astute and professional she was, enclosing an article from an archivist's professional magazine which related that a library worker from the University of Windsor had been arrested, accused, and found guilty of the theft of some extremely valuable Herman Hesse manuscripts from an institutional library in Michigan.

Beth's note read "David, the name you mentioned the other day struck a bell. Could this man be your customer?" The thief's name was Darwin Yarish, and his defense on his arrest sounded eerily similar to Darwin's attitude to my three best books. He wasn't even slightly repentant. Rather, he justified his theft by contending that he, not the library, deserved to own those manuscripts because he revered them. He appreciated Hesse's greatness and he was just liberating them from philistines. A classic justification, one not uncommon from a pathological thief.

Darwin had escaped unscathed because the American library offered a deal. Extradition, if fought, would be very expensive and might take years. Darwin gave back the manuscripts and they didn't pursue extradition.

But, by now, *my* dilemma became apparent. I knew Darwin worked in the area at the University of Toronto where books entered the system before they were processed. In other words, in an area where books could go missing with no record of them having been a part of the collection. What was I to do? The University of Toronto was my major client; I already did a lot of work for them and sold them many books. And here was a known thief working in one of the most sensitive places in the library. And to make my dilemma even more complex, I liked Darwin. He was a true book lover, and to bring in economics again, he was a good customer. And it wasn't like he was a wanted man. He had discharged his legal obligations by relinquishing the manuscripts. I knew that if I reported him he would be fired, and that I would be responsible. While one could not contend that he had paid his debt to society, he had at least mitigated it.

What if he had learned his lesson? And here I was wondering if I had the obligation—or even the right—to ruin his life.

I agonized over my moral dilemma for several days, spending at least two sleepless nights trying to resolve my moral question. I finally managed to deal with it by thinking about it from a reversed viewpoint.

If the positions were reversed, I decided, if I had a known thief in my place and the university knew it and didn't inform me, I knew that I would never forgive them. Put in that light, it would be a betrayal on some basic level, and I now knew what I must do.

I phoned David Esplin.

"David," I began "I have a very unpleasant duty to perform. I have come into information that you have a convicted thief working in a very vulnerable place in your library system. I felt I had to inform you of that."

There was a long pause, then Esplin said, "Are his initials D.Y.?"

"Yes."

"We are monitoring him," said Esplin.

You son-of-a-bitch, I thought. I torture myself for a whole week and finally do the right thing, even as I despise myself as a snitch, and you guys knew all along.

I was starting to understand how huge institutions work. In fact, that's also how governments work too, as we all learn if we're around long enough. Don't make a fuss; don't rock the boat.

I've never accepted that and I hope I never will. But at least my moral dilemma reverted back to their moral dilemma, and I was left with the compensation that at least I had acted properly. Once again my father, the silly banker, was right. *We* know and it doesn't matter what others think.

And in the end I didn't assign to Esplin the contempt I might have had if his methods had offered serious threat to the local book trade. Maybe, I decided, he was trying himself to give Darwin a second chance. Wouldn't it be nice to think so?

Darwin Yarish later became a bookseller, and a good one. He died of AIDS some years after that. I still admire his passion for books, no matter how aberrant.

And now my favourite theft story.

One day a young man came into my Church Street store with four books he wanted to sell. He was a young black kid, a teenager, with a backpack. The books he wanted to sell weren't books in the usual sense—only one of them was.

That one was a facsimile of an illuminated thirteenth-century manuscript produced in France in the 1880s. The French love such things, but I find them unimpressive. I once went to an exhibition of some of William Blake's original and hand-coloured books, which changed my view of art books forever. The Trianon Press was founded in Paris to reproduce, with the best modern techniques, William Blake's original hand-coloured books. They produced some lovely books, but compared to the originals they are insignificant.

No copy can capture the life that is in original art. At best a copy reminds you of the original. The copy can perhaps bring back the emotion you felt viewing the original, but it is a poor substitute for the real thing.

There has been a lot of this done in the twentieth century, printing facsimile copies of early illuminated books, but they all seem bland to me, like an unspiced meal.

So impressed was I by the originals that shortly after seeing the Blake exhibit, I stopped dealing in art books almost entirely.

But the other three books the young man showed me were the real thing. They were original illuminated manuscripts from the thirteenth to the fifteenth century, in beautiful contemporary bindings, stunning in their beauty, with rich primary colours and gilt illumination on the vellum leaves.

I not only had never owned one before, I had never even handled one, every one I had seen being in some exhibition or other. I did have some single leaves framed, at home. One can still buy single leaves from these magnificent examples of medieval art. While some single leaves are very expensive, nice examples can still be found in the $500.00 to $1,000.00 range, pretty cheap for a beautiful example of real medieval art. For years I have found them perfect as wedding presents for family or friends, for their beauty seems to affect everyone and the religious subjects make them appropriate gifts for such solemn rituals.

One can also buy single pages from famous editions of books, like a page of the Gutenberg Bible (which will cost a lot), or the King James Bible (1603), The Nurenberg Chronicle (1493), or a page from the first printing of a Shakespeare play, and these provide for book lovers a tiny reminder of these great monuments to civilization. They are very impressive framed. And, of course, early maps taken out of atlases and framed also make great wall decoration.

The complete manuscripts this young man had were small but magnificent. I knew at once that they were stolen; they had to be. I had no idea what they might be worth, but guessed thousands of dollars each, maybe much more, many thousands more.

He seemed a nice kid, friendly, even naïve. I could tell he hadn't a clue of their value and I knew I could probably buy them for a couple of hundred dollars. But where had he gotten them?

"How do you come to have these?"

"My aunt gave them to me," he replied.

Now I was certain they were stolen; books described as gifted by aunts, uncles and grandparents are always assumed in the trade to be stolen, and almost always are.

"Where was this?" I asked.

"In Kentucky, Lexington Kentucky, where I'm from."

I was still certain of their status, but this kid was too open and nice; he didn't fit the profile of the thief whose lies under questioning usually become obvious.

"Why are you here?" I asked.

"I'm travelling, seeing Canada. I'm hitch-hiking around," he replied.

"Well, these books are valuable. I'd need time to study them, do some research before I can offer you a proper price."

If I'd been more certain that he was a thief I would have simply held them and called the police in front of him, but he still didn't fit any of the profiles I knew, so I asked him where he was staying and suggested he return with them tomorrow so I could properly research and make an offer.

He was staying at the Central YMCA he said, where apparently they put mattresses in the gym so transient kids like him could spend a few days in Toronto during the summer months.

He agreed, left, and I called the police.

As it happened, the Toronto police headquarters was then at the top of Jarvis Street, a block from my store. In fact, I had become friendly with several detectives from there who would drop in on their lunch hour to look at books. I phoned and they sent over a detective. I gave him all the details, explaining these manuscripts were too important and too rare to be unrecorded. It was not possible that they weren't stolen and it seemed inconceivable that Interpol or the FBI or the RCMP wouldn't have a record of their reported loss. He made notes, took a description of both of the books and the kid, and left. Returning the next day he said he had checked with the F.B.I. and Interpol—there were no missing manuscripts reported.

In the meantime the police had gone to the YMCA where the kid was staying and interviewed him. (Well, I thought, that certainly puts a finish to any hopes I had of buying them if they had turned out to be legit; he wouldn't come back to me after I had turned him in.)

The kid had claimed that his aunt, a cleaning lady, had been given them by a client after her husband, the owner, died. A likely story.

All this happened in a small town outside of Lexington and the cop didn't think in the absence of any reported theft that he could justify calling the police in Lexington and asking them to travel all the way out there with no hard evidence.

I was upset.

"The thing is, these have to be stolen," I said, "If not in America, then the most likely place would be Britain or the continent."

In those days the international booksellers had not yet set up the sophisticated system we have now to trace theft, but I decided that normal trade gossip would mean that appropriate members of the British trade would know if they were stolen.

"But I don't have authorization to be phoning all over the world (this was in the days before we all phoned everywhere, every day) just because you think they might be stolen," the cop said.

"I understand that," I said. "But I have a moral obligation to follow this up. If they were my books I would expect any book-seller anywhere to do what's necessary. I'll phone Britain myself and make inquiries."

I could see the cop was upset. Here's a citizen who has been told that there's a limit to what the police can do, accepts it, but says he'll do it himself, at his own expense. I could also see that he was impressed by my refusal to let it go.

"Listen," he said, "hold off for a day or two. I'll see what I can do."

He came back the next day.

"I got permission from my boss to have you call England."

We made an appointment, I came to the station and called Charles Traylen, the only big English dealer I'd had any dealings with. I told Traylen the details. The cop who had examined them had written out a pretty good description of their physical appearance. I joked that if he ever wanted a second career he could probably get a job cataloguing rare books.

Traylen didn't recall any gossip about stolen manuscripts, but he said he would check the grapevine and get back to us. He did a few days later reporting there was no record of any stolen manuscripts.

Before I left the detective told me that his boss, the superintendent, wanted to meet me. I guess that they didn't often get people who insisted on pursuing a solution to stolen goods which didn't concern them personally.

His boss turned out to be Adolphus Payne, famous for having captured the Boyd Gang, who had robbed a lot of banks, killed a police detective, been captured, and twice escaped from the Don Jail. Payne's detective work had located Boyd, who ended up getting twenty years while the men who shot Detective Sergeant Edmund Tong were hanged. Payne shook hands, congratulating me for being persistent.

"You don't remember me, do you?" I said to Payne.

"No, should I?" he said.

I explained that I had grown up three doors down from him on Elm Road, and that his son Doug had been one of my pals in our little neighbourhood gang of friends, until we moved away when I was thirteen. He wouldn't recognize a kid he hadn't seen for twenty some years, but the name clicked. We had a nice conversation, bringing our mutual family histories up to date. His son, my old pal, had become a Mountie and lived out west. And then to compound all these coincidences he told me that his wife had recently inherited some old books they had no interest in, and he asked if I wanted to view them. So a few days later I went up to his house, met his wife again (who as a policeman's wife had often lectured our group as children, warning us of predators and such things). And they had some good books which I bought.

But that wasn't the end of it.

About two months later the original detective came into my store one day.

"I couldn't get that puzzle out of my mind," he began. "I couldn't let it go, so I finally asked my boss for permission to check out that kid's story. I phoned Louisville and they sent a detective out to his town to check it out.

"They questioned the kid's aunt and he checked out. The whole story the kid gave us is true. The aunt remembered very clearly. She was a cleaning lady and one of her clients was a wealthy doctor. The doctor had died and the cleaner told us that the doctor's wife hated her husband's books so much that she wanted them right out of the house, at once. She had given the whole pile of them to her cleaner. The aunt remembered them so clearly because they were all pretty picture books with all sorts of bright colours and gold in the pictures.

"But the reason she really remembered them was because one of her daughters was retarded and very difficult to amuse. She had given the largest book, which was also the prettiest one, to this child, hoping it would keep her quiet for a while. And it worked. The child was amused for several days. She cut out all sorts of pretty scenes of ladies with wings and angels with halos and stuff and pasted them into a scrapbook."

But I hope you have noticed that while I've been recounting stories of cranks and crooks I've not mentioned any crooked dealers, and that's because I have encountered surprisingly few crooks in the trade.

They do show up from time to time, but they are quickly recognized in a trade where the gossip is as international as the trade, and they seldom last long.

In spite of saying that, at least two long-term Canadian booksellers I know of were so crooked as to measure up (or down) to any of the crooks the rest of the book world has ever produced. In case you suspect I exaggerate, one of these men went to jail for stealing books from several libraries in New England. This man, whose name was Borden Clarke, was one of the great characters in the trade, whom I unfortunately never met. He was the proprietor of Old Authors Farm, and there were many stories about him. Whenever you bought books from him in person you had to pack them and remove them at once. If you allowed him to pack your boxes, which he always offered to do, when you got home you'd find entirely different books in the boxes. His catalogues were prefaced with grammatically near-illiterate editorials extolling, not just his books, but his sterling personal qualities. Sometimes, in old magazine articles I've exhumed, he offered elaborate justifications for his unjust incarceration. If you ordered a book you might or might not get the book you thought you were ordering, and it might or might not be the first edition as he described it. It could easily be an entirely different book and in the book club edition, but Borden Clarke would always have a glib explanation. If you complained that you had no interest in the copy of some nineteenth-century clergyman's pompous sermons on the origins of the world that he'd sent instead of the important book you'd ordered, Borden would counter that this man was considered Darwin's most dangerous opponent.

One of Clarke's most famous ploys was to have printed bookplates or rubber stamps made up which he would affix to otherwise worthless books and then sell them as part of some famous person's library. We still see the occasional rubber-stamped ownership of Hannibal Hamlin, the American Vice-President under Abraham Lincoln. The only feasible explanation I can think of as to why he would produce Hamlin's when, had he raised it a notch and done one for Abraham Lincoln, it would have been very lucrative, was because he must have at sometime bought part of Hamlin's library, so he would have a justification for having so many of his books. It was probably a great way to get rid of unsaleable junk.

For Canadians, the most dangerous of Borden's depredations was when he reprinted Sir John A. Macdonald's bookplate, affixing it in his unsaleable Canadian books. I think he may also be responsible for another ownership rubber stamp one still occasionally sees, that of Sir Sandford Fleming, although I have no proof for that one. No one today, except a fool, would add a penny to the price for a Hannibal Hamlin bookplate, but Sir John A. Macdonald is a different story. Sir John's bookplate will increasingly command large premiums on any book where it is found, and the problem is compounded by the fact that MacDonald was a reader, had a library and did indeed have two or three different bookplates that I know of.

In fact, I have in my own library an important book, the first collected edition of Edgar Allan Poe's *Works* in four volumes (New York, 1849), all of which contain Macdonald's bookplates and in two different versions.

I paid quite a bit for this set from a collector who, like me, believed it important, and even though I knew that every Macdonald bookplate should be treated with great skepticism, I myself succumbed for the same reason that dealers and collectors are at such risk when faced with the forgeries which increasingly are appearing in rare book circles. I chose to believe it was real because I wanted it to be real. And it *is* real—at least until I die—for since I won't be ever selling it, I am justified in believing that I own the first collected edition of Poe owned by Canada's first Prime Minister. Another problem for Debbie to deal with when I'm gone.

For many years I have been acquiring as I find them Borden Clarke's catalogues. They were printed on cheap newspaper stock, and I suspect not many had survived. Recently however, I bought a pretty good archive of material relating to Clarke, not just a good run of his catalogues, but considerable correspondence, well demonstrating his nefarious methods, and numerous articles about his activities, wherein he ludicrously extolled his virtues when he got to supply the details to some naïve journalist. But some of the articles do give details of his thefts and incarceration.

Clarke began most of his catalogues soliciting people to simply ship him all those old books from their barn or their father's library, and it seems many people did. There is considerable correspondence in my archive from people he blatantly cheated. Mostly, he never paid any of these people, who innocently shipped him books, and his elaborate justifications for those thefts are very amusing (except, of course, to the people that he cheated). Later on his editorials consisted of attempts to sell his business, the greatest in all of Christendom according to him. Part of his pitch included the offer to train worthy buyers. I would love to know what he asked for it but that was never mentioned.

For quite some time now Old Author's Farm has been owned and run by a quite reputable couple. I expect they bought it after Clarke's death and I guess they would be embarrassed to know all the old stories about Clarke. Only the earliest surviving members of the Canadian trade will have met Clarke; most of the current dealers, including me, never met him. Most of what I know of him comes from the stories of Jerry Sherlock, Grant Woolmer, Phil McCready and Marty Ahvenus, all either retired or dead. So Borden moves into the realm of legend, along with the other famous fraud artist: Raymond Arthur Davies.

Davies, another of the several capitalistic communists I have met and another who would undoubtedly be immediately eliminated if the revolution were to triumph, was a fraud artist of international stature.

Like many of those men, he was brilliant. He not only dealt in books, he wrote several books himself from a far-left slant. I had always wondered if he was a party member or just a fellow traveller, until I recently saw a letter written by a party official warning other members that Davies had no right to use the party letterhead for his personal business, so I guess Davies was a member. Because of his connections, he must have travelled in high circles in the Soviet Union, and when that empire collapsed he found some way to gain access to the libraries of Russian institutions, where he purchased runs of obscure Russian periodicals which he then brought back and sold to North American institutions, where they were much sought-after. There were, however, a couple of problems with this ostensibly clever system. First, Davies would sell them as complete runs, thereby cheating the buyers who paid big prices for what had been described as complete, when they weren't. And when he got paid for them he never paid the Russians, thereby cheating both parties in the transaction. He didn't seem to be concerned that the KGB might come after him, perhaps because he usually had the Mafia after him for money he had borrowed from loan sharks and had not repaid.

Jerry Sherlock told me that every time he entered Davies' office Davies would try to borrow money from him pleading that "the Mob" was threatening to break his legs. When that didn't work he would then try to borrow less, claiming he had no money to feed his kids. Jerry was pretty sure he didn't even have kids. Jerry told me that on one trip to Davies' office, Davies, in desperation, offered him a very substantial discount if he bought a large amount. So Jerry did, spending about $1,500.00 on some important communist material. Just as Jerry finished writing out the cheque the office door opened, Davies' secretary entered (she must have been spying through the keyhole, Jerry thought) took the cheque from Jerry's hand and said, "Thanks. I'll just take that. This man hasn't paid me in two months." And she then left to cash it at the bank.

Davies, of course, then tearfully tried to borrow money from Jerry, but Jerry knew the game and told Davies that the cheque the secretary had taken was every cent he had in the bank.

You also couldn't phone Davies because his phone was usually disconnected for non-payment.

Davies entered my Queen Street store one day in the eighties, unaware that I knew who he was, and handed me his business card. We chatted for a half an hour or so. Like most accomplished conmen, he was extremely charming and had wonderful anecdotes, which were always fascinating, even when one knew that they might not be true.

After half an hour of this he prepared to leave, shook my hand warmly, and then casually added, as though he'd just remembered, "Oh, by the way, I think I'll take those three sections," pointing at the whole of my modern history section, about fifteen feet long, and floor to ceiling high. "Would you just pack it up and send it along with a bill?" he said, as if he was in the habit of buying half a store every time he entered a bookstore.

Since he was quite unaware that I knew his reputation, he may even have believed he had won again, as I, just as casually, responded, "Sure. I'll start packing it up first thing tomorrow."

David Mason

Naturally I did nothing, and, of course, I never heard from him again. Like Borden Clarke's permanent note in his catalogue, "Just ship me your old books and I'll send you lots of money," Davies was also working on percentages. If only one in ten worked it was probably profitable. The archive which I recently purchased relating to Clarke was full of correspondence from people who had shipped him books and received only disdain in return, while Davies, I guess, since he wasn't worried about the Mafia or the KGB chasing him, would hardly feel menaced by a lowly used bookseller.

My supply of anecdotes concerning this sort of bookman is almost endless. If it is true that I, who have recounted stories of a seemingly endless supply of apparent imbeciles, am offering stories with the ostensible motive of amusing the reader, it should be understood that underlying our sly pointing-out of the eccentric foibles of so many bookmen is an enormous amount of true respect. So often, these apparent nuts, who might be incarcerated in mental institutions in a normal world, have a range and depth of knowledge in the areas that interest them which will astound anyone who tests that knowledge.

Here's another example, from another country, another continent, but you may notice, except for the crankiness, it is strangely similar to the case of Mr. Honsberger.

This story was told to me by William Fredeman ("Dick" to his friends), the great collector and bibliographer of the Pre-Raphaelites.

Dick's personal collection, the basis for his important study, *Pre-Raphaelitism: A Biblio-Critical Study* (Harvard University Press, 1965), was a lifetime project, and like all the best of the scholar-collectors he pursued its components with great dedication for his whole life. Once, scouting in England, he was told that there was a man in a village some way away who claimed to be a bookseller, although he was in a house with no sign and nothing to indicate it was a shop. The man was said to be an expert on the Pre-Raphaelites. Dick travelled there with some difficulty and knocked at the door several times before a visibly irritated elderly man finally opened it, stating, "Can't you see I'm busy? What do you want?"

"I'm so sorry," replied Dick diplomatically, not attempting to point out that he couldn't know that the man was busy, since the door was shut and the windows were coated with twenty years or so of grime. He had met this sort before and he knew how to play the game.

"I collect the Pre-Raphaelites," he quickly explained before the man could slam the door. "And I'm told that you know more about them than anyone north of London and that you might have some of their books for sale."

"Well, I might," said the man. "But you can't come in, you know," he added, glaring defiantly.

Dick knew he couldn't come in. After all, if he could, someone might mistake it for a bookshop or something.

"Well," he said meekly, "how can I find out what you might have that I need?"

"Don't you have a list?" the man accused. "I thought you were a collector. Are you a dealer?"

"Oh no," Dick responded. "I hope I don't look like one of *them*. I'm a professor. I teach the Pre-Raphaelites."

"Give me a list," the old man answered. "I'll see what I have."

Dick didn't know what else to do, so he gave him a list of around ten titles, all Pre-Raphaelite rarities, that he had unsuccessfully sought for years.

"Come back tomorrow!" barked the man, slamming the door in Dick's face.

Dick returned the next day with the hopes of a collector, but with little real expectation. The old man answered on only the second knock.

"What do you want? Can't you see I'm busy?"

"I was here yesterday, remember? I gave you my list of books I need. I stayed over hoping you might help me. That you might find some of them."

"Oh, those. Well, as a matter of fact I did," said the bookseller.

"You have some of them?" said Dick—he could hardly believe his luck.

"I have them all," said the man.

"Every one?" said Dick. He couldn't believe it. Books he'd been seeking with diminishing hope for twenty years or so, and they were all here.

"Yes I have them. Which ones do you want?" said the bookseller.

"Well," says Dick, still stunned at his luck. "Well, actually, I'd like everything on the list. I want them all." Not allowing himself to even think of the horrendous price this might entail, knowing he'd be dead before he ever got such an opportunity again.

"Oh no," said our eccentric bookseller. "You can't have them all. You can only have two of them."

By this time, as he recounted his tale, Dick was visibly affected by the recollection of his dilemma. He didn't waste time telling me of his piteous pleas, except to mention his attempt to impress on the man that he was rich—a *very* rich North American, for whom money was no object, an attempt to play on the man's greed.

He and I had both encountered many such people in the book world. We both knew that for whatever demented reason, there would be no way around it. The man was adamant: he could have only two.

"What did you do?" I asked.

"What could I do?" said Dick, near tears. "I did the only thing I could do. They were his books. I chose two." He added sadly, "And to make it even worse, after such a crazy scene, the price he quoted me for those two was almost nothing. I chose two books which I had despaired of ever seeing, never mind buying. He only asked about a tenth of what I was prepared to pay."

Dick stayed over and returned the next day. This time the bookseller didn't even answer the door at his repeated knockings. He probably had a spy hole somewhere in one of those filthy windows.

Returning the next year, hoping he might get another two and if the man lived long enough, maybe all of them, Dick found the house had different tenants, the windows clean. The man must have been dead and his books dispersed.

Dick and I stood in silence for a moment, awed at life and the problems of dealing with crazy booksellers.

My next example comes from Rupert Croft-Cooke, the prolific English writer who published a series of memoirs in the fifties and sixties, one of which relates how, in his youth, he had entered the book trade in England and had successfully held his own in the very competitive provincial trade of that time (in the twenties or thirties). He mentions a man who had a tiny shop in some village who suffered what I have come to call "the Bookseller's disease," in his case the most bizarre manifestation of it I've heard of. The nature of this disease is exactly commensurate to the bookseller's degree of ignorance about his wares. It usually starts when the bookseller sells a valuable book for a fraction of its worth—or when he thinks he has done so, which is an integral part of the syndrome—and becomes progressively more paranoid and sure that every book bought by a more knowledgeable person, especially a dealer, is worth a fortune and that he has been robbed. The only antidote for this mind-poisoning state is knowledge, but curiously, the sort of booksellers who succumb to this disease never want to cure themselves by learning about the books they handle. They prefer to suffer. And, it being a progressive disease, it automatically gets worse with every book sold. That dealer robbed me, says the suffering bookseller, sure that he has been exploited.

I was very lucky in my apprenticeship with Jerry Sherlock, because he constantly reiterated the only known antidote to the insidious progression of that disease.

"Dave, remember the only reason a dealer should worry about selling a sleeper is because it demonstrates his ignorance. And the only reason a serious dealer should want to find out that he has sold a sleeper is to avoid doing it twice. But … you must realize that if you sell a sleeper it's because the other dealer knew more than you. For that reason he deserves to get that book. If you don't like that, then learn your trade. That's the only solution. It's all a game, but it is a game of skill and you need to play by the rules. And accept the consequences—that's what a pro does."

As usual, Jerry was right. And as all dealers learn, no matter how much you study, there will always be many areas where you can't compete with a good specialist or a person knowledgeable in areas which don't interest you. This is the way it should be and even though the Internet seems to have wiped out much of the advantage the knowledgeable specialist has, that is still true. There will always be an edge for the man who knows his subject and there is nothing to match many years of experience which confers subtle benefits no Internet can steal.

"Age, experience and cunning will trump youth every time," says the quote which my father-in-law had pasted over his work station.

The first noticeable manifestation of the bookseller's disease is when the bookseller begins to hide books, usually in the back-room, out of the sight of visiting dealers. There are problems with this method. When the more knowledgeable dealer appears, the bookseller would love to ask what his hidden book is worth, but since he knows that his colleague will want to buy it if it's a good book, he doesn't dare show it, again for fear he will be robbed. He conveniently ignores the fact that his very ignorance means that he himself stole it—albeit due to his ignorance, not his venal-ity—from whatever innocent civilian he bought it from. (Maybe his suffering comes from this; it would be nice to think so.)

We had such a man in Toronto, one of the worst cases I've known personally, made even more painful to witness because this man was an honest, honourable man who would no more have cheated someone than he would have stolen. I considered him to be a very good used bookseller, but he never went over a certain level. He sold general used books and when he started to see some of his special books in the catalogues of more knowledgeable dealers at considerably more money he began to change.

He would hide any book in his backroom which he thought *might* be good, and soon the backroom was full. The backroom began to get bigger, encroaching on the store as it did (book-shelves make great walls in themselves—move them forward, the shop gets smaller, the backroom gets bigger).

Within a few years this man's backroom was 90% of the store, so jammed with bags full of what he believed to be treasures that he couldn't allow any access even if he'd wanted to.

The bookseller Croft-Cooke describes so amusingly was such a dealer, although he suffered a variation of this disease which renders his case my all-time favourite.

This man's peculiar variation of "the illness" came from his notion that other dealers, aware of his hidden treasure trove in the back room, would disguise themselves as a ploy to gain access to its contents.

Consequently everyone who innocently entered the shop was suspect. Croft-Cooke was friendly with the man, perhaps because he understood the futility of attempting to gain access to the hidden stock. Some elderly lady would inquire if he had some old novel and when she left the bookseller would look knowingly at Croft-Cooke and say, "She doesn't fool me. She's really a dealer."

One day Croft-Cooke was in the shop when the postman entered, said good morning, deposited the mail on the desk and left. The bookseller turned to Croft-Cooke, nodding as if in admiration, and said, "He's a clever one, that one. Oh, yes. You probably thought he really *was* a postman."

Chapter 19

The Hemingway Heist

My first reaction was irritation when I put my key in the upstairs lock and got no click when it turned—it was unlocked. As had been the downstairs door. My landlady, Lynn, lived on the third floor so I assumed she had gone out early, leaving the lower door unlocked. Anybody who cared to walk upstairs would have found my store open, one of the best stocks of rare books in the country unguarded and free for the taking. The lights were on but we always left the lights on in the front part of the store so people riding by at night on the Queen streetcar could see the cozy book-lined store and maybe remember later to come in and have a look. I headed first for the money drawer. We always left it half-open with around fifty dollars in it so if we had a break-in the junkies or whoever would find *some* cash and hopefully not trash the place to teach us a lesson. We didn't worry about them stealing books. Junkies need something they can sell quickly and that's not books.

Our daytime theft problems came from the street people who thought they could steal books from one store and sell them up the street, not knowing that the many booksellers on Queen knew each other's handwriting. We caught many petty thieves and drunks this way, which generally served to discourage them.

At night the problem was the junkies: they would throw a brick through the glass door downstairs, run up, throw it through the upstairs glass, run in, locate the cash drawer, grab the money and be out in less than a minute. That's why Lynn had installed the new unbreakable glass doors. We were all sick of calls from the police in the middle of the night to report another $50.00

robbery and a broken door. That's the reason we left the money and why most small business people leave the cash drawers of their tills open, so the thieves don't cost them more in repairs than what gets stolen.

But the cash drawer didn't have any cash in it, so I headed for the safe in the front, now a bit uneasy—maybe someone *had* been inside. I had two safes. A large safe in the front held our most valuable books and another one in the back office held others, including many that were my own, and some not yet ready for sale for various reasons. These safes were really a form of fire insurance rather than theft protection.

I'd had a colleague in Los Angeles who had run his business in a huge red barn in the middle of town and, since naturally no insurance company would insure books and paper in a wooden structure, every year he had spent the equivalent of his insurance premium on fire-proof safes. I had thought that a good idea and copied it (several of my customers did the same in their homes).

You could get a hundred thousand dollars worth of books in one of those safes and every time I filled one I'd buy another. At least, I reasoned, a fire wouldn't wipe us out. And, just as important, it protected these artifacts of civilization from a fate too horrendous to imagine. Booksellers really do come to believe, silly as it sounds, that they are protecting civilization.

This particular morning as I turned the corner, I saw that the front safe was open. The lock was mutilated, one outer hinge snapped, the other barely supporting the badly gouged door, and an untidy heap of books had flowed out onto the floor. I ran to the back office safe and it was the same, lock sprung, the door ajar, valuable books in a heap.

I phoned the police and without touching my valuable books (never tamper with the crime scene I knew from all the police procedurals I consumed voraciously) I tried to see what might have been taken. The first book I saw was an extra-illustrated, sumptuously bound first edition of a Dickens title with the price penciled in—$10,000.00. I relaxed a bit. If they ignored a ten thousand dollar book they must have just been after money.

Debbie always came in an hour or two later than me so by the time that she arrived there were already four or five cops in the store searching, examining and asking an increasing number of precise questions.

We learned that the intruders gained entry through a small window in a small room towards the rear of the shop that looked down three stories into a sunken and deserted area between the buildings, blocked by an iron gate, now ajar. A long extension ladder was still propped against our wall. This was a clever move, for every other window except ours was boarded over. The pit was full of the debris all unused sites accumulate. The ladder belonged to neighbours a couple of doors down and was usually chained to their rear fire escape. The robbers had obviously reconnoitered and Debbie and I got our first creepy feelings. She remembered that her purse, in the back office the previous day, had been open and moved, something she had dismissed at the time since nothing was missing.

Obviously the thieves had been in the store the day before during opening hours checking out the best way to get in. This realization evoked some sort of primal fear that everyone who has ever come home to find that unknown persons have invaded their space will recognize. It's obviously primitive in origin, from times when desecration of your private safe place could have meant horrible consequences—even death.

We didn't realize at first that these feelings would multiply beyond our control. For at least a year afterwards, Debbie couldn't enter the store by herself. She needed to know that I or someone else was already there before she came in. We were getting our first lessons in how the real world works; and it wasn't how we had assumed it would be.

Before we were done we had many of our other liberal illusions shattered as well.

The place now had a steady stream of suited detectives coming in, looking around, especially at the safes, then chatting a bit with the detectives in charge and leaving. It was finally explained that word had gone out, erroneously, through police channels, that the safes had been blown open, a rare occurrence in Toronto, so detectives from all over the city were coming in for a look. When they saw that they had been pried, sawed, and gouged open, not blown, interest faded. It was just another break-in.

The activity went on all morning as we discovered many more pieces of evidence: a crowbar resting on top of books on a lower shelf, a chisel kicked under a safe (other tools appeared behind and on books for the next year or so), a World Series baseball found in the pit under the ladder, probably tossed down and missed during the retreat (by this time we had also figured out that while they'd come in up the ladder, they'd simply exited via the front door, which explained why it was unlocked). Various small messes turned up in the back office, where no doubt some of the thieves had searched while others worked on the safes. A recently purchased copier and a jar of quarters were among the missing items.

Around noon, as we were gradually becoming used to the creepy feelings which came every time we found another part of our private area violated, and while the fingerprint squad put their sticky black stuff all over the safes and the doors—useless although necessary—one of our friends, a long-time customer named Jim Yates who dropped in a couple of times a week on his lunch hour, came in.

"What's going on?" he asked, looking at all the police and their activity.

"We don't know Jim. We had a break-in but we can't figure out what they got, if anything. Maybe they thought we had money in the safe is all we can figure," I said.

"Oh," he said, "so the Hemingway stuff is okay? They didn't get that?"

Complete consternation. Deb and I froze, stunned for a moment. We had completely forgotten the Hemingway material. In our state of shock, it had literally not occurred to us.

Instantly everything became clear and we both ran to the rear office safe even though we knew without any doubt that the Hemingway material would not be there. And it wasn't.

Here was the motive and the explanation for everything. The break-in had been planned to steal the Hemingway material: three books and several letters between Morley Callaghan, Ernest Hemingway and F. Scott Fitzgerald relating to the famous boxing match in Paris in the twenties between Hemingway and Callaghan with Fitzgerald as timekeeper. Fitzgerald had been so amazed that the much smaller Callaghan had been out-boxing Hemingway that he had forgotten to call time. Callaghan had knocked Hemingway down, causing what became an international incident when a reporter published an account in a New York newspaper, resulting in enormous repercussions. There were even a couple of pages of Edmund Wilson manuscript on the subject and other related ephemera.

I had been hired to sell it all by the Callaghan family. Everything changed from that moment on. The police called in their major crime unit and two detectives showed up shortly. I became increasingly panic-stricken, wondering if I might be legally responsible and imagining Barry Callaghan's response when I told him his quarter-million dollar collection was gone. A police officer told me not to worry about personal liability, the law said if I provided security equal to how I treated my own most valuable stock, I was fine. Putting the material in the safes saved me.

Soon we had more detectives in the store because the whole focus was now different. Not much later the newspaper and television people would begin to appear as word got around.

Shortly after, when the news accounts had circulated in most of the English-speaking world, I received a call from a dealer I didn't know in Southern California, telling me that if we were to retrieve the archive he wanted to buy it. So, now I had a customer but nothing to sell him.

Poor Jim Yates was astounded at the furor he had initiated and Debbie and I were really distraught now, all our idle speculation evaporating in the face of this incredible reality.

Most of that morning remains a blur. Almost no one knew the stuff was in the store. When I had spoken of our project common sense had caused me to inform people that it was in a bank safe deposit box and an appointment would be necessary to view it.

My landlady's boyfriend, a young relative of one of my early friends and mentors, knew I had it in the safe and he had asked permission to view it with a couple of his literary-minded friends (one of whom was Stephen Smith, who later wrote an article on the robbery in *Toronto Life*). I had agreed, and had allowed them in to view it a few days earlier.

I told the police that and they took names, but it seemed obvious to us that whoever had broken in was completely unaware which safe contained the material. Of the two safes, one was a modern fire proof one and snapping its lock with a crowbar had been relatively easy and, in fact, had not ruined the safe—my supplier was able to restore it quickly and cheaply. That's where the Hemingway material had been stored. The other safe, an old-fashioned one—a real one—I had bought used. The robbers had demolished it and it must have taken them several hours to do so. It didn't make sense that the robbers would waste several hours of hard work just to allay suspicion. It seemed certain they were unaware that the material was in the fire safe, so we could reasonably assume the young men were not involved.

By now I was pretty hyper, probably in a state of minor shock, constantly jabbering to the cops, offering ideas, suspicions, comments that might help, adding details that I thought might be pertinent to the investigation. Most of it was pointless and irrelevant. I had supposed that our visitors from the day before, seeing the safes, had concluded that we would have huge amounts of cash in them, our take from the many thousands of daily sales we made of rare books to the countless collectors they believed visited us.

I remember making a stupid joke. Going up to four or five uniformed cops discussing details, I approached and said, "I just thought of one suspect we haven't considered," I offered, anticipating their laughter at my punchline.

"Who?" said one of them.

"Me," I blurted with an anticipatory smirk.

A young woman in uniform looked at me and without smiling replied, "Oh no, you were the first one we suspected."

I was completely deflated, all the air sucked out of my silly attempt at humour.

They all looked at me without expression.

The first cop's question had been did I have insurance. Now, I understood why he had seemed surprised when I replied that I didn't.

Only a couple of very good friends, one of whom was Jim Yates, had seen the letters and knew we had them on the premises, so it was fairly obvious that the Hemingway archive had been targeted by people with inside knowledge.

I could no longer put off phoning Barry Callaghan.

He answered and I asked him if he was sitting down.

"We've had a break-in, both safes are burgled, the Hemingway stuff is all gone," I said.

A long pause.

"Do you have insurance?" he asked.

"No," I replied. "Do you?"

"I don't know, I'd better ask. I'll let you know," and he hung up.

No other questions.

I spent the rest of the day waiting for him to show up. He only lived two blocks away and I couldn't imagine he wouldn't want to see the scene of the crime. But he didn't come in, not then, not ever.

In fact, I didn't hear from him again until weeks later when he called to tell me what to say to the insurance adjuster who would be coming to see me.

I did have several visits from the insurance adjuster, and quite a few conversations where some of his suspicions were voiced. I never found out how much Callaghan was reimbursed; I was only told that he got *some* money.

There had been lots of stories about a break-in at Callaghan's house a few years earlier where the house was trashed, many of his manuscripts damaged and his wife's paintings, hanging on the walls, mutilated. This was never solved. It was all very mysterious and gossip and rumors abounded in the literary community. This seemed comparable with our robbery. I don't know anyone who doesn't have a theory, including me and Debbie, but the theories differ—even Debbie and I have distinctly different theories as to what happened. What the police and the insurance adjustor thought we, of course, didn't know, although after countless conversations with them over many months we naturally picked up a fair number of inadvertent hints. Even more of our liberal illusions disintegrated. In all the mysteries I had read the cops figure it out, make accusations, the bad guys confess and we go on to the next thriller. In real life the cops need proof, and even there we get O. J. Simpson. It took years for us to get used to the idea that there wasn't going to be any resolution to this crime, and now twenty years later we know there may never be.

All this began in Paris in the 1920s, but my involvement began around 1970 or so. I'd been reading Morley Callaghan and thought him worthy enough to merit an author bibliography as one of the earliest modern Canadian writers who had acquired an international reputation.

My friend Richard Landon, then learning *his* trade as well, in the rare books library at the University of Toronto, of which he would later become the director, was amenable to my idea of us doing a bibliography together, so we approached Morley Callaghan and made an appointment to visit one evening to discuss our project.

Callaghan was a man lacking all pretensions and vanity beyond his own good opinion of his literary value. We had been warned, however, by people who knew him, that we shouldn't mention Hemingway unless he did. He was sick to death, we were told, of people who came up to see him because of their interest in Hemingway.

We spent a pleasant evening with Callaghan. After a while he became relaxed and expansive and, despite predictions, it was *he* who brought up Paris and Hemingway.

On one of my later visits he told me that his account of the famous fight between him and Hemingway in his memoir *That Summer in Paris* had been purposely softened out of regard for Mary Hemingway. "I didn't want to hurt her feelings so soon after the horrible mess of his suicide," he explained, "so I toned down the ugliness and softened many of Hemingway's nasty reactions. If you saw the letters you'd see how badly both Hemingway and Fitzgerald really acted."

"You mean…? You still have…?"

"Would you like to see them?" he asked.

Would I!

I struggled to appear calm.

Callaghan went upstairs while I chatted with Loretto, his wife. Twenty minutes later he hadn't returned. Loretto smiled, "They're up there somewhere, he'll find them."

After half-an-hour Callaghan came down the stairs triumphantly waving an 8 ½" x 11" letter, the waving causing the letter to flap wildly at the folds. He handed it to me. It was closely typed, the folds weak, evidence of many openings. It was signed, "Hemingway," and was astounding in its content, by turns evasive, hostile, then conciliatory, outright malicious, then friendly. The excuses and lies which, as the written record shows, multiplied hugely over the years were already in evidence here.

At the end of the letter Hemingway says, "In all friendliness and with no idea of anyone being afraid of anyone else I honestly believe that with small gloves I could knock you out inside of about five two-minute rounds although I'm sure you would pop me plenty."

The letter is stunning in what it reveals of the inner Hemingway.

I told Callaghan in no uncertain terms that these letters were of enormous value both as artifacts and as a literary record and strongly advised him to take them all to the bank the next day and put them in a safety deposit box. He told me on a later visit that he had located the other letters and had done what I advised.

After a fair bit of work on the bibliography, Landon and I gradually let things slide and in the end we didn't finish our work.

Then in August 1990 we heard of Callaghan's death. I wondered what would become of all that material, until one day Barry Callaghan came to see me.

I advised him that, in my opinion, the early Hemingway books inscribed to Morley and "The Fight" archive could be safely severed from Callaghan's personal papers without affecting the value of the papers which, of course, focused on Morley's work as a Canadian writer. And that's what happened. Barry Callaghan agreed and made some arrangement with the National Library in Ottawa for Morley's papers to go there, partly purchased and partly as a tax-credited gift. I did the appraisal and then waited for the Callaghan brothers to decide on the disposal of the letters and inscribed first editions. I assessed them, told Barry and his brother what I believed we could ask for them and was hired on commission to prepare a catalogue and sell them. For the only time in my forty-five years as a bookseller I demanded a signed contract before I began.

In preparing that catalogue I made copies of all the letters which, of course, is now the only existent record we have of that famous incident. The trouble is, I don't know where they are; I hope that they are in my papers, donated to the University of Toronto but not yet sorted and catalogued. If the copies are not there, then this invaluable historical record may be lost entirely.

We issued the catalogue, which created some stir in literary circles in North America, but with no immediate results.

I wasn't worried about that: it's not uncommon for a certain amount of time to pass before selling items in that price range. I had told the Callaghans that it might be six months or a year before we had a bite. Gossip filtered back through the trade that told me everyone was aware of the catalogue. I was fairly certain our eventual customer would be an institution.

But with the robbery, fate intervened, and our lives and the literary record were irrevocably changed.

Then things got even more bizarre.

One day, two or three weeks after the robbery, I had a call from a man who claimed he had information on the whereabouts of the archive and might be able to assist in its return—for a reward, naturally. This is what we had been hoping for, the thieves trying to sell it back. I played along and told him I would have to speak to the owners before I could agree.

He thought $10,000 to $15,000 might suffice and I arranged for him to call me again the next day.

I called the detectives and told them I had a recording system I could hook up to my phone and they made an arrangement to trace any call.

The man phoned again and I played along, letting him know the owners agreed and we could arrange a meeting to make an exchange.

By now I was certain from the way he spoke that he was not one of the thieves but a scam artist, who had read about the robbery in the news and was trying his own little fraud.

I took the tape to the police but somehow I'd failed to hook it up properly and the recording was mostly gibberish. They did trace the call, which was, as we'd suspected, from a pay phone; it was located in a motel lobby in Windsor. At least we knew where he was. In a later tape one detective flattered me enormously by saying my interrogation techniques were professional—not for nothing had I read those thousands of police thrillers.

Several calls ensued where I questioned him carefully, hoping to have him reveal things. He said he was in Detroit but we could meet in Windsor for the exchange, but we already knew where he really was. Then during a call he informed me that he would be away a few days because he needed to have a hernia operation. By now we knew he was almost certainly a fraud, all his conversations were cheap cons demonstrating his ignorance of what we were dealing with. But I now wanted to get him, so I phoned a friend, a doctor, and asked him how many hernia operations might be done in a week in a place like Windsor. He guessed there might be around seven and probably all at the same hospital. I figured we had our man. How many of seven or so operations in a smallish city would be on patients who would be found to have a record, probably a string of minor thefts and frauds? As I was sure our man would have.

But the police weren't about to go to all that trouble to catch a sleazy minor conman so when I told him that before the owner and I would travel to Windsor with $15,000.00 in cash we would need to have some proof—a Xerox of the letters—it all sort of fizzled out.

In our last conversation the man finally said to me, "Tell me, who is this Hemingway guy anyway? Is he really that important?"

Our obsession had filled most of six months, then it gradually began to fade, but still, parts of every day were lost to idle speculation...

And regularly, by a stranger's comment or question, a query from the insurance man, or the police detectives who had been on the case so long now they were becoming almost friends, our speculations again surfaced and we would again find ourselves chewing over the details endlessly and obsessively.

We were starting to realize that solving the robbery might take a long time and, although we could hardly bring ourselves to admit it, that we might never learn the truth of what had consumed so much of our lives and thoughts.

One day, two years after the robbery, our obsessions having receded considerably, I had a call late one afternoon. "Mr. Mason, this is Detective Jeff Zammit of 14 Division. I just wanted to inform you that we caught one of the Hemingway thieves."

I was not having a good day and after the initial shock I assumed it was one of my friends making a joke in very bad taste.

"Listen, I'm having a bad day, don't screw with my head. Who is this?!?!" I yelled, very angry.

The voice repeated, coldly now.

"I am Detective Zammit of 14 Division—Toronto Police Force."

I apologized, and Detective Zammit told me the story.

A young man called Robert Pacheco, a known youth gang member, had been caught for something else and revealed that he had been part of the robbery.

One volume of a very pretty leatherbound set of sixteenth-century Italian books and a postcard from Hemingway's sister Marcelline to Callaghan were recovered. I hadn't even noticed that the book had been missing. It was tiny and very attractive, which is why I had probably paid $1,700.00 for it a few years earlier. Only one volume was returned, rendering it now worthless. I figured one of the thieves had stolen it for the same reason I had bought it: it was pretty. Maybe it was to be a gift for his girlfriend.

I later gradually discovered some other important books and manuscript material missing, including the working manuscript of *Airplane Dreams*, the only book by Allen Ginsberg published in Canada. For a long time I hoped these valuable items had been taken by the thieves as their personal bonus and that a careless sale of that material might lead us to the thieves. But it never happened and they're still out there somewhere.

I was elated at Pacheco's arrest. I envisaged a judge saying to him, "Well, you stole these things and we want them back. If you tell us who you were working for and we can recover the material I can be more lenient. If you refuse I will be forced to mete out a drastic sentence."

Isn't that the way it works? Even mob guys faced with huge

sentences turn on their confederates. *Omertà* dissolves faced with forty or fifty years in jail.

We would solve the mystery which had so disrupted our lives for two years, I imagined the pleasure that would follow when Debbie, myself, and all our friends in the trade and the literary community would find out whose theory was correct.

Well, it didn't work out that way. Pacheco committed suicide in prison. Suicide! Facing other charges, he apparently decided that a few years in jail was more than he could endure. Described by a cop who had dealt with him as a handsome, personable young man, he had nevertheless decided at twenty-two years of age that life was hopeless?

I read a lot of police thrillers and I've read considerably in the field of true crime. My understanding of people in the mob or on its fringes is that the odd prison sentence is seen as an occupational hazard. You do your time, your family is supported by the people you didn't fink on and you come out and go on.

Why would this kid choose suicide?

I had a customer who worked as a guard in the prison system. He believes, and I was convinced by his arguments, that prison suicides, with the possible exception of previously respected citizens who are caught out in despicable moral transgressions—like pedophiles—are almost never suicides.

I think the police officer's comments on Pacheco, where he even says he sort of liked him, and was himself shocked by the suicide, are police-speak. He is hinting that he also doesn't believe this kid committed suicide. But, of course, he can't admit that.

My friend the jail guard, speaking privately, had no such reservations. It's almost always murder, he said. Someone who has power, even within the prison system, doesn't want scared kids talking. They could terminate such talk and they did, he thought. So did I. And so do, I believe, the police, even if they can't say so.

Robert Pacheco was part of a youth gang and was obviously hired to steal those artifacts on behalf of someone. Somehow I find it hard to conceive of some unknown wealthy Hemingway collector being in Toronto to begin with, and further having the capability of rounding up a bunch of local gang kids to steal the books and letters.

Someone had to have arranged it who had both connections with local street gangs and knowledge of what the material was, its value, who had control of it, and what could be done with it after it was stolen. Certainly it couldn't be offered on the open market, so the alternatives were either to sell it back to the owners or the owner's insurance company, as happens sometimes with art theft. Or the thieves had to have the sort of international connections which could allow them to discreetly offer the archive to some wealthy Hemingway collector elsewhere in the world.

In spite of the countless thrillers and movies which propose some sinister avaricious collector who covets and steals or buys stolen art to be enjoyed in the privacy of his home, I've never been able to buy into such fantasies. My own experience of collectors, over forty-five years, has demonstrated that perhaps the greatest pleasure they all feel, after the search for and acquisition of their prizes, is to show them off to other collectors. A collector who would be content only with his own knowledge that he had a prize would be missing a large percentage of his pleasure. I never bought that and I still don't.

But finally, after a few more years, we found our obsessions cooled, only rarely did speculation arise and then not for long and finally even details of memory began to fade and facts, once imbedded in our minds, became vague. Except it never quite goes completely away.

Every once in a while something comes up which reawakens everything and all our speculations and anxieties begin again.

And again we measure the years and become more certain we will never learn what really happened and will never see the archive again.

My conclusions seem to have drifted towards this: I suspect that what we generally call "the mob" was behind Pacheco and his gang, but the motives of the mob, their knowledge of the archive's whereabouts, its value, and what happened to it remain a mystery.

And I guess that I blame Barry Callaghan for much of Debbie's and my own mental and emotional turmoil over the years, no matter how unfair that might be.

Callaghan had a serious interest in horse racing and apparently spent a lot of time at the track; he was one of those who studied the racing form and he once told me that he had been able to buy his house because of his winnings. He was serious, too.

I knew a fair number of racetrack habitués in my youthful gambling days; they avidly created "systems" and they invariably struck me as the types who were easy marks for the portable shell games one encountered on busy streets, or for any superficial cheap con. Naïve losers, in fact.

And here was an intelligent man, a writer, seriously informing me that he consistently won large sums betting the horses.

It's one thing to observe the loser who assures you he will win it back next time, or the habitual drunk who denies he has a problem and can stop anytime, but someone who claims to be a big winner on something where only the people who fix things can win is surely a very curious phenomenon.

Mario Puzo, once an admitted degenerate gambler, and who had written about gambling a fair bit, stated categorically that he had never been tempted to bet on the horses, as he thought it was far less dependent on luck than it was on the human propensity for manipulating whatever could be manipulated. Which in racing seemed to be just about everything. As Puzo put it (Horses) "are noble, loveable, and true, but controlled by men not so noble."

It seemed like every time I saw Callaghan at functions or on the occasional television program or panel discussion he was dressed in a black suit and a white shirt. One news photo showed him dressed like that at what was described as "a mafia wedding." He described the groom as a friend, and in a recent article in *Exile* magazine identified the groom as the nephew of a New York State mobster known as "Big Frankie the Mook."

Could Callaghan have unwisely alluded to the value of the archive within the hearing of avaricious ears?

I have spent days, months, years, obsessed by Callaghan's loss, to which he himself seems indifferent.

And in all that time, and with all the mental turmoil we have been through, not once has Callaghan commented on the affair, neither to us, nor, to our knowledge, in any public manner except for the enigmatic quote he gave to Stephen Smith for Smith's article on the robbery in *Toronto Life* (December 1996, "The Purloined Letters").

"What can you say? There nothing to say. These things are not of significance to me. I don't think about them, I don't dwell on them. And I think Toronto should get over this fascination with Hemingway. I think the city should stop milking it. Give it up, get a life.

"I know what the relationship [with Hemingway] meant to my father and what it meant to Hemingway. That's their youth—but it's not mine. And frankly, it's not the city's."

That seems to me to be a very curious attitude for someone who has lost such important literary material that relates directly to his father and to his father's history. Barry Callaghan venerated his father. I could see that clearly in our several meetings. For many years I have observed him guarding and cultivating his father's literary reputation. He has defended his father's reputation ferociously and passionately, his publishing company has reprinted his father's books, and he never misses an opportunity to defend Morley against any and all criticism.

And yet, he is apparently not just indifferent to the fate of the archive, but seriously interested in burying all speculation about this material which, if it were public, would reflect great credit on his father. For the archive clearly demonstrates Morley was a man of acute sensibility and great moral courage.

The mystery remains.

Perhaps it is appropriate to talk here a bit about the actual fight. Perhaps a short review of that famous incident will both clarify the history and afford a greater significance to what we have lost.

First, here are some extracts from Stephen Smith's 1996 article in *Toronto Life*, an excellent introduction:

AFTER MORLEY Callaghan died in 1990 at the age of eighty-six, the work of sifting the effects of a distinguished literary life fell to his son, Barry, the writer. The younger Callaghan donated many of his father's papers to Ottawa's National Archives, kept some for himself and packaged others for sale.

Early in 1991, he approached David Mason—a respected authority who has appraised the papers of Northrop Frye and Robertson Davies among others—with a literary bundle to make a bibliophile's spine turn paperback. It included two painfully rare Hemingway first editions: *in our time* from 1924 and *Three Stories & Ten Poems* (given to Callaghan by Hemingway in 1923 and inscribed "To Callaghan with best luck and predictions"). There were also two Hemingway-to-Callaghan letters predating the fight, one from 1926 signed "Yours always, Hem," full of encouragement: "You'll be a great writer if you keep writing and you'll keep writing."

And then there was what Mason called "The Fight Archive," a collection of letters emphasizing the wilful extremes of Hemingway's ego and how it finally finished Callaghan's friendship with him. There was a letter, first, from Fitzgerald abjectly apologizing for sending the Hemingway-prompted telegram asking Callaghan to correct the press reports. Hemingway opened his account early in 1930 with a letter complaining about the erroneous report of the fight. A further letter, undated but probably from later that winter, culminated in an amazing puffing-out of chest. "In all friendliness," Hemingway wrote, "and with no idea of anyone being afraid of anyone else I honestly believe that with small gloves I could knock you out inside about five two minute rounds although I'm sure you would pop me plenty. I say this not being sore and not in an unfriendly way..."

Together, these few, slightly foxed pages were by far the single most valuable properties Mason had handled in his thirty years dealing in rare books. After three months of research and consultation, Mason valued *Three Stories & Ten Poems* at $60,000; the asking price for the entire lot, books and letters, was $250,000. Sixty-two years after Callaghan jabbed Hemingway hard in the ego, David Mason started calling book dealers and Hemingway enthusiasts across North America. He wasn't surprised by the tremors of collectorly excitement he precipitated. "It's like a Picasso coming on the market," he said at the time.

By 1929, Ernest Hemingway's star was high and arcing yet higher. He published *A Farewell to Arms* that year, adding lustre to the literary reputation that he'd established with the publication of *The Sun Also Rises* in 1926. Hemingway was a full-blown literary event: he was himself *news*. He believed it, and, increasingly, the rest of the world seemed to take his word for it.

In the early summer of 1929, he was back in Paris, a favoured haunt since he'd first gone there in 1921 while still a correspondent roving Europe for the *Toronto Daily Star*. Later, in his posthumously published memoir, *A Moveable Feast*, he recollected those years, using a fond nostalgic palette to illuminate an idyll of pure love, good Cahors wine, roasted chestnuts, literary fellowship and the birth of true sentences.

Also boxing. Hemingway probably saw his first professional fight in Toronto, and by the time he reached Paris, he was a fulltime fan and sometime participant. It was no surprise, then, that one afternoon in June of 1929, Hemingway was to be found at the American Club, about to put up his fists against Morley Callaghan, with whom he'd become friends during his stint at the *Star*. The most reliable account of what happened next, it's roundly accepted by Hemingway scholars, is contained in Callaghan's memoir *That Summer in Paris*. Another of Hemingway's friends, F. Scott Fitzgerald, was enlisted to keep time. The two combatants sparred through a couple of opening rounds without much violence before Callaghan jarred Hemingway with a punch in the mouth. Hemingway bled. Fitzgerald, the story goes, was so surprised or distracted or unsteadied from too much liquor at lunch that he allowed the round to go four minutes, instead of the agreed-upon two. As the round ticked late and later, an unwitting Hemingway got mad—and sloppy. When Callaghan next connected, with Hemingway's jaw this time, the blow knocked his man to the mat.

There the actual fight ended, but its life as legend was only just beginning. The Paris-based *Herald Tribune* and

David Mason

New York's *Post* got hold of the story. Not a very firm hold, it turned out: both reported that Callaghan had knocked Hemingway cold. The mere proposition of such an indignity infuriated Hemingway so much that he instructed Fitzgerald to send Callaghan a telegram demanding that he speak out forthwith to right the printed wrong. At first Fitzgerald refused: he argued that Callaghan would see the article and correct it without prompting. Hemingway persisted, and the spin-controlling telegram was duly sent to Callaghan in Toronto.

Hemingway's manic conduct in the aftermath of a few Parisian punches would eventually alienate a good friend. But he was just warming up; it soon became clear that he considered the story of the Fight to be a work in progress. Two months after the event, he was busy propagating alcoholic excuses, writing to Maxwell Perkins, his New York publisher, to tell of a festive lunch wetted by "several bottles of white burgundy. Knew I would be asleep by five," he continued, "so went around with Scott to get Morley to box right away—I couldn't hardly see him—had a couple of whiskeys en route…"

Hemingway went on to recount Fitzgerald's faulty timing and allowed that Callaghan was able to "pop me and cut my mouth, mush up my face in general." But "Callaghan couldn't hit hard—if he could he would have killed me. I slipped and went down once and lit on my arm and put my left shoulder out in the first round…"

Without Hemingway's wounded fixation, a few minutes' idle exercise would have quickly melted into dusk. Incredibly, twenty-two years later, Hemingway was still editing the past. Writing to Fitzgerald's biographer in 1951, he recalled lunch and liquid and going to work out with Callaghan, "who was a good amateur boxer… but who could not hit a lick." But now he lengthened the overtime round to thirteen minutes, during which he remembered Callaghan hitting him freely. "But he did me no harm and could not knock me down or put me away... I was cut badly in the mouth and swallowed the blood." By this account, Hemingway fought a few more controlled rounds during which Callaghan flailed away at his vastly superior opponent. "I am pretty sure I could have knocked him out," Hemingway breezed, "truly he couldn't hit. But I did not want to knock him out." (With the author's kind permission.)

Back rereading *That Summer in Paris* I found myself again marvelling at the extraordinary contradictions and Hemingway's powers of invention, which Callaghan so clearly illustrates.

Callaghan tells of Max Perkins relating a Hemingway boast about seeing the middleweight champion of France mauling some hapless fighter at a county fair, whereupon Hemingway jumped into the ring and knocked out the champion. Callaghan, kindly, or maybe pointedly, says, "The story sounded incredible to me." But the main point to the anecdote is that Perkins had actually assumed it to be true, but he is recounting Hemingway's version of it to someone who had boxed with Hemingway and knew his limitations.

And we keep getting even more ludicrous things, like the time Callaghan and Hemingway were sparring and Callaghan caught Hemingway with a blow which drew blood, whereupon Hemingway spat blood in Callaghan's face; Callaghan is so astounded at such an insult that he stops fighting, dropping his gloves. But Ernest solemnly informs him that he is merely doing what bullfighters do when wounded. "It's a way of showing contempt," he explains, as if this means his provocative insult is thereby okay.

Callaghan continues to speculate on Hemingway's weird need to pretend that his boxing was the root of his life. Callaghan goes on at some length about how some men have the ability— and the need—to turn their imaginary triumphs into real ones. Hemingway we see is one of those men who need to rewrite their experiences.

More interesting is his observation that, "even today... there will be people who would swear to you that they had seen Hemingway working out like a pro."

When, "the truth was that we were two amateur boxers. The difference between us was that he had given time and imagination to boxing. I had actually worked out with a lot of good college boxers."

Hemingway continues to compose the novel which is his life.

Callaghan then tells us that Samuel Putnam, in his memoir *Paris Was Our Mistress* (1947), recounts a later version which Hemingway had told to Putnam. In this version Callaghan challenged Hemingway to a boxing match and Hemingway knocked him out in one round.

So we have progressed from the thirteen minute round where Hemingway (having consumed six bottles of wine and a couple of whiskys first) accidentally slips and gets knocked down, to a one round knockout by our hero—all in less than twenty years. We can only be amazed.

Maybe that is why Callaghan is so gentle with Hemingway in the end; we are dealing here with a truly pathological inventor, who is recreating himself almost in front of our eyes.

A very melancholy glimpse maybe, into some of the cost of his great gift.

Here I insert, as examples, my entries when I offered the two books in my 1991 catalogue titled "The Fight."

HEMINGWAY, Ernest. Three Stories & Ten Poems. (Paris: Contact Publishing Co., 1923). FIRST EDITION OF THE AUTHOR'S FIRST BOOK. PRESENTATION COPY to Morley Callaghan, inscribed on the e/paper, "To Callaghan, With best luck and predictions, Ernest M. Hemingway." 12mo., grey blue wrappers printed in black.

The first edition consisted of 300 copies printed by Darantiere of Dijon, the printer of *Ulysses*, but published by Robert McAlmon. Hemingway's negative comments about McAlmon's publishing acumen in his letter of July 19, (1926) to Callaghan are presumably based on his experiences with this book.

Covers a bit soiled and darkened, light wear to the spine with minor splits repaired, very small pieces torn off corners of pp. 25-6 and 27-8 not affecting the text. A very good copy. (Hanneman Ala.)

In *That Summer in Paris* Callaghan relates the circumstances around his acquisition of this book with the presentation inscription from Hemingway. This occurred just before Hemingway left the *Toronto Star*. As Callaghan tells us: "I remember our last conversation before he went away. When we met in the afternoon he asked me if I had a copy of his *Three Stories and Ten Poems*. I hadn't. At that time there was a little book-store at Bay and Bloor where Hemingway had left some copies. 'Let's walk up there,' he said. It was a long walk and we loafed along slowly, absorbed in our conversation. I remember we were talking about the great Russian, Dostoevski, and I said 'The way he writes—it's like a forest fire. It sweeps indiscriminately over everything.'

'That's pretty good,' he said, pondering. Then he stopped on the street. 'You know Harry Greb,' he said, referring to the wonderful middleweight champion with the windmill style.

'Well, Dostoevski writes like Harry Greb fights,' he said. 'He swarms all over you. Like this.' And there on the street he started shadow boxing.

We got his little book from the bookshop, then walked to Yonge and Bloor for a coffee. He wrote in the book, 'To Callaghan with best luck and predictions,' and while he was doing it I said wrily that now he was going away it looked as if I was losing my reading public of one—him. 'No,' he said. 'Remember this. There are always four or five people, somewhere in the world, who are interested in good new writing. Some magazines are starting up in Paris,' and he sounded like a bishop and again I believed I only needed to wait." $60,000.00

HEMINGWAY, Ernest. in our time. paris: printed at the three mountains press and for sale at shakespeare & co, 1924. FIRST EDITION OF THE AUTHOR'S SECOND BOOK, limited edition of "170 copies printed on rives hand-made paper this is number 34." MORLEY CALLAGHANS' COPY, SIGNED by him on the pastedown "M. Callaghan."

Tall 8vo., patterned boards printed in red and black. Bookseller's label on the rear pastedown, some rubbing to the spine and edges, some chipping at the spine extremities, careless opening between the title and dedication leaves causing a chip to title with the missing piece retained on the dedication leaf, some occasional smudging throughout but still a very good copy. (Hanneman A2a.)

The bookshop whose label is on the rear pastedown is "The Little Shop Round The Corner." This is the shop where Hemingway's first book was sold in Toronto and this label in the copy of his second book is the only evidence known to us that proves that Hemingway's second book was also offered for sale in Toronto. The shop is listed in Toronto directories of the period as being located at 1184 Bay St. which would be just south of Bloor St. $25,000.00

These prices would be rather higher today; indeed, I'd buy both books myself at those prices. A copy of *Three Stories* with an inscription to another *Toronto Star* friend but of much lesser significance is currently being offered for $125,000 (U.S.).

My own re-reading of both Callaghan's memoir, and several other writers' comments over the years, along with comparisons with my catalogue entries and my now faulty memory, again emphasize the loss to the literary record.

And finally, this tantalizing hint from Callaghan's review of Hemingway's *Selected Letters* in the *Washington Post* (March 1981), which reveals to those who know the background, just how cognizant Morley was of Hemingway's propensity to invent his necessary truths as he went along. For me, it again reinforces how gentle and fair Morley was, and his essential decency towards a man who had so cruelly betrayed their friendship.

ERNEST HEMINGWAY: SELECTED LETTERS, 1917-1961. Edited by Carlos Baker. Scribners. 948 pp. $27.50.

By Morley Callaghan

Hemingway was something more than a natural writer. When nerve-racked, sleepless or desperate, he took to writing letters for relief as another man might take Valium. He wrote strange and sometimes wonderful letters although they have nothing to do with the art of the charming letter. Since he knew he would order that they never be published, most of them come pouring out exuberantly, or furiously, or maliciously, or humorously, the stuff of his own wide gaudy wonderful world.

We get, too, the part of his inner world he wants to reveal; he was always very canny about this. Since he had a searing power to make everything he wrote seem real, the letters are captivating because we can never be sure whether he is telling the truth, or whether he is being seduced by his imagination into believing the legends he created for himself.

There have been quite a few different versions given of that famous fight, most of them composed by Hemingway himself, his varied accounts becoming increasingly bizarre over time. I think it's safe to say that the most accurate one is that given in Callaghan's memoir. A close reading of it shows that Callaghan had no axe to grind. He was a man singularly lacking in vanity and pretension. I never saw any signs in my many conversations with him of any bitterness or spite at Hemingway's grotesque behaviour and manipulations of the truth.

I can picture him again saying such things to me in his living room. "He couldn't help doing these things, don't you know," he'd say, sadly shaking his head.

Morley ended many sentences with that earnest "don't you know," or "don't you see."

And we usually did see. What we also saw was the warmth and generosity of spirit of that wonderful old man. I often got the impression that he felt he had to excuse and forgive Hemingway out of admiration for his great gifts.

But again we are faced with the importance of these missing letters. It was Morley's sympathy for Mary Hemingway's feelings which caused him to leave out the parts that literary history needs. Which we are now deprived of.

Flash forward twenty years from that 1993 robbery in my Queen Street shop.

Earlier this year, while reading J. Michael Lennon's masterful biography of Norman Mailer, one of my youthful intellectual mentors whom I had pretty much stopped reading by the time of his thousand-page novels, I again become interested in that early influence. I returned to the early books, especially the essays, skipping around in *Advertisements for Myself* and several collections, fascinated at how well those early essays held up.

Then, in *Cannibals and Christians*, by chance I hit on something I'd long forgotten reading: Mailer's review of Callaghan's memoir, wherein Mailer continued his compulsive picking at the scab of Hemingway's psyche, probably the obsessive disease of all American writers of his generation, but especially true for such an ambitious one as Mailer.

I was astounded at Mailer's prescience and the depth of his understanding of Hemingway's motives with such limited material as what Callaghan provided in *That Summer In Paris*.

And I found all my earlier speculations returning.

Mailer caught all of Hemingway's insecurities and vanities so well that I could only marvel at his insights.

And he hadn't seen what I had seen, the primary record found in those missing letters.

I read it twice, went back to Callaghan's account, then to the catalogue I prepared when I was trying to sell the letters, now the closest thing to the actual record which remains to us.

Quotes I had put in the descriptions of the letters time after time enticed with their shortness, causing my memory to try and bring back the details I'd forgotten. The details had faded but not the general impression of Hemingway's decidedly pathological response, and here was Mailer seemingly seeing it all.

But while I reread Mailer's brilliant assessment of Hemingway's psyche and compared it to the quotes in my catalogue and my memories of the emotional impact the full reading of all the pertinent letters had left with me all those years ago, I began to realize the real significance of the robbery and what we had actually lost.

It's not just a bunch of autograph letters and signed books of interest to a small group of autograph and first edition collectors.

What's missing, maybe forever, is important evidence relating to the mental make-up of two of the major writers in 20ᵗʰ century American letters.

In the context of American literature, this is an almost incalculable loss. Dozens of books and papers have been written, and many more will be, speculating on the twisted friendship between Hemingway and Fitzgerald, and here we have documents intrinsic to any deep understanding of this relationship lost to posterity because of greed and criminal ignorance.

No writer, and most especially no American writer, can escape Hemingway's influence on literature, ever. And this has nothing to do with what one feels or thinks about this peculiar man or his work. He changed literature forever and he must be reckoned with.

Historians spend lifetimes searching for evidence long after events are generally forgotten in order to place history in proper context. This is what we are now dealing with here. The people who stole this important literary archive stole evidence; evidence literary history needs. Scholars of the future will curse them, those responsible—and those who abetted them—the curse of the scholar will haunt them. As it should.

The old familiar obsessions resurfaced after re-reading Mailer but this time there was a difference. Now given the perspective of time, my view of the events has changed. Now, what once I saw as a crime, a mystery to be solved, the resolution bringing justice and retribution, has come to be seen by me as a sin. Not a crime to be solved, but a sin—a sin against literary history, a sin against the truth: no longer a petty theft, but the stealing of truth from the literary record.

A minor crime has become a major sin.

The truth has been stolen from posterity and now I feel I must point these things out. I left this account out of the first edition of my published memoir because I had no answers, and answers seemed to me to be necessary to justify the inclusion of a mystery. But this no longer seems a mystery to me. I think the nature of the crime is now what's relevant and what must be emphasized.

A weird response, you might say; a life-long atheist speaking of a perceived sin.

I can only quote one of my favourite authors, Brian Moore, another life-long atheist (although he was born a Catholic) who, when asked how he could profess himself an unbeliever when every one of his serious works had themes where the moral dilemmas were deeply Christian, could only answer, "I never had the gift of belief." An appropriate response and a noble one, I think, and I can only concur with that view.

But I believe the sinful aspect needs to be emphasized, if only for the reason that people need to be aware that there *is* posterity, and that time *does* eventually unearth the truth and that there *will* be judgments. And the guilty will be exposed. I am only chagrined that I will probably miss it.

So, in the end, I have to acknowledge all the professional strictures I have claimed to follow in my life as a bookseller. That the mystery will probably remain unsolved during my lifetime is not what is most important. What really matters is that this archive, those letters, those artifacts which are so important to everything I believe in, do survive. That they are still intact somewhere, and that one day they will surface, and go where they should go, to a safe repository where they will illustrate the weakness and vanities of greatly talented men, who, no matter their human frailties and stupid arrogances, created beautiful works of art for humanity. Which is the justification for their lives—and through my life-long devotion to literature, mine—and the only reassuring certainty I can grasp at.

CHAPTER 20

William Hoffer and the ABAC Wars

S ometime in the summer of 1970 I sat in my tiny new shop on
Toronto's Gerrard Street waiting for customers, a common
activity of antiquarian booksellers, then and now. On that day
the empty silence was suddenly broken by a tall gangly figure
resembling a giant demented stork, who came bounding into my
tiny shop, barely able to restrain his flapping arms.

"I hate Toronto," he boomed, not bothering with any preliminaries. "I always get paranoid—every time I come here. Why
do I come here?" he paused, as though awaiting my explanation.
"I'm Bill Hoffer." Still shouting, he paused and glared at me truc-
ulently, daring me, it seemed, to contradict him.

We spent a couple of hours measuring and assessing one
another and discussing the state of the book trade in Canada. His
conversation was constantly interspersed with the many reasons
why Toronto needed to be wiped off the face of the earth.

In spite of his obvious weirdness I found myself liking him.
When he launched into a diatribe, which he did often, he would
become intoxicated by his own rhetoric, then leap up bellowing
and, like an actor, pace the store as though it were the stage of a
theatre. He was, perhaps, the first person I ever met whose voice
merited the word stentorian.

While I've been avoiding it for many years, I have always
known that I must eventually write about Bill Hoffer. The reason I avoided it was because it is widely believed that Hoffer
and I were enemies. It is true that in the last days of his life we
had broken completely; indeed the last time I spoke to him, I
publicly and loudly berated him in a bookstore in Ottawa in

front of a good portion of the Canadian book trade. This was at a pre-bookfair party, meaning everyone in the crowded store was a bookseller or a bookseller's moll, all colleagues of both of us. Hoffer had entered, greeting people as he progressed through the crowd of eating, drinking and jabbering booksellers and, reaching me said "Hello David," with a casual manner, as though all the events of the past couple of years had not occurred. As though the Canadian trade had not been torn asunder, turning friends into enemies, arousing anger and resentment that I expect in some cases will only disappear as people die off. I lost it. His idea seemed to be that we should pretend that his craziness hadn't decimated much of the conviviality which had, till then, existed amongst all the members of the small Canadian trade—as though the ensuing insanity was just business or something, and that here, on a social occasion, we should just ignore the personal repercussions. I yelled at him. "Don't speak to me Hoffer! Go to the other end of the store. Get away from me, goddamn you." I was furious. The store went dead silent—forty or fifty booksellers together, all silent, a rare situation. Hoffer was shocked. He didn't respond, but slunk over to Patrick McGahern at his desk behind the counter, leaned over and whispered something to Pat, then left the store. The hum of talk gradually began again, but everyone avoided looking at me.

I went over to McGahern. "What did he say to you, Patrick?"

"He said he didn't appreciate being yelled at in my store," replied McGahern.

This will be the first of the many contradictions in Bill's character that I will be pointing out. Here's a guy who—admittedly with some help from his friends—had nearly destroyed the Antiquarian Booksellers Association of Canada (ABAC), certainly had created animosities which, in some cases, will never disappear, who was infamous for his attacks on people, blistering letters, loudly conducted insults and ejections from his store, and when someone whom he knows can defend himself yells at him in anger he slinks out like a naughty child who is being sent to his room. We never spoke again.

The fact is that while Hoffer and I had many confrontations and he no doubt saw me as his main adversary in his anti-Toronto, anti-East in general, and anti-ABAC campaigns, we had fairly cordial relations when we weren't involved in one of those periodic eruptions.

The real reason for the perception that we were enemies was that I stood up to Hoffer—I wouldn't let him get away with his insane silly attacks, so I was almost always in the forefront when it came time to battle.

Many amongst those who didn't automatically agree with him avoided those confrontations, some no doubt out of weariness at his incessant provocations, others perhaps because of their own less attractive character traits. And, of course, he had his acolytes, a group, mostly also in the west, who agreed with his paranoid views. But there was also a group which venerated him, men whom he had mentored, who believed they owed much to him for his teaching of them, for imbuing in them the principles of professional bookselling. I actually agreed with that. For instance, every dealer in western Canada whom I consider a very good dealer still pays serious homage to Hoffer as a mentor and a friend, to whom they often publicly acknowledge their own great debt.

I think we have to weigh this against the craziness.

Almost no one in the Canadian trade will remember that a large expansion occurred in membership in the ABAC during the early to mid-seventies, with the bulk of the new members dealers from western Canada. And even fewer would credit that expansion mostly to the combined efforts of William Hoffer and myself, but so it was.

After the war, Bernard Amtmann, a Viennese Jew who had emigrated to Canada after fleeing the Nazis and fighting in the French resistance, set up as a bookseller, first in Ottawa and then Montreal. He had bullied and cajoled several of his colleagues into forming a professional association in 1966, following the examples of the founding of such associations in several countries, such as in the Antiquarian Booksellers Association (ABA) in England and the Antiquarian Booksellers Association of America (ABAA) in the United States. In Canada Amtmann organized it all, paid for everything out of his own pocket, then forced us—in spite of our timidity—into attending foreign book fairs and personally shamed us all into holding the first Canadian book fair ever, at York University.

After he had done this, concentrating on his neighbours in Montreal, Toronto and the east in general, he had approached several western Canadian dealers to join, mostly soliciting their membership based on that age-old system, word of mouth—that is by their reputations, which had filtered east. I have in my own archive a letter from Amtmann to Don McLeod of McLeod's Books in Vancouver announcing that he had been pronounced eligible and asking him to join, telling him he could pay the fees in installments, if necessary. That was typical of Bernard; to assume and acknowledge our mutual poverty and offer ways out before anyone used that as an excuse not to join.

But he had only successfully recruited Hoffer, Hilton-Smith of Victoria and Ned Bowes of Vancouver, although, on Hilton-Smith's recommendation, I believe he also solicited Steve McIntyre of Vancouver, who also didn't join.

I met McIntyre only once, on my first visit to Vancouver. He was amiable, but, I sensed, a loner. I also sensed he had that not uncommon affliction of booksellers, including me in those days, a propensity for drink. This was confirmed many years later when

I purchased an extensive correspondence between him and Al Purdy which dealt pretty much entirely with books and alcohol.

I liked McIntyre. He seemed lonely, with an undercurrent of deep sadness, yet he was eager for the bookselling gossip from the east. He questioned me very closely, nodding as he absorbed my answers. He was both highly respected by Vancouver booksellers and held in great affection by them, and I expect he was a crusty mentor to most. And he was obviously a *real* bookseller.

It must be understood that amongst other social and political realities which Canada shares with the U. S., we have vast expanses and the sense of separation caused by thousands of miles, but unlike our American friends we also have a huge, near-empty prairie and an impressive range of mountains. Canada has a population one-tenth that of the U.S. and, unlike America, whose middle parts are dotted with lots of cities, our major cities are mostly in the lower parts of each province, near the border. So it is much harder to find a city of a size that could sustain large used bookstores in much of that vast expanse, or at least one worthy of a de-planing and all the extra expense that involves. Canadian dealers envy our American and British colleagues, who can hit many different towns in a day or two. Crossing Canada can mean a thousand miles between worthy bookstores. Our two ABAC colleagues in Saskatchewan, for instance, like to announce that only one Canadian dealer has ever visited either of their stores, and that was on a fishing trip. And it was the same dealer. I grew somewhat familiar with Calgary but only because my wife was from there and I frequently visited her family. Being there for other reasons allowed scouting and I generally did well not only because I didn't need to pay for hotels but because other dealers seldom visited.

Consequently the western Canadian dealers looked, and still look, south rather than east for their essential book connections—the average west coast dealer will be far more familiar with the bookstores of Seattle, Portland, San Francisco and Los Angeles than with any eastern Canadian shop.

This exclusionary situation became of great concern to the executive of the ABAC, so when I announced in the early '70s that I would be shortly travelling to Vancouver, Victoria and Calgary I was authorized (I was then an elected director of the ABAC)—in fact ordered—to speak to any western dealer whose shop passed muster, strongly urging them to join our association.

Naturally, in Vancouver I started with Bill Hoffer. We spent a few evenings drinking and arguing about all sorts of east-west crap. I contradicted him bluntly every time he tried to introduce what I considered then, and still do, that petty provincial attitude where regional animosities or jealousies poison people to the point where they somehow see their fellow countrymen, or in this case their co-religionists, as enemies. This enraged me then and it still does, as it is unworthy of civilized people, especially when they are such civilized people as booksellers.

We drank quite a lot. Indeed, we got drunk every night, but we already had formed an essential understanding, one that obviated all the many differences in viewpoint and personality and personal prejudices. While unspoken, it was apparent to us both that we shared one essential characteristic: we were both *real* booksellers. Bookselling to each of us was a vocation, not a job, and we had both embraced it fully, with no doubt that that was what we were meant to be. So, in spite of our differences, we reached a clear understanding. We were both serious in intention and we both shared the essential view that the ABAC should be inclusionary. Any bookseller who passed that crucial test, who was serious about being a professional bookseller, was a potential candidate. Bill and I agreed that for the future of the trade in Canada we should recruit every eligible bookseller.

Don Stewart, who had purchased McLeod's from its founder, Don McLeod, and still owns it, tells me that Bill talked him into joining in 1973. This must be around the time of my first trip west. I really don't remember if that means Don would have joined after the Hoffer/Mason axis was formed, but I would like to think it was a result of our combined efforts. Certainly others did. And while I spoke of the ABAC in every shop I visited and strongly urged each owner to join, I left the real work of persuasion to Bill. Wisely so, for the western dealers, while not unfriendly, greeted me with the reserve and suspicion that foreigners from the east still seem to receive (often from those inhabitants who are themselves refugees from the east). I did the same in Calgary, which was even more isolated from the east than Vancouver, but with more success.

Anyway, after my trip there, the first in some time by an eastern dealer—at least since the ABAC had been formed—I was able to return and report that Hoffer was on the job and that I expected the results to be good. And they were. We got just about every qualified dealer to join except for the two or three contrarians like McIntyre, found everywhere, who never join anything on principle.

Most of the technical problems were easy, and our campaign resulted in several new western members, and our warm invitations to the new and rapidly growing Toronto book fair were accepted by several dealers; following which book fairs were begun in Vancouver, then Victoria, where eastern dealers came and grew to know their western colleagues.

Most important, we quickly voted several westerners onto the Board of Directors so that the westerners also had a stake and say in association affairs. And, of course, personal friendships ensued amongst dealers who previously hadn't known each other well. Then we directed the campaign eastward, first to our

French colleagues in Quebec (we already had the English dealers, because the ABAC had started with Bernard Amtmann initiating it all with Grant Woolmer, Bill Wolfe and several other English dealers in Montreal being bullied into joining).

The east coast followed that, as the Maritime Provinces were dragooned. Curiously, what we never got and still don't have, is any Newfoundland or Prince Edward Island dealer. I've known several Newfoundlanders who dealt in books but every one of them had to make their living elsewhere, while the PEI booksellers I've known never seemed to graduate past selling used paperbacks and books relating to the Island—sad.

Cordial relations with Bill remained for quite a few years. They were always good when you were in his presence, but left to himself in his tiny garret I think his natural paranoia led to imaginary flights which, as often as not, resulted in yet another anti-Toronto or anti-eastern vendetta. And a flow of vicious letters would ensue.

My later problems with Bill came from his constant disruption of ABAC affairs, where he invariably instigated strife amongst the members who cared, then divided them into opposite sides and sat back to watch the strife he had stirred up.

I once spent a night drinking with Bill when he had just returned from a trip to Israel. I think it might have been his first visit to Israel, but I don't really know. He was entertaining a group of booksellers with an absolutely brilliant monologue about Israel, which stunned us all with its incisive wit. It went on for almost an hour, while we all sat in rapt wonder at his insights and perception.

It was wildly funny and incredibly anti-Semitic; which I thought then, and still do, is an important clue to both Bill's character and, to a degree, to that crazy streak that caused so much trouble for him and the rest of us.

I expect that whether a passionate Zionist or not, he was very conscious of being Jewish, for indeed his forebears were Russian Jews. The anti-Semitism he displayed was eerily similar to the wrathful scorn he heaped on what he considered the multiple sins of Canadians (especially easterners and most especially Torontonians). You could say he was at his best when he was attacking his own.

Perhaps this was the root of his rage, the frustration at not having accomplished his dreams of grandeur. All these unprovoked attacks I recount, plus many others I've heard of, convinced me, finally, that Bill's attacks were really manifestations of some painful frustration at his failure to measure up himself to his grandiose view of what he believed should have been his personal destiny.

In an earlier time Bill would have been a religious visionary or a revolutionary. Eventually I came to realize that Bill was another of those few people I have known who were essentially religious people, but who, lacking any belief in the established religions, had to find other outlets for their religious impulses. The most common result of this need many seem to have to believe in something larger than themselves usually ended in political movements, all the "isms" which have cost so many millions of lives.

What I also came to believe—and still do—is that most of Bill's "causes," and the consequent vendettas, were fraudulent. By this I mean I believe he actively sought out causes on which to focus his rage. I also believe that once he had found a cause he sincerely believed in it; he wasn't a hypocrite. I think he manufactured these passions because he *needed* enemies, needed to find those windmills. I don't think his passionate campaign against subsidized Canadian Literature, and by extension the Canada Council, had any basis in his real beliefs. Subsidies were simply an easy target. And life without targets was impossible for Bill. Certainly he cared about literature, and certainly about books and the history of the booktrade. But I always felt that Bill, in his own mind, operated on a very different level. I think he believed, and I do not say this in any disparaging manner, that he was destined for greater things, that his vision of the way things should be in the world was superior to that of others. He believed that his vision was of such importance that he had an obligation to fight for its implementation.

In principle, that's a stance I agree with. The truth is that Bill was brilliant, but there was a problem with his vision: parts of his vision were indeed brilliant, but other parts were obviously demented; the problem was to sort out one from the other.

Bill's shop stock, observed on visits over many years, reflected his personality, as do the stocks of all booksellers, gradually evolving in a manner that also reflected the changes in focus and emphasis that time and experience impose on all of us. In the early years he had a general used stock stressing literature more than other areas, with Canadian literature being the only really impressive part of it. Later his stock of Canadian literature was truly impressive, only Nicky Drumbolis and later Steve Temple and Nelson Ball being able to compete in terms of richness and depth.

But in later years, his hatred for many Canadian writers and the feuds that ensued, his rage at so many of the professors who taught Canadian literature and whose buying practices (or lack of them) caused him to attack them as well, got out of control. He even titled one of his catalogues, full of his succinct opinion of those people, *Cheap Sons of Bitches.* Afterwards he started concentrating on buying more widely in antiquarian books, but it was too late for him to effectively explore other options.

I don't think it was an accident that in his last shop almost all of the huge stock of Can Lit was relegated to the second floor, a sure sign of his anger and disillusionment with his acknowledged specialty.

Much later, after the huge ABAC fight, when many scurrilously nasty letters full of vicious insults were criss-crossing the whole country, tearing the ABAC apart for a generation, one of my own contained what I considered (and still do) a very apt accusation.

"Bill," I wrote, after deliberately insulting him by telling him that I believed that he had only been able to cause so much trouble because his father had given him a half-million dollars or more, "You would be the only bookseller I ever met who purported to despise the only area of books you know anything about."

That was a lovely insult—made more telling, I thought, for being true.

Here are a few more of Bill's self-contradictions. He would invariably be a lively host in Vancouver; but back home vicious slander would filter back or paranoid accusative letters would appear.

He spent a lot of his own money, and an enormous amount of time and energy, on his attacks on the Canada Council, but I discovered he himself had both applied for and received a grant some years before to publish a book. When I inquired if he didn't see a certain irony in this he shrugged it off contemptuously. His vision was too majestic to be concerned with such petty contradictions.

My own view then, and now, about the Canada Council's grants is, so what? I don't mind the thought that future generations of booksellers will have to throw out all that self-indulgent puerile crap purporting to be poetry that the Canada Council paid for. What about the ten thousand other stupid projects the government, like any government, funded in the same period, which flushed away millions of the taxpayers' dollars? If even one great book or painting resulted from all that bureaucratic excess, it's still, in my view, preferable to another mile of freeways or a few more sewers.

For the serious writer, who views his craft in a religious sense, such misplaced patronage must evoke rage as yet another example of the triumph of the mediocre. But booksellers know that time takes care of mediocrity by placing it where it belongs, always.

After Toronto, and other booksellers, Bill loved most to eviscerate those writers he hated. When one had incurred his wrath, for any reason, he never missed an opportunity to attack them, usually trespassing far beyond the boundaries of legitimate criticism and entering libelous territory.

I came to believe that Bill was a born anarchist. The trouble was that he was an anarchist not in the philosophical sense that his co-westerner George Woodcock was, but in of the old-fashioned born-in-Russia fashion, where bombs were the solution.

I began to look more closely at all those Bill attacked and I came to certain conclusions about his hostilities. I measured Hoffer's attacks alongside his constant attacks on me, although I was well aware of his respect for me as a bookseller. Aside from the obvious perceived affronts to his personal dignity, which usually meant booksellers who had offended him, or customers who asked the wrong questions, or innocents who thought a bookstore was a safe haven of learning, where their awe and love of books would protect them, it was mostly writers who suffered Bill's wrath. The pattern I saw seemed to show that the Canadian writers he attacked all had one thing in common: they were the successful ones, often the most famous, Margaret Atwood being perhaps the best example.

It seemed that it was precisely those writers who were becoming highly respected both within and outside of the

The Pope's Bookbinder

country who became the focus of Hoffer's rage. It was not a huge leap to find a connection between his rage at these people and his own perceived failure to obtain a similar status. I began to wonder how much of his vitriol might be born of personal disappointment.

Bill attacked many writers. In his now-famous *Catalogue 80* he attacks half the writers in Canada in his typical cruel and dismissive, but often brilliant, style.

This and other catalogues were extremely amusing no matter what you might think yourself of the authors he chose to skewer. I still reread them with amusement and wonder.

Two authors he loved to attack were bpNichol and bill bissett, both writers whom, no matter your opinion of their work, were widely loved and admired by just about everyone who knew them.

Bill's attacks always became personal attacks; his hatred and contempt for writers' work (or in the case of booksellers, their sins, real or imagined) might not escalate if they were ignored, but if any defense or even response ensued, Bill made it personal and things would quickly escalate to total war.

Bill's scorched-earth method of dealing with adversaries didn't allow for subtlety; if you weren't with him you could expect a devastating response. Many people pretended to be with him rather than risk his wrath, I think.

I find it difficult to imagine that anyone could hate bill bissett, but Hoffer did. He regularly announced his plan to hold a public burning of bissett's books—in fact all the books published by bill at blewointment press—in his parking lot. The attendees would arrive dressed in full formal wear to witness the ceremonial conflagration. Here, incidentally, we see yet another of the many contradictions I noted in Bill over the years. Every bookseller I ever met shares the contempt civilized people should feel towards all censors, but here's Bill Hoffer, who wants to burn books he doesn't like. If you pointed out such contradictions to him, instead of being embarrassed, he would be delighted.

He once told me, and I later heard him repeat it many times, even in print, a very scurrilous anecdote about Atwood. It goes like this. A Vancouver collector, a very cultivated man of East-Indian extraction, who had studied at Oxford, met Atwood at some literary function. During a chat the man mentioned in passing that he had been at Oxford, whereupon Atwood replied—according to Bill—"What were you, a janitor?" Even a cursory examination of this anecdote demonstrated very clearly that Bill's motivation was not just malicious, but ill-thought-out. Bill claimed he had it from the man involved, but one only had to hear it to know that almost no one would act in the manner or use the words he ascribed to Atwood.

It never seemed to occur to Bill that such a response was so unlikely as to be ludicrous. It was obvious that he expected us to understand the anecdote as proof of Atwood's racism. It was even more ludicrous given this man's obviously elegant style and manner of speech. No one would have ever mistaken this man for a janitor. But most ludicrous of all was the idea that even a blatant racist would speak that way during a social encounter with a stranger. The relish with which he recounted it was really a measure of his hate for Atwood and his curious inability to even recognize how inane such an accusation made him appear. I came to believe that these attacks gave a great clue to Bill's character. He was always privately—at least in the first twenty years—respectful, and even deferential towards me, saving his vicious attacks for times of ABAC strife, always magnified by distance (he once referred to me in print as the enemy of his which he considered most talented). I think his attitude was the same towards Bernard Amtmann. Once, trying to understand the vicious attacks on

Amtmann he initiated at any opportunity, I asked him out of curiosity, "Bill—tell me, how well did you know Amtmann?"

"Oh," replied Bill, seemingly indifferent to the import of his words, "I only met him once. For about five minutes."

"Then why," I asked, perplexed, "could you decide a man you only spoke with for five minutes was as evil as you seem to think he is? Did he insult you or something?"

"No," said Bill, "he was very kind and solicitous. I just *knew* he was evil and dangerous."

His attacks on writers, as vicious as they may have been, were nothing compared to his vendettas within the trade, especially the Canadian trade.

I was enraged by Hoffer's repeated attacks on Bernard Amtmann, which were both malicious and in their substance completely erroneous. Bill and I clashed over this a few times, although mostly his diatribes came to me second or third hand. I know Bill was afraid to attack Amtmann openly, just as he was afraid to confront me. And I believe I know why. He knew Amtmann was a man of courage, who wouldn't take shit from anyone, just as he hadn't taken shit from the Nazis, and Bill wasn't about to mess with him, not to his face anyway. But the truth is, I believe that Bill respected Bernard as a man and I came to believe that some frustration at his own personal failure to accomplish what he felt he should have caused him to lash out at people who had made their mark. Like Atwood and like Amtmann.

The primary basis for one of Bill's attacks on Amtmann was the latter's habit of putting out catalogues of Canadian literature which were really just accumulations of whatever had found its way into Bernard's store. Bernard didn't care about Canadian literature; he issued those lists for a very simple reason: to pay the rent. Bill would have seen this as heresy; he really did care about literature and, I think, a good part of his rage was a direct result of the indifference of almost all Canadians to it, as well as the misguided interest in anything that appeared like literature by all these academics who had an institutional stake in the field.

Bill followed his usual style with anyone—writer, bookseller, or customer—who had aroused his ire: he attacked whenever and wherever he could.

Sometime after Bernard Amtmann had died I was slyly shown a letter from Bill to someone else (another example of a disciple stirring things up) which began "I've been waiting ten years for Amtmann to die so we could make something of the ABAC." The problem with that statement, like so many of Bill's, was that it had no basis in fact. Bernard Amtmann founded the ABAC, he made his friends join, he paid all the initial expenses, and having got it going he then bullied us all into attending foreign book fairs. Then he made us run our own Canadian book fairs and he organized the first one. He refused to allow our timidity and lack of self-confidence to keep us from showing an international presence. Once he'd done that, he forgot about the ABAC. He had made the timid kids act like adults and that was enough. After that he barely even bothered to attend any more ABAC meetings. He believed that having jump-started us, we could then take care of ourselves, and he was right. Who knows how long it would have taken us to figure that out on our own, without Bernard's prodding. He had done his duty. He went back to berating the librarians and the institutions of Canada for ignoring Canada's heritage. And he went back to trying to make a living. He had damaged himself enormously, indeed he died broke, deeply in debt, and with many institutional enemies because he insisted on sticking his neck out and demanding that we, the booksellers, be treated with respect by these institutions, because he believed that we were important and what we do is important, and that our cultural heritage, which we search out and sell to those institutions, is important.

He had his admirers amongst librarians, but many others called him a crook. But no one ever has ever gotten away with calling him that in my presence. I know what I and every other bookseller in this country owes to Amtmann, and, indeed, what many of our institutions also owe to his courage and his stubborn refusal to shut up. I have tried to emulate what Bernard initiated, sometimes to my cost, but never suffered even close to the extent that Bernard suffered for his opinions. He regularly forfeited his rightful profits because he insisted on the right of the rest of us to ours. He fought for our legitimacy at the cost of his own. And I will not forget that, nor let anyone else ignore it.

At the San Francisco book fair in February 1979 word circulated amongst the Canadian dealers present that Bernard had died. Several of us found ourselves standing morosely on the floor together, deeply saddened at the passing of this man to whom we all owed so much. I remember six to eight Canadians being there, but the only ones I clearly remember were Grant Woolmer, Alfred Van Peteghem, Hugh Anson-Cartwright, Ned Bowes, Steve Temple and myself. But there were certainly more. Hoffer and Bill Matthews were there but did not join our little group. Some of our American and English colleagues would approach us from time to time to offer condolences, as though we had lost a family member—which, I think, we all felt we had.

We stood there, each no doubt lost, as I was, in his own memories of Bernard; each no doubt aware that we wouldn't probably even be there if it weren't for Amtmann. Curiously, it is one of the times I remember feeling most intensely Canadian, standing there surrounded by foreign dealers, in an American city, feeling terrible, bereft, because a scrappy little Jewish guy from Vienna had died, making me feel like an orphan.

Shortly after this Peter Howard of Serendipity Books in Berkeley, a close friend of Hoffer's and a dealer I consider the best bookseller of my generation, even though I fought with him most of the forty years I knew him, came up to me and asked: "Is it true that Amtmann was the miserable bastard they say he was?"

I knew where that had come from. "Those sons-of-bitches had better not dare say that in front of me. Or any other Canadian here, either," I replied angrily. I then blasted Peter with the tirade I have just written above.

To Peter's credit he didn't reply.

Perhaps here is the place to introduce some interesting points about the behaviour of some of Hoffer's friends. Peter Howard may have actually wanted my opinion when he made that query about Amtmann, to measure it against what he had been told by others; or he may have been doing what several others have done for years, unaware that I have mostly seen through their not-so-subtle ploys. Maybe Peter simply wanted to stir things up. Certainly I have lots of evidence that others did. Many of Hoffer's friends seemed to stay loyal to him whatever he did—even to them.

One important conclusion I arrived at, which continued to surprise me after I figured it out, was that some of Bill's friends were far more dangerous than he was. Because of his style and because he appeared to be the instigator of so many things, it took a while to see the much more sinister nature of some of his followers. With Hoffer, because he was so volatile, you usually knew where you stood. He usually attacked openly. But several of his followers lacked the nobility of aim that he demonstrated alongside his craziness, the craziness that almost always caused him to escalate a worthy thought into the realm of insanity.

Curiously, all these years after Bill's death, I find myself becoming even fond of him again. After a lifetime of admiring outsiders and misfits I find that I am again coming to admire his passionate tilting at the windmills which obsessed him. Maybe he was Don Quixote, as he probably saw himself; or maybe he really was a character from almost any of Dostoevsky's novels, as I and many others saw him.

The *Big Fight*, as it is now commonly referred to in the Canadian trade, erupted over a point in our constitution which stipulated quite clearly that only persons who were full-time booksellers could be eligible for membership.

For years Hoffer had agitated for a new constitution for the ABAC, having convinced himself in one of his many authoritarian moments that the way to make things work smoothly was to make more rules and laws.

I was strongly against this. Our original constitution was very loose, based on the legal obligations provided by the laws of Canada, as per our charter. I believed (I still do) that by sticking with this constitution we were free to do pretty much anything we liked, and that we could deal with problems or change as it came up and pass bylaws to enable us to go in any direction we wanted. During my tenure on the board, some twenty to twenty-five years in every capacity, we have passed quite a few bylaws. The problem—perhaps typically—was that we lost all the files containing the minutes of all those meetings, so nobody seemed to remember, except me, what we had done. Often at our annual meeting a problem or a suggestion would arise and I would point out that we had passed a bylaw twenty years ago relating to it, only to be faced with blank stares. No one else remembered.

Finally Hoffer wore us all down, so it was agreed that we would form a committee to draft and submit to the membership a new constitution.

The committee was composed of Jerry Sherlock, Gail Wilson—then the President, I believe—Larry Wallrich, Bill Hoffer and myself. Bill arrived at the first meeting with a draft

---

David Mason

constitution which he had put together and printed at his own expense and we started to fight it out.

My first problem was that Bill's submission was pretty much an exact copy of the constitution of our American colleagues' association, the Antiquarian Booksellers Association of America (ABAA), with only a few rules based on the most glaring of the differences between American and Canadian law changed. This irritated me. I didn't think that we, as a country which followed the precedent system of the British common law, should be imitating a constitution which was based on U.S. codified law. I felt that his approach would burden us with needless barriers and restrictions. The main area of contention—and the main area of disagreement between Hoffer and everyone else—was the basic qualification for membership. In the U.S. anyone who met the criteria of being a bookseller was qualified, as opposed to ours, which clearly stated that one could only be eligible if one were a full-time bookseller.

I refused to compromise on this point, as I had a fair bit of knowledge about the problems our American colleagues had faced because their law didn't allow such discrimination.

While I had been President of the ABAC, I had been privy to a good part of our American colleagues' problems with their own association. The Americans had been sued by a man who was not full-time, and worse, had a terrible reputation as a slippery crook, although with no record of legal charges relating to his conduct. They had refused him membership based on several objections resulting from his conduct. But he sued, based, I believe, on U.S. Restraint of Trade laws that hamper Americans in so many professional areas.

As I remember it, the ABAA opposed this man, spent some $13,000.00 in legal fees fighting him, and were then informed by their attorneys that they could spend a fortune and would still almost certainly lose. They capitulated and the man, despised by all, was allowed into the ABAA. I saw no reason why we should put ourselves in the same position, where we could face such law-suits, and if I remember correctly so did everyone else excepting Bill and his followers.

After several contentious sessions, we submitted our ham-mered-out draft; it was voted on, and passed.

Long after the new constitution was passed there would still be rumbles of dissent regarding the membership requirements. Finally it erupted again when a librarian in a western univer-sity who had purchased an established antiquarian bookshop in Victoria applied. We assumed that someone would have pointed out to him the constitutional requirement that he be a full-time bookseller, and assumed therefore that the constitution was to be tested. It should be obvious why we had instigated this require-ment. If another requirement in the rules was to be effective, that a bookseller needed to be in business a minimum of three years, how could working evenings and weekends for three full years to qualify constitute that minimum period? And how could that mesh with the experience of a person who actually had run a business full-time for the three years? An obvious problem.

But the real basis of that rule was the belief, shared by me and most of the dealers I discussed it with, that only a man whose whole public livelihood, and hence his reputation, was involved in his business would guard his reputation by acting honestly. If your book business was some sort of hobby business, you might be more prone to succumb to one of the many temptations which occur when you're dealing with people who don't know the value of what they have. A man with a day job to fall back on was not going to be as careful with his reputation as someone whose whole public face was in his book business.

But this librarian applied anyway and after being turned down, applied again later, with his wife named as the owner. Again the application was turned down as improper. Hoffer proposed a constitutional amendment to change the terms of requirement. And the uproar began again. The amendment being proposed was defeated after much exchange of argument and literature.

However, Hoffer continued to pursue it. Indeed, I heard from a friend that he was present when Hoffer boasted to the applicant that he personally would ensure that the man was accepted into the association.

The amendment was proposed again, and then a third time, the rationale being that so few members had bothered to vote that even the majority was a minority. This in spite of what the common law says: that the failure to vote in such cases implies a vote against. The anger continued to fester.

Finally, everything exploded after the third vote when the board of the ABAC, which contained Hoffer's most sinister acolyte Bill Matthews, as well as Hoffer himself as Secretary, issued a proclamation suspending all members who had not voted. They then stirred things up further by announcing that these suspensions would be reviewed at a Director's meeting just prior to the Toronto book fair, with members who had not voted being subjected to expulsion if their excuses didn't measure up. This, of course, meant that affected dealers who were not reinstated would be ineligible to participate in the fair the next day.

These authoritarian pronouncements of the Comintern were contained in a letter by Hoffer to his fellow directors, where he pontificated in such a manner that he appeared to be using the royal we—I choose to do this, I do not choose to allow that. It was an incredible mix of authoritarian bombast and blackmail. One of those directors leaked it to us ordinary members. The result, directed at a bunch of natural anarchists, was equally explosive.

At the annual meeting, which preceded the book fair, once we had covered the multiple motions proposed by irate members, motions which ranged from Hoffer's expulsion to several demands that the entire board of directors resign, the whole nonsensical business was thrown out—although Hoffer's non-expulsion and non-resignation, even from his position as Secretary, caused two public resignations from the ABAC. One of those was Marty Ahvenus, one of the earliest members and a man so gentle and amiable he was universally beloved by all his colleagues; the other, Larry Wallrich, the proprietor of About Books, who was highly respected, having dealt in books in four different countries before moving to Canada.

Friendships were shattered (some remaining so twenty years later) and grudges were held which, I expect, will end only with the deaths of the participants.

Finally, it seemed to me, Hoffer seemed to arrive at some understanding of all the damage he had inflicted on what had heretofore been a group of used booksellers, once mostly friends and now antagonistic foes.

Anyway, not too much time after that, he closed his business, shipped his stock down to Peter Howard in Berkeley and took off for Russia, his family's place of origin, where he married a Russian woman and apparently took up the collecting of Russian folk art.

Well along with these attempts to put Bill into the proper context, I made contact with the Canadian poet Norm Sibum, who had been a long-time friend of Hoffer's. He graciously sent me copies of his long correspondence with Bill after he had given up books and moved to Russia. Those letters, along with a memoir which Sibum himself penned on Hoffer, provided me with a view of Hoffer which was so different from my own experience— and I have to add that of many, many, other people who had to deal with him—that I was astounded.

The Russian letters show a very different Hoffer. Gone was the abrasive, confrontational, messianic madman. The prose was still Bill's; all those unlikely words and phrases he habitually employed, those clever phrases which could shock you with their brilliant juxtapositions of words not expected in normal pedestrian prose—which I came to realize were part of the vocabulary of the religious outsider attempting to impose his vision—were still apparent. But what was missing, seemingly, was the rage. These letters were entirely sane, philosophical even, as though his demons had deserted him. Later he succumbed to cancer and came home to be treated by his father, Abram Hoffer, Huxley's old colleague in the famous LSD experiments, who then was treating various maladies, including cancer, with mega-vitamins.

I later saw copies of letters from Bill when he was sick and probably knew he was dying. They showed same measured calmness. It seemed as if he had attained that philosophical equanimity that we all would hope for at such time, and which we all are virtually certain would fail us.

He died at fifty-seven, and we were finally spared his constant disruptions. But, as I've found so often with other people who caused me so much trouble, I sort of miss him and the startling brilliance mixed with insane outbursts which certainly made things lively.

Some time after Bill's death, John Metcalf wrote an interesting and provocative piece about Hoffer, which appeared first in *Canadian Notes and Queries* (*CNQ*) and then in a slightly revised form in his *An Aesthetic Underground: A Literary Memoir* (Thomas Allen, 2003). This caused me a lot of trouble. John had allied himself to Bill's rather contradictory vendetta against the Canada Council. The primary function of the Canada Council, formed by the Canadian Government to further the arts in Canada, was issuing cash grants to artists and arts organizations, to enable them to relax a bit while they created what was to be the basis of a Canadian cultural heritage. This is not a bad idea, but both Metcalf and Hoffer independently came to believe that such largesse really only fostered mediocrity, allowing every hack in the country to publish their self-indulgent maunderings.

Metcalf in his memoir said several things which led to further writings by others, all of which seemed to be blamed on me by several of Hoffer's cronies and disciples. Metcalf's memoir was both affectionate and laudatory, but John didn't shy away from recounting several things about Bill which offended Hoffer's friends, a predictable result encountered amongst humourless pedants everywhere who only deal in black and white terms.

One of Metcalf's assertions was that Hoffer was, to use a politically correct euphemism, hygienically challenged. I never noticed that, although he was never my house guest and in those days I smoked between eighty and a hundred cigarettes a day (yes, it is possible!), so perhaps I just never noticed. Hoffer certainly drank way too much, especially for a diabetic, and this caused him considerable problems. I remember that he once spent four or five days in hospital in Toronto during a book fair due to a combination of excess alcohol, near-sleepless nights and the frenzied activity which marked a book fair week, at least when we were all young enough to get away with that.

After his stay in the hospital, I kidded Bill. "Did you castigate those Toronto nurses for tending to you so well, Bill?" Or, "Bill, don't tell me a Torontonian saved your life?" And, "Imagine if you had died in Toronto, Bill. What would that have done to your reputation?"

Bill drew himself up in the manner he commonly used when he was about to pronounce something in stentorian fashion. "The wrath of the entire country would have descended on them," he intoned, a slight smile showing. "And the entire international book trade would have demanded retribution—draconian retribution. On Toronto," he added, the smile broadening.

Bill's constant reference to military terms in his campaigns was not just silly; it was a measure of the punitive nature of his rage and frustration. And many of us found his practice of referring to his supposed enemies, in whatever campaign he had thrown himself into that particular week, as "war criminals" particularly offensive, as such ill-thought-out misuse of very emotionally charged words debases the language.

I have come to believe that Bill was really a portrait in frustration, and at the risk of appearing to play at pop-psychology I will elucidate my conclusions. Hoffer, to my mind, is a perfect example of a type fairly common in the twentieth century, one who having lost religion and even political philosophies as a solution to this implacable impulse towards purity, searches compulsively for some cause to which they can pledge their allegiance. Hoffer, I think, sincerely loved literature, indeed, probably all art, so he chose to apply his messianic impulses to attacking the perceived enemies of the art world, envisioning the world as he thought it should be. That he followed in the path of all those other absolutists who have so damaged the human race by attempting to impose arbitrary and harsh rules on people in the name of their vision is to my mind his great tragedy. For he *was* a brilliant man; but, I think, another sad case of one of those perverse twentieth-century examples of one whose passionate vision caused way more harm than good.

Or maybe I'm just trying to grant some measure of forgiveness to a man who, for all his seeming insanity and troublesome propensities, really did care about what I care about.

Chapter 21

Selling Civilization

The sale of the Church Street building meant another move and I, of course, knew where I would be going for sure with this one—to Queen Street, where more and more of my friends were moving and which was rapidly becoming not just the Charing Cross and Fourth Avenue of Toronto but the centre for a whole group of near-penniless young entrepreneurs in all sorts of businesses. I even knew what location I wanted.

Charles Pachter, the artist, had been buying up buildings in that area using, I think, leverage from the banks and nerve, and he had bought the building at 342 Queen Street West where first Temple, then Volume One run by Lockwood and Joyce Blair and operated by them as Abelard Books was located on the first and second floors. Abelard Books had needed the second floor only for extra space so they hadn't bothered to fix it up.

The second floor was dusty and grimy and painted a dingy grey colour, with rugs that sprayed dust with every step. Still, I believed that it had great potential, with its enormous curved front windows facing Queen Street. It had hardly been cleaned, it appeared, since the place was built in 1880.

Pachter had rented the main floor of 342 to an art supply store, but the second and third floors were still available, both of them being around 2,000 square feet. Both of them were for rent at $1200.00 per floor and I would have liked to have both, but moving from $500.00 on Church for store and home to $2400.00 for store alone was more than my business could manage.

I took the second floor, which had its own separate entrance, and began my move. It took an entire month, but my previous moves had taught me enough that I avoided many of the errors I had committed earlier. I had learned that one emptied several sections, took down the shelves, moved and erected them, then put the books back on them. Otherwise one would work in increasingly less space, until it became impossible to move for all of the boxes and shelves.

This new system worked fairly well, but I hadn't counted on my natural propensity, based on the economics of necessity, for using every possible inch of space. This meant that I had crammed way more books than one would think possible into Church Street. It was hard to get everything into Queen in the end, even with twice the space and a closing sale on Church, but eventually I did. But two things happened to complicate things. Trying to get moved and opened before the double rent syndrome caught me, I concentrated solely on the move. For that reason I left the filthy ancient rugs in place even though I knew logic demanded I get rid of them before shelving. I had hired a guy to paint the gloomy grey walls with a couple of coats of white and, as I expected, it changed the appearance radically, white expanding the size, and cleaning making things more cheery.

Putting up shelves, I decided I would have to deal with the floors at the end, stupid as that was—time was more important.

In an incredible bit of luck, when I did come to deal with the filthy carpets by ripping them out, I found not plain old pine boards or worse underneath, but full hardwood floors, which were, of course, filthy with a hundred years of the stains which had seeped through the rugs. But a simple washing of that filth revealed that the original floor was perfect, saved from even a scratch. My time-based stupidity had, for a change, not cost me.

As I had pictured it, fresh paint and proper lights rendered it cozy and beautiful.

I was home again.

And, as has happened every time I've been kicked out of a beloved store, as soon as the horror of the move was over I saw that it had been time, anyway. Having had my future decided by others it seemed my subconscious was not only prepared, but adjusted perfectly to the new situation.

But the major change with the Queen Street shop was that it became the last of my shops which could be seen in any manner as an old-fashioned used bookshop. For better or worse I am now solely an antiquarian bookseller. I continue to make pathetic attempts to pretend that I still have a used bookshop—a small gift section with pretty $10.00 and $20.00 books that no one looks at, a small "clearance" nook with books at 80% off (the old quarter box ploy) but even I can now no longer deny that I'm in the same zone that David Magee was in when I met him all those years ago.

The trouble is, I miss the cheap books, both buying and selling them. And I don't like gin and tonic.

The used book business is in great peril. If the rare book trade seems less precarious, the implications for it are just as ominous because the used book business is the base of the pyramid, of which the rare book is the apex. If the used bookstore survives it will be in a very different form from now. About the only used bookstores that seem to be operating successfully are those where the proprietors seem to know virtually nothing about books. Nor care. They buy for a buck and sell for five, and seem to me entirely lacking in discrimination or any sense of quality. I suspect that even they can only exist by owning their building. I drop in to some of them occasionally, but they are so boring I can seldom force myself to look long enough to find something. I hope they are not the future, but I fear they are; at least in the cities.

Rents in the rejuvenated centers of most North American cities have outpaced a bookseller's ability to pay them. Used bookstores need a lot of space and they need it cheap. After all, used bookstores dealing in recent books at half price, or out-of-print books which are still fairly cheap, need, by their very nature, browsers to seek them out. That means ample space and time, for the books must wait for the person who wants them to come in and find them.

Used & Rare was once a generic term for anything not brand new, although in recent years it has been superseded by the designation Antiquarian (another futile attempt to confer respectability). Used bookstores in the past would usually contain the leavings from the previous hundred or hundred and fifty years—from last year's bestsellers to the reprints of the works of famous writers, the purged books of people moving house, and the libraries of the deceased. While the bulk of the stock in a typical used bookstore would consist of such books, in the last sixty or seventy years the space which paid the rent was the area in front, which sold used paperbacks, the common reading of the young and the impecunious, which heavily outbalance hardcovers in sales. Paperbacks in our time have fuelled the used book business, while the larger general stock of hardcovers gathers dust, sometimes for many years, until the right person finds them.

With the Internet now rendering most used books unsaleable, one finds dealers like me not even buying almost all books from the last hundred years or so. While I hate this, I now have no choice. When we check the Internet sites to find one hundred and fifty copies of a modern book, we begin by not bothering to list our own copy, and it doesn't take long for us to realize that we shouldn't even be buying them in the first place. So now instead of Used & Rare we increasingly find Used disappearing and Rare hiding in offices and homes, appearing only at book fairs.

When the worldwide web started to function, there was a state of near ecstasy in the book trade. Books started to sell to people in places like Tokyo, Singapore, Australia, Eastern Europe. Good books, but ones which previously we would have anticipated might have taken fifteen years for the right person to come along. Pessimists like me weren't so sure this was a good thing, and now we see why. Rare books, being established by their scarceness and intrinsic importance, are less endangered. But there are many cases in the last few years where the Internet has demonstrated that some books, once considered rare, are considerably more common than current owners find comfortable. What I'm saying is that many so-called rare books are not rare. Last year, obtaining a first edition of Samuel Johnson's *Dictionary of the English Language*, I priced it at $30,000.00 and offered it to one of my most serious clients. "No thanks," he said. "I was at the Los Angeles book fair last week and there were three copies there." Johnson's *Dictionary* is not a rare book; it is an expensive book, as it should be, being one of the literary cornerstones of western civilization. Because it was expensive when it was published in 1755, it would have been purchased only by the wealthy, and instead of being read and tossed aside, it mostly languished for a couple of centuries on the library shelves of those huge country houses and survived in great numbers.

But the great books always sell, in fact they are now more saleable than common books. Most dealers will tell you that they can sell a $2,000.00 book more easily than they can sell a $20.00 book.

But what used bookstores need, even more than space and cheap rent, is customers; people who actually come in and browse and find books they weren't looking for but can't resist; or books they didn't know existed by authors they never heard of; or simply a newly discovered book that appeals to their curiosity. The Internet seems to have affected even people's visits to stores. The consensus amongst those colleagues I have talked to seems to be that store sales have been down over a lengthy period, from anywhere between 20% and 50%. It seems that almost everyone uses the Internet to buy most, if not all, of their books. The intricate and I believe essential connection between the buyer and the dealer is thereby threatened, to me perhaps the worst aspect of the entire current situation.

So, used bookshops are closing at a speed which is scary to people who care about learning and civilization. Right now this is mainly booksellers, and perhaps the habitual customers, but the implications seem to me to far exceed the economic concerns of a few guys like me.

A famous writer once said that the degree of civilization of a country could be measured by the number of used bookstores it could sustain. I read a magazine piece, maybe ten years ago, about the British trade, which pointed out that in the previous ten years Britain had gone from 3000 bookshops to less than half that number. This was attributed to high rents, the high streets of British towns having become too pricey for used bookstores. The Internet has exacerbated this situation, but now it is apparent that the Internet is only part of the problem. Friends and colleagues who closed stores to deal from home thinking they could feed their families from the net and the occasional visitor, have often had to send their wives out to work or seek other means of supporting themselves.

But what is most troubling to me in all of this is that collectors need some years of experience collecting to be ready for books in the higher price ranges. And it is my deep conviction that only in the used bookstores can they educate themselves to obtain that level of sophistication which will prepare them for when they are faced with a high price for a book they need for their collection or their library. And what will happen to the education of new collectors when there are no used bookstores? Who will teach them what they need to know?

The large chains, after decimating many of the independents and capturing the average new book-buyer, have staffed their stores with young and ignorant, minimum-wage staff. A friend of mine seeking Evelyn Waugh's *Decline and Fall* was told "try ancient history, you might find 'her' there." Another, wanting Maugham's *Cakes and Ale,* was referred to the cooking section. No one expects a kid working for low wages to have an encyclopedic knowledge of our literature, but your average used bookseller not only knows these things, he can lead you to them or find them for you, and more often than not will recommend similar books that you might not know about. All these changes point more and more to the triumph of bland mediocrity over the personal guidance offered by a knowledgeable bookseller. Every serious reader and collector I ever knew knows that having a knowledgeable dealer to instruct and guide them, especially in their early years, is essential. A friend of mine, a long-time and astute collector, told me recently that years of experience had taught him to start with the best dealers. Although they will often be more expensive, they tend to get the best material and he found after various unpleasant transactions that the high-end dealers often end up cheaper in the long run. A very wise conclusion!

Our job is to search out and buy from remainder tables, from garage sales and the junk heaps, those books which our instincts tell us someone should be looking for, and hold them until that person appears. In other words, we are trained to cull the worthy from the dross. We rescue the past to hold for the future, and if we're wrong we lose money, so we learn to hone those instincts.

Like the blacksmiths, we may be doomed, but let me make a prophecy. We are not going away. If we are doomed, it is only to more of what we have always had to deal with, and we will deal with whatever comes next in the same manner. Fairly soon we will no doubt be selling books as quaint artifacts like antique dealers and we will be selling fewer books to fewer people. But the truth is that most dealers I have known won't much care as long as they can survive to buy another book tomorrow. And read another one tonight.

Even after forty years I still wake up every morning wondering what exciting thing will happen today. And what book I will buy that I never thought I'd own.

I opened on deadline and spent twenty years on Queen West watching the slow evolution (devolution, we thought) from a quaint, lively neighbourhood, with all sorts of great cheap restaurants and interesting neighbours, to the vulgar excesses of the clothes emporia run amok.

Queen Street was vibrant, with more and more bookstores either moving there or opening, including some good small new bookstores, until we had at one count eighteen stores from University Avenue to Niagara Street.

We then had several great years on the street until "progress" took over. The first clue was when the large store beside me, a Goodwill branch, where we all bought our clothes and household stuff, was evicted and a high-end clothing store appeared. It was the beginning of the end, although that wasn't apparent until later.

Within a few years almost all of the small interesting businesses got pushed out, replaced with yet another of the ubiquitous clothing chains, until there was hardly anything left of the old neighbourhood except The Stem, our local mom and pop restaurant where people in the area ate and met. Gossip about the latest outrageous rent one of these clothing empires paid fueled our gossip daily, astounding us.

For several years we would sit on the patio of the Rivoli in the evenings, drinking and watching the passing show. But in the end the passing show became mostly young kids shopping for the increasingly bizarre fashions which told me that I was more and more out of the loop. I had been very lucky in my choice of building though. Pachter, over-extended, had lost most of his buildings in a real estate slump and mine was bought by a woman, Lynn Connell, who moved into the third floor with her three kids. Lynn became a friend and, later, during a bad period when everyone on Queen was going to their landlords with tales of woe, Lynn not only lowered my rent but capped it, never raising it again for the entire time she owned the building.

But everything has an end. Lynn Connell, the closest thing to a perfect landlord I've had, eventually had other plans to pursue and put the building up for sale.

I knew I was done on Queen Street.

As our time approached, Debbie and I started looking for a new space. This was the first time that she had to do so and she learned what I and everyone who needs to find a new business location knows: looking for space is harder and ten times as depressing and takes even more out of you than moving shelves and 100,000 books.

We looked at hundreds of places, some in locations so bizarre that guides would be needed to lead potential customers to us. And others, desirable, but way too expensive for lowly antiquarian booksellers to even consider. It became increasingly apparent that downtown Toronto had no room any longer for booksellers who had stocks the size of ours. We began to look well outside the city, exploring the arc surrounding Toronto in a radius of some twenty-five to thirty miles out. One horrible Sunday in a town a hundred miles from Toronto I stopped the car, we looked at each other in despair and said "What are we doing out here? We're city people. We don't belong out here, no matter how cheap it might be."

We went back to the downtown and started looking for an office in the converted factories still in our area.

But most of them were no longer feasible for booksellers. We had agents offering us space, some so ludicrously inappropriate that we would have marvelled at the optimism of the landlords if we hadn't been so depressed by our prospects. Spaces described as two thousand square feet would be five hundred square feet, and 'newly renovated' meant to some a single coat of paint which barely smudged a hundred years of dirt. The worst of them was a place that even we couldn't find with precise directions, which had been described as a "multi-roomed executive suite." It did have eight or ten rooms, none larger than closet size; shelves would have made any of them impossible to enter.

By this time we were seriously depressed.

We were reduced to wandering every street within a couple of miles of each side of Yonge, by now sure that we were doomed. We would end up, with our books, on the street; our books would be stolen or ruined by rain and we would expire in the gutter, perhaps an appropriate end for our effrontery in thinking that there should be a place in the world for a used bookshop.

Then one day, walking along Adelaide Street West, we saw a sign offering space in a large converted factory. We walked along the hall in the basement (they call it the 'Lower Level,' of course). There were workmen putting up wall board in a large room with the huge two-foot square wooden pillars found in most of these old factories. As soon as we took one look, I knew I'd found my new store. One of the unexpected effects of being a used bookseller is that after a few years it becomes impossible for a bookseller to enter any room without automatically shelving it in his mind. This doesn't just happen in commercial space, it happens everywhere. Women, especially, seem to set up their houses with the concept of how it will appear to their guests. I'm certain that none of my women friends are aware that every time I've entered their houses I've shelved in my mind every room I've entered, ruining their carefully thought-out plans, throwing out all their inconvenient furniture and filling every possible space with books.

When we saw my new store Debbie was doubtful. "It's not right," she said nervously. I had already shelved it in my mind. But she was right in one respect: it was, at some 1800 square feet, smaller than we needed.

I said to the foreman of the work crew who, in fact, was really the superintendent of the whole building and some seven others that the company owned, "It's just what I want but it's too small."

"Well," he replied with a smile. "You can have the room across the hall as well, if you want."

He showed it to me and I began negotiating on the spot. I knew I had found my new shop. A bit of luck intervened here too. I was unaware that most of the upper floors, way too expensive for lowly booksellers, were empty, and that the owners were therefore much more amenable to a deal. We made a verbal commitment on the spot, but were told we needed to submit references and undergo an interview with the landlord before we would be secure.

I made up a packet, a bundle of bullshit based on what I'd learned from dealing with real businessmen and bankers, including a few articles and columns journalists had written about me over the years, and two days later we had a meeting with the owner.

The owner was amiable enough, but he began by informing me that he was a lawyer. Then he showed me one of the articles which had been published on me which he had marked with a yellow marker (which, naturally, booksellers consider a form of desecration). He had underlined a comment I'd made about how all booksellers are so impecunious that they can barely manage the rents.

"We lawyers," he began, laying out the parameters, "aren't really fussy on renting to people who boast that they're not sure that they can pay the rent."

My whining, endemic after all those years, came back to haunt me.

But I responded at once.

"I've never, in forty years, missed a rent payment, nor even been late," I responded bluntly, taking up the challenge. This was my new shop I was dealing with. Losing this negotiation was not an option.

"How long a lease do you want?" he ventured.

"Ten years," I said, trying to hide the fact that I was bluffing.

"Oh," he replied, "we never give ten years. How about five?"

We had done some clever homework—we knew what our two neighbours in the basement (sorry—the Lower Level) were paying, and we knew that one of them, the first basement tenant, had a ten-year lease.

Debbie stepped in at this point with a blunt decisiveness which made me relinquish the entire negotiation to her.

"We need ten years. Anything less is impossible for us. Do you think we're going to go to all this trouble to move again in five years? No."

The landlord had visited the Queen Street shop—he knew what she meant.

I shut up and left it to Deb.

He realized he had met his match, and very quickly too.

She was masterful, and I had the common sense to keep my mouth entirely shut while she not only beat him down on his asking rate, but secured our ten-year tenure.

The deal done, we began our move. That's when disaster struck.

Debbie, who had stayed home feeling weak and dizzy one day, called me to say that she had fallen and was too weak to get back into bed—I'd better come home.

I ran home, and immediately called 9-1-1. Within a few minutes we had six firemen, a couple of ambulance attendants and two cops in her bedroom.

In spite of her weakness Debbie's sense of humour hadn't diminished. Looking at the crowd she quipped that it had been quite a while since she'd had that many men in her bedroom at the same time.

Off we went to the hospital, where after extensive tests she was diagnosed with a blood clot in her lungs. The doctors couldn't understand how this could be with a person her age, especially when she lacked the normal symptoms, the main one being chest pains. She ended up being in hospital for some twelve days and I ended up increasingly demented. Any small business of any duration learns that any problem remains festering in the mind until it's solved. During a move one must make probably a hundred decisions a day, twenty of which will be wrong and need revising on the spot. Norm, my trusty assistant, only with us some months and beginning to use his long-practiced computer skills to set up our website and electronic system, found himself doing the kind of physical labour he probably hadn't done since he was a kid.

He measured up, his unfailing good humour and incessant wisecracks lightening the usual tension. Norm and I would pack up books for a few days and take down shelves until it became impossible to move (I was still doing business then), then I would rent a truck, call in my crew of four and we would move it to Adelaide.

But I was, along with being obsessed with the move, worried sick about Debbie, visiting daily, but incapable of dealing with the real implications of her illness.

Her condition was very serious, but I was essentially in denial; there's only so much the mind can deal with, so I found myself counting on the great doctors in our great hospitals. It became a bit more difficult one morning when I came into her room to find her talking to a sixteen-year-old Chinese man who was about five feet two inches tall. Turns out he was not sixteen, he was a heart specialist, and according to Deb and the nurses I questioned, a very good one. I remembered my old friend and early Church Street client Dachling Pang, who when I first knew him during his residency at a Toronto hospital also looked sixteen years old, in spite of having many years of schooling (he was, and is, a brain surgeon). Meeting Dachling at a San Francisco book fair a couple of years ago, I found that even though he now has grey hair, he still looks sixteen years old.

Debbie, with the hospital stay and the necessary follow-up rest, didn't get back to work for some three months after the move was complete. My obsessional preoccupation with the horrendous move had caused me to be in denial about the real possibilities of what could have occurred. Long after the move, when the actual implications about what could have happened finally sank in, I had a bad period where I became thankful for whatever genetic reaction keeps us going in the face of seemingly insurmountable pressures.

Debbie spent twelve days in hospital while I became even more unstrung, visiting daily but obsessively plowing ahead with the move. I had given my notice to the new owners of the Queen Street building, and rudely too—angry at their years of slippery promises, which they had never intended to keep—and I needed to be out on time or who knows what legal complications could have occurred. By this time I was afraid I wouldn't make it in time, but in the end I did, with two days to spare.

When Deb was released from hospital she went to her parents' for a couple of weeks while she recuperated and finally came home when the move, if not the chaos, was complete.

In all she was off for some six weeks, but the horror of all that plus the exhaustion, no doubt due to my age, made me all too aware that I wouldn't be up for this again, and certainly not when I would be ten years older.

It's a sad state for used bookshops now, not just in Toronto but in every major city in the world. When Debbie and I decided we were city people and intended to stay that way, we knew this decision would be costly. And it has been. We have our main stock in our large two-room shop and live in a tiny heritage house on a residential street, a ten-minute walk away, and it suits us perfectly. But with the considerable overhead this entails it costs us plenty. So many of my colleagues have bowed to economic reality and moved to the country or into their homes, their only access to customers now the Internet or book fairs. Of the glorious days when Queen Street West had seventeen bookstores, only Steve Temple remains, hidden on a second floor in a seedy building, probably the only thing that saves him.

So, I sit here in my mostly empty shop, visited now only by my oldest and most loyal clients, who are still aware of and drawn by the treasures they know I have. Also by the occasional chance visitor, who wanders in and voices their awe by stating, "Wow, I never knew there was a place like this in Toronto." Or those who have been directed to me by other members of the fraternity of book people everywhere, just as I direct those same people where they should visit in all the places and cities in the world where book people can go to find their books.

I've been here now for some six years, isolated in a basement, on a side street, surrounded by what one of the most respected specialists in America has called the best general stock in North America. (And perhaps it was his true view for he said it, not to me, but to someone else; I only heard it at third hand.) That comment cheers me up, as I have always considered myself a generalist. One of my favourite maxims, voiced for many years is, "A good $5.00 book is just as important as a good $500.00 book." And I believe that. One of the inevitable consequences of my lifelong compulsion to buy books whenever I have any money (and, in truth, even when I don't have any) has resulted in me no longer having any $5.00 books. There's no room for them, and even if there were, I get no young browsers anyway.

This is probably an inevitable stage in a bookseller's life, just as is the next stage traditionally followed by older booksellers; move into a bigger house and deal from a separate room, necessitating a small, very select and hence expensive stock, which in itself limits clientele to the upper strata of the collecting crowd, just as it did David Magee when I met him thirty-five years ago.

Curiously, while I was so impressed with Magee's way of dealing towards the end of his life, now that I am faced with the same I find it a bit sad.

I guess I didn't count on the fact that one of my greatest pleasures as a bookseller has been meeting young collectors and recognizing their book-lust and watching them develop their taste and perceptions as they become increasingly sophisticated. I have for most of my career (it actually embarrasses me to refer to bookselling as a career, but you have to refer to a lifetime spent doing the same thing as *something*) understood how important the traditions of the trade are and how imperative it is to pass them on. But it took me until I had lost most of my contact with the young browser at the beginning levels, where they are still just seeking books to read and to own, to grasp this.

I always have understood my mandate to counsel young dealers, to guide the beginners in the proper direction so that they can educate themselves, but I guess I didn't really understand that the collector's progress so closely mirrors that of young dealers.

While I have handled a few important rare books, my aim was never to excel in the flavour-of-the-month sweepstakes. I have tended toward disdain when every travelling dealer who came in asked after Rackham, or those eighteenth-and-nineteenth century coffee-table books with steel engravings, or the hand-coloured botanicals, as those types of books became popular. Even early photography, when it became of interest and then highly sought-after—though I found it fascinating and did pursue it, my pursuit was because of my interest and not the huge rise in prices that all those fads bring along with them.

I have always preferred the out-of-the-way, the curiosities, the areas where I am curious but ignorant, where one buys something and educates oneself researching it.

Every dealer who has written of it (or spoken of it) whom I have respected, has usually mentioned how great is the pleasure of buying a library in an area about which one is fairly ignorant and the enormous pleasure and learning which results. There have been many dealers I've known who chose a specialty all those years ago and stuck with it. These people now have a depth of knowledge in their specialties which will seem incredible to the outsider, but I prefer the excitement and challenge of the new and unknown.

A specialist will spot books in his field in unlikely places and will know their value, and most importantly, he may have a ready customer waiting for that book, but he will also tend to ignore anything outside the range of his specialty. The generalist, on the other hand, will tend to look at everything, seeking books in many fields but, more important, he will be studying everything with the view of its potential. I am of the school which believes that dealers should always be starting and building collections, which only a dealer can properly do, for it takes much searching in shops, at fairs, anywhere in fact, to build a good collection. Actually, I believe collectors should do the same, using the principle Stillman Drake propounded in his marvellous talk to the Amtmann Circle: that a collector pursuing costly important books should also have some minor collections which he pursues just for the fun of it, where the books, when found, are cheap. Doing this affords a lot of fun and ensures that the collector will always have a chance to find something in any bookstore, no matter how humble.

Most important, all book scouting teaches. The lessons learned looking for $5.00 books in junk heaps will teach a collector never to ignore or overlook, no matter how unappetizing the venue seems. That will provide the skills and hone the techniques which will pay off for expensive books too. To think that all the great books are already on the shelves of the greatest dealers and properly priced is a misconception that only the very wealthy can safely entertain.

I have many such collections. Some are serious, like the very good collections I've formed over thirty years of Bulwer Lytton and Marie Corelli. Both these nineteenth-century writers had enormous popularity in their time, meaning they were much reprinted in various secondary editions, and were both pretty cheap when I started. It didn't stay that way, of course, but I got a good head start.

Bulwer was as popular as Dickens in his time and Marie Corelli was perhaps the most popular writer of her time, even though you probably have never heard of her. She was a fraud— short and dumpy, she only published photos of herself as an

ethereal young girl, and her spectacularly vicious attacks on anyone who dared contradict her or criticize her became famous, as
she often published them herself. I have large collections of both
writers, meant to ease the financial problems of my old age. But
I also have quite a few minor collections which afford me great
pleasure, and cheaply. There are several twentieth-century writers whom I read and greatly admire, but not enough to pay the
enormous prices their early books in fine condition command.
So I collect their paperback editions, always in first printing and
only in fine condition. But even with those two strict rules it
is still a very cheap form of collecting and one becomes both
knowledgeable about the advent and progress of the paperback
revolution, and astounded to find how many different editions
have been issued of the books by such people as Waugh, Greene
and Orwell, three people I collect in this manner. And it gets
more complicated—as collecting always does—when one discovered that many publishers changed covers every once in a while,
opening whole new problems. Penguin does this sometimes with
stunning design and cover art so one can have twenty or twenty-five different versions of the same book.

The first three hundred Dell paperbacks I collect not because
of the famous "mapbacks," for which they have been collected
for years, but because the cover art on those early editions is
truly impressive, a perfect example of the use of art to further
commerce. And I collect the first two thousand Signets, arguably the most influential of all the American paperback houses.
But I collect them not for that reason; my reasons are purely
sentimental. For these were mostly my reading of choice when,
as a teenager, I would stop at the cigar store on the way home
from the poolroom every night, seeking the promise of sex
which they offered, often fraudulently, but more than compensated for as they introduced me to much real literature. When

I spot yet another cover of one of those that I remember choosing and reading it brings back wonderful memories of both my naïveté and lack of discrimination, but also the enormous sense of awe when, as I often did, I inadvertently discovered yet another great writer.

CHAPTER 22

What Does It All Mean?

In my early years, when I lived upstairs over my shop, I would generally work late into the night, and often I would spend the last hour looking around my shop while my family slept upstairs. I had built and arranged all the shelves myself, and my stock of books, carefully weeded of dross, I had purchased book by book. I would often walk the aisles looking at the books I had bought, remembering where I had plucked this treasure from some despised colleague, or suffering the embarrassing wince as I saw another of my mistakes or follies accusing me silently from its place on the shelf. Or see part of the library of one of my favourite clients, now gone, and remember so many of our wonderful conversations.

These nightly rituals gave me great comfort and great pride.

This is mine, I would think. I built this myself and it is beautiful. Others see only a bookstore, but I see my own creation, the result of my work, my planning, and my ideas. In times of great stress it would calm me; during periods of upheaval and calamity in my personal life it would sustain me. I have not a shred of doubt that without the stability it conferred I would have ruined myself with drink; it gave me, and still does, my reason and my justification for everything.

Every book had its memories of where and from whom I bought it, what I had paid and how long ago. (These books inevitably resurrected my father, the banker's lectures. *A businessman is supposed to buy and sell. Sell a book for a change—sell it or get rid of it. A book you've had for ten years can never bring a profit, only a loss. If you can't sell it get rid of it.*)

My father was a good man; he meant well; he just didn't understand.

Am I to throw Herodotus in the dump? Is Herodotus in Greek any less important just because hardly anyone can read ancient Greek any longer? Should I dump the obscure, the nut cases, the unpopular and ignored and forgotten novelists who thought they were composing undying art when they were really celebrating those truly undying human emotions, vanity, stupidity, ignorance and obsolescent human sentiments? Or just plain nonsense?

Are we to deny the emotions and dreams which motivated all those silly genteel poets and poetesses who thought they were celebrating the highest human sentiments, when they were actually composing drivel which future generations would justly deride? But who weren't really much different from us?

Don't forget that Newton didn't just write the *Principia*; he also wrote learned treatises on astrology and near-demented polemics on God.

Never forget that Arthur Conan Doyle, whose invention of Sherlock Holmes presented us with the most logical detective ever known, whose celebration of deduction by observation mixed with intelligence continues to fascinate generations, also wrote a book proving the existence of fairies. And that his book on fairies, complete with photographs of fairies fluttering amongst flowers, was based on a hoax perpetrated by two twelve-year-old girls, who sixty years later, while confessing their hoax, admitted that they could never understand how people could have been so taken in by what they had done so lightly as a childish lark. But the creator of Sherlock Holmes *was* taken in.

Does that lessen the brilliance of Conan Doyle—never mind the pleasure afforded to several generations of avid fans of Sherlock Holmes, a creation so compelling that many otherwise imaginative, brilliant people meet regularly, dress up and inhabit Doyle's characters and act as though Sherlock Holmes actually existed? Does this not truly elevate the human imagination no matter how eccentric it might appear?

My old boss, mentor and friend of so many years, Jerry Sherlock, when we had all those wonderful dinners over the years—the food now long forgotten but the conversation, the ideas, still fresh— would always end up in his later years pointing out that we, he and I, and all the people we dealt with during those wonderful years, had been so lucky to be booksellers during the period we have come to believe was the Golden Age of bookselling in Canada.

But when we had these conversations, only possible perhaps with people who have spent a lifetime honing their sense of historical perspective and sense of continuity, it hardly could have occurred to us that we might live to witness the demise of that golden age. Now, with the signs everywhere, we temper our pleasure at the memories of all our wonderful experiences with books and the people who pursue them and worship them with the sad realization that already what we experienced is no more and almost certainly never will be again, the advent of the electronic age rendering us as obsolete as the blacksmith.

Except, except... for the core of it: what will never disappear, what will never be obsolete, what can never desert humanity no matter its latest superficial enthusiasms—the book. The book itself. The book that is, with the possible exception of the wheel, the most perfect invention man has ever created. The book, a small, thick object which one holds, turns a page and continues a dialogue that has existed since man learned to scratch symbols on wood or clay or stone, so that those who came after could know what he thought and felt and believed—and what he thought important enough to pass on. The Gutenberg Bible, the first book printed from moveable type, is considered by book people to also be the most beautiful book ever printed. What other invention of man has ever reached perfection on the first try?

David Mason

One of my father the banker's favourite pronouncements was, "If a bookseller had invented the wheel it would still be square." But to look on the Gutenberg Bible, or even a page from it—all that most of us will ever see—will stun one into an awed reverence. So beautiful, so perfect in execution, and surpassing all else, what it foretold for the future of man.

From the manuscripts previously known, only possible to own for the extremely wealthy or the church, we suddenly had something that eventually gave even the most humble man access to the riches of our heritage. With one book, democracy was also born, even if it took a few more centuries to flourish. The world was forever changed, and I think of that when I see the indifference, even contempt, demonstrated by so many for books these days. And I realize I have worshipped a worthy God all these years, and I am exalted.

So, I'm not really depressed by all of this so-called progress, which seems to render me not just obsolete but irrelevant. I will never be irrelevant because I have devoted my life to passing on the past, so that the future can know what we thought and believed and what we dreamed about. Nothing but a book can allow us to enter the most intimate dreams of another human. You can, through a book, explore the world with Herodotus; conquer the world with Alexander and argue with Plato; suffer the hell of unrequited love with Catullus and two thousand years later with Stendhal; discover God with Augustine and measure human destiny with Darwin and Einstein.

And with the countless imaginative writers literature has produced everywhere, we can measure our lives and our dreams and our lapses against others who have shared our lot.

I've always loved the aphorism, "The storyteller tells lies to show us the truth." Which always reminds me of my early days, when I despised history but devoured historical fiction, completely unaware that it was the history presented in that fascinating guise which really consumed my imagination.

So we come full circle.

The naïve ignorant kid devouring books, completely unaware of what it was really providing him. No different in the end from every other young person who ever wondered why we exist and what is our destiny.

And now, after almost seventy years, it continues. Now an old man, I still take books home every day with exactly the same pleasure and anticipation that I did as a six-year-old, on those long-ago Saturday morning trips with my sister to the library.

And now, let me reveal a final truth....

I don't really think of myself as an old man.

My body is indeed crumbling, my age unavoidably bringing me to the edge of the abyss, but I still retain the same two gifts which set my life on its course and continue to fuel everything I do: curiosity and enthusiasm. And they are as strong and as compelling now as they ever were. I know now that they will only die with me.

So, I must still worship the book, which gave me almost everything I have most treasured.

And as I think of all the books I haven't read, I see that they are like all my sins of omission—the deeds I was too cowardly or too cautious to attempt; or the women I was too timid to pursue. I deeply regret the books I haven't yet read, the dialogues I haven't yet engaged in, the dreams of those fellow dreamers I haven't yet shared. And it is only those unread books that make me a bit sad about the lack of time left. And every day another obsessed dreamer finishes yet another book that I know I will want to read.

But there is still *some* time left.

And while it is nearing the end for me, I also know this: that somewhere, some shy, timid six-year-old kid is going to ask his older sister, "Will you take me to the library today?" And she will say yes and take his hand, and the wondrous dialogue will go on.

Index

Acknowledgments

The old "without whom it wouldn't be possible" phrase certainly applies here. There are two people whose help made this book possible; without them it wouldn't exist.

The first is my editor, John Metcalf, who initiated this and then guided me through the morass of accumulated material, which was approaching the length of *War and Peace* before he applied the editorial skills for which he is justly famous in Canada. He was very kind and gentle as he broke my heart countless times with his ruthless hacking and slashing. He demonstrated not just his editorial skills, but the tact of a psychologist, a priest, a teacher and, not least, a diplomat.

That the result is an actual book that can actually be read surprises the writer more than it might the reader. It helped too, that John is a life-long collector and understands certain things.

I owe John a great debt for his gentle but ruthless guidance in making a book of my endless meanderings and ramblings, and I thank him deeply and sincerely for his efforts, and for teaching me so much while he did it.

The second person is the unsung hero, my assistant Norm Stringer. I can't type and my handwriting is so atrocious that even I have trouble deciphering it myself ten minutes after I have written something. For some unfathomable reason Norm can read my scrawls and has deciphered and typed countless versions and revisions with enormous patience and with his usual good humour and wise-cracks. He also provided innumerable useful suggestions throughout. I owe him a lot too and I thank him sincerely.

And I must gratefully thank my publisher Dan Wells, for his enthusiasm and for his persistence. But mostly I admire him for his stubborn courage in attempting to offer the world yet another obscure book it probably doesn't want, just because he believes they should want it. Another visionary, of which we have all too few in this country. We need more such people. Thank you, Dan.

And I wish to acknowledge my fellow booksellers as well, both new and antiquarian, who through forty-five years have fed my imagination and added to my education, and been generous colleagues, and in many cases my closest friends. And who, not least, provided me with the opportunity to replace my stock through the bookman's favourite sport, scouting their stores. It has been a great privilege to share my vocation with so many of them. I consider it a wonderful gift to have been able to spend so much of my life amongst such a bunch of eccentric individualists, people who have lived their lives as they should have, following their own paths, in spite of the world.

I thank them all, even my enemies.

I must also thank John Elmslie, Reg Innell, Don McLeod and Tom Robe for the kind use of their photographs.

I must also acknowledge Tara Murphy, Chris Andrechek, and Kate Hargreaves, the production team at Biblioasis for their hard work and their impeccable sense of style—they have given me a beautiful book and I thank them.

And finally, I must acknowledge Ginger and her crew, especially the lovely Miss Mandy, at my local, the Bar Wellington, for giving me my private table, supplying me my own special lamp for the dark winter nights, and for keeping my imagination lubricated throughout countless revisions of the text.